Navigating the Spiritual Dimension of Childhood

Focusing on enhancing spiritual development, this book guides educators in thoughtful pedagogy and practice to encourage and recognise young children's spirituality in everyday educational settings.

Young children's innate spirituality is an integral part of their everyday lives, as well as their personal growth and development. This book draws on the Reggio Emilia approach to develop an environment that will nurture the spiritual expression of children. Based on qualitative research, the book presents children's expression of spirituality through flow, creativity, imagination, caring or empathy towards another, attraction to nature and natural phenomena, joy, wonder and awe, curiosity and engagement. It guides the reader in creating environments in which children explore, discover and play, and where spiritual expression can manifest and be nurtured. Each chapter concludes with a variety of practical suggestions to support the reader in noticing and nurturing spirituality in children.

Drawing on interdisciplinary research and perspectives, this accessible book is written for pre-service and in-service educators alike, offering an inspiring way to recontextualise childhood and design pedagogy.

Helena Card is an educator with over 35 years of experience, as a classroom teacher and in significant leadership roles. For many years, she has been involved in facilitating educational workshops and professional development sessions for educators. Recently, Helena has been dedicated to research in early childhood education and completed a Master's by Research thesis. At this point in her educational career, Helena has come to understand and believe that spirituality is an integral part of childhood; it is the way that children express themselves and learn.

Navigating the Spiritual Dimension of Childhood

Theory, Pedagogy and Practice

Helena Card

LONDON AND NEW YORK

Designed cover image: By Megan Tombs

First published 2026
by Routledge
4 Park Square, Milton Park, Abingdon, Oxon OX14 4RN

and by Routledge
605 Third Avenue, New York, NY 10158

Routledge is an imprint of the Taylor & Francis Group, an informa business

© 2026 Helena Card

The right of Helena Card to be identified as author of this work has been asserted in accordance with sections 77 and 78 of the Copyright, Designs and Patents Act 1988.

All rights reserved. No part of this book may be reprinted or reproduced or utilised in any form or by any electronic, mechanical, or other means, now known or hereafter invented, including photocopying and recording, or in any information storage or retrieval system, without permission in writing from the publishers.

Trademark notice: Product or corporate names may be trademarks or registered trademarks, and are used only for identification and explanation without intent to infringe.

British Library Cataloguing-in-Publication Data
A catalogue record for this book is available from the British Library

Library of Congress Cataloging-in-Publication Data
Names: Card, Helena author
Title: Navigating the spiritual dimension of childhood : theory, pedagogy and practice / Helena Card.
Description: 1. | Abingdon, Oxon ; New York, NY : Routledge, 2026. | Includes bibliographical references and index. |
Identifiers: LCCN 2025020505 (print) | LCCN 2025020506 (ebook) | ISBN 9781032887616 hardback | ISBN 9781032887609 paperback | ISBN 9781003539575 ebook
Subjects: LCSH: Children--Religious life | Early childhood education--Religious aspects
Classification: LCC BL625.5 .C36 2026 (print) | LCC BL625.5 (ebook)
LC record available at https://lccn.loc.gov/2025020505
LC ebook record available at https://lccn.loc.gov/2025020506

ISBN: 978-1-032-88761-6 (hbk)
ISBN: 978-1-032-88760-9 (pbk)
ISBN: 978-1-003-53957-5 (ebk)

DOI: 10.4324/9781003539575

Typeset in Optima
by SPi Technologies India Pvt Ltd (Straive)

Contents

Acknowledgements and dedications	vi
1 Introduction	1
2 Young children and spirituality	27
3 The Reggio Emilia approach and pedagogy	65
4 Another way to understand young children	118
5 Discovering spirituality	141
6 Spirituality: A natural phenomenon in children's lives	206
7 Revelations: What research is telling us about young children and spirituality	233
8 What can we do? Nurturing spirituality in young children while understanding our own	247
9 Weaving the tapestry of spirituality	251
10 Creating the spiritual tapestry	254
References	257
Index	278

Acknowledgements and dedications

Figure 0.1

I would like to thank and acknowledge the following people who have been an integral part of this journey.

To my husband, Peter Card, for being my beloved partner and strength throughout this whole research and for being there, with his mind, heart and spirit: I thank him for believing in me, loving me and supporting me throughout the difficult and tormented travails and my emotional times as I worked through my research and for his devoted understanding in the times when I would zone out and withdraw into the melding of writing, thinking and emotion. I thank deeply him for his patience, for listening and for his way of empowering me and strengthening my resilience in pursuit of this book. His belief in the intention and purpose of my work and this book supported the times when I agonised and became disillusioned throughout the journey towards completion. My work and research and this book could not have been achieved without him by my side.

Acknowledgements and dedications

To my parents, who provided me with the most wonderful childhood in which I could discover the world through play, delight and wonder: I thank them for their love and their cherished view of children, always telling me that I could do and be whatever I wanted, and for believing in me. This has remained with me throughout this journey.

To Ann Bliss, my friend since the age of five, with whom I spent many years of playing, discovering and enjoying moments of joy, wonder and awe in our childhood years: a wonderful lifelong friend who has believed in my dedication and who has empowered and respected my ability and perseverance as a researcher and author.

To Lisa Burman, as academic colleague and a very dear friend who has supported my research and journey with this book and listened, guided and believed in me throughout the journey: she has shared her individual beliefs and experiences with me in conversations and enjoyable get-togethers, always providing exciting and passionate opinions about education and children. She is inspirational in her work with young children. Special thanks go to Lisa Burman, who introduced me to the Reggio Emilia approach and who was there with me as a colleague and friend during my first visit and study tour in Reggio Emilia. She opened up a new outlook towards childhood.

To Professor Deborah Harcourt, who is truly an inspiration. Her work and advocacy with children is endless. Highly regarded globally, she values childhood and rich pedagogical practice. I admire all her wonderful work and am grateful to acknowledge her as a wonderful colleague and friend.

To the wonderful educators who participated in my research and who are so dedicated to the rights of children and childhood: their respect, honour and value of children and childhood are a true credit to them. I thank all of them for allowing me to enter their everyday settings and conduct my research. Their environments provided wonderful and extraordinary moments and encounters for children every day.

To Gail Mantel and Craig Fosdike, who were instrumental through their leadership in bringing the Reggio Emilia approach to life within an educational setting. Their belief in the strong and capable child was seen in all their work. They are inspirational educators who have been a treasured part of my journey.

I thank my beautiful daughter, Megan. As a child, she was curious, sensitive to the natural world, with an abounding love for animals and nature: she had an intrinsic sense of the world and of wanting to know about how it worked from the moment she was born.

As a young neonate, from the earliest moments of her life, Megan engaged with the world, wanting to know and connect with others and the things around her. Her spiritual, imaginative and creative mind has remained strong and powerful and has sustained her interest and passion, unleashing her wonderful ability to be so creative. She has become a strong and fervent advocate for children and is a beautiful and wise person. As a mother, she now cherishes and honours her own beautiful children. Megan has been supportive throughout this whole journey and I thank her for her patience during the

Acknowledgements and dedications

times when I have withdrawn into myself and the way she has intuitively allowed these times to occur. Her belief in me and my research and book journey has been a foundation upon which I relied throughout my work.

To my two beautiful grandchildren, Emma and Jackson, you bring to life this book, you are the wonderful spiritual human beings who demonstrate to us daily and delight us all with your quest for being, your creativity, joy and curiosity for knowing and understanding the world. You are both a gift and so dearly loved and adored; you both continually surprise me with your wisdom and knowledge. Thank you for your lovely illustrations throughout this book. Thank you for being a precious part of my life.

Figure 0.2

Introduction

Figure 1.1

Spiritual moments and spirituality happen and exist every day. All we need to do is accept it and understand it.

Helena Card

I have been a dedicated educator for over 35 years, working as a classroom teacher and also in various leadership roles, including as a Principal. Throughout my journey in education, I thought that I knew children and how they interacted in their learning environments. As I began to understand more about the Reggio Emilia approach to learning, I found the encounter with this pedagogy would shape and influence my own journey as teacher, educator and researcher. My encounter with Reggio Emillia opened up some questions in my mind about an innate capacity that, I believe, all children have. They are spiritual beings who express their spirituality in the extraordinary moments of their everyday settings. However, we must be open to construct learning and pedagogy that invites and ignites young children's spirituality. As adults, if we do not take time to understand this dimension of children, then we are missing out on fully understanding their inner being. We not only miss out, but also denying children their right to spiritual expression. I was determined to find out and explore more about the spiritual dimension of children and embarked on a thesis and higher degree research. Through my research, I hope to present provocations to educators about how they can allow this innate spiritual capacity of children to flourish. In this hurried world, with so many demands on young children and the pressures of society, let alone a society influenced by social media, I believe we need to allow some time to stop and give children time for awe and wonder, to discover and connect with moments in time. Among the fundamental beliefs which I have in relation to young children and spirituality are the following:

- Spirituality is innate and present in young children.
- It is essential that this innate spirituality and dimension must be nurtured in order to flourish.
- Pedagogy plays an integral role in the nourishment of spirituality in young children.
- All children have the right to engaging, beautiful spaces in which to learn and interact.
- Young children are extremely capable and competent.
- Each child is an active agent in their learning.
- Children have a more holistic way of seeing and understanding things; they don't analyse as much so their perception, connections and interactions take on a more mystical quality.
- Young children's innate spirituality will develop when the adults in their lives understand and are willing to engage with, observe and listen to spirituality

My own perception of childhood changed as I put into practice the Reggio Emilia approach to teaching and learning. I began to see children in a different light; their spiritual dimension became evident to me and I was eager to make connections between pedagogy and spirituality. I did not want this spiritual dimension of children to remain unnoticed. In order to preserve spirituality and keep it noticeable, it is essential that we do not lose sight of holistic approaches to learning. If we, as educators, provide time and space for the interplay of cognitive, authentic and spiritual learning to be enabled and afforded, then we will be able to create the potential for today's students and learners to become balanced, insightful and curious citizens of our world who are nurtured in every facet of their being.

I offer you this book, which encompasses my research. I explain and take you through the process of my research and how I came to the deep understanding of children's spirituality. Throughout the book there are provocations and considerations for educators. I have woven a series of Learning Stories. Within the Learning Stories is where I documented, observed and recorded children's interactions in their natural learning environments. I invite you to read through these and also to read through the interpretive summary of the observations. In Chapter 5, I provide a detailed discussion about each of the Learning Stories and some conclusions and findings from my study. My book has embedded my research which offers the reader some grounded evidence about spirituality in childhood.

This book proposes ways for educators to recognise and navigate the spiritual dimension of children. At the end of each chapter, I offer some provocations for educators and some recommendations to relate to their current practice and suggest contemplating some changes to pedagogy and thoughts about children and childhood. The last few chapters offer my thoughts about spirituality and also propose some ideas and implications for educational practice and professional development.

1.1 Listening to, and engaging with, spirituality: dancing with the spirit

If I can create a space that nurtures children's senses, creative minds, wonder, awe and curiosity, our souls can connect with each other, then I can truly value and respect each child as a spiritual being. I can dance alongside their spirit.

Helena Card

This book offers a trajectory for rethinking childhood and holistic child development which includes their spiritual dimension. It opens up our minds to listen and notice children as they interact with their environment and supports us in recognising that each child has an individual spiritual capacity, language and expression that, at times, can inadvertently become unrecognisable. My research has served a purpose to support my belief that spiritual expression in young children is alive and present and can be nurtured. Our challenge as adults and educators is to be truly present and to be prepared to adopt the approach of listening to and engaging with spirituality so that we can navigate the rich tapestry of spirituality. My hope is that this book will inspire people to go beyond the simplified idea of merely being with and teaching children, into a more complex and more hopeful place where listening and being with young children, becomes a pedagogy and a way of researching life. This life is the holistic nature of young children which encapsulates spirituality, that we can listen to and engage with and help nurture, as we support children to live full and wonderful lives.

The Reggio Emilia approach is one which is held in the belief that children are strong and full of potential and the pedagogy is grounded in the strong image of the child. If children are to be given the opportunity to develop to their full potential, then fostering their innate spiritual capacity and nurturing this dimension must be part of the process and in the rhythm and the flow of caring for them. In this way we can construct a vision of childhood which invites dialogue centred around the spiritual dimension.

This book takes you through the journey of my research. It provides a framework for the discussion of spirituality in the lives of our young children. I pose some guiding questions throughout my analysis of my observations which support and make evident a deep understanding of young children's spirituality. The book also offers a holistic look at pedagogy which brings to life the spiritual expression of children. I offer you a way to look at your educational setting and to take time to look for spirituality in the everyday interactions of young children. In the practical domain, this book offers provocations for educators and whole staff who work alongside children and want to go deeper into the understanding of young children. It lends a hand in creating environments that nurture the spiritual dimension and keep spirit at the core and centre of early childhood education. Throughout the book, I have entwined my Learning Stories, which are the observations of young children who are immersed in the rich pedagogy inspired by the Reggio Emilia approach. These Learning Stories are analysed through the lens of Reggio Emilia and provide the evidence that this rich pedagogical approach cultivates the spiritual expression of young children. My research allowed me to collate an overview of how these two elements: pedagogy and spiritual expression are, definitely, present.

By understanding spirituality in young children, we are offering them the right and the opportunity to be fully heard and acknowledged as exceptional human beings. Today, I believe that spiritual development and nurturing is absent from most early childhood programs. Knowing that children are spiritual beings and that they have an innate expression of spirituality will, therefore, transform how we interact, learn alongside and afford children's experiences in early childhood education. Childhood spirituality opens up a window into the nature of childhood. It can help us to be critical of the theories, ideas and practices which suggest that children are empty vessels waiting to be filled. Children are already vessels filled with a delightful treasure of knowledge and innate capacities. We can advocate for a dance, a worldwide dance, a partnership, with spirituality and work towards truly understanding and navigating this dimension in young children.

1.1.1 My research and study

Children express spirituality throughout their lives. This can be nurtured if significant others in their lives are alerted to its features and to how it can be developed. However, without a theoretical foundation and a practical means to facilitate or accommodate spiritual expression specific to young children, the area can remain complex, neglected, unseen or unrecognised in educational practice. For educators who wish to nurture or enrich this dimension of children's lives, this presents a problem. To address this problem, my research and case study explores the understanding of young children's spirituality and how it can be interpreted in an early childhood setting. It investigates how to make this dimension more comprehensible through children's everyday contexts.

In this chapter, I explain the position of the researcher, describe the contemporary concept of spirituality and explain how it is presented throughout this research. I present the overall research question and the aims of the case study in exploring the phenomenon of young children's spirituality, and set out the guiding questions. I next provide the background to the study and discuss the significance and purpose of the research. I describe the case study used to explore the overall research question, using qualitative naturalistic study methods, explaining the case study design, the methodology used and the purpose for exploring the qualitative indicators of the expressions of young children's spirituality.

Furthermore, several theorists (Boyatzis 2005; Hay & Nye 2006; Spilka & McIntosh 1997) claim that the area of children's spirituality is under-researched, to the very point that Boyatzis (2005) acknowledges that '[t]his is not a case of "yet another topic" but is in fact a serious problem' (p. 136).

My research sets out to explore children's spirituality and to understand the ways in which the Reggio Emilia approach can provide a context to recognise, identify and facilitate the spiritual capacity of young children. This research takes place with young children aged four to six within an environment inspired by the Reggio Emilia approach and suggests contexts, concepts and conditions that recognise indicators of expressions of spirituality as they exist in an early childhood setting. This inquiry explores and investigates how aspects of the Reggio Emilia approach to teaching and learning practice with young children may offer a theoretical framework for nurturing and navigating the spiritual dimension of the child.

Although empirical studies have been conducted on children's spirituality, this case study attempts to build on areas suggested for research. Crawford and Rossiter (2006) have suggested that, to truly enrich children's spirituality within education, it is necessary to use a pedagogical approach that is multidimensional and holistic. Within Australia to date, very little research has been conducted in relation to young children's spirituality. Furthermore, within an Australian context, research is particularly lacking in the area of exploring expressions of spirituality through the Reggio Emilia pedagogical lens.

1.1.2 Aims of the research

Contemporary research has focused on the specific nature of spirituality, suggesting that young children exhibit spirituality in a variety of ways (Champagne 2001; Hart 2003; Adams, Hyde & Woolley 2008; Hyde 2008a). The current study suggests that children's interactions in early childhood settings can be described as spiritual. The study not only identifies what the concept of spirituality looks like in four early childhood cohorts in an everyday setting, but also explores how spirituality can be present in relation to specific contexts and to a specific pedagogical approach in early childhood education. In contrast to studies undertaken on the subject of young children's spirituality, the current research will identify why a specific pedagogical approach such as Reggio Emilia can assist in further understanding spirituality as a natural dimension of the child in early childhood education. The uniqueness of this case highlights a particular context in which expressions of spirituality are exhibited by children. The aim of my study is to suggest that once spirituality is seen and understood within an early childhood pedagogical context, it can then be nurtured and supported. My case study is guided by the overall research question and four guiding research questions.

The overall research question is:

> What indicators may be used to identify expressions of spirituality by four- to six-year-old children, and how can the Reggio Emilia approach to education offer a context for recognising and nurturing children's spiritual capacities?

The four guiding research questions are:

Question 1: What are the qualitative indicators of expressions of spirituality that may be demonstrated by young children in their everyday early childhood activities?

Question 2: In what ways can the Reggio Emilia pedagogical approach provide conditions for the expression of children's spirituality?

Question 3: How can young children's expression of spirituality be described?

Question 4: What are the specific elements of the Reggio Emilia pedagogical environment that nurture children's spiritual dimension?

1.2 The Reggio Emilia pedagogical approach

The Reggio Emilia approach has been recognised as a holistic pedagogy (Rinaldi 2006) and the attention that it gives to the physical space incorporates all the senses as children encounter the elements within the environment. One overriding factor which is distinct to the Reggio Emilia approach is the image of the child. Within this approach, the fundamental belief on which the image of the child is constructed is that of the child having rights rather than needs (Malaguzzi 1993; Rinaldi 1998a).

Rather than seeing and considering the child as an empty vessel waiting to be filled with knowledge and information, Reggio Emilia educators consider the child to have unlimited potential who is eager to interact, understand and contribute to the world. The teacher works alongside children as a researcher and co-constructor of knowledge with an attitude of listening to children, not only to their spoken words but also to their unspoken expressions as they interact with their environment. The Reggio Emilia educators recognise that children desire to communicate through both spoken and unspoken expression, communicating in many different languages: the child is referred to as the capable child with a hundred languages (Malaguzzi 1998; Rinaldi 2006). Learning environments are constructed to provide multisensory materials, allowing for multiple possibilities.

Underlying the Reggio Emilia approach is the view that the child is driven by curiosity and imagination, that each child has many ways to express their interactions and learning and that this must be listened to by educators. Within the Reggio Emilia approach, the child is viewed as an active constructor and co-constructor of knowledge and meaning-making. In addition, Malaguzzi (1993) maintains that the image of the child is continuously changing through sociocultural influences within particular contexts.

In recent years, Professor Carla Rinaldi, the president of Reggio Children from Reggio Emilia, worked alongside the South Australian government and in collaboration with the Adelaide Thinkers in Residence program (2012–13), sharing views about childhood with the hope of reconstructing and re-imagining childhood (Rinaldi 2013). Professional development in connection with the Reggio Emilia philosophy is currently being constructed in the hope of influencing early childhood education, not only in South Australia but also with the intention of filtering through early childhood education throughout Australia. Within the early childhood education curriculum, it is anticipated that the findings of the current research can offer ways in which teaching and learning environments can be inspired by the Reggio Emilia approach. This approach provides an authentic learning environment in which to promote a holistic pedagogy (Edwards et al. 1998) and a climate for learning relevant to the child, the adult and the culture of the school, with this becoming visible through the values, identity, tradition and ethos of the school. Educators within the schools and educational centres in Reggio Emilia stress the importance of understanding the context of individual communities and of being aware of 'the historical and sociocultural context of a community that can influence the ways that teachers view children and ultimately interact with children' (Hughes 2007).

Understanding the image of the child is integral to understanding how it is defined in the current study. Terms such as 'strong', 'rich' and 'powerful' are frequently used and applied to children in the Reggio Emilia municipal schools. This view and image of the child contrasts with the conventional view of the child as weak, dependent and limited in capability. The image of the child within the context of the Reggio Emilia approach is:

> A way of being with children that orients adults to seeing strengths and capabilities that can be encouraged and built upon, rather than seeing the child as being comprised primarily of deficits. The teacher sees the child as capable, rich in ideas ...
>
> (Scheinfeld, Haigh & Scheinfeld 2008, p. 3)

Emerging research (Goodliff 2013; Adams, Bull & Maynes 2015) has suggested that the Reggio Emilia philosophy and pedagogy can provide '... a theoretical framework for understanding spirituality' (Adams et al. 2015, p. 7). Furthermore, Goodliff (2013, as cited in Adams et al. 2015) suggests that the philosophy of Reggio Emilia offers a way to 'embody the holistic understanding of children's spirituality' (p. 7).

My research explores the notion that the spiritual dimension cannot be removed from discussion about the image of the child and its implications for pedagogy and practice. As a result, the current study provides some avenues for what spirituality looks like in early childhood settings and how it can be identified, aligned with aspects of pedagogy, which nurture the strong image of the child and their spiritual capacity. This study aims to investigate and contribute to the overall understanding of the child's encounters in the everyday normality, in a particular early childhood setting, that makes visible their spiritual expression.

1.3 Spirituality as a growing interest of empirical study

The concept of children's spirituality has been a topic of empirical study among scholars over the last 25 years (Adams et al. 2008; Champagne 2001, 2003; de Souza 2009; Hart 2003, 2006; Hay & Nye 2006; Hyde 2008a; Nye 2009; Ratcliff 2010; Rossiter 2010a, 2010b; Wane, Manyimo & Ritskes 2011).

Most studies and research in the field of spirituality have been undertaken with older, primary school-aged children (Hay & Nye 2006; Hyde 2008a). For example, the study by Coles (1990) is the result of five years of research with children between the ages of six and thirteen. Research to date indicates only a few studies which have a focus on how preschool children experience or express spirituality: Bone (2007), Champagne (2003) and McCreery (1996). Other studies involve younger children, such as the study by Giesenberg (2007), who considered spiritual characteristics of preschool children, and Goodliff (2013), who focused on spirituality in children from birth to the age of three. Although much more is now understood about children's spirituality, there is limited understanding and empirical research concerning how children in preschool and in the early years of schooling, between the ages of four and six, express spirituality.

Several scholars (Chan 2010; Etheridge 2004; Guss 2011; Matthews 2004; Rogers 2011) are responding to the need to rethink the pedagogy and practice in early years' settings. Their view of young children encompasses the child as an active agent, with a pedagogy required that recognises each child's full potential as they actively search and construct meaning about the world. Alongside this view is the guiding principle of the Reggio Emilia philosophy, the image of the child. This pedagogical approach values and observes children, their contemplation and theories, recognising that within young children there is a search for meaning. The Reggio Emilia philosophy offers an image of the child who, from the moment of their birth, is engaged in developing a relationship with the world and is intent on experiencing and making meaning of the world (Rinaldi 2006).

1.3.1 The concept of spirituality

The identification of spirituality in young children has been made fraught by the variety of terms by which it is described. Through their empirical research in 1996 and 1998 in the United Kingdom (UK), Rebecca Nye and David Hay (Hay & Nye 1996; Nye & Hay 1996) introduced and opened up the concept of spirituality and children. In Champagne's (2001, 2003) scholarly work, she offers three insights into spirituality which she describes as children's expression of modes of being. Champagne's research refers to children's experiences of spirituality and relates this to the everyday events and experiences of childhood. Champagne's work focuses on the children's different expressions of being: 'attention was given to words, facial expressions, attitudes and gestures, as well as the *inner dynamics* they expressed in a way objectively observable' (Champagne 2003, p. 45).

In Hyde's work (2008a), spirituality is described and termed as characteristics which he identified in primary school children. He refers to spirituality as ontological and a natural human disposition, positioning both adults and children within this reference to spirituality. Hart (2003) offers spirituality as more elusive, suggesting that it takes on many forms, some of which may be non-verbal. He suggests that the spiritual dimension manifests itself through children's experiences of joy, wonder and wisdom. Hart's (2003, 2006) research identified four types of experiences and capacities which he refers to as 'ways of being in the world' (2006, p. 65): wonder, wondering, relational spirituality and wisdom. Goodliff (2013) describes aspects of children's spiritual dimension as behaviours. All of these researchers have offered a description of spirituality which comprises the spiritual dimension of childhood.

1.3.2 The spiritual debate

Spirituality has been suggested as an innate human quality (Hart 2003, 2004, 2006, 2009; Hyde & Rymarz 2009; O'Murchu 1998) and as manifesting itself within each of us as a desire to interconnect with the world (Hay & Nye 2006). In relation to contemporary research, various scholars adopt a broader definition (e.g. Adams et al. 2008; Hay & Nye 1996; King 2009), recognising spirituality as fundamental to human experience.

The human condition can be interpreted in many ways; however, I am referring to what has been considered a fundamental human condition—spirituality. In this research, I argue and advocate that spirituality can be considered as an innate quality. The many scholars from a variety of disciplines who have endorsed this aspect of our human condition (Eaude 2005, 2009; Hogan 2009; Zohar & Marshall 2000) also recognise that young children have an innate spiritual capacity and spiritual dimension.

The notion and understanding of spirituality, particularly in young children, have been discussed from many viewpoints and this is expanded in the literature review, with a similarly wide discussion on the connection between spirituality and a variety of disciplines.

Coles (1990), O'Murchu (1998), Champagne (2001), Hart (2003), Hay and Nye (2006) and Adams et al. (2008) are among the scholars who have suggested that spirituality is an integral part of a person's being and can be viewed as an intrinsic human disposition. Therefore, 'spirituality', as the literature suggests, belongs to each person's being (Adams et al. 2008, p. 15).

Within scholarly research, spirituality has been identified as intrinsic (Benson, Roehlkepartain, & Rude 2003; Champagne 2001; Crawford & Rossiter 2006; Groome 1998; Hardt et al. 2012; Harris 2007; Hart 2003; Hay & Nye 2006; Hyde 2008a; Kirmani & Kirmani 2009; Myers 1997; Palmer 1998; Rodger 1996; Watson 2000) and naturally existing in young children.

The debate distinguishing religion and spirituality in relation to young children is further explored in the review of the literature which articulates the ongoing debate on positioning and defining spirituality. Knowing and talking about God do not automatically produce spiritual experiences, with this view supported within the work of Hay, Reich and Utsch (2006) in which they state that 'spirituality is universal, found in all human beings whatever their formal religious beliefs, or lack of them' (p. 50). According to Love (2001), spirituality and religion are interrelated; however, they do not overlap. When positioning children within the discourse of spirituality, spirituality remains distinct from religion.

According to Bone (2010), in reference to spirituality in early childhood, 'the whole is more than the sum of its parts; it is this quality that makes it difficult to articulate' (p. 403). Motha (2011) argues that despite the disparities within the spiritual debate, spirituality is 'an organic total integration of the individual, regardless of race, gender or religion' (p. 63). Young children express their spirituality through their everyday encounters: according to Motha (2011), this warrants an understanding of what this may look like in order to nurture this aspect of their being.

1.3.3 Defining spirituality in young children

The definitions and interpretations of spirituality have been widely contested and discussed and, according to Cole (2011), there are contentious epistemological and ontological debates among academics. However, also according to Cole (2011), definitions and assumptions made by adults may hinder the ability to understand the spiritual nature of children. It is important and integral to my study to clearly define a position on children's spirituality.

In my research, I consider a variety of scholarly positions regarding young children's spirituality, and I pose my own position. I adopt Goodliff's (2013) argument that children are spiritual beings and that spirituality and spiritual expression are part of their natural identity. The study also espouses Hay and Nye's (1996) premise that young children have an intrinsic natural capacity for spirituality. The position of spirituality within this research does not limit spirituality to religion.

When defining spirituality in young children, I also argue that the spirit of children is depicted when spirituality is understood as an 'inexhaustible web of meaning interrelatedly connecting self, other, world and cosmos' (Myers 1997, p. 109). Furthermore, the essence of spirituality in young children is mysterious; at times, it is necessary to fully understand how they experience and express their spiritual nature. Hart (2003) supports this mysterious quality of spirituality and describes it as an unquantifiable force which animates and connects all things.

Within this research, along with Hart's view of spirituality, I support Cole's (2011) definition of spirituality: that it is something intimate that helps children to expand their understanding of themselves and their place in the world. Furthermore, scholarship suggests that, rather than spirituality being finitely defined, spirituality can be considered with a broader understanding than merely being described in terms of its attributes and characteristics and what it may look like (Grajczonek 2012; Harris 2007; Roehlkepartain, King, Wagener & Benson 2006; Tacey 2004).

Spirituality can be understood as a shift towards humanistic knowledge and a sense of identity with one's community and the world (Miller 2007; White 1996). Champagne (as cited in Hyde 2008a) supports Hart's (2003) work on the spirituality of children, suggesting children have a high capacity for abstract conceptions of wonder and relational connections between the self and others. Champagne states that 'spiritual experience is human experience' (as cited in Hyde (2008a), p. 53)'. Binder (2011) states that within young children, spirituality is the ongoing pursuit of a sense of one's place in the universe which enables the child's capacity for more abstract conceptions of wonder and relational connections between the self and others. This then extends to something greater and a search for bigger questions and ideas. It is here that I situate my own understanding of spirituality in this research. The position regarding children's spirituality in this research, and in my view, is that; it is intrinsic, that spirituality is an integral part of each child's being. This research also supports the position that spirituality in young children appears as an inbuilt curiosity, questioning, wonder and awe about where they came from or how they exist in relation to their everyday world. Furthermore, my study, and this book, supports my belief that spiritual expression and spiritual capacity is part of young children's natural identity.

1.4 Implications for early childhood education in Australia

Adopting this notion of spirituality in children poses some thought-provoking questions in relation to the places where young children are educated and also to early childhood pedagogy. It is timely to suggest further investigations, especially within Australia, where the Early Years Learning Framework has included a definition of spirituality in relation to children in their early years of learning. A number of factors have contributed to a growing interest in the field of young children's spirituality, in particular, the inclusion of spirituality in *Belonging, Being and Becoming: The Early Years Learning Framework for Australia* (Australian Government Department of Employment, Education and Workplace Relations [DEEWR] 2009). Within this framework (Australian Government Department of Education, Employment and Workplace Relations [DEEWR] 2009, p. 44), the meaning of spiritual 'refers to a range of human experiences including a sense of awe and wonder, and an exploration of being and knowing'. More recently, in version 2 of this document: 'Spiritual: refers to a range of human experiences including a sense of awe and wonder, or peacefulness, and an exploration of being and knowing' (Australian Government Department of Education [AGDE] (2022), p. 68) Spirituality in young children and the nurturing of this dimension are mentioned as part of the holistic approach to teaching young children within the current framework.

In South Australia, the Department for Education and Children's Services (DECS) *Learner Wellbeing Framework* (Department for Education and Children's Services [DECS] 2007) positions a link between wellbeing and spirituality with spirituality stated as being a dimension of wellbeing. The framework also states that wellbeing is influenced by the context of four domains which it identifies as: '… the learning environment, curriculum and pedagogy, partnerships and policies and procedures' (Department for Education and Children's Services [DECS] 2007, p. 7).

The *Melbourne Declaration of Educational Goals for Young Australians* (2008) supports the view that schools play a vital role in the spiritual development of young Australians.

Further discussions in relation to policies and early childhood education in Australia are presented in the review of the literature. While the policies within Australia which have associated and mentioned spirituality present some ambiguity, they offer a broad perspective on the identification of spirituality, what it can look like or how it can be developed through a particular pedagogy. This has opened up an area for research to present some rigour and 'a more comprehensive understanding of spirituality in early years' education particularly within Australian contexts' (Adams et al. 2015, p. 12).

1.5 Identifying a gap in contemporary research

The unique aspect of this research is to view spirituality through the lens of the Reggio Emilia pedagogical approach, an area which has not yet been widely researched. The emerging research from both Goodliff (2013) and Adams et al. (2015) in relation to young children and spirituality suggests that further exploration is necessary to fully understand spirituality. This study intends to fill a gap through exploring a specific pedagogical approach in relation to young children's spiritual expression.

This research involves young children, and presents to the reader the suggestion that certain characteristics relate specifically to children's spirituality. Research to date has focused on the specific nature of spirituality, suggesting that young children exhibit it in a variety of ways (Adams et al. 2008; Champagne 2001; Hart 2003; Hyde 2008a). This study suggests that the everyday experiences of children, as observed in this early childhood setting, are spiritual. It not only identifies what the concept of spirituality looks like in four everyday early childhood cohorts, but also explores how it can be present in relation to a specific context and pedagogical approach in early childhood education. In contrast to the literature reviewed and the studies undertaken on the subject of young children's spirituality, this research identifies why a specific, holistic approach is necessary to assist in further understanding spirituality as a natural human dimension of four- to six-year-old children in early childhood education.

In addition, my research and case study is differentiated from other research involving young children's spirituality for the following reason. It follows recommendations made by recent researchers in the field, such as Schein (2013) and Mata (2014), who suggest that, in order to learn more about spiritual development in young children, studying how it is visible and recognised is required (Schein 2013), and that when spirituality is understood as a natural expression in children, then it is necessary or appropriate to include spirituality in early childhood education (Mata 2014).

Within Australia, as previously mentioned, discussion of spirituality is included in the document *Belonging, Being and Becoming: The Early Years Learning Framework for Australia* (Australian Government Department of Education, Employment and Workplace Relations [DEEWR] 2009). Version 2 (Australian Government Department of Education

[AGDE] (2022) of this framework makes explicit references to children's spiritual lives, recognising and considering the roles of the spiritual in children's learning.

This book aims to present a territory not yet covered, to unpack what spirituality specific to young children looks like. What pedagogical and philosophical approaches nurture this in young children is still an area which requires further research. A unique aspect of my case study, and this book, is that it looks specifically at a particular early childhood context in which the Reggio Emilia approach inspires pedagogy, and at how this approach has been implemented within this sociocultural context. The case study explores how expressions of spirituality are exhibited within this early years environment and how this dimension of young children's development can be not only navigated but also nurtured. It builds on suggestions from other scholarly work, such as the studies by Grajczonek (2012) and Cole (2011), that when a person's spirituality is expressed through daily activities within early childhood, it is then that their spirituality can be nurtured.

1.5.1 A different lens through which to investigate young children's spirituality

The contribution of this book, and my research, is that it explores a different viewpoint on young children's spirituality which has not been widely explored. The Reggio Emilia approach is a philosophy which has been described as a holistic approach to early childhood teaching (Goodliff 2013; Ludlow 2014; Rinaldi 2006; Rudge 2010). This case study builds on Bone's (2010) study and her notion whereby spirituality is transformed through metamorphosis or made evident through pedagogical conditions in early childhood. This study aims to provide evidence that elements of the Reggio Emilia approach and philosophy provide an opening and conditions for children's expression of spirituality to be made evident. The description of Reggio Emilia as a holistic pedagogical approach suggests that it is connected to spirituality: 'spirituality is a truly holistic subject …' (Bone 2010, p. 403).

In my research, I use the lens of the Reggio Emilia pedagogical approach and the work done by Ceppi and Zini (1998), who expand upon the principles of the Reggio Emilia approach. Through this lens, the research explores the expressions of children's spirituality.

This case study is situated in an educational setting which is inspired by the Reggio Emilia approach in the way in which learning environments are designed for the children and the way that childhood is understood, that is, by recognising the powerful image of the child and that each child has a hundred languages (Malaguzzi 1998; Rinaldi 2006). Therefore, the pedagogy and practice within this site are different from those in other educational settings. Another unique aspect of the research to highlight is that the approach to pedagogy and practice is integral in relation to children's spirituality. Through the lens of the Reggio Emilia approach, the case study explores a juxtaposition or a viewpoint, suggesting that a pedagogical approach of this style is optimum for spirituality to be evident and may therefore contribute to spiritual nurture and development.

Within this research, indicators or expressions of children's spirituality capacity evolve as the case study and observations of children are analysed. The indicators or expressions of spirituality are drawn from and reinforced by the review of the literature. The data are collected from four cohorts at an optimum time in the teaching program, which is inspired by the Reggio Emilia approach.

1.5.2 Contribution of this study

There is little research focusing on exploring spirituality in four- to six-year-old children in a context inspired by the Reggio Emilia approach. My work and this case study provides a sociocultural context through this lens for understanding children's expression of spirituality. This research investigates a unique insight through the data analysis of particular features of the Reggio Emilia pedagogy which contributes to an interpretive understanding of spirituality and young children. My work, and this book, argues for a broader situating of spirituality in early childhood education. The development of an innovative methodology within this research strengthens its potential contribution to knowledge, offering a juxtaposition, a different viewpoint and a broader understanding about how pedagogy can contribute, not only making visible the expressions of spirituality but also suggesting how to provide contexts which nurture spiritual development in young children.

It can also be noted that spirituality in young children is a coherent fact of their being. As educators and people who learn alongside children, there is a need for them to be fully understood. Throughout my study and through my loyalty to children and childhood, it is my belief that listening to others and being open to them offers an opportunity to go from what is known to the unknown. This is how I undertook my approach in this study, to truly be open to children and to listen to their ways of being, which allowed me to explore the innate spiritual capacity that they have. Children have a biologically predisposed tendency to communicate and to exist, be and live in relation. Children interact and be in learning environments; as adults we can learn more about their intrinsic nature and disposition and as they live and learn. Once this is understood, we can nurture children's spiritual capacity within the learning environments.

1.6 Personal interest in the investigation

I have worked within education for over 37 years and wanted to investigate how pedagogy and practice can respect the image of every child and engage their spiritual nature, or to make suggestions for understanding this dimension outside religious doctrine and teaching—in children's everyday encounters.

My visit to the Reggio Emilia municipal schools and centres in Italy presented me with the opportunity to see how young children can express themselves through many different media. As a visitor to the municipal schools within Reggio Emilia in 2008 and again in 2013, I could see the prospects for the provision of many learning opportunities for young children by taking the view that the image of the child is valued, powerful and full of potential. Rinaldi (1998a) reflects on the experience and philosophy of Reggio Emilia:

> The cornerstone of our experience, based on practice, theory and research, is the image of the children as rich, strong and powerful. The emphasis is placed on seeing the children as unique subjects with rights rather than simply needs. They have potential, plasticity, the desire to grow, curiosity, the ability to be amazed, and the desire to relate to other people and to communicate.
>
> (p. 114)

The review of scholarly literature on this subject provided further avenues for thought and investigation: it seemed that the empirical research to date may lack some explicit details in the explanation of pedagogical contexts which may nurture spirituality. The review informed a starting point for exploring the spiritual expressions of young children. It seemed that some attention could be dedicated to thoughts about how children's spiritual characteristics, expressions and dispositions appear in their everyday encounters with the world and, in this case, within early childhood settings inspired by the Reggio Emilia approach.

1.7 Position of the researcher

At the time of the research, I became a participant observer in this case study and also the assistant principal and curriculum coordinator in the school in the research. I was also a regular participant with a teaching role in the learning areas. The teachers accepted me as another colleague who has participated alongside them in projects and learning experiences and the children know me as another adult and educator across the learning cohorts.

For the purpose of this case study, my researcher's intent was to explore the intrinsic nature of childhood, its spiritual capacity and where the Reggio Emilia pedagogy and practice served as a medium for understanding the spiritual expressions of young children. Through the study, understandings have also been explored and suggested of how children spiritually express themselves and how the spiritual dimension of childhood can be described and recognised within this particular context.

One key principle of hermeneutics is to acknowledge my own role within the research. This case presents a hermeneutic view of young children and spirituality through the lens of Reggio Emilia. This case study has been developed from a perception and particular view of the world held by the researcher. My researcher's personal experience, preconceptions and knowledge are not factored out of the research design. According to Sargeant and Harcourt (2012), it is through understanding and acknowledging the influences and opinions held by the researcher that 'the data that emerge have even greater richness' (p. 8).

As previously stated, the position of the researcher is that of participant observer. I was aware of ethical issues which could be raised within this research and ensured that '[r]esearchers have a responsibility to act in the best interests of the participants' (Cullen, Hedges & Bone 2009, p. 116). In addition, I was mindful to adhere to Cullen et al.'s (2009) guidelines for conducting ethical research in early childhood, with this adherence crucial to maintaining my ethical position as the researcher. Edwards (2002a) suggests that when the researcher employs an interpretivist methodology, this then allows for responsible research to occur.

This intention of the research was made clear to the teachers so they knew that their own personal work and pedagogy were not being judged or criticised. The teachers were invited to comment and contribute to the research to inform the inquiry. Throughout the research, I entered each of the learning cohorts 'as an outsider who sought to combine authentic enquiry with respect for professional knowledge' (Broadhead 2010, p. 42).

To support my role within this research, I draw on previous insider/outsider research such as that of Unluer (2012), with his view that there are distinct advantages in being an insider/outsider within research. Unluer (2012) states that, through his role as teacher researcher, he is able to determine the case, enter the research site, define the researcher's role to the participants under study and survive in the research site. Accessing data is easily done, colleagues may be supportive and helpful, the researcher does not have to go to other research areas, and the whole school may benefit from the research results.

The role of participant observer and the duality of insider/outsider are supported in relation to the issue of addressing ethics. This is explained and outlined by Bonner and Tolhurst (2002), who outline three key advantages of being an insider within a case study research domain: a superior understanding of the group's culture; the ability to interact naturally with the group and its members; and a previously established, and therefore greater, relational intimacy with the group. Within my case and the existing culture of the school, to be a co-learner, researcher and investigator was a familiar aspect of the school's culture. My position was not unusual in the overall context of the school.

In addition, according to DeLyser (2001), Farnsworth (1996) and Harklau and Norwood (2005), some insider researchers choose to conceptualise themselves as co-investigators, co-learners, facilitators or advocates, rather than researchers: this is in an effort to minimise the power differential between themselves and those participating in their research. This was clearly the situation within this research. My position as researcher and an insider/outsider is validated by the work of Herr and Anderson (2005), who claim that the insider/outsider role of the researcher enables a deep understanding of the lived experience and the flexibility to shift within these multiple roles throughout the research.

1.8 Field of this research

This research takes place in an early learning setting, which has been inspired by the Reggio Emilia approach to pedagogy and learning. This philosophy encompasses a social constructive framework (Fraser 2006). In order to understand the foundation of this philosophy and approach, a historical background is provided. One cannot replicate the approach in its entirety, but educational settings can adopt some of its guiding principles and this inspires their pedagogical beliefs and practices. The elements chosen from the Reggio Emilia approach were interpretations and were aligned with wider research and theories within early childhood. A detailed description of each principle is clearly explained within the literature review, bringing in relevant connections from global perspectives on the approach and the guiding features which impact on early years settings. Alongside the interpretation of the approach and the distinct way in which the approach advocates for childhood with its beliefs in the strong and capable image of the child, it was acknowledged that it was essential to frame perceptions of childhood and a contemporary image of the child according to current theorists and advocates of childhood.

1.8.1 Theoretical orientation

This research is oriented from a sociocultural perspective. It is essential to note the sociocultural teaching practice and learning for this research in order to determine and analyse the spiritual capacity of young children. Within this culture, the child is able to construct knowledge and meaning outside the boundaries of the scientifically accepted constructions. It becomes a learning process for all those involved as they encounter the child's ideas (Dahlberg Moss & Pence 1999).

Both Dewey (1910) and Vygotsky (1962) agree that the human condition is based on social interactions. Humans are initially social beings who slowly develop their individual selves through their relationships or experiences with others (Glassman 2001, p. 5).

The Reggio Emilia approach to, and philosophy of, teaching and learning have largely been influenced by both Dewey (1910) and Vygotsky (1962), and this view of the child supports the sociocultural view of learning and researching. 'Dewey believed that children learn best when they interact with other people, working both alone and co-operatively with peers and adults' (Mooney 2000, p. 5).

Vygotsky's (1962) notion of children and learning supports the sociocultural aspect and purpose of this study. Through his work, he outlined that 'social and cognitive development work together and build on each other' (Mooney 2000, p. 82). Gardner's (1999) thoughts, theories and reframed multiple intelligences for the 21st century provide a foundation and the substance for this research and its connections to the hundred languages of children (Malaguzzi 1998; Rinaldi 2006). Gardner (1999, p. 45) states that 'we have a unique blend of intelligences'. He suggests that 'the big challenge facing the deployment of human resources is how best to take advantage of the uniqueness conferred on us as the species exhibiting several intelligences'.

This research is oriented within a sociocultural theoretical framework which encompasses a child-centred pedagogy. The case study observes children embedded within a theory of pedagogy which is referred to by Robertson and Gerber as 'firmly embedded in the everyday experiences of the child' and where Dewey's philosophy of education is built on humanism and is centred on the child (Robertson & Gerber 2001, p. 60).

1.9 Research methodology

A qualitative naturalistic case study approach involving children in an early learning setting was used in my research. The qualitative data were collected through field notes, digital photographs, interviews with teachers, observations of children, conversations with children and a collection of children's artwork and creative experiences, with these collectively organised into Learning Stories or accounts and documentation of my observations.

The qualitative nature of this case study research was valued due to its ability to provide information about a particular phenomenon (Major & Savin-Baden 2010). The research report is a 'rich, thick description of a snapshot in time and place' (Major & Savin-Baden 2010, p. 15). Fundamental to this case study was the hermeneutic interpretation of the observations of the children. Hermeneutics is the reading and interpretation of the messages of texts. Sargeant and Harcourt (2012) suggest that when 'researching the child, the world of the child is experienced through the interpretation of their language in all forms' (p. 8). Through engaging hermeneutically with the child's world or context, language provides understanding and knowledge (Dowling 2004). Sargeant and Harcourt (2012) state that 'any text must be read in order to make sense of it, but that as the researcher, one must know the language in which it is constructed; that being the language of the child' (p. 8).

Natural settings and contexts which, in this case, were the classroom and preschool, are desirable and were used when collecting the various data mentioned. A natural setting is preferred when conducting qualitative research as it typically involves 'a study of things as they exist' (Lichtman 2006, p. 11). The intent of this research was to observe and collect data related to behaviour within a natural setting for, as described by Creswell, 'qualitative research occurs in natural settings, where human behaviour and events occur' (2009, p. 195). The researcher observed and collected data which suggested the phenomena of the indicators of expressions of young children's spirituality as they interacted within a Reggio Emilia-inspired learning environment.

A hermeneutic, multi-layered approach was used in the data analysis process. The study involved interpretive analysis by the researcher, with the data analysis framed by both deductive and inductive phases in this process.

1.9.1 The case study

The research was designed as a case study with the following boundaries:

1) An inner suburban site was selected as the setting as it espoused a Reggio Emilia approach.
2) At the site, there were four groups (cohorts) of four- to six-year-old children in the same school (one preschool and three Reception/One [Year One] groups).

The particular pedagogy being observed (during Exploration Time) in the preschool and the Reception/One classes is inspired by the Reggio Emilia approach. This study attempted to explore and investigate what the spiritual capacity of children may look like within a particular approach to early childhood education.

According to Lichtman, 'it is the researcher's task to identify the case and to set the boundaries of what is being studied' (2006, p. 71). This case study identified a particular group of children, teachers and parents who helped to produce the data which were used for analysis to determine the research findings. A case study was proposed in this situation to conduct an in-depth exploration of the spiritual capacity of children and the Reggio Emilia pedagogical approach. 'A case study could be proposed if you are conducting a study that gets you close to a particular individual, group, school, program or event' (Lodico, Spaulding & Voegtle 2010, p. 175).

My focus was on how the children themselves participate in constructing and demonstrating the spiritual through their relationships and everyday activities and interactions in this particular setting. In summary, a case study using an ethnographic approach was used to investigate the phenomenon (Yin 1994) of spirituality and how it is expressed by four- to six-year-old children.

The human condition can be interpreted in many ways; however, I am referring to what has been considered a fundamental human condition—spirituality. The many scholars from a variety of disciplines who have endorsed this aspect of our human condition (Eaude 2005, 2009; Hogan 2009; Zohar & Marshall 2000) also recognise that young children have an innate spiritual capacity and spiritual dimension. The case is presented as a lived experience, a description and a portrait of a culture, a place and a context. My strong belief is that throughout my interactions with children, not only for my research, I position myself to listen to spirituality and engage with spirituality. I believe that children should be held in this mode of listening to and for spirituality, for it is then that we are truly open to their ways, their being and their natural human condition.

Further discussion in relation to spirituality as a natural human condition is in Chapter 2.

1.9.2 The participants

The participants were 66 children between 4 and 6.5 years of age from four early childhood cohorts, ranging from preschool through to Year One. A series of visits were conducted across the learning groups and I was the participant observer. I observed children during inquiry play-based activities and listened to and recorded conversations in my field notes. Attention was given to the environment of the learning setting and the various ways that children encountered their learning and experiences.

Throughout the study, the children are identified by number only so that they remain anonymous, as agreed with the children's parents. For the purpose of this book, I have collated the observations into a format: Learning Stories with Narrative Observation. I share these with you at the end of some of the chapters and I provide you with an interpretive summary of the Learning Story and Narrative Observation. Furthermore, there are chapters which analyse these Learning Stories through various lenses, which have created evidence to support my belief about spirituality and young children.

1.10 Some provocations to consider

Every day encounters need to be seen as spiritual moments

Helena Card

- *Spirituality exists as an innate capacity and dimension in young children which needs to be a topic of more conversation and considerations in early childhood education.*
- *To truly navigate this dimension, we as educators need to fully understand what children's expressions of spirituality look like and how they appear in naturalistic everyday early childhood environments.*

- *How can you become a participant researcher and observer in your educational setting to explore the phenomenon of spirituality in young children?*
- *What benefits would an investigation into spirituality accrue for your early childhood educational setting?*
- *If spirituality is considered as an innate capacity in each child, why is this not a topic of more conversation in early childhood settings?*
- *What is your understanding of spirituality in young children?*
- *How do you observe children? Is documentation and observation used as a tool for dialogue and discussion?*
- *Does this dialogue and discussion promote opportunities for planning and extending the experiences of young children?*

Learning Story 1

Music in the preschool: Narrative Observation 1

Child 1 was observed exploring the music area. She used a variety of instruments that produced different sounds. I was present observing Child 1 and asked her a question.

When asked about what she was doing, she answered, 'It makes me feel happy.' And looked down at the instruments with which she was playing.

Child 1 continued to explore the music for about five minutes; she picked up various instruments and tilted her head to listen to them. I asked if she would like to draw what she was doing.

She agreed and moved over to the creating or making table and began drawing and using the materials on the table. She continued drawing and creating for about 20 minutes. Other children came and went from the creating table and Child 1 did not interact with them. She said out loud, 'Me happy', and looked down at the drawing. This was written on the drawing for her by a co-educator who was working nearby.

Child 1 then proceeded to express her learning through symbolic interpretations and patterns which appeared to be swirls and squiggles.

I questioned whether these were associated with the music; she nodded and stated that the music looked like 'waves and swirls'.

She looked down at another creative representation. Her creative interpretation was a bird which appeared to have a flap. Child 1 then stated out loud, 'and this is a bird. It flaps to the music'.

This observation was about 35 minutes.

Introduction

The interpretive summary of Learning Story 1

Indicators of spirituality	Interpretations from Narrative Observation 1
Curiosity and interest in mysterious things	Child 1 used her natural disposition for curiosity; Child 1 used a variety of instruments that produced different sounds; her head is tilting as she listens to the sounds
Flow	Child 1 appeared to be involved in drawing and creating for about 20 minutes. She appeared to be undistracted by the other children who were in this learning space.
	She continued drawing and creating for about 20 minutes. Other children came and went from the creating table and Child 1 did not interact with them.
Creativity and imagination	Through self-discovery and creative processes, Child 1 was participating in a state of flow and freely using her imagination.
Pedagogical Condition: Reggio Emilia approach	**Interpretations from Narrative Observation 1**
The hundred languages of children	Child 1 proceeded to express her learning through symbolic interpretations and patterns which appeared to be swirls and squiggles to communicate her language, which can be attributed to the hundred languages of children. Child 1 is purposeful and resourceful as she creatively designs a picture and attends to the details required to complete this activity; she does not leave her activity uncompleted.
The environment as third teacher	The learning environment engages prior and further learning through aesthetic and engaging materials which were present within the room. The free movement of the child in the room and the accessible materials lead to further learning experiences, allowing the child to be independent and for children to use self-expression through their hundred languages.
	The learning environment was designed with a variety of aesthetic materials, as shown in the photograph, with these arranged so the child could independently choose the materials. Once Child 1 was at the creating or making table, she independently chose the materials.
	On the creating table, as shown in the photographs, chairs were arranged and materials were placed to provide the children with many opportunities to express themselves in a creative and imaginative way. Child 1 used these materials to make the bird with the flap and her symbolic representations.
The image of the child	Evidence in the data suggests that Child 1 is an active constructor of knowledge to make meaning.
	A suggestion was made to Child 1 about representing her learning. This was then attended to independently by Child 1 as she represented the music as 'waves and swirls'.

Learning Story 2

Preschool materials for outdoor play: Narrative Observation 2

The preschool was involved in play-based activities. Provocations and learning materials were set up inside and outside. Outside there was a wooden table set up with dinosaurs: natural pieces of bark, wood, small pebbles and parts of plants: spiky balls (acorns), pine cones, leaves and small acorns and material were set over the top of the table. Many materials were set on the table from which the children could choose in order to create.

Four chairs were arranged around this table; children came and went as they chose.

I was outside and I noticed Child 2 sat at this table which had materials in what looked like a diorama for dinosaurs.

Child 2 was singing and arranging dinosaurs using the materials.

I noticed that he arranged all the bigger dinosaurs with smaller ones next to them.

He suddenly said aloud:

Child 2: "Oh there's a little one with a broken back. I'll get your mummy; we'll fix you and take care of you."

He carefully placed the dinosaur on another dinosaur's back as if to carry the injured baby.
He placed natural materials around the dinosaurs, arranging and rearranging.
He was singing and humming as he created and arranged scenes.

Child 2: "Come on; go with your mother."

He carefully placed more babies next to their mothers.

Child 2 said aloud: "They need to be protected and looked after." (He was referring to the babies.)

He then started looking at and touching some pine cones and some spiky balls which had been on a tree.
He was placing the spiky balls inside the grooves of the pine cone.

Child 2: said aloud "Lots of spiky acorns, hanging in the tree."

As he was arranging the spiky acorns, his eyes were down watching the materials, feeling them, touching them and looking at them from different angles.

He was engaged with these materials and he remained at the table for a sustained period of time (20 minutes).

The interpretive summary of Learning Story 2

Indicators of spirituality	Interpretations from Narrative Observation 2
ImaginationCare and attention towards another	Child 2 used his natural disposition for imagination when, through play and the materials, he imagined a role play. The dinosaurs were the characters of mothers and babies in the role play.
	I noticed that he arranged all the bigger dinosaurs with smaller ones next to them.
	He suddenly said aloud:
	'Oh there's a little one with a broken back. I'll get your mummy; we'll fix you and take care of you.'
Flow	For the period of time that Child 2 was involved with the role play, he did not appear distracted but was focused in the imaginative dialogue.
Connection with nature	The child was connected to the natural materials and was interested in them as the following evidence suggests:
	He then started looking and touching some pine cones and some spiky balls which had been on a tree.
	As he was arranging the spiky acorns, he was closely watching the materials, feeling them, touching them and looking at them from different angles.
Pedagogical Condition: Reggio Emilia approach	**Interpretations from Narrative Observation 2**
The environment as third teacher	The learning environment was set up with a variety of materials: provocations which included aesthetic natural materials, as shown in the photograph: the dinosaurs, the material and the natural materials were arranged in a tray.
	These were arranged so the child could independently choose the materials. Once Child 2 was at the table, he independently chose the materials to construct his imaginative play.
	He was engaged through the handling of the materials and his gaze and attention to the materials seemed to indicate that he was enjoying the sensory experience as he was: 'feeling them, touching them and looking at them from different angles.'

The image of the child	Evidence in the data suggests that Child 2 is an active constructor of knowledge to make meaning. This is supported by the evidence suggesting that he is able to draw on prior knowledge about families, in particular, mothers and babies, and the evidence suggests that he has an understanding of the relationship between a mother and a baby through his display of caring. 'Child 2: "Oh there's a little one with a broken back. I'll get your mummy; we'll fix you and take care of you." He carefully placed the dinosaur on another dinosaur's back as if to carry the injured baby.' The interpretations of the data suggest evidence that Child 2 is orchestrating his ability to purposefully create a scenario for a role play.
The hundred languages of children	Child 2 was able to express his understanding of caring through play and the materials; he was also able to express his imagination and his understanding of caring vocally and through the materials in the role play. This provided a multidimensional entry point for opportunities for engagement and expression.

Young children and spirituality

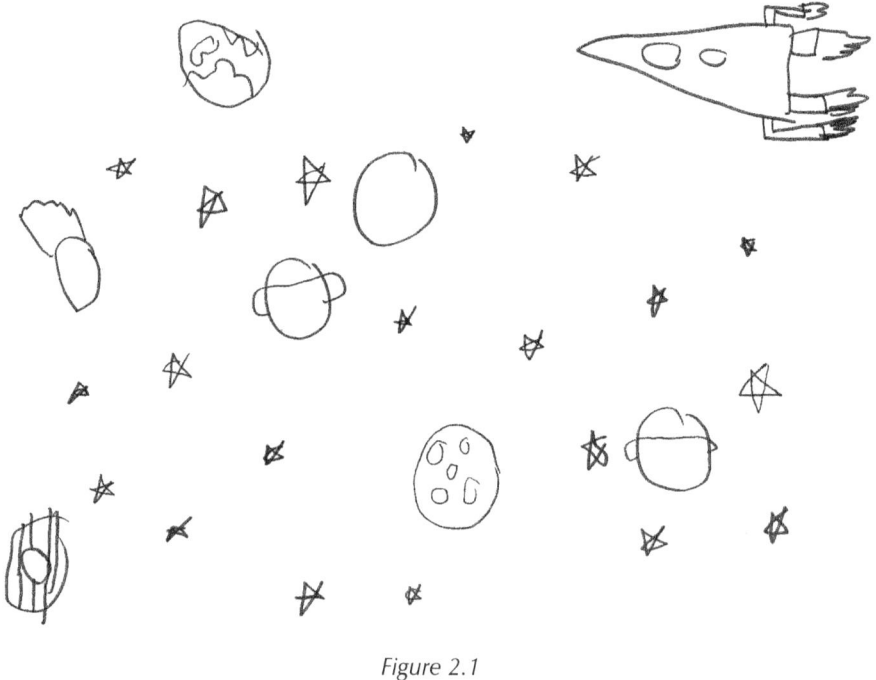

Figure 2.1

❧ *The idea that young children's spirituality "sees what is unseen" is a profound way to describe how children often engage with the world in a deeply intuitive, imaginative, and spiritually open manner. Adults see the world as it is. Children see the world as it could be.* ☙

Helena Card

2.1 Introduction

The field of children's spirituality is broad and vast; therefore, this review attempts to synthesise the scholarly input to present an overview and critique for this particular inquiry. The notions of spirituality, spiritual development and, certainly, of children's spirituality have received attention that has been acknowledged and recognised through the contemporary research and will be highlighted in the review. The literature has indicated some recurring themes and concepts which have provided a suitable theoretical foundation for this inquiry, proposing a conceptual framework for understanding children's expression of spirituality within education.

This section of the literature review presents an overview of current trends and contemporary research in relation to spirituality. With regard to the main guiding questions of the research, the review has sought to provide a thorough grasp of the current position taken towards young children's spirituality in education which then serves to locate this case study as an extension of research incorporating the fusion, analysis and critique of the literature.

The review begins by proposing a view based on scholarly input that spirituality in young children is an innate capacity. The review continues with a discussion which suggests a position regarding the connection that spirituality has with religion or whether spirituality is an ontological concept, an innate human characteristic which can then be transformed and developed through religious tradition.

The starting point for this section traces the understanding of spirituality through a variety of disciplines and the connections to qualitative research paradigms involving the investigation of spirituality and young children. It offers an understanding of spirituality today.

It is followed by a discussion in reference to scholarly reviews about the connection of spirituality and religion—a necessary inclusion within the review which highlights the disparity and confusion between the two ideas. It is pivotal and crucial to be sensitive to the fact that spirituality means different things to different people (Bone, Cullen & Loveridge 2007).

A key aspect of my study is to identify and clarify spirituality and the association with religion providing a context for how it is encompassed and important in a broader sense within education (Kessler 2000; Miller 2000; Palmer 1998). This section of the review is essential as it provides the reader with an idea of the position of the researcher within this inquiry.

The review of academic theories (which are outlined in the literature review) connected to spirituality serves as a guide and a 'scaffold' in attempting a definition of spirituality in young children and a position on their spirituality within this research inquiry. The review draws together global research, perceptions and understanding about spirituality and childhood.

2.2 Spirituality in young children described as ontological

The meaning of the ontological concept positioned within this research in relation to young children is based on research in which it was presented by Hay et al. (2006) and Hyde (2008a) that children have an intrinsic way of theorising how they exist in relation to the world and how they engage their whole self with their experiences and everyday encounters. Children's experiences of spirituality, from this description, suggest an innate spiritual dimension. According to Hart (2006), there has been a growing body of evidence indicating that children do have a spiritual capacity. He states that the critical role of this capacity has 'gone largely unrecognised in the annals of child development' (Hart 2006, p. 163).

2.3 A fusion of past and future: phases of research into understanding spirituality

A past and present fusion of phases of research into conceptualising spirituality is a necessary component of the review which identifies a gap in this area: it serves to indicate and suggest a new phase and platform for innovative research to take shape. Some disparities and anomalies within spirituality in education are reviewed in light of some insights into future recommendations for more research. The review continues to critique some aspects of multidisciplinary approaches in researching children's spirituality.

The analysis of spirituality and research with regard to children has a long history which is connected to qualitative paradigms that link scholars from various disciplines in psychology and sociology who applied procedures of natural science to the study of humans (Ratcliff 2010). Scholars, such as Ratcliff (2010) and, more recently, Boynton (2011), claim that the foundation in understanding spirituality in childhood has been formed by attention to the various disciplines which have influenced understandings of spirituality and those that may have started with theological connections. As the current research is conducted in the present, this may lead to a future conceptualisation of spirituality in young children and a discovery of how to understand the ways in which spirituality presents itself today within childhood.

Ratcliff (2010) presented four phases in the scholarly study of children's spirituality, including religious development. Ratcliff's reference to the four phases is important because it assists in posing the question: 'what was gained at each phase, and what continues to be instructive from the four phases?' (Ratcliff 2010, p. 10)

In the first historical phase, a holistic approach was placed on the child, bringing some new insights to the world, insights in which there is a distinctive orientation to theology which places the child at the centre of divinity (Ratcliff 2010). Theology in relation to this insight is explained as children who are made in the image of God having the right to respect, value and dignity (Rahner 1966, as cited in Bunge 2006) and where children are honoured as part of God's purpose (Bunge 2006; Mercer 2005). All aspects of the child were considered and present correlations with today's current trends and understandings in which spirituality is understood as part of the whole child.

The second historical phase had an emphasis on statistical evidence and records. Within this phase, according to Ratcliff (2010), the relationship between religion and spirituality was not considered permanent and momentary. Within this phase, it was the aspects of spirituality that could fit under enumeration that came into discussion and were given priority. However, as the research progressed, informed by the work of Ratcliff (2001) and Hyde (2008a), it was agreed that this quantitative method for presenting a phenomenon, such as spirituality, presented limitations and that careful study was required, rather than simply using quantitative methods. For example, according to Ratcliff (2010), in the second historical stage, an important consideration to highlight is that the emphasis on religious knowledge also presents some limitations. As was supported by the work of Hay et al. (2006, p. 50), having knowledge about God does not automatically produce spiritual experiences. Hay et al. (2006) state that 'spirituality is universal, found in all human beings whatever their formal religious beliefs, or lack of them'. Considering this fact in the second phase, Ratcliff (2010) poses a crucial consideration for today's understanding of spirituality in young children and how knowledge about God, across sectors, may not necessarily influence spirituality. In other words, spirituality in this phase is considered innate and occurs with or without God (Ratcliff 2010).

Thirdly, the cognitive historical stage brought about some sequencing of religion and faith. The growing complexity surrounding spirituality during this phase was overlooked: instead, there was a trend to oversimplify and to classify children's faith. This brought about a realisation that the theories proposed did not account for the child's experience of spirituality. Johnson and Boyatzis (2006) stated that this phase posed a limited view of the child with regard to spirituality, whereby it did not take into account the fact that cognition and spiritual development are entwined, not through the acquistion of more knowledge, but from the meanings which children construct which connect them to reality.

Ratcliff's (2010) fourth historical phase introduced an emphasis on the cultural and religious influences on the child and constructed a more universal concept of spirituality. This universal concept of spirituality encompassed both religious and non-religious people. The nature of experiences may be influenced by the social and cultural context.

In light of this, it could be argued that contemporary views influenced from a variety of disciplines have opened up the research of children's spirituality into a new realm and understanding. The phases of spirituality, as outlined by Ratcliff and presented here, have shifted the research to a current contemporary view in this area and into the future. Boynton (2011) agrees:

Children's spirituality is an area that requires ongoing theory and research that embraces differing epistemological stances. Both quantitative and qualitative methods and the varying epistemological stances are helpful in developing a more thorough and integrative understanding of spirituality in children.

(Boynton 2011, p. 122)

In regard particularly to young children's education, as suggested by contemporary scholars (Boynton 2011; Hay et al. 2006; Ratcliff 2010), it seems that, through the literature reviewed and described in this section, the next phase of understanding spirituality is offered where further inquiry and research can provide some illumination. Given the strong interest in spirituality, as offered by Hay et al. (2006), to fully expand the understanding of this dimension in childhood, more research is likely to provide further insights and 'lead to a more fruitful dialogue' (Hay et al. 2006, p. 55).

2.4 The critical spiritual phase of research

The emergence of critical spiritual education could be considered the next phase of understanding and researching spirituality. From his investigation of the literature, Wright (2000) suggests that society is becoming more interreligious or secular than religious and moving towards pluralism. Therefore, as Wright (2000) indicates, there is a moving urge to create some universal ground in the quest for an understanding of spirituality and, specifically, if spirituality is to be redefined and understood within education. One pathway towards this re-identification is what Wright (2000, p. 139) refers to as a 'spiritual pedagogy'.

The three aspects offered by Wright (2000) within a model for spiritual pedagogy involve a shift in thinking: firstly, spirituality is inclusive of historical, cultural, linguistic and social tradition; and, secondly, it seeks the spiritual truth and the ways in which it manifests or is exhibited. Thirdly, critical thinking and wisdom are valued in our knowledge and developing relationship with the world. There is a strong relationship with wisdom and knowledge in this developmental process.

In summary, Wright (2000) proposes some provocative initiatives and thinking through additional research in order for education to nurture spirituality. These require a shift towards highlighting tradition, truth and critical thinking that is necessary for work in developing a universal landscape in understanding spirituality.

2.4.1 Spirituality and philosophy

This section examines the discipline of philosophy in relation to understanding spirituality. Philosophy, according to Giesenberg (2007), has the capacity to ask questions about the everyday which increase the interest in, and wonder of, what lies beneath what is actually seen. Philosophy and the connection to spirituality can be interpreted as a connection to the mystery of life and discovery beyond what is seen and known: it cannot be considered apart from living and life.

According to Scheibel (1995), naturally wondering about existential questions is a human characteristic. As stated in reference to Plato and Aristotle, Stewart and Mickanus (1990) and Matthews (1980) maintain that '[p]hilosophy begins with wonder' (Stewart & Mickanus 1990, p. 5; Matthews 1980, p. 2). In scholarly work in which spirituality is discussed, one of the most common spiritual characteristics is wonder (Carey 2003; Myers 1997; Nye & Hay 1996; Smart 1996). It is claimed by Stewart and Mickanus (1990) that philosophy is a spiritual process or activity and that the core of human personhood is the action or activity of philosophising. Stemming from this understanding, Giesenberg (2007) states that '[s]pirituality in philosophy is thus closely connected with everyday life' (p. 54). Each person, including children, philosophises and wonders about everyday things and events which are related to their spiritual nature (Giesenberg 2007).

2.4.2 Philosophical explorations of spirituality outside religious contexts

Developing a broad understanding of spirituality involves exploring the philosophical perception of spirituality outside religious contexts. The scholarly work of Haldane (1992), Jacobs (2003) and McGhee (1992, 2000) offers a view of spirituality and whether it can be understood independently from religious boundaries. As noted by Haldane (1992), spirituality has traditionally been associated with religion.

However, in contrast, Haldane (1992) considers ways in which spirituality might be brought within moral philosophy and acknowledges that it is a central aspect of philosophy itself. Spirituality is connected with some of the topical and great debates of philosophy, such as the mind/body dualism associated with Descartes. From a philosophical perspective, the notion of the spiritual self can be positioned and made visible through the lens of metaphysics. This form of philosophical thinking is concerned with the world beyond the physical. It maintains that belief systems are underpinned by the understanding that human beings are considered above other products of nature. The metaphysical realm was described by Plato, who presented the concept that human beings inhabit a world which is likened to a cave full of shadows and that the reality out in the sun is beyond their comprehension. In relation to the metaphysical philosophies, there is the assumption that something is always outside or beyond our perception.

In contrast, a materialist perspective is opposed to the metaphysical. A materialist view of the world is described as an acceptance that all entities and processes are composed of, or can be reduced to, matter, material forces or physical processes (Stack 1998). This philosophical point of view is described as a reductionist view of human nature.

2.4.3 Spirituality and virtue

The scholarly work of Jacobs (2003) explores the possibility of developing a conception of spirituality that draws on virtue ethics. The notion of virtue is connected to what is naturally pleasing. Jacobs describes this as follows: 'the pleasure of a virtuous activity is not a distinctive sensation but an appreciation of the activity and the object of the activity' (Jacobs 2003, p. 62). He continues by asserting that spirituality enters by the active agent having an awareness of the 'inexhaustible richness of meaning and value that is in the world' (Jacobs 2003, p. 62).

Jacobs (2003) states that spirituality is made accessible by one's knowledge and active enjoyment of goods that are tangible or accessible through virtue. He maintains that this virtuous understanding is underpinned by one's acknowledgement of the world and one's relationship with the world, and that we are completed by this relationship to the world. Jacobs offers the view that we can only live distinctively human lives by conceptualising the world and ourselves in a rich and complex variety of ways. The virtuous agent's appreciation of this view can have a spiritual dimension with this found to be a source and a focus of wonder and delight.

2.4.3.1 Postmodernism

Wright's (2000) scholarly work explores various philosophical traditions which have shaped contemporary spirituality. According to this work, postmodernism embraces the freedom to create and recreate our spiritual values. Lyotard (1984) introduced the term 'metanarratives', which were considered to be comprehensive world views which contribute to the claim to explain the whole of reality. Within the postmodern tradition, worldviews of religion, materialism and romanticism are all dependent on metanarratives and neither God, elements of the material world nor our immediate experience can provide answers to the human condition.

According to Foucault (1989, 1991) and Norris (1987), postmodernism looks at the conception of what is truth and reality and offers a freedom of thinking and an elevation of human consciousness. They maintain that the truth and reality open a 'freedom to roam through the postmodern cultural playground in which everything is permitted' (Wright 2000, p. 21). Postmodernism can be described as a picture of humanity as a fiction which is destined to be erased or removed 'like a face drawn in sand at the edge of the sea' (Foucault 1989, p. 387).

Derrida (1976) offers a postmodern view of spirituality in which not every reality or word we read or discern is related to God. For Derrida, words are not labels, nor associations nor 'divine', 'physical' or 'mental' objects: instead, they are all interconnected to a never-ending web of language. According to Derrida (1976), we have the freedom to read a text using our imagination and to derive our own meaning and interpretation as we wish.

In summary, Wright (2000) proposes that viewing spirituality through a postmodern perspective offers an emancipation from religious and secular ideals and narratives and the desire to obtain the absolute truth. Thus, it offers us the freedom to reconstruct our own spiritual identities in relation to our own feelings, partialities and instincts.

2.4.4 Section summary

In summary, spirituality needs to be situated in the philosophical field. Each person philosophises about everyday things and events; this is also connected to their spirituality where there is an ongoing contemplation about the purpose of life. Overall, to view spirituality through a philosophical lens broadens the understanding and places it as an evolving conversation with its place within society. Equally impacted is education, which is encompassed within the realities of the existing society. In regard to young children today, who exist within a pluralistic, secular society, adopting a philosophical understanding of spirituality opens an ontological and epistemological position for research. Within this position, spirituality is viewed as not tied to religion. According to Watson, de Souza and Trousdale (2014), research from a variety of different disciplines has led to 'a recognition of spirituality as a vital element in human life' (p. 11). Including philosophy alongside psychological, cognitive, theological and educational disciplines leads to a broader understanding of spirituality.

2.5 Spirituality: religious or not?

This section debates the varied views concerning spirituality and religion. The current perception of spirituality in young children (Champagne 2001, 2003; Hart 2003; Hay & Nye 2006; Hyde 2008a, 2008b; Kessler 2000; Mountain 2007; Upton 2009) has become a significant conversation and topic within scholarly research and writing. Before attempting a definition of spirituality, it is necessary to investigate the ongoing debate about segregating spirituality from religion. Initially, scholarly research was geared towards adults and adolescence; however, recently the focus has centred on young children and their spirituality and spiritual development. Across a variety of disciplines, not only is the personal, physical, cognitive, social and emotional development of children regarded (Boynton 2011; Crompton 1998; Crawford & Rossiter 2006; Eaude 2009; Roehlkepartain et al. 2006; de Souza 2009), but spirituality has become recognised as a significant attribute in young children's development, and the inclusion of the spiritual element in their development has raised some scholarly interest and research.

According to Liddy (2002), some children also bring prior religious understanding to their educational context. Scholarly literature by Hay and Nye (2006) and Tacey (2006) has suggested that children are innately spiritual. The changing view and perception of children in early childhood education (as discussed later in this chapter), and the inclusion of many preschool and child care settings associated with a religious context, whether it is Catholic or Christian, propose that there is an understanding of the spiritual dimension in young children.

In reviewing the concept of young children's spirituality, an acknowledgement of the debate about whether religion and spirituality are entwined is essential and understanding the nature of their relationship is necessary in order to establish a position within this research. The following theories are related to scholarly analysis and research: further investigation on the relationship between religion and spirituality is discussed later in the chapter.

The literature and debate on spirituality (Eaude 2003; Harris 2007; Hyde 2008a; Liddy 2002; Tacey 2004) or a clearly articulated definition around spirituality are surrounded by many anomalies. One position supported by scholars is that spirituality is defined or categorised within a secular and humanist understanding. Therefore, spirituality may be described as different from or separate to religion; however, it can still find a place and be expressed outside as well as within a religious tradition (Rossiter 2010a; Tacey 2006).

Within a humanist or secular stance on spirituality, there is the understanding that one seeks to find meaning and purpose in a universal experience, rather than in a religious experience (Meehan 2002b). Another outlook or viewpoint within the humanist perspective is that spirituality is related to wholeness and connectedness (or relationship) with oneself, others, nature and the world but not with a Divine or Greater Source (Eaude 2005; Hay & Nye 2006).

On the other end of the debate is the view that spirituality is affiliated with religion which includes some aspects or traits from the humanistic and secular domain, but, to differentiate, there is also one's relationship with the Divine or Greater Being. In addition, it seems that research to date has suggested some overlap between the nature of spirituality and the nature of religion. The other domain or stance on spirituality is that some strong connections exist between religion and spirituality which aligns with the view of Hay and Nye (2006) that teachers require an understanding and consideration of young children's innate spirituality before considering the religious education program.

Taking this one step further is not only to determine young children's innate spirituality and what this may look like, but also to discover how to nurture this capacity through a pedagogy that is relevant to young children. In addition, a promising prospect is the inclusion of the word 'spiritual' within (Australian Government Department of Education [AGDE] (2022), p. 68), which has some favourable outlooks for the inclusion of the spiritual dimension within early childhood across many sectors. This is explored further in the literature review.

The following discussion helps to define and develop a foundation for understanding spirituality. In order to do so, we have to lend ourselves to a full understanding that, within the process of learning, we engage the elements of perception (Myers 2002) through the senses, with our feelings and our intuition. Myers elaborates this notion of perception and describes that we 'process vast amounts of information off screen' (Myers 2002, p. 15). He expands on intuition by stating that we respond to stimuli which are inspired by intuitive thought and action. Myers (2002) deduces that intuition is alive and vibrant in each person and that our minds are continually processing infinite amounts of information outside our consciousness and beyond verbal interaction. Infants possess amazing intuitive capacity long before they develop language skills:

> (Infants) prefer to look at objects eight to twelve inches away, which, wonder of wonders, just happens to be the approximate distance between a nursing infant's eyes and its mother's ... Babies also have an intuitive grasp of simple laws of physics. Like adults staring in disbelief at a magic trick, infants look longer at a scene of a ball stopping in mid-air, a car seeming to pass through a solid object, or an object that seems to disappear.
>
> (Myers 2002, p. 18)

As these young infants enter our early learning settings, we can build on Myers' deduction and become aware that understanding intuition is integral to understanding the spiritual dimension of children and the implications for early childhood curricula.

Reflecting on what Tacey terms as 'new spirituality', we can begin to recontextualise where spirituality corresponds in our daily interactions with young children (Tacey 2006, p. 208). Subsequently, there is a suggestion that to become more intuitive is to become more aware or to allow mysticism to enter our classrooms and pedagogy (Tacey 2006). We can establish a place and relevance for spirituality. Tacey offers the thought that inward imagining *is* intuition and that 'intuition is a faculty that is vital to the work of soul-making' (Tacey 2006, p. 208).

When inspired by a pedagogical approach, we can allow the most ordinary moments, as suggested by Tacey (2006), to be embellished and enriched by the intuition and wisdom of young children:

> Certainly, part of our problem is that we work from defective or incomplete models of education. We carry an old prejudice that students are empty vessels and they do not have innate wisdom. I think much education begins with the faulty premise that we are vessels that need to be filled, to be directed, corrected, shaped, and conditioned, all from outside. We forget that the people we are addressing are not just young people in need of information, but souls and spirits who need to remember who they are and what they already know.
>
> (Tacey 2006, p. 209)

In relation to pedagogy and to Tacey's perspective, there is also the subject of constructivism in connection to young children's spirituality. Constructivism, when applied within pedagogy, allows children to socially construct meaning. Boynton (2011) states that 'constructivist studies have been instrumental in unearthing some unique features of spirituality for children that include meaning-making ...' (Boynton 2011, p. 122).

Through the insights of Krauss (2005) and Piaget (1976), the idea is conveyed that constructivism supports the belief that each human being is able to interpret and construct meaning and knowledge through interactive internal and external learning experiences which, in turn, provide explanation and guidance. Benson et al. (2003) maintain that constructivism is integral to spiritual development: they define spiritual development from a constructivist lens as:

> the process of growing the intrinsic human capacity for self-transcendence, in which the self is embedded in something greater than the self, including the sacred. It is the developmental 'engine' that propels the search for connectedness, meaning, purpose, and contribution. It is shaped both within and outside of religious traditions, beliefs, and practices.
>
> (Benson et al. 2003, pp. 4–5)

The understanding of spirituality as an essential aspect of establishing identity and relationships with others and the world is indicated by the work of Adams (2009) and Myers (1997). In respect to relationships and spirituality, Adams explains that, within the spiritual aspect, relationships are 'considered in the context of how the child finds their place in the world which in turn shapes their identity' (Adams 2009, p. 116). Where there are significant adults in children's lives, Myers (1997) emphasises that children's development as human beings is dependent upon their relationships with people who are open to loving and guiding them and listening and responding to them.

To broaden this discussion even further, other theorists (Grajczonek 2011; Hyde & Rymarz 2009; Nye 2009; Ratcliff 2010; Ratcliff & May 2004) have all put forward the discussion and relationship posed by spirituality in the context of religious tradition in education and have left this open for interpretation and discussion. A further discussion centred on relationships in light of pedagogical approaches in early childhood education occurs later in this chapter and adds to the breadth of understanding about the place of relationships in regard to spirituality.

Research has posed questions to early childhood centres belonging to the Catholic tradition in consideration of the pedagogy that nurtures the spiritual capacity of children (Grajczonek 2011). The proposal by Grajczonek (2011) questions whether the current *The Early Years Learning Framework for Australia* (Australian Government Department of Education, Employment and Workplace Relations [DEEWR] 2009), and also version 2, requires careful attention to spirituality in the context of Catholic education.

In summary, there is a dualistic aspect to consider: it has been established, as highlighted by the scholarly investigations, that if spirituality is innate, then religious tradition may offer a pathway to come and know the God of that faith. On the other hand, without considering the affiliation of spirituality to faith, as de Souza (2009) points out, there is a 'pressing need to explore a contemporary understanding of spirituality and its implications for education and learning' (de Souza 2009, p. 1129).

2.6 Defining children's spirituality

The meaning of spirituality in relation to young children is sometimes described as the exuberance of a child and a child who has spirit (Harris 2007). In other situations, spirituality can refer to a mystical sense of otherness of a child that may be intangible and vaguely described. Spirituality has been considered an elusive word with a variety of definitions (Palmer 2003). A lack of consensus has been confirmed by Greenstreet (1999): he states that these definitions are variable and do not reflect a consensus of thought.

Spirituality can encompass aspects of human development and has been defined as the 'living out' of the story of one's life (Bennett 2003). All humans have a spiritual essence which incorporates the narratives of our lives, and the consistency of living them out is an intrinsic part of human nature (Atkinson 1995; Burkhardt 1989; Hyde 2008a, 2008b; Ratcliff 2004). Spirituality can be understood as the ability to experience connectedness and to construct meaning in one's life (Fried 2001). According to Palmer (2003), spirituality evokes feelings and human yearning to be connected with something larger than ourselves.

In scholarly attempts to define spirituality, other scholars, such as Fowler (1981) and an element of his thought, have focused on moral development and the effects of behaviour towards others. Furthermore, Hart (2006) suggests that young children have demonstrated the capacity for thoughtful inquiry into the bigger questions, asking about proof and the source of knowledge: they can reason through problems, question their values and reflect on their own identity within the world.

In summary, the varied scholarly views, which have underpinned definitions about young children and spirituality, have a wide scope that incorporates many areas of their development and their existence. As an early childhood educator and researcher, my intention is to appreciate and understand children's spirituality and, within this inquiry, it is my intention to explore the expressions of young children's spirituality. This review of definitions assists in the formulation of an evolving understanding of spirituality in young children.

2.6.1 Towards a working definition

A landscape of opinions and definitions of spirituality has been proposed by a variety of contemporary scholars and theorists (Benson & Roehlkepartain 2008; Champagne 2001; Crawford & Rossiter 2006; Groome 1998; Hardt et al. 2012; Harris 2007; Hart 2003; Hay & Nye 2006; Hyde 2008a; Kirmani & Kirmani 2009; Myers 1997; Palmer 1998; Rodger 1996; Watson 2000). Considering these contemporary definitions and research around children's spirituality, it is essential for this study to formulate a viewpoint on spirituality on behalf of the researcher.

Each of the definitions over time poses a particular view and stance, indicating that ambiguity still presents itself in association with the notion and concept of young children and spirituality. Several researchers have expressed the view that there has been no clear definition of spirituality in relation to young children (Hart & Ailoae 2006–07; Hay & Nye 2006; Hyde & Rymarz 2009; Ratcliff 2010; Ratcliff et al. 2004; Wright 2000). As suggested by Ratcliff and May (2004), one might consider that determining a definition of spirituality may restrict some further thinking and contemplation in expanding the meaning. 'If children's spirituality is to be considered as involving the whole person, every area of the child, perhaps there is benefit in deferring the definitions' (Ratcliff & May 2004, p. 10).

The following scholars, Carr (1995), Coles (1990) and Eaude (2005), have all expressed some hesitation towards the possibility of establishing a clear definition of spirituality and suggest that allowing further discourse and a more widely shared meaning seems a more positive approach.

However, as Bone (2007) suggests when undertaking her research on children's spirituality, research about spirituality in the context of early childhood education is highly justified. Expanding on this, Bone (2007) implies that research into spirituality is an attempt not only to eliminate the speculations and phrases used in recent research when relating spirituality to young children, but also to open up an understanding of what this may look like, how it exists and what indicators or expressions contribute to children's spiritual capacity. In her research, Bone (2007) presents a working definition to position herself as the researcher within the inquiry and describes spirituality in the following way:

> ... a force that connects people to each other, to all living things, to nature and the universe. Spirituality is a way of appreciating the wonder and mystery of everyday life. It alerts me to the possibility for love, happiness, goodness, peace and compassion in the world.
>
> (Bone 2007, p. 8)

In education, spirituality has been defined both as being affiliated with religion and as falling outside religious boundaries (Carson 1956; Champagne 2001, 2003; Coles 1990; Hyde 2008a, 2008b; Liddy 2002; Ruddock & Cameron 2010; Wright 2000).

These scholars have also presented these affiliated views on spirituality and have critically reflected on how spirituality is revealed within children.

Therefore, in summarising their accounts, it can be stated that, in education, spirituality is viewed as a quest for knowledge and meaning-making in the everyday (Hyde 2008a, 2008b; Kennedy & Duncan 2006; Moriarty 2011; Webster 2004) and, in the psychological discipline (Hardt et al. 2012), it entails the quest for a meaningful existence. Spirituality opens up a personal consciousness and awareness about everything and attempts to make meaning from wondering, along with the questions and answers that are pondered (Coles 1990; Hart 2003).

At this point as this case study research progresses, it is important to acknowledge that the findings may provoke a reconceptualisation or a rethinking of spirituality in young children. In line with Benson et al.'s (2003) belief, a working definition is influenced by the culture and context in which it occurs (Ratcliff & Nye 2006). Supporting Ratcliff and Nye's (2006) notion involves taking up their argument, which is in support of future research requiring a 'synthesis of the multiplicity of definitions' from prior research (p. 478). Underpinning this research is the intention to rethink and to recognise young children's spirituality within a particular context, rather than forming a definition.

2.7 Spirituality: mapping/charting the contemporary landscape

The review of the literature suggests several insights into spirituality and, through consideration of these insights, and in light of this exploration, it is necessary to present a summary of where the understanding lies in regard to spirituality as an innate capacity.

Much of the contemporary research suggests that spirituality is:

> ... concerned with a person's sense of connectedness or relationship with self, others, the world (or indeed the cosmos) and for many, with a Transcendent dimension—God in the Christian tradition.
>
> (Hyde & Rymarz, 2009, p. 45)

As mentioned, this broad statement does not offer a clear and concise explanation of spirituality before the entry of religious affiliation. However, it is stated that:

> ... if children's spirituality is to be considered as involving the whole person, every area of the child, perhaps there is benefit in deferring the development of an ultimate definition, and entertaining a multiplicity of definitions.
>
> (Ratcliff & May 2004, p. 10)

While spirituality may be considered as involving the whole person and has a multiplicity of definitions, various scholars have advised that children are capable of having profound spiritual experiences from an early age (Champagne 2001; Hart 2003; Hay & Nye 2006; Hyde 2008a). The notion of spirituality has received considerable attention in research and the diverse scholarship (Eaude 2003; Tacey 2004; Upton 2009) suggests a kaleidoscope of descriptions in terms of attributes and characteristics of spirituality, rather than offering an explicit and defined clarity.

2.8 Contemporary research into children's spirituality

An interesting point to consider is that, while it has been indicated that children are innately spiritual (Champagne 2001; Hay & Nye 2006; Hart 2003, 2006; Tacey 2006), and if their education in the early years is within a Christian context, then this may present a starting place for further spiritual development affiliated to the Christian tradition. This is supported by Hay and Nye (2006), who have argued that educators should firstly contemplate and understand young children's spirituality in order to nurture further spiritual development.

It has been considered by Hart (2003) that although all people have a spiritual capacity, it seems that children may be even more open to this capacity. Adams et al. (2008), Champagne (2001), Hart (2003) and Hyde (2008b) have proposed that the spiritual dimension exists and cannot be divorced from children. They also concur that the spiritual dimension is most evident and visible in the everyday.

Within education, spirituality has been viewed and described as a quest for knowledge and the making of meaning (Carson 1956; Coles 1990; Fowler 1981; Hyde 2008b; Kessler 2000; Liddy 2002; Palmer 1999a; Steiner 1995). When relating this to children, spirituality can manifest itself through wonder, imagination and the experience of their world. A fusion and amalgamation of the above theorists' descriptions and views on spirituality denote that children's spirituality is then a personal consciousness and awareness about phenomena, a pursuit to make meaning and connections from the answers or theories that one has when wondering and contemplating.

For scholarly input, I have chosen a collection of contemporary scholars who offer some emerging themes that propose various indicators or capacities of spirituality. For the purpose of this research, these current scholars offer a foundation or a starting point for further examination of children's expression of spirituality.

2.9 Categorising children's spirituality

Research into spirituality by Hay and Nye (2006) conducted in British schools encompassed the interviewing of children of primary school age, and culminated with the claim that all children have an innate spirituality with which they are born. Their study led to further investigation into children's spirituality which opened up a wider sphere of comprehension and recognition of spirituality. Hay and Nye (2006) referred to a spiritual sensitivity which comprised three categories: awareness sensing, mystery sensing and value sensing. These categories were made evident as they observed children interacting with their daily activities. Awareness sensing refers to those times when young children are completely absorbed in whatever they are doing and can be described in terms such as flow, focusing or tuning. Mystery sensing, b contrast, includes children's sense of awe and wonder and also includes imagination, which they use in response to complex issues or in observing phenomena. The last category, value sensing, is observed in children as they respond to various experiences and try to make sense of the meaning of those encounters.

Branching further into their research is yet another proposed identification or characteristic of spirituality named by Hay and Nye (2006) as 'relational consciousness'. This relational consciousness was observed during those times when children articulated their awareness of many things but, most significantly, these things were always in relation to someone or something.

The rudimentary core of children's spirituality seems to lie in this relational consciousness, out of which can arise aesthetic experience, personal and traditional response to mystery and being, and mystical and moral insight (Hay & Nye 2006, p. 114).

2.10 Modes of young children's spirituality

Champagne (2001) opened up some unique directions in exploring young children's spirituality. The notion of language and voice as the sole means of understanding spirituality placed her research in a different sphere whereby spirituality could be described as 'going beyond words' (Champagne 2001). This was related to Rogoff's (2003) educational theory in which spirituality is part of a more 'nuanced' communication that involves gaze and gesture (Rogoff 2003, p. 310).

Champagne, like McCreery (1996), conducted her research with small children, proposing a focus on spirituality as communicated 'without words'. As a result, her intention was to widen this aspect in her research with young children (Champagne 2001, p. 82).

In terms of shifting thought and concepts related to young children's spirituality, Champagne's work offered an alternative angle. Her work favoured and explored the theory around listening to and for spirituality (Champagne 2001). Her later work went on to present a condition of listening for spirituality whereby the participant became involved in the everyday experiences of young children and presented the challenge of being open to recognising spirituality.

The work from Champagne's (2003) study suggested modes of spirituality and a holistic, sensitive attitude towards spiritual awareness in young children. Champagne's (2003) research extends the phenomenon of spirituality into a holistic perception of children's ways of being in the world and a broader context for considering and appreciating the manner in which spirituality exists in young children. Her metaphorical and rhetorical research into this dimension suggests an outline or framework of a 'spiritual form' of the child's being which may help to define and affirm the relevance in developing an understanding of 'the spiritual dimension in day to day living' (Champagne 2003, p. 44). Her work provides a platform for further research in early childhood and in the reconceptualisation of childhood in light of the spiritual dimension as children 'participate in their existence' and 'manifest essential facets of being a child' (Champagne 2003, p. 44).

In summary, Champagne's research into the modes of spirituality focused on facial expression, gestures, words and attitudes: her work did not extend to include factors within the environment or how the environment entwined as the children interacted. Also excluded were the style and pedagogy of the everyday learning setting. Consequently, her research offers a platform for this case study and for further research into the breadth and many features of children's spirituality, including factors of the environment which may influence children's ways of being.

2.11 Expressions of spirituality in young children

The following section identifies and collates the contemporary scholarly literature with regard to the various expressions of spirituality in young children.

2.11.1 Spiritual experiences of wonder, wondering, relational spirituality and wisdom

An investigation into the childhood experiences of spirituality by Hart (2003) also recognised the challenges of listening to the spiritual: in this investigation, he conducted in-depth interviews with more than 100 individuals and gathered written accounts from hundreds more children and adults. These narrative accounts of life experiences were collated in his research. His process is described as 'trying to hear the delicate and often the very private spiritual moments that can shape a life' (Hart 2003, p. 4). When investigating these childhood experiences of adults, his study demonstrated its significance by indicating and concluding that families and teachers have an impact on the spiritual experiences of children.

Furthermore, Hart's (2003, 2006) research identifies four types of experiences and capacities which can be referred to as ways of being and existing in the world (2006). These capacities present themselves as wonder, wondering, relational spirituality and wisdom. In relation to young children, Hart (2006) proposes that these capacities 'may help provide a multifaceted definition of spiritual life, demonstrating the diverse ways in which spirituality manifests' (Hart 2006, p. 165). His research points out that these capacities or characteristics are not always present all the time in every child. They may present themselves at different stages and at different times. The next section explores the capacities of wonder, wondering, relational spaces and wisdom.

Wonder, according to Hart's (2006) description, entails a 'constellation of experiences that can involve feelings of awe, connection, joy, insight and a deep sense of reverence and love' (p. 165). Hart claims that children's insights are comparable with those of the great mystics of the world and that they could shape a world view or the course of someone's life (Hart 2006, p. 168). Hart's description of wonder encompasses the asking of the big questions about life and meaning that can include knowing and knowledge, truth and justice, reality and death. He relates it as being 'a spiritual quest' and a passage of entering into a form of discourse with the mysteries of life.

A significant aspect of Hart's research was his high regard for children and their wonderings: he advocated that these were to be taken seriously, while acknowledging that, in the past, they had been discounted or unappreciated (Hart 2006, p. 168). He comments that time for children to wonder is valuable as it allows one to see in 'a more immediate, open, and less categorical fashion' (Hart 2004, p. 43). The time for wonder and total absorption in the learning environment, according to Hart, is essential in order to satisfy this innate capacity and need in young children.

Furthermore, adding to Hart's (2006) scholarly theories, and his views on the spiritual capacities of young children is what he refers to as relational spirituality or the 'spirituality which is lived out in the intersection of our lives': the 'between you and me' (Hart 2006, p. 172). In young children, this can begin as an experience of empathy and then leads into deep understanding. Hart contends that relational spirituality is:

> ... about communion—a profound sense of interconnection with the cosmos; connection – a sense of intimacy with someone or something; community—a sense of belonging to a group; compassion – the drive to help others.
> (2006, p. 174)

Hart (2004) strongly advocates for concern in respecting and enhancing children's spiritual capacities. Hence, within early childhood education, this bears considerable contemplation of and action in understanding childhood. He continues by stating that the capacities of children reveal a spiritual intelligence which, like any intelligence, is diverse. All beings possess this and he maintains that '[i]t can emerge at different times, and it may require cultivation in order to be brought to full bloom' (Hart 2004, p. 47).

In addition, he states that any encounter with divinity through awe and wonder does not wait and that: '[w]e live it as children, and it forms a centre point for our lives; even, perhaps the deepest source of human motivation' (Hart 2004, pp. 47–48).

Furthermore, Hart asserts that young children have a capacity for wisdom, contrary to the view that wisdom is related to experience. He suggests that children are able to access 'profound insight and acting wisely' (Hart 2004, p. 39).

Wisdom portrays many entities and meaning; however, Hart's (2004) explanation in regard to young children is related to their spiritual nature. He explains that it has connections to how we live and what we know, but becomes more as it embodies knowledge and compassion in our lives. Relating this to young children, they have knowing which connects to remarkable insights. Hart's view and theory are bounded in the recognition that wisdom is an entity:

> ... it is an activity of knowing, perhaps most simply named as a shift in a state of consciousness. In some moments, children find remarkable insight as they access this contemplative knowing that complements the rational and sensory.
> (2004, p. 40)

In summary, Hart's advocacy for recognising spiritual capacities in young children places great emphasis on knowing and understanding the inner world of children. While respecting the everyday perceptions, feelings, connections, questions and ways of being in the world (Hart 2004) which young children express, we open ourselves to understanding their spiritual life.

Openly considered and stated by Hart and aligned scholarly colleagues is the fact that spiritual capacity has been described as ontological (Hay et al. 2006; Puhakka, Hart & Nelson 2000) or as an innate and intrinsic quality of each person. Scholars (Adams et al. 2008; Coles 1990; Hart 2003; Wills 2012) have suggested, in relation to an ontological view of spirituality, that it is a perception and way of being in the world, in relation to and connected with the world and 'an essential aspect of being is an essential aspect of humanity' (Heidegger 1978, p. 228).

In Hart's (2003) research, he advocates for a challenge to religious doctrine, tradition and values to first understand children and how children are and exist in the world before religious doctrine is taught or discussed. He debates that having this recognition changes perspectives and practice in education. Hart's significant debate and theories raise the possibilities of first considering pedagogy and practice which nurture spiritual capacities and value children. What happens later is that their minds can be open to religious traditions, values or doctrine.

Most importantly, Hart contests the view that the consideration and understanding of children's innate spiritual capacities challenge education, questioning '... what the point and the practice of education is or should be?' (2004, p. 48).

In summary, Hart (2003) offers an ontological viewpoint on children's spirituality. He outlines some capacities in young children, such as wonder, wisdom and wondering, as children connect with the experiences and actualities of the everyday. These capacities are the ones that Hart conveys as important to consider and nurture, challenging religious tradition to primarily consider these aspects and to recognise spirituality before considering other aspects related to doctrine and further spiritual and religious development (Hay & Nye 2006; Vialle, Walton & Woodcock 2008). In relation to young children's spirituality, Hart's (2003) research connects with proposals and research offered by other scholars whose insights recognise that children are innately spiritual and that, while a person may be spiritual, this is not necessarily connected to religion (Grajczonek 2012; de Souza 2009; Rossiter 2010b; Tacey 2000). As suggested by Watson, when considering spirituality, a broad perspective is required: she states that 'the term, 'spirituality', can be stretched to encompass a broad area well beyond the religious' (Watson 2003, p. 12).

2.11.2 Spiritual characteristics

Building on Hay and Nye's (2006) earlier studies, Hyde (2008a) has conducted work within Australian Catholic schools with his work related to primary school-aged children.

Insights into the spirituality of children can be gained by focusing not only on their use of religious language and concepts, but also on the perceptions, awareness and responses of children to what might be classified as ordinary and everyday activities (Hyde 2008a, p. 60).

The research and scholarly input from Hyde reaffirm the spiritual capacity of children: he offered four categorisations and characteristics of children's spirituality, namely, the felt sense, integrating awareness, weaving the threads of meaning and spiritual questing (Hyde 2008a). Hyde's theories generate overlaps with and connections to previous research, in particular to Hay and Nye's (2006) earlier studies.

In summary, he concedes that spiritual characteristics are detectable in children and can be nurtured by the adults within their lives. While he has identified children's spiritual capacities, he also proposes that: '[f]urther research is needed to determine these, and to provide further signs for adults to effectively enable them to nurture the spiritual dimension of children's lives' (Hyde 2008a, p. 172).

2.11.3 Spirituality and pedagogy with young children

In an exploration of spirituality and pedagogy, the work of Eaude (2003, 2005, 2009) posed the view that how teachers understand spirituality is linked to how they provide for it (2005). An angle within the qualitative, ethnographic research which he undertook noted that the work has significant implications towards pedagogy and practice, suggesting that it is necessary to consider spiritual development when designing programs and approaches which cater for young children. Moreover, this idea is affirmed and supported through Eaude's academic hypothesis and research with regard to every aspect of school life and the curriculum: '[w]hile some activities offer particular opportunities for spiritual development, the emphasis needs to be more on environments, relationships and pedagogy than on techniques, content or lesson plans' (Eaude 2005, p. 247). The conclusions and themes raised from his study proposed the following:

> For teachers to look at their teaching environment, planning and interactions with, and assessment of, children through the lens of spiritual development may provide new, and creative ways of enriching children's experiences and self-understanding.
>
> (Eaude 2005, p. 247)

The work of Eaude (2009) continued with the culmination of knowledge around children's spiritual capacities, with this related to mental health. He claims that there are three characteristics attributed to, and necessary for, children's happiness and wellbeing.

Firstly, there is the capacity, to which Eaude refers as the 'sense of search', which he argues is related to the existential questions which children ask. For example, 'Who am I? Why am I here?' These questions are associated with 'identity, place and purpose' (Eaude 2009, p. 189).

Secondly, there is the search for meaning related to making sense of difficult situations (Eaude 2009, p. 190). Eaude insists that children need to make sense of what is hard to comprehend in life as this presents a continual challenge they have to face. He argues that it is unnecessary to protect children from questions which do not have definite answers and that this may prevent them from asking the constant questions they have that are related to the search for meaning (Eaude 2009).

Thirdly, Eaude's work defines another characteristic—connectedness. Here, he has used the work of Hay and Nye (2006), where they identified connectedness under four categories. Within this characteristic, the children recognise 'both their independence and interdependence' (Eaude 2009, p. 190). This is also characterised by children developing a sense of identity and how they exist in the world.

Eaude's work recommends that inviting children to encounter challenges and to make sense of, and search for, meaning contributes to happiness and flourishing. The opportunities where children have a sense of agency and resilience 'to cope with adversity' (Eaude 2009, p. 195), in his opinion, contribute to a healthy state of mental health and happiness. He concludes that for children to flourish and for their spiritual aptitude and dimension to exist, they require opportunities to explore, search and to reflect (2009).

In summary, Eaude's work seeks to suggest that as children encounter their world through child-centred pedagogies, they are able to express themselves as they seek to wonder about themselves and make meaning of the world. His belief is that:

> … young children have important capacities like openness, curiosity and joy, the teacher must allow, and enable, these to flourish. Among the qualities that this

demands of teachers are flexibility and sensitivity, too easily underestimated if planning becomes over-focused on content and a transmission model of learning.

(Eaude 2005, p. 247)

According to Eaude, the expressions and capacities of children are aligned with positive emotional and mental wellbeing; they are also connected to their spiritual development. To consider a pedagogy that nurtures these capacities is to promote an understanding of children's spirituality.

2.12 Children and their spiritual life

The review of the spiritual life of children leads to a deeper insight and understanding of this concept and phenomenon. In support of this, Liddy (2002) points out: '[s]uch insights may enable us to think more holistically about them and teach them in more spiritually meaningful ways' (p. 13). Liddy offers a culmination of thoughts extracted from contemporary scholarly research and scrutiny (Coles 1990; Hay & Nye 2006; Kessler 2000) in which her own account of young children's spirituality is summarised. Through her scholarly inquiry, Liddy attests that contemporary research indicates that spirituality is intricately connected to the meaning and purpose of life and that, as we develop our insights, it may 'enable us to think more holistically' about children and to 'teach them in more spiritually meaningful ways' (Liddy 2002, p. 13). Furthermore, Liddy argues that if this is the terrain of children's spirituality, 'the vast majority of children enjoy rich and challenging spiritual lives that are at the centre of developing self-understanding' (Liddy 2002, p. 18).

In summary, Liddy's intention is a fine-tuning of research bringing to the forefront the view that a recognition and an ability from teachers are crucial to identify the dimensions of childhood where spirituality is likely to appear and exist (2002). In her key point, she argues that there should be great emphasis placed on the recognition of children in a spiritual sense and she states that: '[i]t is far more important to acknowledge the child as an intensely spiritual being and find ways to discover the language and images they are using to be in relationship in the world' (Liddy 2002, p. 19).

2.13 Key indicators and characteristics of children's spirituality

The scholarly input has produced some key characteristics or indicators of children's spirituality. One core indicator or disposition is relationship or connectedness (Adams 2009; Adams et al. 2008; Hart 2003, 2006; Hay & Nye 2006; Nye 1998). This indicator or characteristic is expressed through the child's relationship with the self, with others, with the world and, in some children, with God or an Ultimate.

Identity and a sense of belonging have also been identified as fundamental characteristics of children's spirituality. They are reflected in how children come to know and find themselves in relationship with others and are expressed and related to children seeking to find meaning in the many experiences they encounter in their everyday (Adams 2009; Coles 1990; Eaude 2003, 2005, 2009; Hay & Nye 2006; Hyde 2008a).

Another indicator of children's spirituality and spiritual life is their sense of awe and wonder (Hart 2003, 2006; Hay & Nye 2006; Hyde 2008a). Two other indicators have also been recognised: imagination (Hay & Nye 2006) and wisdom (Hart 2003, 2005). These researchers have presented a landscape and key points to further develop and research in light of young children and education. Moreover, a point not to be overlooked is the literature which strongly advocates that recognising the indicators or dimensions of spirituality must also be in relation to educators. Further research presents a challenge towards understanding how spirituality appears and presents itself in the everyday, how it is listened to (Champagne 2003) and how to find ways to discover the language, images and expressions which children use within their spiritual dimension (Liddy 2002).

If we accept that spirituality is a part of each child's connection to the meaning and purpose of life (Coles 1990; Hay & Nye 2006; Liddy 2002), then young children have an intensely spiritual capacity. It may, therefore, be possible to suggest that spirituality has to do with the essence of the human condition (Kendall 1999; Liddy 2002). As children seek to express their place in life, each child has a capacity for spirituality which can present itself through indicators as children interact with each other and make meaning of their world.

The contemporary views on spirituality and young children, as highlighted in this review, pertain to the view that spirituality is a natural human disposition. Groome (1998) presents the argument that spirituality is a human 'universal possibility' (p. 332) and that spirituality belongs to every person's being. He states that it is more accurate to 'call ourselves spiritual beings who have a human life, than human beings who have a spiritual life' (Groome 1998, p. 332).

> If spirituality can be related to children's expression of being, if it is related to children's being, it may be possible to recognise it in different concrete situations, and even more so in their activities of daily life.
> (Champagne 2003, p. 44)

This conceptualisation of spirituality is to contemplate it as the essence of our being: it is related to the wonder and awe of life and ordinary activities (Hart 2003). It is a fluid entity that presents itself differently and through people's identity and experiences.

If spirituality is viewed as a truly holistic concept (Bone 2010), then could it be suggested that a connection to those philosophies that favour holistic approaches to education could help us to continue to define or to reconceptualise spirituality in young children?

2.14 Understanding childhood and spirituality

In seeking to fully understand and respect the notion of childhood and, as suggested, the spiritual indicators and characteristics which children express, we are urged to find a pathway to understand and value the spiritual rhythms of their nature (Lindner 2004). The potential for being 'spiritually arousing' is brought within the ordinary experience of everyday childhood. Understanding childhood, according to Nye (2009), means that we need to allow ourselves entry points within children's everyday experiences which then open up the door to further thinking: as Nye suggests, this is a 'fundamental element' in understanding childhood spirituality (Nye 2009, p. 8).

Nye's (2009) work in Britain, and her scholarly research, have conceptualised three different entry points for understanding, firstly, childhood and then spirituality, with these entry points described below.

2.14.1 Children's ways of knowing

Children present us with a more holistic way for the perception and interpretation of things. They do not seem to analyse things as much and therefore their insights and observations have a more mystical quality (as discussed in the next paragraphs). Insights from Cooke (1994) remind us that human awareness is more than what may touch us: it involves a perception of the world which Cooke likens to the mystical and describes as 'mysterious and wondrous' (Cooke 1994, p. 11). Children are particularly open, curious and inquisitive about their world. They have a natural and intrinsic capacity for wonder.

2.14.2 Children in their daily encounters

Children in their encounters and endeavours of learning and discovering are comfortable with the *noetic*, which is about 'being granted new understanding' (Nye 2009, p. 8). According to Nye (2009), most studies of childhood spirituality have been restricted to verbal exchanges and what children can talk about. Through familiarising ourselves with the theories and constructs of childhood, we build a deeper understanding: this implies being open to the notion that many approaches, not only the verbal approach, are integral to understanding this dimension of childhood. This warrants attentive contemplation as the spiritual dimension is embraced and comprised in childhood as a part of their being. As reinforced by Champagne: '[s]pirituality inhabits the being. It is expressed through the being' (Champagne 2003, p. 52). This concept of 'the being' that has been identified and clarified in research, as Champagne (2003, p. 52) advocates, 'can make us better witnesses of young children's spirituality'.

2.14.3 Children's ways of being

The child's day is one of encounters, exploring, discovering, inquisitiveness, wondering and inventiveness (Kind 2010; Matthews 2004; Olmsted 2012). If we want to honour spirituality, then we must be open to offering children many ways of 'being' and opportunities to express their spiritual dimension (Bellous & Csinos 2009; Kirmani & Kirmani 2009). Reinforcing this is Hardt et al.'s (2012) investigation, which presented the core dimensions of spirituality from a psychological discipline that characterises a feeling of being at home in the world as an integral part of this dimension to which we must be responsive.

2.14.4 The Reggio Emilia approach and spirituality in young children

This section offers an understanding of the Reggio Emilia philosophy and approach. It provides some angles which draw on further scholarly input to support this proposal. What require further investigation and are pertinent to this research are a pedagogy and practice that offer a platform for childhood to expand and to include its spiritual potential. This section explores an approach to education that, first and foremost, places the child at the centre. A pedagogy inspired by the Reggio Emilia approach may offer this platform for understanding, observing and valuing the spiritual dimension of childhood and may offer a reconceptualisation of spirituality within early childhood education.

In order to have a sustainable early childhood learning environment which enriches spirituality, it may seem that it is imperative to adopt a view about the need for educational nourishment which goes beyond written curricula and outcome-driven systems (Bosacki 1999; Chandler 1992), but serves to preserve and foster desirable commodities and capabilities which naturally exist. These commodities or capabilities, according to Helminiak (1996), may include the ability to thoughtfully regulate, express and channel emotions and creativity—to synthesise oneself in relation to life and to be considered as an authentic human reality. This requires nourishment in a supportive environment throughout life (Helminiak 1996). The understanding of spirituality in young children presents a deep connection to some essential and desirable intrinsic capabilities necessary for their whole development as citizens within today's society.

The Reggio Emilia approach invites educators to perceive children and childhood in a way that encompasses humanity. This is illustrated and reinforced by Rinaldi (2006):

> ... childhood is not a separate phase of life or of human identity. Childhood is the loveliest metaphor for describing the possibilities of mankind, on the understanding that we let it exist, that we recognise it and that we cease all these processes of acceleration and imitation that, in denying childhood, destroy not childhood but man.
>
> (Rinaldi 2006, p. 176)

The Reggio Emilia pedagogical approach has offered us a different way of viewing children. As stated by Malaguzzi (1994), the founding educator of the approach, the child is viewed in a positive way, not with deficits and in need of care and moulding, but as a strong image of the child (Malaguzzi 1994; Rinaldi 2006) and children.

The Reggio Emilia approach presents a way of learning with children that not only recognises this strong and powerful image of the child (Malaguzzi 1994; Rinaldi 2006) but, in accordance with contemporary theories regarding spirituality, in this light of encompassing humanity, must bear some forethought in recognising the spiritual image of the child. De Souza's (2009) research into young children's cognitive understanding recognises that students learn both consciously and unconsciously and that the way in which information and learning are presented should engage the senses which provide different kinds of memory. This notion of learning presents us with a holistic approach to understanding children and providing programs which engage and enhance every aspect of their senses. Rinaldi offers us the view that: '... Reggio has widened the idea of language into what they have called "the hundred languages of children" ...' (Rinaldi 2006, p. 7). This provides a holistic framework for learning which engages the senses in young children and allows interpretation through many modes and expressions.

Miller (2000) states that, when we look at holistic education, an education which nourishes the soul, we need to clearly identify the term 'soul' from a non-sectarian point of view. The term 'soul' may often be used in connection with religion but, to introduce a more postmodern understanding of soul, we can use the term in a manner that allows for a broader and more inclusive approach to spiritual education.

A more recent and contemporary study of young children's spirituality has offered suggestions that spirituality is an awareness and consciousness of everything, seeking engagement and meaning-making from the answers which one gains from wondering and curiosity (Giesenberg 2007). In considering this research, the Reggio Emilia approach is considered as a philosophical approach which allows young children to express themselves through a variety of media and to make sense of their experiences (Gardner 2001).

Together with the approaches of Steiner (1995) and Montessori (1964), the Reggio Emilia approach is European in origin: it holds similar views of children as capable, full of potential and as 'active authors of their own development, strongly influenced by natural, dynamic, self-righting forces within themselves' (Edwards 2002b, p. 5). This research has identified that there may be potential through current literature in the pursuit of an understanding of spirituality in young children and the connection to the Reggio Emilia approach.

For this research, and through the examination of the literature, I have proposed the view that spirituality is a natural human disposition (Adams et al. 2008; Champagne 2003; Hart 2003; Hay & Nye 2006; O'Murchu 1998). Contemporary views on spirituality and young children consider that spirituality is a natural human disposition also present in children. If spirituality can present itself in children, the Reggio Emilia approach may offer a field for the observation of spiritual indicators in young children in early childhood settings.

It is important to establish that this research aimed to clarify and confine spirituality to young children, what this might look like, how it may present itself in educational learning situations and how spirituality can be expressed by young children. This is where the connection with the Reggio Emilia approach to teaching and learning unfolded as the research and inquiry proceeded.

A more recent study conducted within Australian preschools has offered suggestions that spirituality is an awareness and consciousness of everything, seeking engagement and meaning-making from the answers which one gains from wondering and curiosity (Giesenberg 2007). This author's research offered an innovative look at young children's spirituality: the results indicated that a well-balanced teaching program, one which attends to all aspects of child development, including the spiritual, is essential and concurred that preschool children do display characteristics of spirituality. However, it did not consider, investigate, name or clarify what could or may constitute a well-balanced program and the connection to young children's spirituality.

An investigation undertaken in Australia by Nemme (2008) incorporated young children's spirituality. Her work extended the work of Hay and Nye in attempting to shift Gardner's (1983, 1999) work with multiple intelligences and, in particular, with reference to existential intelligence. Her research supported the narrow space that encompassed spirituality and suggested that it was related to religious and theological theoretical frameworks, posing the challenge that religion and spirituality are not the same but can work independently or in connection with one another. The study underlined that influences other than religion can be associated with spirituality, opening the door to a link with educational influences: hence, it is a useful investigation to bring to another realm of contemplation and the rationalising of children's spirituality.

Nemme's (2008) work is recognised as contemporary, with it acknowledged that her theory and investigation maintain that spirituality exists and can be exhibited by young children. However, her study, although undertaken in three educational settings, neglected to consider the connection between the educational environments and failed to offer any insights into a pedagogical approach which may nurture spirituality and influences from the educational environment.

2.15 Spirituality: psychology and human development

Another body of literature explores spirituality from psychological perspectives. Spirituality can be placed within the sphere of psychological science as it is a synthesis of thinking skills linked to creativity which presents a connection to research in the field of education (Hogan 2009).

Thinking and consciousness can develop through different stages—this has been acknowledged by several developmental psychologists (Fischer & Bidell 2006; Labouvie-Vief 1994; Pascual-Leone 2000). In early childhood education and in young children, consciousness develops and centres itself on bodily sensations and extends out to the physical and social world (Hogan 2009). It begins to be centred in the world of language and memory. If we take this notion of consciousness coupled with imagination, the human person is offered a limitless palette of mental freedom and perhaps a 'profound, universal connection' which can allow ideas to flow into a state which can be likened to 'a transcendental, spiritual state of being that is somehow above and beyond the material world, free from all material constraints' (Hogan 2009, p. 139).

Developmental psychologists like Pascual-Leone (2000) propose categories of spirituality representing a high state in human cognitive and emotional development together with modes of thinking and feeling associated with wisdom. Hogan (2009) insists, therefore, that spirituality exists as 'states of consciousness and associated abstractions (i.e. ideas, values and beliefs) that pertain to the concept of spirituality in "human systems"' (Hogan 2009, p. 139), suggesting that it is part of our challenge to understand it.

Any research must bear this in mind, by encompassing this knowledge from a psychological perspective to provide a reliable investigation. Accordingly, this research is designed to address the cognitive and emotional aspects of the human condition through a balanced investigation which includes multidisciplinary outlooks in an attempt to fully comprehend the notion of spirituality and the impact it has on young children's lives.

2.15.1 Intelligence reframed as spiritual intelligence

Gardner (1983), through his multiple intelligences theory, referred to spirituality as the possibility of intelligence, with this proposal existing within his early work in 1983. Later, in 1999, he emphasised a belief in a 'spiritual intelligence' and suggested this as a topic for further research. His book, titled *Intelligence Reframed* (Gardner 1999), revisited the concept of spirituality and, in reference to Gardner's theory (which he continued to develop), ascertains that spiritual intelligence is concerned with cosmic or existential issues expressed in an interest and inquiry about experiences.

The multiple intelligences theory of Gardner (1999) includes existential intelligence. Someone with existential intelligence has the:

> ... capacity to locate oneself with respect to the furthest reaches of the cosmos ... and the related capacity to such existential features of the human condition as the significance of life.
>
> (Gardner 1999, p. 60)

These experiences are not understood in the physical sense, but involve bigger questions. Gardner (1999) continued the pursuit of refining the concept of spirituality and, in *Intelligence Reframed*, he proposed three distinct senses of the spiritual. In summary, these senses of the spiritual are, as Gardner proposes, associated with an intelligence that 'explores the nature of existence in its multifarious guises' (Gardner 1999, p. 60).

Zohar and Marshall (2000) have added to Gardner's work in existential intelligence and provide an explanation of spiritual intelligence, which 'is an internal innate ability of the human brain and psyche, drawing its deepest resources from the heart of the universe itself' (Zohar & Marshall 2000, p. 9). Their research and findings include the understanding of the neural basis of transcendence. Their meaning of transcendence is confined to a fundamental and humble suggestion, namely, the experience that takes us beyond that which is in the present moment: 'It takes us beyond the limits of our knowledge and experience and puts these things in a wider context' (Zohar & Marshall 2000, pp. 68–69). This notion is linked to the work of Singer and Gray (1995), who suggest that there are bundles of neurons all over the brain which oscillate simultaneously at similar frequencies to provide a unity to our perceptions. 'At a neural level, this unity can be described as a transcendent dimension to the activity of individual neurons' (Zohar & Marshall 2000, p. 71). Through Zohar and Marshall's work, they present us with the concept of thinking about the human person, and that every single thought or emotion has a transcendent dimension that exists against a wider oscillating background. Furthermore, in relating this concept to young children, the ways in which it is identified, observed and how young children express this concept adds to the complexity and possibilities in researching their spiritual capacities. Moreover, it provides an intention and direction for this research that is not to be disregarded. It also supports Myers' (1997) explanation of transcendence in which she relates that young children always seek to transcend the boundaries of their world from the known to the unknown: they have limitless boundaries as they seek to engage and transcend to different understandings. This thought bears serious consideration in view of the spiritual dimension when investigating human and, in particular, child development.

In light of this, the work from Adams et al. (2008) offers some broad recommendations for recognising spiritual intelligence and for assisting in nurturing this phenomenon. In particular, they mention the ordinary and extraordinary spiritual experience which children have in their everyday and upon which children draw to address problems of meaning and value in their lives. These authors propose that 'when children do this, they may be using their spiritual intelligence' (Adams et al. 2008, p. 100).

One cannot dismiss the groundwork of Coles (1990) in the exploration of children's spirituality. His work on moral intelligence (Coles 1997) offers some consideration. The perspectives and work opened up by Coles in the moral archaeology of children (1997) inform us that children expand their moral intelligence through wonder and speculation about everyday circumstances, valuing some consideration towards a spiritual dimension and demonstrating not only a moral, but a spiritual intelligence.

In the discussion of spiritual intelligence, a more recent opinion is expressed by Painton (2009). She bases her opinion on her work with children and employs the view that spiritual intelligence is a capacity to 'be awake and aware of a deeper dimension of themselves' (Painton 2009, p. 368). Her background in clinical play therapy correlates to children's development and supports the innate spiritual nature but proposes that this spiritual nature encompasses a spiritual intelligence which requires a sensitivity and understanding from adults.

In contrast, another contribution to the discussion of spiritual intelligence is that of Emmons (2000), who presents an argument which confers the view that spirituality does meet the criteria for intelligence. However, he continues to suggest that, while abilities in the spiritual realm contribute to being a purposeful human, the question of spiritual intelligence is debatable. How it sits within the construct requires further research and conceptualisation (Emmons 2000).

Work that seeks to strengthen the research foundation of children and spirituality requires an outlook over the whole spectrum of what spirituality may look like in relation to young children. Evidence of prudence and forethought is shown by reflecting on the work on spirituality which includes spiritual intelligence (Emmons 2000; Mayer 2000; Painton 2009; Singer & Gray 1995; Vaughan 2002; Zohar & Marshall 2000) then persisting to find the many ways and the depth in which spirituality may present itself and connect with how learning environments and pedagogies are constructed. Similarly, scholarly writers (Lindner 2004; Palmer 1999a, 1999b; Ruddock & Cameron 2010) offer some broader thoughts and claim that, rather than paying attention to pedagogical approaches which endorse the accumulation of knowledge and correct answers, the development of spirituality should be given higher priority. The implications for consideration by educators are the need to recognise child development from a multidimensional perspective (Lim 2005) and to enhance all domains of learning and intelligences.

2.15.2 The interplay of cognitive and spiritual dimensions

De Souza (2009) states that, within each human person, there is the aspect of spirituality and that the role of spirituality within a learning context must be distinct:

> If we accept that human spirituality is about relationality—expressed through the different levels of connectedness and meaning that a person experiences in his/her life, we need to investigate elements in learning programs that relate to these aspects.
>
> (de Souza 2009, p. 689)

In addition, de Souza (2009) recognises that students learn both consciously and unconsciously. Therefore, the way that information and learning are presented should engage the senses which provide different kinds of memory. De Souza (2009) maintains that a more holistic approach to learning can lead to transformation and deeper learning.

Scholarly work discussing the association of conscious and unconscious learning (Buchanan & Hyde 2008) suggests that the trend within education to separate mind, body and spirit has a detrimental impact on holistic learning. In recognising that educational systems must attend to the cognitive functions of learning, the omission of the spiritual dimension is something that needs attention. The interplay of a curriculum and a pedagogical approach which recognise both spiritual and cognitive dimensions is worthy of analysis and discussion. This gives some thought to the precedence of holistic education, not only in the religious sense of a faith-oriented school, but across all education. In ascertaining the avenues for transformative knowledge that should be present within the teaching and learning of children, the inclusion of spiritual development in the curriculum requires recognition and prominence (Iannone & Obenauf 1999). From the onset of children's educational experience within the early years, a holistic approach to education is essential to establish the pathways for meaningful learning and developing lifelong learning skills (Lim 2005). Pedagogical approaches which will complement this style of learning are those that move beyond 'analytical and left-brain ways of thinking' (Iannone & Obenauf 1999, p. 740). An approach pointed out by Iannone and Obenauf (1999) is where spirituality is found in the 'intuitive, emotional, right-brain ways of thinking' (p. 740).

Johnson and Boyatzis (2006) have highlighted the importance of nurturing and encouraging spiritual development and cognitive processes. An early childhood curriculum, such as their model, requires attention to be given to the environment and reciprocity, valuing the different styles of learning and intelligences which children present, and focusing on how to 'scaffold' and observe this transformative stage of young children's learning (Johnson & Boyatzis 2006).

2.16 Spirituality within contemporary early childhood education in Australia

2.16.1 Spirituality and early childhood education

Equally important in a discussion on the varied aspects of research centred on young children's spirituality is presenting an understanding of those educational approaches that acknowledge children's spirituality.

Within early childhood education, the two well-known approaches, both with European origins, are those of Waldorf and Montessori. They can be viewed as an inspiration for progressive educational reform (Edwards 2002b). They parallel one another with various underlying beliefs and views about children. These approaches are both founded on the belief and vision of helping children to 'realize their potential as intelligent, creative, whole persons' (Edwards 2002b, p. 3).

Rudolf Steiner acknowledged spirituality in young children within his holistic outlook and philosophy of education and his interests 'intersected spiritual and scientific planes' (Edwards 2002b, p. 3). Within Steiner's philosophy, he proposes that 'genuine thinking is alive; it is an intense spiritual activity' (Dahlin 2009, p. 542).

The Montessori education system acknowledges the school community as a whole in which parents and teachers 'work together to open the children to the integration of body, mind, emotions, and spirit that is the basis of holistic peace education' (Edwards 2002b, p. 8). Montessori deliberately included spirituality in her educational writing about children (Bone et al. 2007). Her philosophy acknowledges the child as spiritual. According to Bone et al. (2007, p. 346), Montessori's view of the child can be interpreted as '… the growing child is spiritual and that spirituality can be conceptualised as developing in an orderly way given the right conditions'.

Moving away from the European influence on early childhood education, we can look at New Zealand and the early childhood curriculum: *Te Whāriki: he whāriki mātauranga mo ngā mokopuna o Aotearoa, Early childhood curriculum* (Te Whariki). Within this curriculum, the notion of holistic education is woven through the underpinning principles. This document advocates for the hope that children are supported in growth 'in mind, body and spirit' (Ministry of Education 1996, p. 9). The curriculum supports the idea that spirituality should be acknowledged and recognises the important place of the spiritual dimension in the development of the whole child (Bone et al. 2007).

In addition, it is useful to decide whose model or approach is best suited for early childhood education. Watson's (2000) review that reflected an argument about the inclusion of spirituality in education within a pluralistic society has posed an aspect for further consideration. In recognising the diversity in understandings of spirituality and the fact that our society is becoming more pluralistic, Watson points out that careful questioning about the validity of spiritual development is paramount. Within her study, she offers the view that supporting spiritual development is crucial and, in the conclusions from her study, she suggests:

> Education, therefore, has assumed both that; spirituality is a universal, naturalistic human attribute, which is experientially based, and that this inherent spirituality can be developed by general, naturalistic (classroom) methods.
>
> (Watson 2000, p. 96)

Consequently, questions arise with regard to the pluralistic nature of society. This generates further thought on the contextual aspects of early childhood influencing how pedagogy and practice are attuned to the cultivation of the spiritual dimension in the many diverse ways it manifests itself in young children. Developing an understanding of what children's spirituality may look like and how it is recognisable within early childhood can provide a pathway for nurturing this dimension and understanding spirituality as part of the human condition. Watson et al. (2014) state that once spirituality in education is understood then there is a place for further development which is responsive to both global and local contexts. Within this case study, spirituality is viewed through the lens of the Reggio Emilia approach and within a particular context.

2.16.2 Addressing diversity within Australia

Australian society is becoming increasingly secular and multicultural, with its indigenous population also recognised; therefore, it is necessary to clarify some points concerning this particular case study. The case study was situated in a faith-based school: the community was not affiliated with the faith tradition, with community members coming from a variety of backgrounds. While most children were from an Anglo-Saxon heritage, it was recognised that children from a range of family backgrounds, including both secular and religious ones, attended this school. The review of the literature addresses and acknowledges cultural diversity and sensitivity to secular and non-secular contexts and draws on scholarly research based on both contexts, including different cultural backgrounds. Fundamental to these scholarly investigations within this literature review is the view that spirituality is a part of the human condition regardless of religious affiliation (Nemme 2008). Zohar and Marshall (2000) point out that spirituality is a natural human disposition which is embedded in life itself, and is not affiliated with religious or cultural influences. Scholarly research by Binder (2011) extends this view, claiming that spiritual expression in children is embedded in a sense of ownership that children develop while exploring their inner lives through everyday creative experiences.

2.16.3 Early Years Learning Framework

The question about the provision of a framework, curriculum and overview for developing the 'whole child' seems never-ending. With it affirmed as an absolutely necessary component of a learning environment (Best 1996; Binder 2011; Iannone & Obenauf 1999; Miller & Athan 2007; Yust 2007), the fostering of spiritual awareness has evolved into a contemporary discussion. Key pedagogical processes and contexts lack clarity and is in need of careful deliberation. Work within Australia in New South Wales by Vialle et al. (2008), and a summary of this investigation which involved building on contemporary work around children's spirituality, still failed to complete an overall context for nurturing spirituality (Hemming 2013; Rose 2001). The work relayed many disparities around spirituality and expressed the view that the work and research require further data and a hope that 'the developmental trajectory for spirituality will become clearer' (Vialle et al. 2008, p. 156).

The work by Grajczonek (2012) offers a perspective for understanding the spiritual nature of children and how, through the initiation of the Early Years Learning Framework (Australian Government Department of Education, Employment and Workplace Relations [DEEWR] 2009), educators and pedagogy respond to young children's spiritual aspects. In relation to early years' education and spirituality, Grajczonek (2012) emphasises that:

> The reference to children's spirituality is an important one as, for the first time at the Australian Federal Government level, an official educational document acknowledges the spiritual dimension of children's lives and learning, advocating holistic approaches to children's learning, advocating that holistic approaches to children's learning must include attending to the spiritual, as well as to the physical and cognitive aspects. The document also assigns responsibilities to early childhood educators related to this spiritual dimension.
> (Grajczonek 2012, p. 152)

Grajczonek (2012) emphasises that the document is too general and that it is essential to fully understand both the nature of young children's spirituality and the pedagogical response.

2.16.4 Spirituality within a Catholic early childhood context

It is important within this study to identify the understanding of spirituality from a Catholic perspective and, for the purpose of this research, to relate this to the context of young children and their learning as a foundation for this study. This aim of this study is not to contest the tradition and ethos of early years education in a Catholic setting. Sensitivity is recognised in this particular study as the location is within a Catholic setting. The study, through its clearly defined questions, has a specific intention and purpose; however, the literature review identified the disparities concerning spiritual development and religious development and how they may need some further research and clarity. For example, Fowler and Dell (2006) impart the view that a child may either nurture a transcendent relatedness or derive this from exposure to religious practices. This perspective suggests that the transcendent experiences may come first, derived from social practices and relationships, and later move to the divine (Fowler & Dell 2006).

Hyde's (2008a) research suggested a difference in meaning-making for children and that children's spiritual sense of wonder in meaning-making depended upon cultural traditions and other world views outside of religious ones.

Prominent in this study is how spirituality is visible in young children in their way of being in the world and how pedagogy and practice can nurture children's development, including their spiritual dimension.

The particular view of childhood that is portrayed in, and integral to, this research holds the child at the centre of learning and discovering:

> The search for life and for the self is born with the child, and this is why we talk about a child who is competent and strong, engaged in this search toward life, toward others, toward the relations between self and life.
>
> (Rinaldi 2006, p. 112)

For early childhood educators, and within the purpose of this research, recognition of the spiritual characteristics of young children and the provision of learning situations that engage them have implications for the way in which we teach, instruct and understand young learners. This research anticipates offering findings on how a teaching and learning environment inspired by the Reggio Emilia approach can provide an authentic learning context in which to promote a climate of learning relevant to the child, adult and culture of the school, with this highly relevant to early childhood curricula.

> This principle reflects the central Catholic conviction that God mediates Godself to us and we encounter God's presence and grace coming to meet us through the ordinary of life – through our minds and bodies, through our works and efforts, in the depth of our own being and through our relationships with others, through the events and experiences that come our way, through all forms of human art and creativity, through nature and the whole created order, through everything and anything of life.
>
> (Groome 1996, p. 2)

Groome (1996) states that, in order for this principle to be considered and relevant to students, the rigours of our curriculum should be constructed so that children are allowed to stretch their imagination, to always question and creatively search for more. Academic rigour, according to Groome, can be enhanced by the commitment to sacramentality and by urging students to search for other meanings and ways of expressing their relationship to life. Parallels with a child-centred approach already exist within a Catholic anthropology (Groome 1996).

For a school influenced by a Catholic ethos and tradition, questions may be raised about whether the Reggio Emilia approach can be related to cultivating the spiritual dimension of childhood. As pointed out by Grajczonek (2011), in those early childhood settings connected to faith, traditions require some reflection on nurturing spirituality first as a possible trajectory towards faith development. Based on this assumption, this research may form a basis for not only understanding the innate spiritual characteristics of young children but also raising questions in accordance with how this presents itself in a Catholic school setting:

> Children try to understand not only what is happening to them, but why: and in doing that, they call upon the religious life they have experienced, the spiritual values they have received, as well as other sources of potential explanation.
>
> (Coles 1990, p. 100)

Furthermore, this study may illuminate the question outlined earlier in the literature review about how the innate capacity of spirituality can be nurtured and to consider the implications of the influence of a Catholic tradition in early childhood education today. Beckwith (2004) states that postmodern children are different thinkers with diverse and distinctive ways of seeing the world:

> These children will not value the same things we value. These children will not understand the things that happen around them in the same way we do. They will not view concepts about truth and reality in the same way we do. This does not mean their outlook on life is wrong and must be changed. It's just different. If we are to minister to these children ... we have to understand their way of thinking and change our ways of doing things.
>
> (Beckwith 2004, p. 29)

Considering the ways in which children comprehend and perceive their world perhaps clarifies the necessity for understanding and nurturing children's expressions of spirituality; for selecting the pedagogy which is implemented; and for where this is positioned in relation to religious development in the early years of childhood.

Crompton (1998) and Eaude (2003) have claimed that if young children's spirituality is not nurtured, it will diminish and disappear. When considering this within early childhood faith-based and Christian settings, other scholarly insights have offered that, in determining the starting point for young children's religious education, this should be a point that pursues and develops their spirituality (Hay & Nye 2006; Hyde 2008b; Liddy 2002).

2.16.5 Spirituality, connecting people and communities

As stated in this chapter, a discussion on spirituality must propose the argument that spirituality in today's western secular society is distinct from religion. Ritskes (2011) states that spirituality is separate from religion, citing the reason that religion's rigid ideology and exclusivity do not accept or allow true connection or the identity of a person. In order to fully acknowledge indigenous culture and identity, spirituality must then exist external to a religious regime. When this is the case, indigenous spirituality and identity are given the space to emerge as part of the student's identity. In relation to education, Ritskes (2011) argues that the multiple identities in the classroom or learning environment related to the students' lived experiences and their own spiritual journey affect how they will create meaning and knowledge in the classroom. Scholarly literature (Dei 2005; Kessler 2000; Ritskes 2011) claims that to fully accept individuals and how they express their spirituality, education must provide a space which allows for different experiences, such as play, creative learning or silence. This scholarly input further argues that educators who are interested in bringing spirituality into learning spaces need to provide possibilities and spaces where students are able to explore for themselves. This offers a more inclusive approach and context where spirituality can be recognised, regardless of cultural or indigenous heritage.

2.17 Summary

This chapter has provided an overview of contemporary research on children's spirituality. It covered key contemporary research by scholars associated with children's spirituality. The chapter explored how the phenomenon of spirituality is demonstrated by young children. It explored the scholarly research which describes the characteristics of children and how researchers have identified and related these characteristics to the spiritual dimension of young children. The chapter suggested that spirituality is an inherent quality of human beings, both adults and children, and that spirituality is an integral part of child development and is essential to the whole life of the child, part of their natural identity. In addition, the chapter discussed what is distinctive about religion and spirituality and the important distinctions between the two concepts. Religion can be viewed as an organised faith system which is grounded in institutional standards and core beliefs, while spirituality can be experienced within or external to formal religion and is inclusive of individual heritage and culture. Spirituality is also stated as a natural part of human capacity which can find expression in every dimension of life. In conclusion, the chapter offers a broad understanding of spirituality and what it may look like, whereby young children's spirituality can be reflected in the normal activities of everyday life.

2.17.1 Provocations, considerations and pondering for Educators

- *I believe that spirituality is not synonymous with religion. Spirituality is an ancient primordial predisposition of human beings. Out of this capacity and experience a religion or a religious response may emerge. What are your thoughts as a collective group working and learning alongside children?*
- *Make yourself comfortable with the understanding of spirituality.*
- *Commit yourself to offer children more than a hundred ways to see and explore the world. Use a broad and interesting array of artistic materials. What would this look like in an educational setting?*
- *Do you respect and honor children's verbal and non-verbal questions, manifestations and intrigue as thoughts and reflections of their intellectual curiosity and their spiritual expression?*
- *How do you approach the big questions that children ask? Spiritual nurturing occurs when children are asking questions and discovering answers. This is not based on a correct answer from an assuming adult.*
- *Children require settings where they can express themselves and need reassuring adults to walk alongside them plus a learning environment that feels secure, where children are listened to. Do you listen with purpose with children?*
- *What kind of environment do you provide for your children? Are you someone who walks alongside and learns with children, rather than be the holder of all knowledge?*
- *Do you allow children to ask questions and be curious?*

The Reggio Emilia approach and pedagogy

Figure 3.1

> *If we recognise the capacity for spirituality, it is then fundamental and vital to also ensure how this capacity can be nurtured through our pedagogy and practice within education*
>
> Helena Card

The following section of this literature review provides an overview of young children's capacity for spirituality and elements of the Reggio Emilia pedagogical approach which may nurture this spiritual capacity. The chapter provides a historical overview of the origins of Reggio Emilia and how this educational project and experience are an interpreted experience within each culture and context outside Italy.

This chapter delivers some explanations, clarifications and descriptions of terminology unique to this philosophy, with this section of the review also serving to enlighten aspects of the guiding principles of the Reggio Emilia pedagogical approach. This section of the review analyses and details the aspects of the approach which are relevant to young children's spirituality and this case study.

In addition, this section of the review presents and describes a view of children, as described by the Reggio Emilia approach, in a manner which presents the child as one of potential and possibilities rather one who is needy and deficient in capabilities.

A review of educational theorists guides the reader into an understanding about the theoretical foundations which underpin the Reggio Emilia philosophy and practice. Subsequently, this review refers to current early childhood educational trends in Australia and other countries that incorporate this approach. It portrays pedagogical conditions in which children are encouraged to be active agents and protagonists in their learning and in the construction of identity and knowledge. The position of educators (based on scholarly literature) who honour children's capabilities and listen and learn alongside them is discussed and reviewed. The way that environments are designed to engage and provide multi-layered experiences for children is detailed.

The intention of this section is to provide the reader with knowledge of the Reggio Emilia approach and how this philosophy and belief affect the way in which the full capacity of children is respected, supported and nurtured within a particular philosophical methodology. It analyses contemporary early childhood pedagogy and reviews the changing perspective on childhood and the educational conditions we provide for children in the early years.

3.1 Origins of the Reggio Emilia approach

The groundwork for what is now referred to as 'the Reggio Emilia approach' (Edwards et al. 1998) is deeply connected to and has its origins in Italy.

Reggio Emilia is a small city in Italy's Emilia Romagna region in northern Italy. The philosophy of the city-run schools began at the end of World War II. The first schools of the city started immediately after the war as parents and other citizens in sections of the city had decided that there was a need to build schools for their children.

Reggio Emilia is seen as a municipality that supports preschools and infant and toddler centres. The work within Reggio Emilia has attracted attention and challenged some of the contemporary interpretations of early childhood education (New 2007). The nature of the work and their interpretation of how children learn have provided a context for Reggio Emilia to contribute 'to the discourse on the "what" and the "how" of an early childhood education' (New 2007, p. 9).

The visionary for this education system within Reggio Emilia was Loris Malaguzzi: the system evolved from a parent cooperative system into a city-run system. Malaguzzi was the educational theorist and leader of the Reggio Emilia educational project, which he led for 40 years. The project is ongoing. The foundation and formation of the Reggio Emilia approach influenced and led in many areas throughout Europe and, increasingly, North America. It now extends through Asia, Australia and New Zealand.

The first local government preschool opened in 1963 and the first infant–toddler school for babies/children from birth to three-year-olds opened in 1970. Today, the city is a medium-sized affluent city with infant and toddler centres for babies from birth to six months and, through the dedication and belief in a municipal approach, is committed to offering centres fostering a quality childhood.

For the past 30 years, the system within Reggio Emilia has evolved into its own distinctive and unique style and system of philosophical and pedagogical theories and beliefs, employing methods of school organisation and principles of environment and design. These are all considered 'as a unified whole' which can be referred to as the Reggio Emilia approach (Edwards et al. 1998, p. 7). The Reggio Emilia approach promotes the relationship between parents, educators and children. Within the approach, young children are encouraged to explore their environment and express themselves through all of their available 'expressive, communicative and cognitive languages' (Edwards et al. 1998, p. 7), and, in so doing, to utilise many different modes (words, movement, music and drawing). These languages are associated with the Reggio Emilia approach as 'the hundred languages of children' (Malaguzzi 1998; Rinaldi 2006) and this aspect of the approach is discussed in this chapter. Play and problem solving are an integral aspect of the approach and children's interests are followed and developed to expand learning. A fundamental element to consider about the Reggio Emilia approach is that the educators ensure that children have the time for deep exploration and are able to experience the 'joy and satisfaction that comes from such freedom' (Kennedy 2006, p. 92).

This pedagogical approach has been adapted throughout the world within the context of various early childhood settings. The city of Reggio Emilia and its approach to education have been a focus for many countries in their pursuit of establishing a quality early childhood program. In terms of current and past literature demonstrating an understanding of this approach or accounts of educational programs assimilated within it, there has been a strong interest in sharing accounts. Comprehensive resources have been written and collated to offer interpretations of and insights into this pedagogical approach (Edwards 2002b; Fraser 2006; Katz 1998; Millikan 2003; Wurm 2005).

3.1.1 History and context of the Reggio Emilia approach

It is necessary to point out that the Reggio Emilia educational project and the associated approach are uniquely situated in a cultural and historical setting which cannot be replicated or copied in other contexts. To understand the Reggio Emilia approach in an

Australian context and the work of the educational project within another cultural setting would be of only limited use (Millikan 2003). The educational project is continual and there is a changing impression of the work and theories to which the teachers and educators are committed in researching and developing in relation to young children and learning.

Recognising the vast interpretations and literature about the Reggio Emilia approach suggests, however, that pedagogical practices and beliefs centred on early childhood education can be inspired by this approach. According to Millikan (2010, p. 13), it has developed 'as one of the most important early childhood experiences in the world'. Several researchers have expanded upon a variety of aspects of the approach which have captured their interest (Moran, Desrochers & Cavicchi 2007; Hewett 2001; New 2007). All have advocated in a similar fashion that the Reggio Emilia approach is not a 'set of guidelines and procedures to be followed; therefore, one cannot or should not attempt to simply import it to another location' (Hewett 2001, p. 99). In support of this statement and view, my own research and investigation highlight the inspirations taken from the Reggio Emilia educational project and define aspects of the approach. This is by no means an interpretation of the authentic, multi-layered and evolving educational project which is unique to the municipal schools and centres in Reggio Emilia.

3.1.2 Philosophy behind the Reggio Emilia approach

The Reggio Emilia philosophy of teaching and learning derives its pedagogical framework from Vygotsky (1962), Dewey (1910) and Gardner's (1983, 1999) multiple intelligences. Others have also influenced the pedagogical approach. The way in which this influence is derived and is today cultivating global principles and theories related to early childhood education and contemporary convictions associated with childhood is discussed and reviewed later in this chapter.

The Reggio Emilia approach to pedagogy is a constructivist approach to early childhood education as it recognises and provides avenues for diverse learning opportunities in order for young children to make meaning and to be the co-constructors of knowledge: '... we understand that children naturally and actively engage in the search for meaning and, in doing so, are in a constant process of constructing meaning' (Kinney & Wharton 2008, p. 3). This approach to teaching and learning offers a social context for the observations and interactions of young children. Many would consider this to be the main thread or core of the philosophy, whereas work by Rinaldi (2006) and interpretations of the approach and work by Fraser (2006), Kroeger and Cardy (2006) and, more recently, Moran et al. (2007) present a persuasive argument suggesting that the philosophical assumptions together with the theoretical framework are far broader.

Through a collection of writing, speeches and interviews, Rinaldi's insights into the wider implications of Reggio Emilia's theoretical influences offer a convincing and authentic interpretation of the approach by one of the leading authorities. Carla Rinaldi began working in the region in 1970 as a *pedagogista* or pedagogical consultant and became the pedagogical director of the municipal early childhood services. She was president of Reggio Children and the Loris Malaguzzi Foundation, an organisation established by the municipality of Reggio Emilia. Her role was to manage and maintain the relationship between the municipal schools of Reggio Emilia and the rest of the world. As a leading expert and authority on the approach, Rinaldi was to the fore as a respected academic whose legacy will endure and continue to inspire educators globally. Dewey's principles of spaces for childhood, interesting materials, and the design and scope of the environment were considered by Rinaldi to be 'vibrating with life' as she reflects on the spaces of childhood in Reggio Emilia (Rinaldi 2006, p. 77). Furthermore, this supports the understanding of the construction of spaces within childhood. The way in which this influences the current study is clarified later in this chapter.

Through Rinaldi's interpretation and work, Fraser (2006) outlined that the founding theorist, Loris Malaguzzi, established strong connections with the work of John Dewey (1897). He stated that children would develop a central core of motivation to learn from their own investigations. Fraser encouraged teachers to plan and program according to the child's interests. His ideology maintained that children should learn to live in a democratic society. In relation to play, Dewey considered fostering this as a means by which all children imagine and recreate their own experiences. This connection between Malaguzzi and Dewey is what Fraser stated to be crucial:

> … embedded the Reggio Emilia approach within the mainstream of educational ideas, which reach back to Jean Jacques Rousseau (1788–1802), Johan Heinrich Pestalozzi (1746–1827), and Friedrich Wilhelm Froebel (1782–1852) … The principles that have evolved in the preschools in Reggio Emilia, therefore, have meaning to many other early childhood programs.
>
> (Fraser 2006, p. 8)

In addition to Fraser's work, Kroeger and Cardy (2006) recognise that an elementary aspect of the Reggio Emilia-inspired teaching is the constructivist tradition. Pertinent to this is how teachers come to know the child in a 'way that supports deep relationship' (Kroeger & Cardy 2006, p. 390). In their work around the documentation of children's work, a constructivist attitude is essential in documenting and discovering how children think, their emotions and how they come to know and make meaning. They advocate a belief in the constructivist theories of teaching young children and provide some substantial reasoning and examples of how the adaptation of Reggio Emilia-inspired forms of documentation can 'enhance the qualities of children's experiences' (Kroeger & Cardy 2006, p. 393). The work of the educators in the region is also deeply rooted in the socio-political image of the child. The educators advocate giving each child the democratic right to be listened to and also giving them the recognition as a citizen in the community. It is necessary to pursue an examination of Kroeger and Cardy's (2006) work in relation to my research and inquiry, and how documentation is positioned within the case study. Documentation, the image of the child and the constructivist approach are all fundamental to the approach; however, this is unique to the culture and practice of the Reggio Emilia educational project. This presents a challenge regarding whether using documentation may present limitations when trying to authenticate the style of the educators in Reggio Emilia. A question can be raised as to whether all the affordances (see Glossary) through the exploration of media and capabilities of children can be recognised through an attempt to adopt this style of documentation. Are there valuable considerations about which teachers should think carefully in the choice of particular documentation styles and forms? These convincingly valid questions are raised by Kroeger and Cardy (2006). Similarly, they also raise a thoughtful rationale around the intention to research and observe children along with choosing a suitable documentation tool that justifiably illuminates children's meaning-making and learning interactions.

In a similar fashion, the research by Moran et al. (2007) states that the Reggio Emilia approach is based on a constructivist theoretical perspective influenced by Dewey (1910); Gardner (1999), Vygotsky (1962, 1978) and Piaget (1929, 1968, 2002) with these influences comprising the approach's basic principles. Stemming from the fundamental ideas and principles of the Reggio Emilia approach, particularly in the areas of documenting and observing children, Moran et al. (2007) have also indicated that applying the theoretical perspectives can be simple. However, their adaptation and examination of the principles and practices require very careful attention and analysis in order to truly aspire to the authenticity of the educators in Reggio Emilia.

3.2 Child theories related to the Reggio Emilia approach

As mentioned, Dewey, Piaget and Vygotsky's influences have formulated the theories of the Reggio Emilia approach. The following theorists are integral to the educational project as they offer a platform for identification with a culture of childhood and a particular image of the child.

3.2.1 Piaget's child

Jean Piaget, a Swiss theorist, is well known for his exploration in the field of epistemology and the study of the process that children and adults undertake to become knowledgeable. His cognitive development theory has three key parts: order, structure and process. Within the first part, he illustrated that children move through various levels of developmental stages. Within each key part, the significant sequences of development are noted. His work contributed largely to the field of early childhood in opening up an understanding of how the child comes to know. He highlights the functions of mental thought intrinsic to children. The explicatory function is where the mind turns to the external world and the implicating function is where the mind turns inward to analyse the intentions and their relations (Piaget 2002). Although this presents only a brief summary of Piaget's theory, the point I mainly highlight is how his work contributes to the construction of an image of the child. This is attempted in the following quotation regarding the mind of the child: '[t]he explicatory functions arise out of the need felt by the child, as soon as he becomes conscious of intentions, to project these into the world around him' (Piaget 2002, p. 237).

Piaget goes on to explain that once these intentions meet the outside world, interactions and phenomena, the implicating function becomes active and the child must endeavour to search for why and how things occur (Piaget 2002). Although not all of Piaget's theory is acknowledged by the educators in Reggio Emilia, they do recognise the contribution of his cognitive development theory. However, they also contest Piaget's view of the egocentric child (Fraser 2006). In summary, focusing on the cognitive development theory and the functions of the mind, a very capable and curious image of the child is portrayed through Piaget's theory.

3.2.2 Dewey's image of the child

The Reggio Emilia approach, according to Fraser (2006), has extended John Dewey's ideas in their representation of the hundred languages (Malaguzzi 1998; Rinaldi 2006) or the symbolic interpretations and representations which children use. Dewey (1910) stated that, through play, children are able to connect and unify meanings in a coherent way to make sense of things. He describes an attitude of inviting and allowing children to play and discover meaning in their everyday natural settings. Dewey's image of the child is one where he emphasises 'a larger acquaintance with life', where the child constantly questions and is curious about the elements and functions which exist around them (Dewey 1910, p. 32).

3.2.3 Gardner's influence: the child with multiple languages

The work of Howard Gardner has been a consistent influence on this approach. His outline of the multiple intelligences has strong connections to the Reggio Emilia principle of a hundred languages (Malaguzzi 1998; Rinaldi 2006). Gardner's provocative theory of multiple intelligences has captured educational institutions. The Reggio Emilia educational project has endorsed Gardner's work, which has been assimilated in the notion that children have a hundred languages (Malaguzzi 1998; Rinaldi 2006) through which they can transmit knowledge and meaning-making. While Gardner's multiple intelligences' theory centred on expanding the view of aptitudes, he claimed that 'we as human beings are better described as having a set of relatively autonomous intelligences' (Gardner 2011a, p. 7).

He maintained that we have human cognitive capacities in various areas which he categorised as intelligences, for example, bodily kinaesthetic intelligence, interpersonal intelligence, spatial intelligence, etc., adding to the six categories he devised in 1983. Gardner continued to expand on his suggested intelligences with more categories devised including existential and naturalistic intelligences.

Throughout the period 1993–95, Gardner extended his theory and proposed some distinct uses of the term 'intelligence' which he described as, firstly, 'a property of all human beings' and, secondly, as 'a dimension on which human beings differ' (Gardner 2011b, p. 15). Gardner's assumption is that each human being has a different capacity and, therefore, intelligence: Gardner's theory stressed that it is applied to all people and is represented and used in different ways.

Furthermore, the hundred languages of children resonate with this theory. Malaguzzi (1998) refers to the different languages used by children: these can be either graphic or symbolic. Through symbols, children are able to transfer concepts from one situation to the next and they are able to relate to several symbolic languages at the same time (Malaguzzi 1998). Recognising this in children opens up a reconceptualisation of how children construct meaning and the view that many languages are associated with symbols. This symbolic language is not restricted to reading, writing and mathematical notations: instead, Malaguzzi describes symbols that are 'used by children to acquire culture, grow and communicate' (Malaguzzi 1998, p. 93).

In addition, when working as researchers observing young children, a grasp and openness towards the many symbolic languages and intelligences which children own and exhibit present us with a challenging landscape for research and analysis and provide an essential angle to this current inquiry. Supporting and synthesising the views and work of Malaguzzi (1998) and Gardner (2011b) provide some extensive characteristics when applied to the image of the child.

Together with the many perspectives presented to date by theorists is the influence of Jerome Bruner, one theorist who had previously lived and worked in Reggio Emilia. Bruner's influence on the region's educational project cannot be overlooked as he presented the perspective of a theoretical framework that contributes to the position of the Reggio Emilia approach.

A major theme in Bruner's (1977) theoretical framework is his belief that learning is an active process in which each learner constructs new ideas and concepts based upon their current and prior knowledge. Centred within his theoretical framework is the connection to child development and cognition, which builds on Piaget's work.

The notion of the quality and intellectual aims of education is reinforced by Bruner. His philosophical view does not permit education to abandon this stance, while his ideology in the process of education is to perceive teaching as an act of training citizens to live within a democratic society (Bruner 1977).

The contribution of each of these theorists to the theoretical background of the Reggio Emilia philosophy is fundamental in influencing and defining one of the core principles and values within the Reggio Emilia approach, that being the image of the child.

3.2.4 The postmodern perception of childhood

When considering the description of the image of the child from a Reggio Emilia-inspired perspective, it is suggested that we place ourselves in the position of 'destabilizing' (Guss 2011) or rethinking our perception of childhood. Placing this suggestion within ourselves when researching with young children is a critical discursive element to view and observe the child and value their full potential.

Adopting a postmodern perspective on childhood has been advocated by Dahlberg et al. (1999). It encourages educators and those associated with early childhood programs and institutions to take a broader attitude in designing learning for young children, an attitude which encompasses children as 'active co-constructors of their own knowledge' (Dahlberg et al. 1999, p. 83). Their postmodern view of childhood advocates new experiences: it also advocates that practitioners, educators and researchers deepen their knowledge about children.

Postmodernism places an emphasis on understanding the complexity of the world and being open to the multiplicity of the world (Dahlberg et al. 1999). When adopting a postmodern stance on researching and viewing children, an important consideration is to recognise identity as a social construct (Janzen 2008). A lens on childhood through an approach like Reggio Emilia assists in the reconceptualisation of and new insights on children and childhood fostering a postmodern view of childhood which honours children's perspectives in learning.

3.3 The Reggio Emilia approach and the image of the child

3.3.1 The image of the 'rich' child

Within the Reggio Emilia approach, the image of the child is a focal point and integral to understanding the place of the child within the current research. The Reggio Emilia philosophy is based on an image of the child as a social being from birth; a child who is competent, intelligent and who learns and is in relationship with others (Rinaldi 2001).

Loris Malaguzzi, the philosopher and founder of the Reggio Emilia approach, stated that:

> It's necessary that we believe that the child is very intelligent, that the child is strong and beautiful and has very ambitious desires and requests. This is the image of the child that we need to hold. Those who have the image of the child as fragile, incomplete, weak, made of glass, gain something from this belief only for themselves. We don't need that as an image of children. Instead of always giving children protection, we need to give them the recognition of their rights and of their strengths.
>
> (Malaguzzi 1994, p. 56)

Ceppi and Zini have also presented us with a view of the child which underpins the Reggio Emilia philosophy:

> The image of a child who, right from the moment of birth, is so engaged in developing a relationship with the world and intent on experiencing the world that he develops a complex system of abilities, learning strategies, and ways of organizing relationships.
>
> (Ceppi & Zini 1998, p. 117)

This construct of the 'rich' child underpins the pedagogy of Reggio Emilia. As stated by Goodliff, this construct of the child offers 'the possibility for recognizing within their imaginative play, meaningful expressions of spirituality and creativity' (Goodliff 2013, p. 1055).

If we consider the child to be 'rich', as did Malaguzzi, the foundational figure in the establishment of the Reggio Emilia approach, then it opens up the possibilities and capabilities of the child. It is essential, therefore, to establish a firm understanding and belief today in the type of child who exists in early childhood education. In addition, within the current research that evolves within an early childhood environment, a clear position must be stated. The view of the child within this research defines a pedagogical approach which allows avenues for all children to express and make meaning of their world through the co-construction of knowledge. Accepting and valuing this view of the child paves a crucial pathway for thinking about and considering children in relation to learning and, more broadly, with regard to the intent of early childhood education.

In conjunction with defining an image of the child, attention is required around what Anning (2009) terms 'constructs of childhood' (p. 69), a genuine image of the child that can be obtained by observing the magnitude and diversity of research in relation to socio-theoretical perspectives on childhood. Many researchers have connected to this field (Anning, Cullen & Fleer 2009; Edwards & Hammer 2006; MacNaughton 2009;

Rogers 2011; Spodek & Saracho 2003; Wright 2010). One message presents a key point and train of thought throughout their diverse thinking and influences in early childhood education and research. Considering their work in this field, it is clear that all attempt to promote an image of the child which is positive and of a child who learns through a social and cultural context, a child who is not deficient in ability: through their research, they propose theories and visions for an early childhood pedagogy that fosters this image. As stated by Spodek and Saracho (2003), in reference to their overview of the traditions of early childhood education, 'educators need to be aware of their own ideological preferences and their own values, of their ideas of what we want our children to be and to become' (Spodek & Saracho 2003, p. 9).

Through this review of the trends within early childhood theory, the extent to which the Reggio Emilia approach to education is mentioned indicates that it stands as prominently recognised to sustain this vision. The aim, prevalent in this research, is to view the child through the lens of the educators and philosophy of the region. Earlier in this section, when defining a construct of childhood, I refer to taking theoretical perspectives even further by viewing children as 'social actors in their lives' and indicate that this social interaction plays a role in young children's learning (Kim & Darling 2009, p. 138). This image considers the child to be a natural researcher who has the curiosity to ask and discover questions so that the child's nature is taken seriously (Kim & Darling 2009). This constructs an image of the child that is authentic to the Reggio Emilia philosophy in which each child is considered to be powerful, competent, creative, curious and full of potential (Malaguzzi 1998). The current research is aligned with this image of the child and a pedagogical approach which, as Whitfield (2009) strongly implies, 'focuses on what children can do, rather than what they cannot do' (Whitfield 2009, p. 160).

3.3.2 The hundred languages of children

The Reggio Emilia founding educator, Malaguzzi (1998), describes children as having a 'hundred languages' with which they express themselves. One of the most important contributions to education from Malaguzzi and the educators and researchers in Reggio Emilia is 'in extending our awareness of how many languages children can use to express themselves and represent their world' (Fraser 2006, p. 250). The Reggio Emilia approach and philosophy to learning have provided a lens for this research which takes us beyond the traditional modes of meaning-making and provides an avenue for observing how young children can make meaning and connect to understanding their world. It provides an avenue for the documentation and observation of young children and their learning which forms the methodology for data collection in this research.

Scholarly research (Caldwell 2003; Dahlberg et al. 1999; Edwards et al. 1998; Fraser 2006) seems to suggest that the Reggio Emilia approach can provide an avenue for a more creative and collaborative approach to teaching and learning with young children and allow us to observe children's expressions and interactions. When relating this to spirituality, we can then consider the insight that 'the child's voice is not always a verbal one in matters of spirituality' (Adams et al. 2008, p. 38). Hart (2003), in relation to spirituality, has observed that young children have an endless capacity for creativity and imagination that needs to be observed by adults.

Nye (2009) has the view that, within research, spirituality has been restricted to verbal expression. She supports the view that we need to be careful not to restrict the understanding of childhood spirituality to a verbal approach when researching spirituality within children. Through the Reggio Emilia approach to learning, children are able to make meaning and express their innate spiritual capacity and translate this into the hundred languages (Malaguzzi 1998; Rinaldi 2006).

Just as Howard Gardner has broadened our view of intelligence beyond valuing only the logico-mathematical and linguistic aspects of intelligence, so have the educators in Reggio Emilia increased our understanding of how children use graphic, verbal, literate, symbolic and imaginative play 'and a hundred hundred more' languages in making meaning of the world (Fraser 2006, p. 250).

3.3.3 The Reggio Emilia approach and the pedagogy of listening

According to contemporary theorists (Clark, Kjorholt & Moss 2005; Burman 2009; Fleer & Richardson 2009; Fraser 2006), the pedagogy of listening is significant in early childhood education. Scholarly insights demonstrate that the notion and understanding of listening can permeate every aspect and feature of early childhood education and warrant attention and importance in offering an understanding of the complexity of young children's thinking.

Clark et al. (2005) maintain the opinion that there is no simplified view of listening. They draw attention to listening in a more complex form in which listening affects the ways in which we conceptualise how children interrelate and learn in their environments: we can listen to how they explore their environment with the hundred languages (Malaguzzi 1998; Rinaldi 2006).

The Reggio Emilia approach encourages educators to listen and learn from young children as they attempt to make meaning through the pedagogy of listening and provides an overall umbrella of thought which poses a valid and critical angle to my research. The pedagogy of listening opens up profound possibilities for understanding others. If we act upon the inspiration and insights of Rinaldi and view listening as an 'approach to life' (Rinaldi 2006, p. 114), this merits some careful consideration of how we listen and whether we are open to listening as a predisposition towards change as we invite ourselves to be broadened by new knowledge (Rinaldi 2006).

Contemplating this pedagogy and action in the light of research with young children presents many opportunities to understand their thinking and learning, and this research provides sensitivity in perceiving and interpreting their spiritual expression.

At a conference in Australia, Elena Giacopini, an educator at Reggio Emilia, stated that listening to young children is 'to go from what is known to the unknown and it involves listening with all senses' (Giacopini 2010). The pedagogy of listening opens up the opportunity to understand how children see themselves in relation to others and their world and how we, as adults, can seek to identify young children's relationships and encounters in their everyday world.

In the review of the literature by Clark et al. (2005), a persuasive argument is presented and suggested which states that the pedagogy of listening can be used as a tool and a method of inquiry to discover children's active involvement proficiencies within a natural learning environment. The pedagogy of listening that is situated within this research 'is understood as a pedagogy and a way of researching life ...' (Clark et al. 2005, p. 13).

In addition to the previous intention and situation of the pedagogy of listening, we can draw from Davies' (2011) work and what she describes as 'open listening'. She provides an example where she observes a young girl and describes this as listening, watching her actions, how she explores the space she is in, her movements and watching as the young girl learns from the result of her actions. The pedagogy of listening also goes hand in hand with a philosophy of inviting children to take time to explore their environment which is a concept that is further explored in this chapter. As children engage and are allowed to explore their environments, Davies encourages open listening and emphasises that educators need to think of this as the 'void' in education that can transform our thinking. Her reference to the word 'void' means 'open to the not yet known' (Davies 2011, p. 131). In doing so, we are allowing the space (or 'void') to become visible. The work by Davies affirms the view that broadening our interpretation of listening and becoming open listeners involves listening to the other without judgement and 'with openness of mind that does not rest on the fixing of one's own, or the other's identity' (Davies 2011, p. 131).

Bearing this view in mind, situating it within the current inquiry and drawing even further into this open listening, the understanding is to recognise that children are active participants, curiously pursuing and wondering in their daily encounters. To deny the authenticity of the validity of children's experiences is to pose a barrier to their innate spiritual development. Cupit (2002) suggests that the understandings and issues of spirituality within young children engage them deeply as 'active participants rather than passive recipients' (Cupit 2002, p. 5).

With regard to children's spirituality, as situated within this research, the application of this pedagogical approach and understanding is essential. Hay and Nye (2006) suggest that the only way to map or appreciate spirituality within young children is to listen:

> In the end, the only way an accurate map can be drawn is to listen to what children have to say and, from what we hear, to create an empirical account of the contexts of childhood spirituality.
>
> (Hay & Nye 2006, p. 64)

The perception of listening and the broadening of this understanding into a tool and a method for researching spirituality have been mentioned by numerous authors (Champagne 2001; Hart 2003; Hay & Nye 2006; Liddy 2002; Mountain 2007). In relation to this, as we observe children and their spiritual experiences, moments of awe and wonder, curiosity, imagination, creativity, wisdom and flow of consciousness can all be considered and, as the above authors concur, are viewed as experiences of spirituality. When considering pedagogy and spirituality, Watson suggests that the challenge for educators is to acquire a space for listening:

> Spiritual pedagogy must involve space for a listening encounter with [the] other; for children to encounter themselves and reflexively engage with [the] other. And I would argue, then, that the teacher needs the 'sense', bodily depth and groundedness, to be able to confidently clear a space, and to listen.
>
> (Watson 2013, p. 127)

Being receptive to utilising listening in a more innovative style when researching contributes to a pioneering attempt in this field.

3.4 The Reggio Emilia approach and the hundred languages of children as an expression of meaning-making

The Reggio Emilia philosophy describes the many ways in which children can express themselves as 'the hundred languages of children' (Millikan 2003). Just as there are multiple styles or modes of knowing, the Reggio Emilia philosophy acknowledges that there are multiple ways of expressing, demonstrating and interpreting knowledge (Malaguzzi 1998; Hewett 2001; Rinaldi 2006). With many forms of knowledge or meaning-making in relation to spirituality, young children remind us that children have a wide variety of spiritual experiences and ways in which this is expressed (Adams et al. 2008). Reggio Emilia educators maintain that the hundred languages are parallel to Gardner's theory of multiple intelligences (Gardner 1994). His theory outlines that children have the ability to make meaning through manipulating systems of symbols. He maintains that the use of symbol systems is the major developmental event of the early childhood years and that 'within a short period, the world of the child becomes a world of symbols' (Gardner 1994, p. 129). The hundred languages model provides a different optic for viewing learning, allowing children to explore, experiment and play with materials and also allowing them to become literate through different modes of communication and symbolic representation (Edwards et al. 1998).

Within the Reggio Emilia approach, numerous media have been offered to children to represent their understandings: '[o]ver time these symbolic representations, typically regarded as art activities, were reconceptualised by Malaguzzi as among the "hundred languages" of children' (New 2007, p. 8). Malaguzzi (1998) suggests and offers another dimension for understanding symbolic language and how young children express meaning. He outlines that young children weave between verbal dialogue and graphic representations and that children have an amazing ability to relate to several symbolic languages at the same time (Malaguzzi 1998, p. 93).

In order for young children to express this voice, they must be given the opportunities through many modes in order for their meaning and expression to be heard. This is where the creativity of the hundred languages (Malaguzzi 1998; Rinaldi 2006) and modes of expression in children offers a catalyst for meaning-making, and suggests some parallels for recognising and engaging with the innate spiritual capacity of children. Binder, in support of this point, maintains that children require alternative forms of expression and that, through these modes, young children find 'the spaces that revealed a deep understanding of their inner landscapes and the world around them' (Binder 2011, p. 22). This determines how we construct the spaces and environments for learning and engaging with children.

Dahlberg et al. (1999) open up the conversation about viewing the child as a co-constructor of knowledge, then offering children opportunities to allow this construction to flow and occur, providing an angle for further investigation into unravelling the many dimensions of childhood, including the spiritual. Their view involves 'understanding young children as active co-constructors of their own knowledge, as critical and imaginative thinkers and as the possessors of many languages …' (Dahlberg et al. 1999, p. 83).

In addition, according to New (2007), as children have multiple forms of knowing, they also have multiple ways of demonstrating and expressing, with these ways potentially including aspects of their spiritual dimension and capacity.

3.4.1 The Reggio Emilia approach: documenting and observing children

Within this research, the methodology of documentation, inspired by the Reggio Emilia approach as a tool for recording children's learning, is considered and discerned in the current literature, with the review also exploring the ways in which this methodology has been interpreted. Documentation is a process that makes more visible how children learn and what they are learning (Kinney & Wharton 2008).

From a Reggio Emilia perspective, documentation is linked to a pedagogical approach and is viewed as:

> A procedure which sustains teaching because of the interaction it makes possible with the learning processes of the children. It makes visible the interweaving of both adults and children and provides the possibility of improving the quality of communication and interaction, in a process of reciprocal learning.
> (Rinaldi 1998b, p. 28)

Documentation is used as a tool not only for recording but also to discern children's conversations: it involves a process of interaction and respect for the child as an active participant in learning. It also regards the teacher as a researcher and active participant within the child's learning. Millikan (2003) states that the documentation method and process 'engages teachers in processes that enable them to become researchers, to learn, to perhaps challenge widely accepted theories and practice ...' (Millikan 2003, p. 87).

It is essential to establish at this point that the kind of pedagogical approach involving documentation gives the educator a role in which the educator is not the director of children's learning, but is instead in a relationship with the child. My position as the researcher is to use an aspect from this design of documentation as part of my data collection: this determines that it is necessary for my role to be not a mere observer, but a teacher–participant–observer within the research.

The many interpretations around documentation (Berger 2010; Burman 2009; Carr 2001; Edwards et al. 1998; Goodsir & Rowell 2010; Kroeger & Cardy 2006; Rinaldi 2006; Turner & Krechevsky 2003), after initially posing a quandary or disparity in interpretation, have engaged me in a reflective and critical analysis of the available array of literature. Once again, I draw on the perception and construction of childhood, and the image of the child (Malaguzzi 1994; Rinaldi 2006) is the governing overlay in my own interpretation. Evidence from Rinaldi (2006) provides a justification for using documentation as a means of interpretation. The notes and photographs become fragments of the memory of situations that can be subjectively deciphered by those who are documenting. This is only one use and explanation of the documentation process and I am aware that, within the Reggio Emilia educational project, a much broader context is constructed.

Introducing some dilemmas which educators have faced, Kroeger and Cardy (2006) provide some critical points and nuances when conceptualising and contemplating how to interpret and use documentation and, in particular, when determining, as a researcher, how best to employ this as a method. The work of Kroeger and Cardy (2006) endorses the thoughts of Turner and Krechevsky (2003), who maintain that documentation is a process and a tool that assists in getting closer to children's thinking processes. Their contribution through a well-thought-out table and matrix outlines limitations and solutions and poses more questions about documentation. This table and matrix are a resource that any researcher contemplating a form of the documentation approach would find worthy and credible.

Another consideration in the deciphering of documentation is to acknowledge the thread between listening and documenting. If we are uncovering children's thought processes, then a clear intent and position are necessary. I draw on Burman's work in which she recognises and refers to the many languages of children as a 'voice' with these voices requiring responsive listening. Her thought-provoking equivalence of voices to languages filters our lens and attention to the thinking and learning which take place when young children are present:

> Once you decide to value the learning and thinking that happens through languages such as art, construction, dramatic play and movement, you can't help but notice more and more of what is happening during these moments.
> (Burman 2009, p. 153)

Combined with her distillation of documenting and listening, Burman also offers some suggestions for how to record it. Burman's (2009) work offers further interpretation of the documentation approach as a tool for research and for comprehending young children, adding to my overall decision on how to implement such an approach and how to interpret documentation reliably within this exploration and inquiry:

> This enables educators to use their professional judgement to interpret children's learning habits (known as 'dispositions'), based on the educator's knowledge and observations of children and their interests.
> (Goodsir & Rowell 2010, p. 12)

'Learning Stories' present an alternative form of documentation that has been thoroughly investigated by Carr (2001). Her persuasive angle about the intent of Learning Stories and the link between skills, knowledge and dispositions provides further thought about documentation. Carr (2001) developed views on dispositions in learning situations: 'learning dispositions are about responsive and reciprocal relationships between the individual and the environment' (Carr 2001 p. 22). This viewpoint by Carr (2001) resonates with the emerging themes deduced from the literature on spirituality in young children and the ways in which spirituality can be expressed as children interact with their environment. In addition, Carr's work offers an interpretation of documentation when researching and working with children: further discussion in this chapter clarifies and enlightens this viewpoint.

Hatherly and Sands (2002) put forward the opinion in which they describe a Learning Story as a form of narrating the instances of children's learning. They derive this from the premise that '[n]arrative is a viable and useful approach to recording children's learning' (Hatherly & Sands 2002, p. 9). Within their interpretation of Learning Stories, they illustrate that the documentation process can provide an overall picture of a child within particular learning contexts and a story of the child's learning.

Taking this to another level and paradigm of thought, Berger (2010) adds a significant view of documentation and a distillation of this concept. A critical interpretation of pedagogical narration is proposed by Berger (2010) as she builds on the insights of Malaguzzi (1998) Dahlberg, Moss and Pence (1999) and Arendt (1998; cited in Berger 2010). She posits that within 'the process of pedagogical narration, educators make decisions about choosing an experience to be narrated and reflected upon' (Berger 2010, p. 66). In deciphering Berger's thought, I concur that 'through the process of pedagogical narration, educators become participants, co-constructors of the documented experience' (Berger 2010, p. 66).

Within the context of my research and this book, the purpose of the utilisation of any form of documentation is to recognise the spiritual indicators which young children display as they construct knowledge. An adaptation stemming from Learning Stories and the collective insights of the above authors has contributed to this decision, and also to the decision to name the form of documentation 'Learning Stories with Narrative Observations', which is authentic and considered conducive to my research.

Supporting this decision are the insights from Rinaldi (2006), who recognises documentation as a pathway to understanding children's ways of knowing:

> Documentation, therefore, is seen as visible listening, as the construction of traces (through notes, slides, videos and so on) that not only testify to the children's learning paths and processes, but also make them possible because they are visible, and this is the relationship that are [sic] the building blocks of knowledge.
> (Rinaldi, 2006, p. 51)

3.5 The Reggio Emilia approach and the environment

Harris (2007) states that as educators it is necessary to reconceptualise how young children learn and how we can interact, engage and co-construct knowledge with them. Her view is that spirituality cannot be divorced from the normal curricula and pedagogy. Harris stresses the need for a reciprocal environment which nurtures the spiritual capacities of young children.

Here, I draw parallels with the Reggio Emilia approach to teaching where one of the basic elements and principles of the approach is 'the environment as third teacher' (Fraser 2006; Malaguzzi 1998) where the environment acts as a catalyst for the beliefs, values and identities of the learners, respecting and valuing the rights and images of all individuals. Millikan (2003) gives a perspective to this principle as she states that 'the physical space influences the intellectual space, including the thinking, culture, and the experiences within the classroom'.

The Reggio Emilia approach places particular emphasis on the view that an aesthetic environment which highlights beauty and nature connects children to learning and offers engagement, curiosity, wonder and awe. Spaces are created with careful attention to beauty and how materials are arranged. This is a very different notion to traditional teaching spaces and is integral to the context of this research: '[e]very corner of every space has an identity and a purpose, is rich in potential and to communicate, and is valued and cared for by children and adults' (Caldwell 2003, pp. 4–5).

Children naturally interact with their environment, as shown when Marrero (2000) conducted a research study around spirituality in Latino children in the United States (USA). Marrero's study offers some theological correlations about the child and the environment created. Through Marrero's study and his appropriation of the Reggio Emilia approach, he identifies that when children are engaged through wonder, this brings the child to question and to deepen their awareness of God in the present. If we take out the mention of God and replace this with attention to a connection with transcendence, this opens a discussion about the significance of aesthetics or giving attention to the environment to a perceptiveness of spirituality:

> The spaces we create for children reflect how we conceive education and learning in childhood. The space we create will mirror how we view the experience of childhood, one where the child develops 'a sense of self as a creator'.
> (Goouch 2008, p. 99)

The Reggio Emilia approach to learning allows learning to be an emergent process with the environment integral in providing a rich, multifaceted and multisensory space inviting learning, encounters and experiences. Within this multidimensional space are many provocations or stimuli that engage children. As children weave, navigate and interchange within the multisensory environment, there is a sense of freedom in discovery with no expectation to attain the right answers, but support for children in their construction of knowledge. New knowledge can stem from an encounter with different materials, stimuli or provocations. Provocations are an invitation to ask children to 'see situations from multiple perspectives' (Tarr 2003, p. 11).

Caldwell (2003) offers a rich interpretation of this element of the environment as '[s] ensory navigation that exalts the role of synaesthesia in cognition and creation, fundamental to the knowledge building process and the formation of the personality' (Caldwell 2003, pp. 108–109). This merits considerable thought when researching children and taking the view and theories proposed in the review of the literature that spirituality is an intrinsic capacity within each personality.

My explanation of provocations, and of the way that provocations are situated and understood within this research, is influenced and inspired by the Reggio Emilia approach. I describe a provocation as an invitation to engage with thought and imagination. This analogy and description of provocation comes from Gianni Rodari (1996). Rodari was influential in advocating for and making imagination a strong perspective and ingredient in the Reggio Emilia approach.

Through synthesising the review of the literature, I explain a provocation as a construction of ideas with materials from real life (Rodari 1996). Rodari states that the imagination is only constructed from things that exist in real life and

> ... it is necessary that children be able to grow up in an environment rich in impulses and stimuli to nurture their imaginations, and to apply the imagination to appropriate tasks that reinforce its structures and expand its horizons.
> (Rodari 1996, p. 113)

For my research, a distillation of the notion of provocation is also described as follows: 'provocations for learning mean a stimulus that arises naturally within a learning experience or one that is provided by the adult to extend the learning within an episode or project' (Kinney & Wharton 2008, p. 7). The provocations can be provided by educators, not to control the learning experience (Hewett 2001), but to provoke occasions of discovery which may lead to new knowledge, new wonderings and new discoveries.

In my study, natural and aesthetic elements within the environment are a space for children to observe and with which they can interact, in anticipation of enticing wonder and awe. Later in this review, elements of the environment which may lay a foundation for nurturing spirituality in young children are explored.

The term 'provocation' is used within the Reggio Emilia approach as a word to explain an artefact, thought, question or idea which engages children and sparks endless possibilities with no single desired outcome. According to Millikan and Giamminuti (2014), educators within Reggio Emilia and educators inspired by the Reggio Emilia approach have long used the term 'provocation'. It provides educators with a word which becomes a tool or a focus for observing and interpreting in early childhood settings. Millikan and Giamminuti (2014) explain that provocations broaden the scenario for educators in early childhood settings with the focus not on the end point but on the journey, turning points and discoveries in the steps of the journey. In addition, Millikan and Giamminuti state that:

> Both 'provocations' and 'possibilities' are linked to an image of the child as a constructor of knowledge and creator of culture, and an image of the educator as constructor of knowledge and creator of culture.
>
> (2014, p. 69)

Provocations spark possibilities for engaging children's interest but do not expect direct answers or intended outcomes. They invite new possibilities to occur, in which the child is constructor of what comes next and where there is the prospect of the unexpected to occur. Provocations have no prescribed outcome.

3.6 Teachers as researchers within the Reggio Emilia approach

The educators in Reggio Emilia have been involved in many research projects and their learning is documented and made visible (Millikan 2003; Kinney & Wharton 2008; Fraser 2006). The Reggio Emilia approach to documentation and research into children's learning helps the educator be more effective in hearing, seeing and feeling what children are communicating (Kinney & Wharton 2008). The particular process of observation, interpretation and documentation used by the teachers in Reggio Emilia offers a powerful tool for researching and understanding children (Millikan 2003). It is essential to establish that, for this research, my position as researcher and adult is to take an active role with children as I document, observe and interact with them.

The term 'researcher' in relation to this study, within the context of this inquiry, is embodied and inspired by the Reggio Emilia approach whereby the pedagogy of relationships and listening is integral, not only to the role of researcher but also to that of participant observer. Here, the work and scholarly input of Warming (2005), Adler and Adler (1987) and Atkinson and Hammersley (1998) aid in the refinement of this definition, as they describe participant observation as a methodological approach whereby the aim is to learn about 'the other' through participant observation. It is important to define 'the other' (Warming 2005; Dahlberg et al. 1999). To clarify this term, 'the other' is described as 'relational and anti-essentialistic meaning, otherness being regarded as a product of processes of social construction' (Warming 2005, p. 66) and 'the other means not treating the other as the same as or having some universal or generalised character' (Dahlberg et al. 1999, p. 39). Warming (2005) maintains that this initiates enormous potential for the pedagogy of relationships and listening. She maintains that participant observation and entering into a relationship with the child will allow the observer to study children's interactions with each other and the physical environment (Warming 2005).

The essence of the role of the participant observer is also guided by the pedagogy of relationships within the Reggio Emilia philosophy which is explored in the next section.

3.6.1 *The pedagogy of relationships*

The pedagogy of relationships as described and contextualised by the Reggio Emilia philosophy concerning the child and the adult is embedded and based on the idea that children and adults learn from each other (Fleer 2006). From the adult's perspective, this pedagogy is about listening to children, letting go of any personal truth that we consider to be absolute and being open to possibilities (Rinaldi 2001).

In considering relationships, we can also consider encounters: as adults, encountering children requires attention to receptiveness and to not knowing meaning ahead of time (Kind 2010), with entering into the relationship or the encounter marked by a question or further possibilities. A deeper insight into relationships is allowing 'diverse dialogues that engage heart and mind' (Elliot 2010, p. 17) which generate new thinking and understanding.

As children interact and encounter their environment, they are also in a relationship with everything that is within that environment: this includes both the physical attributes and the human attributes (Rinaldi 2006) and can be explained, as Rinaldi proposes, as a common desire intrinsic to children to understand and to know. She uses the example of a flower. For a child, as Rinaldi explains, in the flower, there is the meaning of life: she further clarifies that 'in the relationship with a flower there is the search for the meaning of life' (Rinaldi 2006 p. 113). The adult role in this kind of relationship is embedded in the practice of collaborative and co-constructive inquiry where it seems that receptiveness to the other is paramount (New 2007). This genre of relationships can also be described as 'relational practice' where the adult allows the child, as the child plays and interacts, to experience 'a new mode of becoming' (Yeu 2011, p. 127).

In connection with spiritual development, the pedagogy of relationships corresponds to the teacher's responsiveness to nurturing the spiritual dimension (Baumgartner & Buchanan 2010). Inviting children to encounter an awareness and appreciation of the unknown and enabling them to discover this within their world require a relationship that respects children's preferences and interests, allowing them the freedom to question and to move beyond what is 'unknown to the new known' (Baumgartner & Buchanan 2010, p. 92). Harris (2007) advocates that when meaningful relationships with others, including adults, are established, a child's spiritual development is nurtured.

In reflecting on the notion of 'the other' in a pedagogy which values relationships, Hart's investigation into an integrative spiritual pedagogy has strong connections to the Reggio Emilia-inspired type of relationships and the other. To understand 'the other' is to cross boundaries towards intimacy and empathy opening the door to a richer perception (Hart 2009). This concept of understanding, as argued by Hart (2009), 'requires a fundamental shift in the process of knowing' (Hart 2009, p. 1156). He explains that understanding comes when we 'empathise with the other …' moving '… from an 'I–It' relationship …' towards a more reciprocal one (Hart 2009, p. 1156).

In terms of offering a holistic environment that values reciprocal relationships and enhances the spiritual dimension, Ferrer (2002) suggests that participation in the co-creation of knowledge is vital. His theory advocates for and matches the context of the Reggio Emilia-inspired experience of the pedagogy of relationships:

> Participatory refers to the role the individual consciousness plays during transpersonal events. This relation is not one of appropriation, possession, or passive representation of knowledge, but of communion and co-creative participation.
> (Ferrer 2002, p. 21)

Through the investigation and review of the literature, there is an emerging consensus proposed in relation to early childhood education. The analysis of scholarly input strongly suggests a reciprocal relationship which embodies or is associated with the philosophy of Reggio Emilia. This relationship is one where knowledge and meaning-making exist in a reciprocal, respectful and relational dialogue through shared and equal endeavours where knowledge, questions and possibilities are contemplated and valued, leading to further theories and meanings (Copple 2003; File 1995; Fraser 2006; Podmore 2009; Soler & Miller 2003).

In summary, a pedagogy inspired by the Reggio Emilia approach encourages sensitivity to the possibilities of allowing the other to go beyond the known to the unknown: it suggests that this genre of relationships encompasses a pedagogy which allows the spiritual characteristics of children to emerge.

3.7 Phenomenology in researching children's spirituality

The scholarly input in relation to phenomenology and children's spirituality warrants some focus and attention. The daily encounters that children offer us encompass their innate spirituality and present a challenge in connecting them to methods of research. The challenge is with respect to how the method is utilised, and leads to the question of who has presented credible research using this method in relation to young children and their pedagogical surroundings.

Aspects of phenomenology were essential and crucial for this research to maintain the integrity and nature of the work with young children. Brearley (2001) employed phenomenology to offer and reflect on the richness and originality of the data and this, in turn, provided multiple prisms through which to explore the experience. In relation to this case study, the children's thinking and complexity need to be reflected providing multiple prisms through which to explore the experiences which, in this case, are their expressions or indicators of spirituality and how these are influenced by the Reggio Emilia approach. In reference to Brearley's (2001) research, this study can be viewed as phenomenological for the following reasons. It combines the concepts of empathically engaging with another human being's experience (Bentz & Shapiro 1998, cited in Brearley 2001); exploring the essential and perennial themes of the human condition (von Eckartsberg 1998); merging cognitive and non-cognitive ways of knowing (van Manen 1997); and the interpretation of phenomenology which seeks to tap the unique nature of human experience and invite us into the experience of another (van Manen 1997).

In this study, it was decided that there is an element of phenomenology, with this becoming evident. One essential consideration for this case study was that it needed a clear position: hermeneutic phenomenology. There was an incentive to give justice to the collected data which would not detract from the child's sophisticated ability and the powerful image of the child (Malaguzzi 1994; Rinaldi 2006) who has agency that deserves to be listened to and who has given advocacy for the present moment (Aird 2004, Dahlberg et al. 1999, Lindner 2004, Rinaldi 2006). It is a vital and critical element of the methodology used in this research to allow spirituality to be understood. 'To understand spirituality in a valid and complete way, methods must account for the multiple ways children perceive, experience and express spirituality' (Boyatzis & Newman 2004). The understanding of the expression of spirituality is through the indicators which have been collated for this inquiry. The hermeneutic aspect of phenomenology is then connected to the insights derived by the researcher and the interpretation and responses based on the findings of the data analysis.

3.8 The context of play and the early years child

This section builds on the existing understanding of play, taking it to a new level of interpretation where we may begin to understand and grasp the child's world. In light of the spiritual capacities and how this is evident in the everyday, play offers a threshold for this manifestation: throughout this discussion, the understanding of this concept will be illuminated. The section also outlines the notion of play viewed through the Reggio Emilia approach and the pedagogy that it inspires.

Within early childhood settings, the discussion, interpretation and commitment to play encounter some uneven boundaries: thus, play has been both questioned and supported through theory and research (Wood 2009). In relation to young children, it becomes essential to establish, through the broad interpretations and research into play, where this inquiry is situated in regard to young children and play.

The context of play, situated within this study, is a worthy discussion in light of developing insights into how children think, learn and understand their world. It is through play that interpretations are developed about life and where children 'confront reality and accept it' (Rinaldi 2006, p. 118). The dimension of play is where children construct their theories and interpretations about everyday experiences, and it is a dimension which is 'an essential element of human beings (Rinaldi 2006, p. 118). Accordingly, Rogers (2011, p. 9) supports this by interpreting play as something 'unique to humans' which 'lays the foundations for crucial life skills such as empathy, problem solving, creativity and innovation'.

According to Fraser (2006), one important fact to consider and on which to reflect is that, within the Reggio Emilia approach, the emphasis is not on the notion of play but rather on the encounters that children have in their everyday. It is more important, as she highlights, that teachers participate in this play or these encounters through listening and documentation. The teacher should be open in order 'to find in the intuitions of the child the roots of systematic knowledge' (Bruner 1996, p. 57). Within the Reggio Emilia approach, the distinct nature of the understanding of play is not solely and ultimately for the child, but rather a reciprocal relationship between child and teacher where the latter comes to know the child. I perceive this, based on Fraser's description, as being how the teacher is positioned alongside the child, whether that be by interacting or observing.

When young children participate in uninterrupted play, in which they are engaged, involved and participating in their environment, there is the perfect opportunity for educators to watch and observe them. Correlating this with Vygotsky's (1978) well-known position on play, we can also see how a child perceives their world. The importance and impact of play in the child's life are essential to their development. Through play, as Vygotsky (1978) explains, the child perceives things in a different light:

> The child sees one thing but acts differently in relation to what he sees. Action in an imaginary situation teaches the child to guide her behaviour, not only by immediate perception of objects or by the situation immediately affecting her, but also by the meaning of this situation.
>
> (pp. 97–98)

In relation to child development, Vygotsky points out how play is a stage in young children's lives and the way that it contributes to their overall development. He claims that, although play is not the only important process, it is fundamental to their development.

3.8.1 Play theorists

In reviewing the literature, one cannot disregard the influence and reference to play theorists. Consequently, I refer to play in the context presented by Miller (2000), in which he recognises that 'within each person there is an unconditional, timeless element (i.e., the soul) that needs to be nourished and sustained if we truly want to educate the whole person' (Miller 2006, p. 89). This notion generates opinions from other similar theorists (Bellous & Csinos 2009; Moffett 1994; Kessler 2000; Myers 1997; Miller 2000; Moore 1996) who view play as a holistic framework for children, giving them unhurried time to enjoy, encounter, make meaning of their lives, wonder and discover connections to their world.

Acknowledging the importance of play through surveying the scope of the literature leads this discussion in a distinct direction. From the insights gained, it is therefore essential to conclude that play may be one of the media through which young children can express their spiritual characteristics. I next present an overview of these characteristics in the light of play and spirituality.

3.8.2 Play and spirituality

As early as the 1900s, play was associated with spirituality: it was Froebel (1887) who claimed that 'play in young children is the purest, most spiritual activity of man and typical of life as a whole' (Froebel 1887, p. 55). His theory on allowing time for children to play has influenced the line of thought in the association of play with spirituality.

Play as an aspect of children's spirituality is mentioned by various scholars (Berryman 1997; Hay & Nye 2006; Nye 2004). Csikszentmihalyi (1997) claims that play offers the potential for children to experience a flow of consciousness when they are fully immersed in an activity. Such an assertion suggests that the capacity for a child to achieve their intellectual and creative potential can occur through play.

In summary, if we view play as an essential component of children's everyday experiences, then it is imperative to have a clear understanding of what play can provide. Play is a medium for children to explore their world: '[p]lay and exploration go hand in hand' (Olmsted 2012, p. 182). As Olmsted goes on to point out, children engage with their environment and 'follow their intuition to new spaces' (Olmsted 2012, p. 182). The association between exploration, holistic timeless learning and spirituality leads us to a discussion about the spiritual characteristics and physiognomies children may display and express.

Of course, play is often perceived as a recreational activity which should be regarded as external to the educational setting (Youngquist & Pataray-Ching 2004). Within early childhood education, however, the concept of play is given a different understanding, being valued for the way in which it contributes to children's cognitive, social and psychological development (Johnson, Christie & Yawkey 1999). Saracho and Spodek (1998) observe that in early childhood education, play is 'highly valued and contributes to young children's cognitive, social and psychological development'. As Youngquist and Pataray-Ching (2004) state, it is within this light that a shift in the interpretation of play from being merely a recreational activity highlights its importance within early childhood education.

Through this extension of the understanding of play, Youngquist and Pataray-Ching's (2004) research project offered the view that inquiry is entwined within play, but the response from educators was also discussed. Suggestions were made that educators can also use a mode of inquiry to understand how children learn: '… so they may understand the complexities of and rigor in young children's inquiries as well as the implications for schooling and lifelong learning' (Youngquist & Pataray-Ching 2004, p. 171). In light of pedagogy and practice conducted along the lines of the Reggio Emilia approach, teachers researching into young children offer a sound basis for observing the complex investigative traits which children display. Similarly, with regard to the exploration of spirituality through inquiry and play, this approach strengthens the argument that we can assume that play is a powerful medium through which children gain an understanding of their world.

Lillard's (1998) position opens up a broader understanding of play in relation to theories on children, portraying the image of the child as capable of exploring and understanding their world. Following observations of various play activities, Lillard (1998) argues that children develop theories about their world, thereby contributing to their theories of mind.

3.9 The pedagogical environment: nurturing spirituality

This section summarises some emerging themes in relation to children's spirituality, along with the characteristics which children display and how these may be manifested. As portrayed in the literature, in order to understand spirituality, there is a requirement to recognise the characteristics, physiognomies, dispositions and indicators (Champagne 2003, Binder 2011) which young children display within an educational environment.

3.9.1 Creativity and imagination

It has been stated that spirituality can be enhanced when time and energy are given to developing imagination through creative experiences (Mountain 2007). Creativity invites curiosity and imagination, allowing young children to experience a flow of ideas and expression. When we allow time for flow, when there is a willingness for a sense of surprise, an openness to the experience of mystery and an uncertainty about where the process is going, the power of creativity is unleashed (Mountain 2007). Young children are often in a flow of creativity.

Howard Gardner, when looking at creativity, reminds us that:

> Surprise is an experience that plays a part at the birth of an idea and during the work itself ... Open-mindedness, flexibility, willingness to trust hunches, and curiosity are factors that emerge repeatedly as facilitating and favouring creativity.
> (Gardner 1983, p. 382)

Both Mountain (2007) and Gardner (1983) have reflected and suggested that valuing the time for creativity within all young children's environments is essential when offering a pedagogical attitude to learning, suggesting that, within the environment, this time is recognised and valued in relation to young children and their experiences. Wright (2010) considered creativity to be a 'personal trait' of a young child and that it is 'the process of generating ideas' (Wright 2010, p. 3).

The research outlined by Adams et al. (2008) suggests that, in supporting this natural trait of creativity possessed by all children, we are also offering them a way of identifying themselves in the world through 'being' and 'doing' (Adams et al. 2008, p. 55). They outline that, in allowing these moments for children to absorb themselves in their own being, these moments are often unpredictable, capturing a spiritual experience.

In addition, Csikszentmihalyi (1997), in his notion of 'flow', articulates that flow happens when someone becomes immersed in an experience. He continues by elaborating that it this a time when people focus their attention without distractions. Some parallels can be assumed and are suggested between Csikszentmihalyi's (1997) theory and the work of Adams et al. (2008) in relation to children identifying themselves through being and doing in their everyday experiences. The flow experience is described by Csikszentmihalyi as a state in which one is immersed in learning; he asserts that there is a state of awareness that occurs in flow which assists the person in achieving new perceptions and skills (Csikszentmihalyi 1997).

In addition to developing an understanding of the intrinsic nature of creativity, Kessler (2000) offers insights that categorise creativity as a universal way for every child to express themselves. Kessler's theory offers us the observation that creativity can help to connect young students. It offers them an escape from the busy demands of everyday routines and expectations, and that it values their own uniqueness. She goes on to point out the relevance of creativity and of accepting individual children as she describes creativity as accommodating different learning styles, listening to divergent thinking and being tolerant of cultural distinctions (Kessler 2000):

> Creativity flourishes most often as a synthesis or integration of many modes of knowing – left brain/right brain; reason and intuition; imagination and observation; and physical, emotional and conceptual ways of knowing.
> (Kessler 2000, p. 104)

Kessler's position and study highlight the importance of creativity as the bridge between the 'ordinary and the extraordinary' (Kessler 2000, p. 104) and, in her view, 'is vital to both the survival of soul and the success of learning' (Kessler 2000, p. 114).

The British researchers Hay and Nye (2006) have offered a domain for understanding spirituality in relation to children. They offer the view that spirituality is a part of the child's experience, a kind of inner knowing, which is different to the cognitive knowing of formal education where so often there is one correct answer. Allowing children to experience an environment where learning and imagination go hand in hand can nurture the spiritual domain and provide a rich and dynamic learning environment. Imagination, according to Knill (2004), can be described as part of an effective reality, a reality that is a tool essential for living and is a part of the human sense of living engagement.

Spirituality and imagination cannot be divorced, but can be viewed 'as inner aspects at the core of human being' (Mountain 2007, p. 194).

In summarising the literature outlined in this section, correlations appear to be suggested between spirituality, imagination and creativity. Moreover, when placing importance on creativity in an early childhood pedagogical environment, we are also nurturing the spiritual capacity of young children (Upton 2009).

The literature has suggested some correlations between imagination as an expression of spirituality and the philosophy and pedagogical approach of Reggio Emilia. This is supported by Malaguzzi's (1998) statement: '[c]reativity should not be considered a separate mental faculty but a characteristic of our way of thinking, knowing and making choices' (Malaguzzi 1998, p. 75).

Furthermore, he suggests that creativity is a part of a child's everyday experience as they 'construct and reinvent their own ideas continuously' (Malaguzzi 1998, p. 75). The Reggio Emilia approach advocates imagination and creativity as an aspect of the child's ordinary everyday experiences and expressions when they interact with and encounter their world. Malaguzzi (1998) supports this through advocating that: '[c]reativity seems to express itself through cognitive, affective and imaginative processes. These come together and support the skills for predicting and arriving at unexpected solutions' (Malaguzzi 1998, p. 76).

It appears that the Reggio Emilia approach not only enhances this creative imaginative process but also offers a domain for extending creativity into a profound experience where children are able to express themselves, according to Malaguzzi, with 'a sense of freedom to venture beyond the known' (Malaguzzi 1998, p. 76).

In addition, creativity in the Reggio Emilia approach is endorsed by Rinaldi (2006) as an attitude towards the child who 'searches every day to understand something, to draw meaning, to grasp a piece of life' (Rinaldi 2006, p. 112). According to Rinaldi, the creative process is a learning process whereby children are able to construct new meanings and 'connections between thoughts' (2006, p. 116). Her insights into imagination and creativity suggest that the creative process 'needs to be recognised and legitimised' (Rinaldi 2006, p. 119). One attitude which the Reggio Emilia approach adopts in nurturing this creative expression is advocacy that creativity has a right to exist: it is part of everyday life. For children, Rinaldi argues that 'the creativity of daily life should be the right of all' (2006, p. 120).

Within the Reggio Emilia approach, creativity is given precedence through the unique elements designed to nurture its expression. The approach emphasises a space for artistic materials and media (*atelier*) and encourages the presence of a trained art teacher (*atelierista*). These elements within the approach are intended to assist in capturing expression, creativity and imagination which are highly valued and regarded within the approach and essential for young children. This is articulated by Gandini (2005):

> Expressivity is a structure that is intrinsic to the individual. Therefore, the cognitive and the imaginative inevitably go together. The atelier within the school places expressivity inside the process of understanding giving life to a structure that is more complete, more human.
>
> (p. 142)

An approach such as Reggio Emilia offers a philosophy about children and learning which encourages creativity. Within each of the municipal schools of Reggio Emilia, the *atelier* and a professional *atelierista* are a common asset to the pedagogical approach which is presented within these settings. *Ateliers* are spaces that offer opportunities for techniques and expression. In these spaces, creativity is encouraged and takes precedence while many possibilities are nurtured and facilitated. A typical *atelier* space within Reggio Emilia would be:

> ... large enough to contain several children and activities and connected visually and otherwise with the rest of the school. It will be equipped with tools; tables, containers for materials, computer, printer, digital cameras, easels for painting, surfaces for working with clay, an oven for ceramic work, tape recorder, a microscope ... there will be a large quantity of traditional materials: different kinds of colours for painting and drawing in different consistencies and shades ... wire in different thickness, cutters, recycled and discarded materials ...
>
> (Vecchi 2010, p. 4)

The aim is for children to enter the area of the *atelier*, where they have access to tools and materials that make it possible for them to have experiences in which thinking is able to take on different forms: visual, musical or verbal. This makes it apparent that there is a connection between imagination and creativity. For creativity to flow, it is imperative that creativity is valued and possibilities for creativity, aesthetics and expression are made viable:

> [A]mong Reggio pedagogy's most original features is an acceptance of aesthetics as one of the important dimensions in the life of our species and, therefore, also in education and in learning.
>
> (Vecchi 2010, p. 5)

The Reggio Emilia approach clearly creates a viable environment that fosters creativity, imagination and aesthetics. This may lead to an encouraging view in assuming that this pedagogical approach supports and develops the intrinsic spiritual dimension of the human disposition. Within the Reggio Emilia approach, the aesthetic dimension is discussed in relation to learning and education:

> Perhaps first and foremost it is a process of empathy relating the Self to things and things to each other. It is like a slim thread or aspiration to quality that makes us choose one word over another, the same for a colour, a shade, a certain piece of music, a mathematical formula or the taste of a food. It is an attitude of care and attention for the things we do, a desire for meaning; it is curiosity and wonder; it is the opposite of indifference and carelessness, of conformity, of absence of participation and feeling.
>
> (Vecchi 2010, p. 5)

The importance of imagination in its relevance to perception is worth discussing: if children are spiritual beings who constantly try to make meaning and see their world, then it is necessary to review the relevance of perception (Dewey 1980). As every human lives their experience, there is a constant interchange with their environment and, as Dewey points out, this is when 'experience becomes conscious, a matter of perception' (Dewey 1980, p. 283). His theory highlights that, when one encounters meaning, this is when imagination provides 'the only gateway through which these meanings can find their way into a present interaction' (Dewey 1980, p. 283).

The literature from authors such as Kind (2010), Wright (2010, 2012) and Elliot (2010) has indicated support for imagination and creativity as crucial aspects of early childhood development.

Wright has suggested that young children's 'creativity is surfaced through the act of meaning making' (Wright 2010, p. 2). Her further exploration and work within creativity and art have led to some discussions on the existential nature of arts pedagogy. She states that: '[t]he arts give shape to formless ideas and are a vehicle by which we can express our growing awareness of ourselves and the worlds in which we live' (Wright 2012, p. 207).

Aligned with early childhood education are Kind's (2010) views about art. She found that her work as an educator and an artist offered the fusion between arts and creativity, lifting it into a different realm. She states that, in order to take artistic exploration seriously, the arts need to be seen 'as integral aspects of children's inner world or creativity' (Kind 2010, p. 113).

For educators, Elliot's (2010) opinion on imagination provokes some thought in relation to pedagogical approaches. She expresses the view that imagination includes our emotional, rational, historical, experiential and cultural selves as a unified whole: each of these elements influences the other. In offering this view, she includes the opinion that understanding imagination and the acceptance of imagination as a part of each person's being requires a degree of receptivity or, as Elliot describes, 'an attitude of openness and empathy' (Elliot 2010, p. 14).

3.9.2 The environment: engaging wonder and awe

The literature has suggested the space that we create in which children live and learn may be a spiritual endeavour (Hart 2003), especially when these environments consider children to have a 'rich and informative spiritual life' (Hart 2009, p. 1150). Appearing frequently in the literature, the notion of 'wonder' appears to be a recurring spiritual characteristic (Beck 1986, 1990; Carson 1956; Elkins et al. 1998). Furthermore, inviting and allowing children to wonder is tending or nurturing their spiritual nature (Kessler 2000; Nye 2009; Adams et al. 2008) and, as educators, we can provide 'settings where awe and wonder can arise' (Miller 2006, p. 155).

Likewise, the Reggio Emilia approach pays particular attention to constructing children's environments, thus inviting their natural capacity to be curious and to wonder, and to engage their senses (Curtis & Carter 2003; Strong-Wilson & Ellis 2007). In respecting the joy and learning which children display, the grounding philosophy of Reggio Emilia considers these as values to be highly regarded (Gandini, Hill, Caldwell & Schwall 2005). The Reggio Emilia approach advocates that children come to us with many expressive competencies: as educators, a fundamental principle is that it 'is essential to preserve in children the feeling of wonder and surprise' (Gandini 2005, p. 8). The approach considers all children to be 'rich, powerful and competent' (Fraser 2006, p. 108) and it is bearing this view in mind that Fraser suggests that environments are designed to nurture and mirror this image (Fraser 2006). Building on the notion of the powerful image of the child (Malaguzzi 1994; Rinaldi 2006) are Claxton's (2002) ideas and views on building learning power in children. He contends that we can nurture and build the child's mind and capacities. Recognising the capacities of 'resilience' and 'resourcefulness' involves 'harnessing the capacity for children to imagine, question, and reason' (Claxton 2002, p. 17). The above views provide some agreement that educational environments offer a nurturing 'scaffold' for the natural, intrinsic capacities which young children display and this, as is made evident from contemporary literature, includes the innate spiritual capacity.

Hart describes children's ways of being in the world as showing how spirituality presents itself, and that one characteristic of spirituality is wonder (Hart 2006). In addition, he states that 'wonder includes a constellation of experiences that can involve feelings of awe, connection, joy, insight ...' (Hart 2006, p. 165). He then links this to a pedagogical approach that values children and the environment: how this is designed can attend to these experiences and to what Rinaldi refers as to 'create a space for life' (Hart 2006, p. 80).

Similarly, Harris (2007) illustrates that wonder cannot be taught: furthermore, in order for children to develop this sense, they require opportunities to discover, engage and experience mystery and questioning (Harris 2007, p. 271). She refers to environments which enrich this capacity and states that when educators provide these:

> They [children] are given abundant opportunities to explore their curiosities and expand their multidirectional, multiethnic and multidimensional development growth. A child's spiritual development is nurtured within this type of educational setting ...
>
> (Harris 2007, p. 271)

This section leads into, and forms, a connection to the next section, which further investigates and develops the notion of elements within the environment that nurture the spiritual capacities, expressions and characteristics of young children.

3.9.3 Aesthetics and beauty in the environment: an essential element to nurture spirituality

The literature suggests that a number of points of connection exist between spirituality and aesthetics (McMurtary 2007; Upton 2009; Miller & Athan 2007; de Souza 2009; Crawford & Rossiter 2006; Wright 2000).

While Wright endorses aesthetics as a 'reality of our spirituality diversity' (Wright 2000, p. 20), he tends to refer to aesthetics as a domain for spirituality: he views this through the lens of romanticism, in which we are rejecting materialism in attending to the aesthetic elements of life. Others, such as de Souza (2009), place aesthetics as part of the human experience (Baumgartner & Buchanan 2010; Crawford & Rossiter 2006) and indicate that environments should promote 'responses to beauty and creation' (de Souza 2009, p. 1137) in order to stimulate the spiritual by perception through the senses.

Similarly, Baumgartner and Buchanan (2010) assert that an aesthetic environment offers children the time to wonder. They emphasise the importance of supporting children's spiritual dimension and that, through sensitively inventing and creating environments for children, we can then evoke an awareness and appreciation of the unknown. Children need to know that the world is full of interesting things to discover. Children share with all human beings an appreciation of beauty and mystery (Baumgartner & Buchanan 2010, p. 92).

In emphasising the spiritual connection to beauty and aesthetics, Crawford and Rossiter acknowledge that 'the aesthetic dimension to spirituality has to do with the appreciation of beauty ...' (Crawford & Rossiter 2006, p. 196). Some sound evidence from the above scholars validates the strong connection and essential consideration of aesthetics and the spiritual dimension. This literature offers some pertinent and valid key points illustrating how this may implicate environments designed for early years' education in relation to young children's spirituality.

Subsequently, I have highlighted some broader links to the early childhood field and draw on the work of Apps and MacDonald (2012). They view aesthetics as integral in designing early learning environments and consider that this is interrelated with pedagogical experiences which impact on teaching and learning (Apps & MacDonald 2012). Their view is that 'the design and aesthetics of a pedagogical space can be a point of entry into how the classroom and curriculum are activated, engaged with and embodied' (Apps & MacDonald 2012, p. 49). A key point raised by these scholars in relation to aesthetics is that: '[a]esthetics in connection with classroom design and curriculum generates implicit and explicit messages and contribute[s] to the process of teaching and learning' (Apps & Macdonald 2012, p. 49).

Equally, Curtis and Carter (2003) favour and recommend aesthetics in the environment through paying careful attention to the materials that are offered to children. They see the materials providing aesthetic entry points for 'sparking children's imagination' (p. 16). Their view is that an aesthetic environment in early childhood is a way of 'provoking wonder, curiosity and intellectual engagement' (Curtis & Carter 2003, p. 17). Correlations appear to exist between what are also known as the characteristics of the spiritual dimension. In addition, creating spaces in a holistic manner is related to a living pedagogical space which is created 'in a manner that honours the personal, visual and sensed aesthetics' which contribute to the living existence within the classroom or learning space (Apps & MacDonald 2012, p. 58).

Lastly, Lim (2005), in her study within early childhood settings, asserts that aesthetic experiences are a crucial and vital domain in children's development. She emphasises that it is important for young children:

> to be exposed to a variety of aesthetic qualities in the world, natural and man-made, structured and chaotic, all of which ultimately inspire a sense of wonder and serve as a basic source of their aesthetic experience.
> (Lim 2005, p. 369)

Likewise, the Reggio Emilia approach values the aesthetic attention to the space, the beauty and the materials in the environment, emphasising the aesthetic element of learning spaces (Ceppi & Zini 1998; Giamminuti 2012; New 1998: Ridgeway & Hammer 2006; Rinaldi 1998b, 2006; Vecchi 2010). Within the Reggio Emilia approach, the aspect of beauty in the environment is considered to be a right for every child: it is articulated as an essential component of the aesthetic spaces which the educators create, but the notion of beauty is aligned with a value that requires respect for young children (Rinaldi 2006). The practice of teaching and learning inspired by the Reggio Emilia approach is challenged with the concept of the environment and, as Rinaldi suggests, requires us to be challenged in how we choose to construct these spaces. A key point is that if these spaces value the aesthetics as the right of children to enjoy and in which to learn, then the existing literature which highlights the connection of the spiritual and aesthetics places a critical emphasis on designing a pedagogical space which develops the spiritual dimension. This is highlighted by Rinaldi: 'the aesthetic dimension thus becomes a pedagogical quality of the scholastic and educational space' (Rinaldi 2006, p. 81).

The Reggio Emilia approach, and the pedagogy it inspires, also consider that the spaces which are created are conducive to providing encounters with possibilities for children to engage, discover, wonder and be curious, all of which are characteristics of spirituality (Kessler 2000; Nye 2009; Adams et al. 2008).

When attending to the aesthetic dimension through a Reggio Emilia-inspired approach, we are also carefully developing environments which Harris (2007), in her work on spiritual education, describes as those spaces which 'spark children's interests' (p. 273). Thus, it is important to realise that these spaces nurture a child's 'head, heart, spirit and soul' (Harris 2007, p. 273).

The notion of the 'environment as third teacher' in Reggio Emilia-inspired environments is explained by Strong-Wilson and Ellis as a marketplace which generates a context where teachers can 'become more thoughtful about how they can provoke children's interests' (Strong-Wilson & Ellis 2007, p. 45). They emphasise that, within this context, 'the objects, placed in relationship with one another within the classroom, can carry messages that invite children to engage with the world' (Strong-Wilson & Ellis 2007, p. 45). It is appropriate to also draw attention to the work of Strong-Wilson and Ellis in early childhood education: they expand on the notion of the Reggio Emilia-inspired aesthetic environment and state that the 'aesthetic and transparency draw our attention to how children are attracted by and curious about anything that engages their senses' (Strong-Wilson & Ellis 2007, pp. 44–45).

If we acknowledge that the young child is a spiritual child (Hart 2003; Hay & Nye 2006) then attention to their spiritual dimension is crucial. The above literature has indicated correlations between the aesthetic and the spiritual: consequently, what Reggio Emilia offers through their pedagogical environment is noteworthy. The inclusion and understanding of the aesthetic dimension within this philosophy have implications for their view of life. I draw on Vecchi to support this concept: she expresses that 'among the Reggio pedagogy's most original features is an acceptance of aesthetics as one of the important dimensions in the life of our species' (Vecchi 2010, p. 5).

Lastly, the Reggio Emilia approach offers us a choice to consider in our construction of learning environments which nurture aesthetics and beauty and, therefore, the spiritual dimension. Giamminuti expands on this by stating that '[b]eauty is a choice; it is a value' and within Reggio Emilia, '... there has been a conscious choice to value beauty' (Giamminuti 2012, p. 207).

3.10 The sociocultural influence

The following section summarises the main points that underpin sociocultural theory and thus influence how we view or perceive childhood, according to the writings of Malaguzzi (1998), Cullen (2009) and Anning et al. (2009). Language, communication and the formation of relationships are central to learning. Within sociocultural theory, there is an understanding that childhood is a social construction and, therefore, that children's multiple ways of development are influenced by social and cultural specifics. Children are active constructors and contributors to their development, providing a context for adults to research and comprehend.

This theoretical view is embedded in practice within education and positions adults and competent peers alongside children, 'scaffolding' and supporting their development through task and/or demonstration. This reinforces the sociology of childhood as viewed through a sociocultural lens with educators in daily practice working alongside children, the adults researching and documenting children's learning in multiple ways and acknowledging children as active agents in their own right (Anning 2009). With this in mind, when acknowledging children as active agents, a position on listening is highly regarded: this position involves listening to children through hearing and observation while adopting an open mind (Clark et al. 2005).

Bearing in mind these perspectives, a construct of childhood is presented in which children are active contributors and thus create their worlds through interactions with others who assist them with learning how to learn. Given that this study is positioned where the Reggio Emilia philosophy inspires practice, I take this even further by suggesting the inclusion within this theoretical paradigm of the 'other' that assists or extends children in the instances of their learning, with the 'other' being the environment. This is where the analogy of the environment as the third teacher (Fraser 2006; Fleer 2006) holds a powerful position in the cultural and theoretical implications of its sociocultural effects on the pedagogy and practice of a place.

3.10.1 Constructivism and social constructivism

As young children embrace the world, they learn to construct their own meanings around the many cultural artefacts that exist (MacNaughton 2009). In extending this theory, MacNaughton directs our attention to the fact that as children construct the meanings of these artefacts, 'through these artefacts, they are able to manipulate meanings according to context (MacNaughton 2009, p. 53).

Positioned within the concept of social constructivism is the Reggio Emilia-inspired perception and belief in the child 'as an active constructor of knowledge' (Hewett 2001). In Hewett's examination of the Reggio Emilia approach, she asserts that the child is understood as having an innate desire to understand and make sense of the world (Hewett 2001). The word 'protagonist' is used by the educators within this region and can be interpreted as the child as the central character or as the leading person in a learning situation.

It is vital to have a distinct portrayal and understanding of the shift from constructivism to social constructivism and of the fine divisional line that exists in the Reggio Emilia approach and where it exists on the continuum. As New (1998) points out, while the educators in the region recognise the knowledge construction by children, the social context cannot be ignored. Similarly, New describes the influence of Loris Malaguzzi and how, as educators in Reggio Emilia, they 'focused on the processes and potentials of the children's learning, the symbolic meanings assigned to that knowledge, and the ways in which adults might use such knowledge in the children's best interests' (New 1998, p. 264).

The term 'co-construction' places an emphasis on the child as powerful and competent within his or her learning experience (Jordan 2009). When viewed as a co-constructor, the image of the child is one which is 'rich in potential, strong, powerful, competent, and, most of all, connected to adults and other children' (Malaguzzi 1993, p. 10). For the co-construction of knowledge to flow, a conscious effort is required of the teacher or the adult in their awareness of what the child thinks and understands: this requires a sensitive understanding of the child's body of knowledge (Jordan 2009) and the manner in which adults 'scaffold' and support learning (Anning et al. 2009).

In summary, the child is an active agent of learning and discovering through their inter-relational experiences and encounters, and also a constructor of knowledge. Moving to a different paradigm of co-constructing knowledge with peers and/or adults primarily requires a focus and a respect for children where the power remains communal (Jordan 2009).

3.10.2 The child as an active agent

Building on the notion of a communal understanding of the co-construction of knowledge requires that attention be directed towards understanding the child as an active agent within a community of learners (Etheridge 2004). The individual differences of learners and their ways of knowing and meaning-making are respected within this experience of a community of learners (Etheridge 2004; Surman, Ridgeway & Edwards 2006).

A lens on childhood that respects children is one which advocates the child as an agent (James 2004). Taking this lens into a broader perspective also filters the child's agency in light of their spiritual dimension, whereby children are nurtured as agents of their own spiritual development (Lindner 2004).

3.10.3 Reconceptualising children's spirituality

In view of reconceptualising children's expression of spirituality, the notion of children as agents plus viewing children as capable of perceiving their own world has many implications. Expanding on this assumption, Hyde, Yust and Ota (2010) posit a construct for children as co-creators which:

> ... has many implications for the ways in which their spirituality might develop and for the ways in which we as adults might seek to nurture their spirituality. If children can be thought of as co-constructors of their own childhood, then they are also co-constructors of their spirituality. While all children are spiritual, they exercise agency in terms of how they nourish and choose to express this quality of their lives.
>
> (Hyde et al. 2010, p. 1)

In summary, when children are respected elements of the community (Lindner 2004), their voices as agents offer opportunities to explore and understand the theories of the world and the serious questioning about the world which they contemplate (Matthews 2004; Lindner 2004). Thus, they are spiritual beings wanting to connect with the world: forming theories and exploring and enjoying moments of mere wonder.

3.11 Beauty and the Spirit

As you read through this book, you will see that there is so much that we can do to contribute to nurturing children in a holistic and genuine way. We can offer an avenue in education that develops the mind, body and spirit. My research offered many definitions of spirituality and I have been fortunate enough and confident enough to now offer my own working definition of spirituality in young children.

Spirituality is an innate human trait and is expressed as young children play and discover in their everyday lives. Spirituality can be nurtured with careful attention to aesthetics and the pedagogy that is constructed in the learning environment.

The following points also need to be considered as early childhood educators work and learn alongside children:

- All children require and need interesting and beautiful spaces in which to experience life.
- Young children are competent, skilled and capable learners from birth. They have absorbent minds with an extraordinary ability to learn and take in nuances from the environments and people in their environment.
- Spiritual development plays an important role in the holistic learning and growth for all children.
- Nurturing spiritual development and expressions of spirituality is inter-related with all other domains of development

I was lucky enough to conduct fieldwork in an educational setting which was inspired by the Reggio Emilia approach. The evidence collated from my fieldwork concluded that this approach provides a learning environment which nurtures the spirituality and the spiritual expression of spirituality in young children.

3.12 Inviting beauty

3.12.1 Beauty, aesthetics and spirituality

One of the significant factors of environments which are inspired by the Reggio Emilia approach is the beauty and aesthetic nature of the learning environments. Beauty is an essential force in our lives which adds zest, joy and happiness to a moment. Opportunities to have sensitivity to beauty is an avenue to wholeness. Sensitivity to beauty also brings about sensations of awe and wonder, which are indicators of expressions of spirituality. Early childhood educators can foster children's aesthetic sensitivity by supporting children to experience beauty in many rich and diverse ways; they can provide a pathway for beauty to enter the daily lives of children, thus nurturing their spiritual development and expression.

3.12.2 Beauty: hard to define

The definition of beauty is hard to define and has been discussed through the eyes of poets and philosophers. Throughout history, beauty has meant different things to different people, but one sustainable thread of discussion in relation to beauty is that beauty evokes the senses. The definition of beauty has even been referred to as 'moving target'—something that may change over time (Gardner, 2011b, p.192). What can be said and known about beauty is that it resides more in the subjective, abstract or transcendent aspects of reality than is what is objective, concrete and measurable (Gendler, 2007). In some moments and instances, beauty is ephemeral or fleeting.

3.12.3 Beauty: a basic necessity of life

There are many theories which support the understanding that beauty is a basic need and desire in our human life. Some scholars, including Abraham Maslow (1954, 1968, 1971) and Howard Gardner (2011b), suggest that beauty is a basic human need and a value which defines the essence of who we are. According to Maslow (1954), humans have two major types of needs: deficiency needs and being needs. The deficiency needs include basic physical needs such as food, air, water, shelter, security, esteem, friendship and love. Maslow also suggests that there are 'being needs', which are related to self-actualisation: becoming all that you can be or reaching your full potential. He states that needs in this area include creativity, spontaneity, beauty, independence, self-expression and morality. Maslow's theory supports the theory that beauty is one of the 'being needs' and states that this promotes human development. As early childhood educators who promote holistic development including spiritual development, then beauty is an essential element of an early childhood environment. The work of Howard Gardner (2011b) questions the need for beauty. His own response suggests that beauty is fundamental to our condition as human beings and the search for beauty signifies a crucial part of life.

Gendler (2007) relates to beauty as a 'bridgebuilder' and can be a pathway to wholeness, which helps us to make connections between ourselves and the world. Gendler also states that beauty is something that opens up the door to creativity and wisdom. These, as my research has suggested, are indicators of expressions of spirituality. Additionally, beauty puts us in touch with truth and invites reflection on the more spiritual aspects of life (Chawla, 1990; Gardner 2011b; Kemple & Johnson, 2002).

3.12.4 Beauty and early childhood education environments

Carroll (1999) considers the aesthetic experience as a way of encountering stimuli that involve attention, contemplation and thoughtful perusal that must involve being open and attentive. Through this understanding, aesthetics is capturing of attention and wonderment.

One of the most prominent examples of beauty and aesthetic sensitivity occur in human characteristics such as perception, imagination, observation and creativity. All are synonymous with expressions of spirituality. These characteristics can be nurtured and fostered through early childhood programs and learning environments. With a very strong emphasis on beauty in the physical environment, the Reggio Emilia approach, when implemented or inspiring the learning environment, provides numerous examples of how to foster and nurture young children's aesthetic sensitivity. Among the environmental aspects and elements of the learning environment used in the Reggio Emilia approach are light, colour, overall softness, smell and sound (Ceppi and Zini, 1998). These are aspects of the learning environment which are unique to the Reggio approach. The following contribute to the aesthetic sensitivity of young children.

The *atelieristas*: The *atelierista* is an art teacher who works closely with educators to suggest, supply and arrange the materials and tools in the *atelier* (art studio) and other places around the school to invite and observe children's creative and learning processes.

The *atelier* (art studio): The *atelier* is a purposely designed space equipped with a wide variety of art materials. It contains paint, pens, paper, clay, wire, beads, shells, and other natural materials. Children use these materials to create short- and long-term projects to express themselves through the 'hundred languages' of children.

The 'hundred languages': This refers to the many modes of expression children use to express their discoveries about the world around them. Their many 'languages' include words, movement, drawing, painting, sculpture, shadow play, collage, and music (Edwards, Gandini, & Forman, 1998). This also includes the language of spiritualty. In conjunction with engaging the children to learn and discover about the characteristics of different art-related materials, the *atelier* also offers beauty, space, and time for children to research and ask big questions (Schein, 2018). It allows them to connect to nature and natural phenomena and search for meaning-making. This nurtures their spiritual dimension.

3.12.5 Inviting beauty and aesthetic sensitivity into early childhood environments

The Italian cultural sense of aesthetics in the learning environment has been evident in the design of the preschools and childcare centres of Reggio Emilia. The influence from these educational spaces has been felt globally and has influenced many educational settings across Australia and New Zealand. The beautiful environment interpreted from the Reggio approach is a 'relational space' and a holistic, consisting of 'an environmental fabric rich in information, without formal rules. It is not the feel about it ... the aesthetic quality depends (also) on the quality of connections (the aesthetic of the links)' (Ceppi and Zini, 1998, n.p.). This, in effect, is the spiritual aspect of these environments, the connectedness of all things made possible by the 'aesthetic of the links' (Ceppi and Zini, 1998, n.p.).

3.13 Provocations and recommendations for early childhood educators, creating spiritual spaces

Nature:

Not all early childhood programs are in a position to provide art studios and art teachers. However, there are many things to nurture young children's aesthetic sensitivity. It has been suggested that the most powerful way to foster a sense of beauty in young children is to connect them with nature. Sandra Duncan (2011) states that nature is a 'gift to our senses, minds, and hearts' and suggests that one of nature's greatest gift 'is giving children a beautiful and creative perspective of the world' (p. 12). She suggests to educators that we can help children to assume the roles of gatherer, observer and creator as they interact and connect with nature.

- *As gatherers, children can collect gifts from nature: simple things like shiny rocks and pebbles or a crumbly piece of tree bark or leaves.*
- *As observers, children can take the time to explore their collections and make decisions about how to display them.*
- *As creators, children can express their feelings and ideas about nature's gifts through such artistic modes and expressions such as sculpting, painting, and drawing.*

Surround children with beauty:

- *Add plants, river rocks, and other natural materials to the indoor environment. It's optimal, and offers a sense of agency, if children are involved in gathering some of these materials. Children can be counted on to find objects of beauty in nature in the outside area or on field trips. You can also invite parents to help their children find beautiful natural materials during their outings together.*
- *Use real aesthetic art works to provoke discussion and provocations to decorate the room.*
- *Look for aesthetics; real-life examples of nature are best.*
- *Use tablecloths, curtains, materials and attractive rugs to enhance the décor of the room. Bring textures into the environment.*
- *Enhance and call attention to the natural features of the outdoor playspace. Try grow a variety of plants, including different types of trees, fruits, vegetables, and flowers. Use logs for benches and tables. Add decorative windsocks and bamboo wind chimes to draw attention to the element and sensation of wind. Invite local wildlife with a bird bath, a bird feeder, and create a butterfly garden.*
- *Encourage creative expressions and related discussions. Provide a variety of art-related materials in an organised space. These materials can be used both indoors and outdoors and should preferably include natural materials such as leaves, seeds, and different textured stones.*

- *Follow the children's interests with materials, allow them to go deeper into exploration and discovery of materials and mediums.*
- *Provide child-friendly workspaces where child agency is encouraged, and they can participate in projects that are child-centred and can be continued over time.*
- *Display children's work in an attractively arranged gallery and always arrange their work in aesthetic ways which honours their work and not merely contribute to the clutter and visual noise of the learning environment.*
- *Children's work, when attractively displayed, adds beauty and values the image of the child.*
- *Listen attentively to children, be present to their many languages and modes of learning and exploring, notice their gestures, their non-verbal times, their awe and attraction to inquiry and finding out more. Respect their questions and their curiosity.*
- *Introduce children to the cultural diversity of beauty.*
- *Create spaces for quiet and stillness for children to contemplate, sit and ponder.*

As early childhood educators, we are at the forefront of providing beautiful environments for our children. In so doing, we are allowing and respecting their right to beauty and nurturing their innate spirituality.

3.13.1 The right to spirituality

We can be at the forefront of honouring the child's right to spirituality as we work and learn alongside young children.

> The spiritual dimension of children's development is part of a holistic understanding of the needs and rights of children, young people, families and communities.
> (Sedan, 2005, p. 4)

We can be inspirational in our views and how we construct pedagogy and learning environments for children. Spirituality involves a sense of connection with the world and its creatures, a search for awareness of the meaning of life. Generally, innate spirituality is linked with a sense of awe and wonder, with compassion and creativity. It involves affording children the time 'to be' to play and discover thus igniting their imagination, awe and wonder.

3.14 The portrait of a place

As our knowledge about young children's spirituality grows, I offer to the following provocations to consider when designing places for children to learn in early childhood settings. I offer these provocations for you, as educators, to construct your own 'portrait of place'. Let the provocations be the palette to paint your portrait and learning environment.

Educators can:

- *provide a community of care where young children make connections, have a sense of belonging and learn about understanding and empathy, giving and gratitude, faith and hope*
- *respond to and explore children's awe and wonder at tangible things, such as nature and music; and intangible things, such as beauty and love*
- *support families' expression of their spirituality through talking with them and their children and giving opportunities for families to share their different rituals and special occasions*
- *help children enjoy the history of beliefs in the world and what they mean, through stories and myths*
- *have rituals that support concepts such as joy, beauty, gratitude and empathy. For example make a card for a child who is unwell or a welcome back ritual for a child who has been away, a special place to put objects of awe or beauty, be thankful for a lovely day, have quiet times for meditation*
- *listen to children's questions and thoughts about big ideas like life and death and what it all means to them—make spaces for their voice to be heard and respected*

Children learn their spiritual values from who we are and what we say and do, and we need to be intentional and careful in this regard. By their questions and their interests, their beliefs and their wonder, children offer us the opportunities to support this important part of their being. As educators seeking to nurture this innate aspect of all children, we should bear in mind the following: spirituality is about listening more than telling, wondering rather than knowing, respecting others in our learning environments, connecting with others and with the world.

Creating a portrait of a place to nurture spirituality is our privilege as early childhood educators. We can make a difference in our ever-changing world, where children are not faces on data spreadsheets, or specimens to collect grades and achievements by which to judge ability and human quality according to educational standards. It is the opportunity to understand how wonderful and capable children are.

3.14.1 Provocations for educators

Inspired by the educators in Reggio Emilia, I believe that all children have a right to beauty and that beautiful environments nourish the soul, igniting the tapestry of children's innate spirituality to come alive. Environments require particular attention to beauty. Beauty can entice a more attentive and observant eye; beautiful environments invite a more empathetic relationship and approach to interactions within the learning space.

What is your image of the child?
As educators of young children, how can we achieve the following goals?

- Create an environment which invites curiosity and interest for all who enter and provides experiences which embrace and nurture the potential for every child
- Honouring the rights of every child to a stimulating aesthetic environment. Is this a priority in your setting?
- If children have a right to spirituality and spiritual expression, how do we as educators need to change the way we interact with children?

An environment and pedagogy that ignites the spiritual expression of children, in my opinion and supported by my research, is influenced and inspired by the Reggio Emilia approach. The environment as third teacher is an important catalyst for spirituality to flourish and builds a delightful way to understand and navigate the tapestry of spirituality in young children.

- *How do your environments support and nurture spirituality to flourish?*

The following checklist may help educators to reflect on their learning environments (Table 3.1).

Table 3.1 Learning Environment Checklist for Educators in Early Childhood
Setting:_____Name:_____

The environment and the beliefs of your school	What are your actions and initiatives?
What is the relationship between the physical environment of your setting and the beliefs of the school?	
How is this represented?	
Does the environment welcome the community to be a part of the child's learning?	
Every space has a particular purpose	
Does the space provide for and invite student engagement?	

Do you document children's work? How do you make learning visible? How much time to do you spend listening to and observing children?	
Design and flexibility	
How much attention can you see paid to light, shadow, colour, texture, smell and sound?	
Is beauty and aesthetics present in the environment? How can the learning environment be less institutionalised? Are materials plastic and uniform, or open-ended and engaging?	
Inside and outside	
How do the spaces you see engage with the natural world? Is there value indicated inside and outside which ignites a curiosity for the natural world? Are materials varied so that natural materials are used and respected?	
The image of the child	
How is the classroom/learning environment respectful of the child's identity?	
Do the spaces in the classroom/learning environment value the child?	
How is the ownership of the classroom/learning environment indicated e.g. Is it a teacher's classroom or the students? Is there an overall softness whereby there is an ecosystem for diversification, stimulation and welcoming?	
What indicators are there for inviting head, heart and hands to engage?	
Enhancing children's learning Intellectually Physically Emotionally Spiritually	

How is your setting invitational for children? - Are shelves, provocations, materials at children's height? - Do they offer and invitation to interact, to discover?	

3.15 Summary

This review of scholarly literature and work has explored spirituality from a philosophical and psychological perspective. It has explored contemporary early childhood pedagogy in the Australian context and the Catholic context and, in particular, has investigated the Reggio Emilia approach. Through presenting scholarly perspectives, this chapter has outlined the key elements of the Reggio Emilia approach which are relevant to this case study. It has highlighted and described the interpretation of the hundred languages of children (Malaguzzi 1998; Rinaldi 2006) and the many media in which children can express themselves which may include their spiritual expressions.

The literature has provided knowledge regarding the environment and how the environment not only offers physical attributes but also how attention to aesthetics and materials with open-ended possibilities opens up avenues for awakening the senses and the potential for expression in multifaceted ways.

The chapter has described the meaning of the image of the child (Malaguzzi 1994; Rinaldi 2006) and has provided an analysis of major current theoretical perspectives on the changing face of the child. It provided an overview of the theorists who have influenced the Reggio Emilia approach and contributed to the changing face of early childhood education. This chapter offered an analysis of the views of children, childhood and children's learning and how pedagogy can influence the spiritual capacity of young children. It offers a definition of spiritualty and emphasises that we, as educators, can be at the forefront of nurturing this innate capacity in young children. The consideration of beauty in learning environments is important if we want to truly educate the whole child, both intellectually and spiritually. I believe that all children have the right to a beautiful learning environment and what my work has advocated is that this right to beauty is an activator for the spiritual voice or expression of children. The chapter explored the notion of beauty as a provocation to igniting the spiritual capacity of children and offered some ways in which we can design environments to encourage the development of this dimension.

This chapter invites teachers to think deeply about their practice and how they work with children. The provocations and questions in this chapter are merely a guide for professional discussion and reflection. If we are going to truly understand the spiritual dimension of childhood, then I invite you to open up these provocations and discussions in order to reflect on how we are providing the most optimum conditions for nurturing spirituality.

3.16 Recommendations, thoughts and provocations for educators

- *Adults need to carefully consider how learning environments can engage children's senses in many ways. The environment needs to be a guide, a teacher, a starting point for further discovery, encouraging questioning. An environment that values children's natural fascination and inquisitiveness.*
- *The following provides some Narrative Observations which document children in their natural setting. There is an interpretive summary at the end of each which provides a lens to view children through the Reggio Emillia approach and with the openness to look at how they express themselves.*
- *You can use these as a means of discussion and consideration. Is the spiritual dimension being nurtured in the observations and documentation?*

Learning Story 3

Nature in the classroom: observing guinea pigs: Narrative Observation 3

The Reception/One A classroom had some live guinea pigs which they had been looking after and this was set up as a provocation for the children to observe and with which to interact. The children were invited to represent and design their own guinea pig in various ways. One table had a sign on it which asked the children to draw a guinea pig; a variety of materials was placed on the table for them to use. This was during Exploration Time, which is a play-based discovery and learning time. I noticed that Child 3 was sitting at the table in front of the guinea pigs. She had drawn a guinea pig on a piece of paper. Child 3 was watching and staring at the animals. She represented her ideas through drawing, not seeming to be distracted by the surroundings and the activities which occurred around her. Child 3 looked carefully from the guinea pig to the drawing and spent a long period of time looking down and forming the details for the hair and legs of the guinea pig.

The interpretive summary of Learning Story 3

Indicators of spirituality	Interpretations from Narrative Observation 3
Imagination and creativity	The children were invited to represent the guinea pigs through the mode of drawing and materials were arranged for the children to access. These are evident in the photograph: paper on the table, pots with pens.
	This activity occurred during Exploration Time which is a play-based discovery and learning time. Child 3 chose to represent the guinea pigs through drawing:
	'Child 3 looked carefully from the guinea pig to the drawing and spent a long period of time looking down and forming the details of the hair and legs of the guinea pig.'
	It appeared though that Child 3 was absorbed in the flow of consciousness, and it was stated that she was 'staring' at the guinea pigs. She then chose to represent her ideas through drawing and was in her own sphere of consciousness, not seeming to be distracted by the surroundings:
	'Child 3 was watching and staring at the animals. She represented her ideas through drawing, not seeming to be distracted by the surroundings and the activities which occurred around her.'
Connection to nature	This staring and her visual gaze could suggest that Child 3 was captivated and in awe of the animals and that there was a connection to nature.
Pedagogical Condition: Reggio Emilia approach	**Interpretation Narrative Observation 3**
The environment as third teacher	There were many opportunities for engagement in various activities which had been arranged in this learning area. I noticed that there appeared to be a strong connection and theme throughout the classroom which was associated with nature: the photographs show that the guinea pigs were positioned on the tables, with plants a part of the learning environment. The environment and the provocation of the guinea pig provided an entry point for Child 3 to interact with the guinea pig through observation but also to then represent the guinea pig: all materials were flexible and accessible.
	There were particular aspects of the classroom environment that emphasised and respected nature: as shown in the photographs, between the pencils and materials were natural plants. Many provocations were around the room to engage children, such as the plants, the guinea pigs and other natural materials and textiles; this added to the aesthetics of the environment. These all appeared in the natural daily activities of the classroom environment.

Learning Story 4

A rainy, stormy day in the preschool: Narrative Observation 4

The children were playing outside when the weather started to change and a storm was brewing.

Child 4 was dancing around saying:

"I saw the storm clouds coming, they were like giant people coming going, rah, rah, rah."

HC: "Where do you think they (the storm clouds) come from?"
Child 4: "They come from God."
HC: "How do you know?"
Child 4: "Because everything comes from God because my mum told me."

It had begun to thunder again. Child 4 was looking up and listening.

HC: "I wonder what makes the thunder."
Child 4: "The fan in the sky."

It started to rain.

Child 4: "Yeah I love rain!"
"I just love it!"

Child 4 began dancing around.

Child 4: "I just love storms because I get to jump in puddles."

Child 4 continued to dance around.

Child 4: "I just love it!"

Hail began to fall and one of the educators prompted the children to have a look at the hail that was gathering on the outer part of the verandah. Child 4 picked up the hail and stared at it for a period of time. She collected more pieces of hail. Child 4 explored the hail by touching it with her finger; her facial expression was looking down at what she was doing and there was a smile on her face. She took time to explore this phenomenon and stared at it.

The interpretive summary of Learning Story 4

Indicators of spirituality	Interpretations from Narrative Observation 4
Connection to nature or a natural phenomenon	Child 4 is dancing around and claims, 'I just love storms.' Her sustained interest through touching and exploring the hail also suggests this connection to nature and a natural phenomenon.
Wonder and awe	It appeared that Child 4's sustained interest and happy facial expression could be interpreted as an expression of wonder and awe. In the second photograph, her eyes are lifted up, her mouth is open and her expression is that of surprise. She displayed an expression of wonder with the hail as 'She took time to explore this phenomenon.' Child 4 is interested in the hail and seeks to explore the sensory qualities as she is 'touching it with her finger; her facial expression was looking down at what she was doing and there was a smile on her face.'
Talking about God or a greater being	Child 4 draws on prior knowledge and relates this phenomenon to God. The researcher asks a question which was open-ended. Child 4 responds with the connection about the storm clouds to God because her mother had spoken to her about God.
Curiosity and joy	Child 4 has an animated face with a smile on it as she gazes toward the sky, which can represent an expression of joy. She claps her hands and is described as excited and she dances around with a smile on her face. Her gestures and movements suggest joy.
Pedagogical Condition: Reggio Emilia approach	**Interpretation from Narrative Observation 4**
The image of the child	Child 4 was able to use prior knowledge and relate this to her own theories about the thunder and about God. She stated that everything came from God because her mother had told her. She identified that the noise of the thunder sounded like a 'fan in the sky'.
The hundred languages of children	Child 4 had many expressions, such as: clapping her hands; lifting her eyes to the sky; and dancing around as she announced her theories and as she heard the sound of the thunder.

Learning Story 5

Playful moments in the preschool: Narrative Observation 5

Child 5 was playing in the home corner. I noticed he was engaged in his role play with another child in the preschool. He seemed to be directing the play and their interactions. Child 5 had assumed the role of an adult. His facial expressions were sensitive and attentive towards the other child who assumed the role of a minor in the play.

Child 5 was playing around in the home corner with a briefcase. There was a child in the bed who said out loud that she was the daughter. Child 12 came over to the bed and began to tuck the child in. This went on for a while in the home corner area. The other child then said that she had to go to school now.

Child 5: "I need my keys."

"Baby, here is your bracelet," and Child 5 gave the child in the bed a bracelet.
He bent down and looked at the other child and asked:
"Do you want to come for a walk? You have to hold my hand," and looked into her face.
He took her hand carefully and they walked a small distance away from the home corner area to an area which he termed 'Children's School'. He dropped her off at the pretend school area, and looked her in the eye and said, "I will be back to pick you up at 1:30."
When Child 5 returned to the home corner area, I decided to ask him a question about where he took his baby.

HC: "Where did you take your baby?"
Child 5: "To baby's school."

He then went back to the girl in the pretend school area, saying to her:
"It's 1:30, I am here to pick you up," looked her in the eye and took her hand.
They then went back to the home corner area.

The Reggio Emilia approach and pedagogy

The interpretive summary of Learning Story 5

Indicators of spirituality	Interpretations from Narrative Observation 5
Demonstrating care for another	The interaction between Child 5 and the other child who was the baby was very intimate and tender. Through his play, it was demonstrated that he presumed that this was the way to care for another and make sure that they felt safe and secure.
	'"Do you want to come for a walk? You have to hold my hand," and looks into her face.'
	There is evidence of empathy and care as Child 5 takes the child's hand and drops the child off at the school, then looks her in the eye as he reassures her that he will be back to pick her up.
	'He took her hand carefully and they walked a small distance away from the home corner area to an area which he termed "Children's School".' He dropped her off at the pretend school area and he looked her in the eye and said, "I will be back to pick you up at 1:30."'
Pedagogical Condition: Reggio Emilia approach	**Interpretations from Narrative Observation 5**
The image of the child	Narrative Observation (NO) 5 demonstrates that the image of the child is one in which they make connections to learning within their world as they play and interact with each other and their environment.
The environment as third teacher	The way in which the environment was set out facilitated this opportunity for the role play of a parent caring for a child and taking them to school. The home corner was set up and there was time for uninterrupted play.
	The conditions in the environment were such that Child 5 could experience relationships and his own identity through play where he created a real-life situation with which he connected and which he understood. The environment offered conditions for relational exchanges between the children.
The hundred languages of children	The hundred languages of children were evident as the children interacted and interpreted real-life situations through the medium of play and their relationships with each other.

 Another way to understand young children

Figure 4.1

Extend an invitation to open the window of your mind's eye. Allow the fresh viewpoints, new insights and new truths to enter and be seen.

Helena Card

4.1 Introduction to the research

This chapter addresses the outline of the research method in relation to the study of children's expression of spirituality and the connections to pedagogical context. Within the chapter, there is a description of the use of case study methodology to investigate the contemporary phenomenon of children's spiritual capacity within naturalistic settings.

The research questions which guide the inquiry are clearly outlined for this case study. The bounded system unique to this case is rationalised and defined. There is an explicit attempt to preserve the unity of the case, and how the case is refined to clearly define the focus is addressed.

4.2 Research questions

In order to answer the research questions, this chapter provides a construct for the reader to understand how the data were collected and collated. The guiding research questions were:

Question 1: What are the qualitative indicators of expressions of spirituality that may be demonstrated by young children in their everyday early childhood activities?

Question 2: In what ways can the Reggio Emilia pedagogical approach provide conditions for the expression of children's spirituality?

Question 3: How can young children's expression of spirituality be described?

Question 4: What are the specific elements of the Reggio Emilia pedagogical environment that nurture children's spiritual dimension?

4.2.1 The lived texts in children's lives

The research which I undertook employs case study methodology to identify the phenomenon of the expression of children's spirituality, within the Reggio Emilia approach. The case study embraces empirical research and, within this, there is an implicit and explicit research design which is logically sequenced, connecting the empirical data to the study's initial research questions and eventually to its findings (Yin 2012). The intention of this research is to explore the ways in which children may demonstrate, express and indicate spirituality as they interact within their natural settings. The purpose of this naturalistic case study is to analyse data related to children's spirituality within a Reggio Emilia-inspired educational setting. In light of this, the researcher employs the pedagogy of listening whereby rich volumes of rich and descriptive data are recorded. Children's body language, facial expressions, physical settings and interactions are noted and recorded in the field notes.

Observations and field notes are collated in a narrative form in the style of Learning Stories with Narrative Observations which are explained in detail within this chapter. The rich descriptions within the Narrative Observations are then analysed and interpreted by the researcher who is the 'prime filter and interpreter' (Goodwin & Goodwin 1996, p. 111).

Case study methodology enabled the researcher to examine the orientation of the phenomenon: children's spirituality within the lived experience or the 'texts of life' or the hermeneutics which exist (Creswell 2009). Through this method, as researcher, I was able to analyse essential themes which examine the phenomenon (Creswell 2003) and allowed ideas and findings to be made visible in relation to children's spirituality, examining how this offers a connection to the Reggio Emilia approach. Using a case study approach, multi-layered and multifaceted perceptions from the landscape could be included for this specific research. The case study approach illuminated the unfolding experiences which formed the researcher's position about spirituality and young children. The researcher allowed the research design and the data generation to guide and direct her own position. The data analysis assisted in reshaping recurring themes drawn from the data to provide new insights and concepts related to the research questions.

The case study approach has not been widely employed to explore the area of young children's spirituality and, therefore, this study endeavours to shed new light on a previously underutilised approach. As suggested by Sagberg (2008, p. 367) in relation to pre-school children in the Norwegian context, there seems to be a 'universal fog' surrounding children's spirituality which would need some additional and broader hermeneutical approaches in order to contribute to an extended understanding in this area. By specifically focusing on collecting observational data that involved children between four and six years of age, this study sought to address a gap in the research. Ratcliff and Nye (2006) suggest that the aspirational goal for the study of children's spirituality requires a rigour that brings about greater academic respectability and acceptance of children's spirituality. In order to contribute to this outcome, the current study explored a particular pedagogical approach and how this influences children's expression of spirituality.

4.2.2 An exploration of the phenomenon of spirituality

Case study research enables the exploration of particular phenomena. The case study enables exploration of a particular phenomenon and of the nature of the data collected and observed which informs the question about the phenomenon within a setting. The case study approach was selected for this study to explore 'phenomena occurring more widely, in the expectation that the fine-grained exploration that case study allows will assist our general understanding of the phenomena' (Edwards 2001, p. 126). Case study research is related to phenomenology as it permits the researcher to venture beyond the limits of materialistic or naturalistic realities (Stewart & Mickanus 1990). In relation to children's expression of spirituality, phenomenology allowed the researcher to wonder about experiences, to study the lived experience, in this case, spirituality, and to understand the essence or the structure of the phenomenon (Stewart & Mickanus 1990; van Manen 1984). When exploring children's spirituality, the phenomenological approach by Coles (1990) evokes elucidation into the spiritual lives of children; thus, this research is aimed at highlighting children's expression of spirituality in their everyday, natural settings and understanding the quality and depth of children's spiritual capacity. It is important that this research is rigorously framed with phenomenology as the theoretical lens used to explore and encounter the phenomenon in new and fresh ways (van Manen 1990):

> If the description is phenomenologically powerful, then it acquires a certain transparency, so to speak; it permits us to 'see' the deeper significance, or meaning structures, of the lived experience it describes.
> (van Manen 1990, p. 122)

In this study, children's spirituality is intended as a defined and clear area of phenomenon: 'researchers focus case studies on defined portions of the phenomenon of interest' (Riemer, Quartaroli & Lapan 2012, p. 244). The object of this case study is to examine the observed spiritual capacity of young children, including the deep significance of how it exists, is expressed and is demonstrated in everyday experiences of an early childhood setting.

4.3 Researching through many entry points: reconceptualising children's spirituality

The umbrella of qualitative methodology allows many entry points and much variety in the exploration of the research questions: the expressions of children's capacity of spirituality and an approach to early childhood pedagogy (Punch 2005). Case study research is a form of qualitative research where the researcher looks for the detail, the characteristics and the particularity of a single case (Stake 1995). The qualitative, holistic and naturalistic methods chosen for this case study are aimed at providing clarity around the anomalies that exist within the definition of the term 'spirituality'. The qualitative methodological orientation of this current study allows an authentic entry point for the exploration of the expression of young children's spirituality.

In qualitative research, the observation of children in their natural settings captures the everyday moments that exist in children's interactions in learning settings, requiring a design in which the ethnographic nature of collecting and generating data allows the study to capture human behaviour and propose a field of inquiry to analyse. The basic message, in qualitative research, referring to Punch (2003), is that human behaviour related to hermeneutics and phenomenology allows the researcher to view human behaviour which is based on meanings brought to the situation by the people involved.

This behaviour is not forced or caused; rather, it is constructed and reconstructed by the people within the situations. With this in mind, the lived nature of the study aims to provide an understanding of the essence and phenomenon of the experience.

As the literature review identified, authors to date have distinguished spirituality in adults (Elkins et al., 1998; Fowler 1981). However, previous studies have not employed or acknowledged tools and methods that assist a researcher in determining young children's spirituality. In order to best support expressions of spirituality, a unique research design with the capacity to consider a variety of perspectives within a pedagogical approach was needed.

A case study approach has been chosen to observe things as they exist and to offer a construction of 'a clearer reality', not to discover but to offer a sophisticated reality which will endure 'disciplined scepticism' (Stake 1995, p. 101).

The case study approach serves to propose a reconceptualisation of the phenomenon of how spirituality in young children is expressed and to answer the intent of the first guiding research question: What are the qualitative indicators of expressions of spirituality that may be demonstrated by young children in their everyday early childhood activities? It will also serve to answer the second guiding research question: In what ways can the Reggio Emilia pedagogical approach provide conditions for the expression of children's spirituality?

4.3.1 Naturalistic settings: a catalyst for spirituality

A case study occurring in a natural setting is preferred as it typically involves 'a study of things as they exist' (Lichtman 2006, p. 11). This research involves the natural setting of the classrooms and preschool within the school site which are considered desirable for collecting the data and observing children as they engage, communicate and interact. From the data generated, it is envisioned that, as the researcher, I would gain insights into the complex meaning of spirituality, how it presents itself through children's expression, how it exists in relation to young children and how it can be encouraged or nurtured.

As the case study researcher, I positioned myself 'to understand individuals' perceptions of the world' (Bell 2010, p. 5). This research involves young children as the individuals, and explores how they present indicators of spirituality and how they interact socially and construct meaning from situations and particular phenomena presented to them. As the research progressed and data were analysed and summarised, this allowed general interpretations to become narrowed and detailed. Punch verifies this and provides an important distinction of the case as a form of qualitative research:

> Qualitative research not only uses non-numerical and unstructured data but also, typically, has research questions and methods which are more general at the start, and become more focused as the study progresses.
> (Punch 1998, p. 29)

Case study research enables the description of the natural setting where children interact. Recognising the strong image of the child (Kinney & Wharton 2008; Malaguzzi 1994; Rinaldi 2006) is an essential paradigm to understand when implementing this research and is imperative to interpreting the research. The child must remain at the centre of the research. This research draws on Warming's (2005) explanation of participant observation in which the researcher aims to learn about, '"the other" by participating in their everyday life' (Warming 2005, p. 1). The case study methodology highlights listening to children as the potential within the study. It is necessary for the design and method in this research to clearly present the position and meaning of listening, as recommended by Clark (2005).

4.3.1.1 The case: exploration of the spirit

The case consists of the terrain of spirituality and how children's expression of spirituality can be 'seen' or recognised: a case study seems to present the most suitable method for answering the research questions and for collecting and generating data.

The case study is used in early childhood education research as it allows the researcher to investigate and deeply scrutinise a specific situation of intrinsic interest (Hill & Millar 2015). In this particular case study, the specific situation comprises the expressions of spirituality, thus formulating the existing phenomenology within this and the pedagogical approach of Reggio Emilia.

The focus in a case study is on one particular instance of an educational experience: in this case, it is 'Exploration Time' where the play activities are influenced by the philosophy of the Reggio Emilia approach. Within this case study, observation during these play activity times offered the researcher a time in which to focus and gain theoretical and professional insights from a full documentation of that instance (Freebody 2003). This empirical research within a case study was within a unique setting which adopted a particular pedagogical approach. The dimension of this case study requires clarity, along with a description and details of how it was conducted. According to Coolican (2004) and Edwards (2001), the dimension of this case study sits within the definition that the research through this case study was conducted as a 'snapshot' at one particular point.

The case study has boundaries: in this study, the research was designed as a case study within the following boundaries:

1) The research is restricted to a particular pedagogical approach: Reggio Emilia.
2) Childhood spirituality in four- to six-year-old children has been selected as the capacity for spirituality may be more evident within this age group, in terms of data collection.

(Nye 2009)

As stated by Lichtman, '[i]t is the researcher's task to identify the case and to set the boundaries of what is being studied' (2006, p. 71). This case study is identifying a particular group of children through various methods which aid in exploring the research. The case is presented as a portrait.

The details of the Learning Stories and Narrative Observations have the intention of transporting the reader into the research site, giving them an overall description of the children and the environment. This offers a means to communicate the essence of the research situation, illustrating the participants' actions and voices (Stake 2006). The uniqueness of the site, being a preschool to Year One setting, allows the study to be bounded and confined to the age group of four- to six-year-old children. The site is also committed to implementing aspects of the Reggio Emilia approach. A case study was proposed in this situation in order to explore in depth children's spiritual capacity and the pedagogical approach of Reggio Emilia. 'A case study could be proposed if you are conducting a study that gets you close to a particular individual, group, school, program or event' (Lodico et al. 2010, p. 270). The case is presented in a narrative style and as a portrait of a place, thus transporting the reader into the lived experience of the setting and giving the reader a sense of being there.

Presenting the case as a portrait with the many facets and elements which characterised the bounded inquiry was decided with the intent being to 'solve the problem that the case set out to address as precisely as possible' (Swanborn 2010, p. 125). Throughout the portrait of the case, some salient themes and patterns emerged and, as Lawrence-Lightfoot and Davis (1997) suggested:

> the researcher does not search for the exhaustive and mutually exclusive categories of the statistician, but instead to identify the salient, grounded categories of meaning held by the participants in the setting.
>
> (p. 116)

The data are presented through a narrative analysis 'to illuminate' the particular meanings and experiences of the case (Punch 2005, p. 218).

The case was set in a natural setting and this provided the researcher with a clear aim and purpose: to quote Gillham, 'the naturalistic researcher is more concerned to give an account of the reality of the research process' (Gillham 2000, p. 96).

4.3.1.2 Phases of the research to define the case

In order to define the case, the phases of the research needed to be clarified. The first and second phases of the study were when the researcher entered the field through negotiated visits to the learning setting where the researcher observed children and collected field notes from the observations. The field visits occurred within a setting inspired by the

Reggio Emilia pedagogical approach. The first and second phases constituted the data collection which involved field visits to the learning setting and also interviews with the teachers. The interviews with the teachers began in the early phases of research and continued throughout the phases at regular intervals to ensure that the time set for the interviews was when the teachers, the artist in residence and the school principal had time in their schedules and did not feel pressured or coerced into the interview. In the second phase of the research, the field notes were constructed into the Learning Stories, and the indicators of spirituality and the pedagogical environment were explored. The third phase was the data analysis: the fourth phase was formulation of the findings from the analysis. The aim of this case, in accordance with Stake, was 'not to discover but to design and construct a clearer reality and a more sophisticated reality' (Stake 1995, p. 101).

From the structure of the phases, it was anticipated that the case would begin to refine, spiral and emerge as the research provided a rigorous overview of the findings. In the fourth phase, this would also allow the findings within the case study to emerge and provide an account and a study of 'things as they exist' (Lichtman 2006, p. 11).

4.4 The importance of listening and valuing young children

The children and the teaching environment formed the landscape for this research, with views of children and of listening and valuing children, such as those of Hay and Nye (2006), Hyde (2004) and, more recently, Giesenberg (2007), helping to guide the study into a new terrain. This has been explained and referred to within the literature review, showing how it is situated within this research. In addition, the case study is used as a tool and a method of inquiry to discover children's active involvement proficiencies within a natural learning environment. This case study 'is understood as a pedagogy and a way of researching life' (Clark et al. 2005, p. 13). As children interacted in their environment, the researcher observed and listened through the of recording field notes and collecting and documenting data. These were then collated into Learning Stories which are outlined later in this chapter.

The methods employed in this research support the view of the strong image of the child and the view that as adults we need to listen to the many ways that children express their encounters with the world (Rinaldi 2006). Children have their own sophisticated and theorised ideas about the world around them (Barbarin &Wasik 2011) and they express these theories through the hundred languages (Malaguzzi 1998; Rinaldi 2006; see literature review in Chapter 3). Listening to and documenting these moments broaden our understanding of young children. It was anticipated that children's theories and ideas, as observed and documented by the researcher, would be of assistance in providing a different perspective and angle for this study of children.

4.4.1 The teacher as researcher and participant observer

It is imperative that the position of the researcher is clearly defined. The Reggio Emilia approach to teaching and learning advocates the mode of learning in which teachers are researchers. Carla Rinaldi (2006), the executive pedagogical consultant in Reggio Emilia, explains the role of teacher researcher and states that:

> Learning does not take place by means of transmission or reproduction. It is a process of construction, in which each individual constructs for himself the reasons, the 'whys', the meanings of things, others, nature, events, reality and life. The learning process is certainly individual but because the reasons, explanations, interpretations and meanings of others are indispensable for our knowledge building, it is also a process of relations—a process of social construction. We thus consider knowledge to be the process of construction by the individual in relation with others, a true act of co-construction.
>
> (Rinaldi 2006, p. 125)

In this case, the research site was the learning area of children within the preschool and Reception classes and the individuals were the students. My role became that of participant observer with varying stages of participation as is outlined by Creswell: '[q]ualitative observers may also engage in roles varying from a non-participant to a complete participant' (Creswell 2009, p. 181). As the researcher, I employed observation, and took field notes and digital photographs of the children as they were interacting in the learning setting.

The research site chosen for this exploration has an existing pedagogy which is child-centred and is a site with which the researcher was very familiar with established professional relationships with the teachers: the researcher was also familiar with all the children in the setting. Prior to this study, the researcher has participated in various projects within the site and within the classroom settings. The existing culture within the school is conducive to adults researching alongside children. This presented a natural process for me as the researcher in conducting my own research within this field. The limitations of being an employer within this field are explored later in the chapter. It is made clear that my intention was, as Kemp (2001, p. 528) describes, to recognise 'what is going on here': this was done within the boundaries of the case, not to judge or criticise the teachers or children.

4.5 Tools and methods for the collection of data

4.5.1 Observations of the children: a delight to witness and see

All children were observed in, and examples taken from, naturalistic settings. It is essential to mention that the situations for observation were not contrived or staged. They occurred as part of the weekly and everyday structure and routine of the schools. Naturalistic observations 'are undertaken in the everyday setting of the participants' (Mukherji & Albon 2010, p. 106) which, in this case, comprised the classrooms and learning environments. As explained, the children were observed during Exploration Time. The importance of play in spirituality is highlighted by many writers (Berryman 1997; Elkind 1988; Myers 1997) who all claim that, for a child's spirituality to grow and develop, a child requires and must be allowed to play and contemplate the situations which he or she may be in at a given time. Play, and its significance to this research, are addressed in the literature review. Vygotsky (1962) states that through play, the child is a free agent and that play is the young child's main activity. For a child to develop a sense of wonder, Haiman (1991) states that it is essential for the child to play. With regard to spirituality, as the child wonders and is free to contemplate and wonder, they make meaning of the world. It is through this natural instinct to make meaning and connect that expressions of spirituality may emerge and be observed in a play situation. It was imperative to this case study that, as the researcher, I observed the children during these times where play was valued and accepted as part of the daily routine.

4.5.2 Observational field notes

Observational field notes were taken while observing the children interacting in their natural setting and these notes served to inform the Learning Stories. The observational field notes were transcribed into a narrative and a commentary in which the author/researcher expressed her own commentary (Yin 2012). It is important to establish and note that the Learning Story method for collecting data within this case was chosen by the researcher through the understanding of case study in which: '… a case study, in itself, is not a method of collecting information but it is an approach within which one can choose to use a variety of data collecting instruments' (Mukherji & Albon 2010, p. 81).

This research involved listening to children, or 'a pedagogy of listening' (see literature review), which became a tool in the methodology. This is one of the guiding principles of the Reggio Emilia approach: a comprehensive overview of this area is provided in the literature review. With the research's alliance with hermeneutic phenomenology within a case study, this tool was used to distil the data generated and to understand how spirituality was expressed. It is imperative to this research to mention and highlight this tool and method within this inquiry. Contemporary research undertaken by Champagne (2001) with regard to children's spirituality posited a critical point to consider when listening to children. She suggests that, while we can listen to the expressions of spirituality that children may reveal through conversations, it is necessary also to listen for the spiritual aspects which underlie their everyday lives. The depth in understanding children which is implied in the Reggio Emilia principle of listening allows for this entry point into the spiritual aspects of daily lives and the spiritual experience which Champagne states is the everyday human experience. The underlying intention of this method of observing children assisted in the credibility of the research by generating authentic data of the everyday experiences of participating children.

4.5.3 Construction of Learning Stories

For the purposes of this study, I, as the researcher, decided to use a hybrid of the 'Learning Stories' tool to record my observations. As the researcher, I had documented the children interacting in their environment through observational field notes which became the narrative for the Learning Stories written as a reflection of the observations and serving as the tool for data analysis. (A comprehensive explanation of documenting and observing children, of the origins of this tool and of how it is situated and adapted for this study, is discussed in the literature review.) Case studies are undertaken in naturalistic settings (Mukherji & Albon 2010) and this also supports the Learning Story approach that offers a narrative of the everyday interactions and gives a feasible way of collecting data (Punch 2005). The everyday interactions of the children in the classroom offered a platform for naturalistic observation and for recording what the participant said or did (Mukherji & Albon 2010).

Learning Stories were chosen for this case study as a way of interpreting the observational field notes collected throughout the research. As described by Carr (2001), the narrative approach to Learning Stories 'can capture moments' within children's daily interactions and development. For the purpose of this study, and to generate and collect data, the notion of Learning Stories was adapted from Carr (2001). According to Lee (2006), the intent of Learning Stories is an open and evolving process which provides opportunities for the viewer to make visible the learning as it is valued within that setting. My Learning Stories encapsulating a narrative observation of children interacting in the everyday.

For this study, the researcher decided to utilise and create a particular style of Learning Stories in order to illuminate, clarify and provide a refinement in understanding the phenomenon of children's innate spirituality and what this may look like in connection with a particular pedagogical approach. The adaptations to the Learning Story style incorporated and opened up prospects and distinct scenarios pertinent within this setting and the boundaries of this case study. The 'Narrative Observation' style of Learning Stories suited the naturalistic inquiry of this research and, through adapting the style and creating a hybrid of the original style and layout of Learning Stories, assisted in emphasising and defining the boundaries of the case and the intent of the researcher in answering the research questions.

4.5.4 Interviews

Interviewing one or more participants is popular in qualitative research (Creswell 2012), as is the offering of unbiased, open-ended interview questions that are 'essential sources for case study information' (Yin 2009). The purpose of the interviews with the teachers was to provide professional insights about the natural everyday experiences of the children within the early years environment. Interviews with teachers who consented to be involved in the research were undertaken and audio-recorded. These were transcribed and written up by the researcher. If there were any examples of children's work provided by the teachers that would assist in answering the questions, they were either collected or photographed by the researcher. The school principal was interviewed. He is an educator with over 30 years' experience and is also very familiar with the Reggio Emilia approach to teaching and learning.

In addition, the researcher decided to interview a visiting artist who had worked in this setting on various art projects over the last two years with different cohorts of children. It was anticipated that he would provide a different perspective and avenue for the interview questions. He is familiar with the Reggio Emilia philosophy and was able to articulate this knowledge through his visual arts and artistic background and training. With respect to the interviews undertaken within this case study, as Swanborn (2010) points out, it is essential that the people chosen for the interviews are 'informants' or 'key personnel', and that this forms part of the protocol of conducting and choosing the people for the interviews (Swanborn 2010, p. 74). As an important aspect to add to the quality of this research, the teachers and those interviewed were considered to be key personnel due to their involvement with the social phenomenon explored within the case study.

Informants, firstly, supply general information about the phenomenon and the social processes in which they are involved. Their personal experiences are, for the time being, less central. However, they may also report their own experiences, social relations, perceptions, attitudes and behaviour (Swanborn 2010, p. 74).

Their perspectives also supported the validity of this research. This qualitative case study required input from other individuals to present other perspectives, viewpoints and outlooks which would assist in presenting multiple insights into the research. A characteristic of qualitative research is to allow for 'discovering and portraying multiple views of the case' (Stake 1995, p. 64). Other people's observations are viewed with a different lens and different objectives (Punch 2005; Stake 1995).

Much of what we cannot observe for ourselves has been or is being observed by others. Two principal uses of case study are to obtain the descriptions and interpretations of others. The case would not be seen in the same way by everyone (Stake 1995, p. 64).

4.6 The participants: protagonists in the portrait of a place

The case study took place in a setting that incorporated a preschool and a school. The site was selected because the staff and the school principal have a commitment to, and an understanding of, the Reggio Emilia approach and the school community is similarly inspired. In this case study, 41 children were involved: four teachers were interviewed along with the school principal and an artist, contracted to the school, who worked alongside the children.

The site is an inner-city school with two campuses. One campus has the Year Two–Year Seven site, the other has a preschool–Year One site. It was at this latter site that the case study was conducted and this added to the uniqueness of this case providing a cohort of children from four to six years of age.

The Reggio Emilia approach inspired the pedagogy and practice within the early years setting of this school. The children attending preschool and early years schooling were able to transition into the school setting with a consistent approach and pedagogy influencing the teaching and learning. The school is a Catholic faith-based school and the socio-demographics of the location include professional working families with mainly Anglo-Saxon backgrounds.

4.6.1 *The field visits*

I visited 10 of the Exploration Time sessions across different cohorts of children. Three cohorts of children were in the Reception–Year One group and there was one preschool group. This site is in South Australia, where the first year of school is called Reception. Across Australia, the age at which children begin school varies. In South Australia, at the time of the study, a child would enter their first year of school in the term after their fifth birthday. Within this site, there are four school terms: during the time of the study, there were Reception intakes across the four terms. If a child began school in the first two terms, they would enter Year One the following year. If a child entered Reception in the third term, they would complete two terms in Reception and four terms in Reception the following year. (Note that since this study was conducted, changes have been made to school entry and there is now only one school intake into Reception each year in South Australia.)

Within this site, at the time of the study, the structure of classes included composite classes; for example, the Reception/Year One composite class consisted of some continuing Reception students, due to complete six terms in Reception, who commenced their third term of school at the beginning of the year. There were also Year One students in this cohort, plus new students beginning school. Visits to the preschool cohort were negotiated differently due to different preschool regulations.

Within the funding agreement called the *National Partnership for Early Childhood Education*, all four-year-old children have access to 15 hours per week of preschool (Department for Education and Child Development [DECD] 2013). This agreement began implementation within this preschool site last year at the beginning of Term 3. In these government agreements, preschool for all four-year-olds across Australia is called 'Universal Access', which essentially means that families choose five days across a fortnight for their child to attend preschool, so individual children will not be at the preschool on certain days. As the researcher, I conducted 10 visits to the preschool, with these occurring at various times over the three terms: I checked with the preschool coordinator each week to see on which days those children who had permission to be involved in the study were present. In line with parent consent, only certain children were observed across all the cohorts.

My visits to the classrooms of the two Reception/Year One classes and the Year One class were between 30 and 40 minutes in length. Exploration Time generally ran for 45 minutes to an hour each week, so it was within this time that the data were collected and the children were observed. The most coherent way to design these visits was to check with the class teacher to see how and when the visits could occur during Exploration Time. I visited each learning cohort once a fortnight, with a total of five visits for each cohort across the three terms of school and preschool: 25 visits spanning 30 weeks made up this phase of the data collection.

The plan was to observe as many children as I could across the cohorts and to collect the observational field notes for the Learning Stories which would inform my case study. Altogether, 41 children were involved in the case study and 66 Learning Stories were collected.

4.6.2 Exploration Time

'Exploration Time', as it was called by the educators in the Rec/One (Year One) and Year One classrooms, was a time of day offered as many times as possible throughout the week which allowed uninterrupted time for play, inquiry and discovery. This time was for children to explore, interact with and investigate their learning environment. This was a dedicated time in the day for which the teachers advocated: they wanted uninterrupted time that was not associated with particular lessons, aims and outcomes, but which was child-centred, and based on play and inquiry. Attention was centred on the children: following their interests, engaging with the provocations in the environment and finding opportunities to discover, to construct knowledge and to enjoy the experience of interacting with the environment and with each other. The children chose their interactions, what they wanted to do or in which they wanted to be involved and engaged.

It was a timetabled time, which ranged from about 45 minutes to an hour. During Exploration Time, the teacher provided and designed elements in the environment with various provocations to engage the children: at times, these were related to their ongoing learning while; at other times, they were unrelated. It was a time inspired by the Reggio Emilia approach and in which the child was an active agent in their encounters with the environment. Sessions varied according to teachers' timetables. Exploration Time for Year One was first thing in the morning and children were engaged as soon as they entered the classroom. In Rec/One A and Rec/One B, Exploration Times were at various times during the day, usually after a break, recess or lunch: this depended on each teacher and when they chose to allocate this time within their timetable. At the end of each Exploration Time, the children and the teacher would pack up the provocations if they were laid out on tables. Either the children's creations and constructions could be placed in a secure area to return to at another time or the children could choose where to store or place their creations. When the children had artefacts from

Exploration Time that related to an ongoing project or that were merely artefacts from their inquiry and discovery, these were kept in a secure location or they were left in an area for the children to go back to and to continue their ongoing exploration, discovery and inquiry. During Exploration Time, in the classroom contexts for Rec/One A, Rec/One B and Year One, if Education Support Officers were in the room, a teacher was always present. Children were inside the classroom areas, unless stated, and were able to go into adjoining areas. The preschool environment was more fluid: children were either inside or outside, and exploration and play-based inquiry formed a natural part of every day. The number of adults varied depending on the level of attendance for each preschool day. One teacher was always present and, if Education Support Officers were involved in an activity, this is stated in the Learning Stories.

4.7 Allowing for spiritual moments in space: provocations for educators

My research highlighted to me the importance of time in the day to allow children to 'just be'. So often in our present-day lives, everything become prescriptive with deadlines, data collection and academic pressures. My overall wish for my research was to conduct it in the most natural way. Fortunately, I was able to relish in a Reggio Emilia-inspired environment and observed children who naturally encountered spiritual moments in their everyday activities. Another fortunate aspect which is essential to finding spiritual moments was that teachers were good listeners and observers of children. They used this playful time in the classroom and preschool to listen to the hundred languages of children. The hundred languages of children was able to flourish and be noticed, this included the spiritual language.

Spiritual moments in learning environments require deep listening and intentional practices which allow children's spirituality to occur. Spiritual moments occur in an environment that is aesthetically pleasing and beautiful, spaces where real objects, rich language and authentic experiences are intentionally provided and created. This kind of environment is often filled with moments of awe and wonder.

Provocations for educators:
- *What would you consider to be a beautiful learning environment/space?*
- *Are you able to draw or describe this space?*
- *What qualities would that space need?*
- *How can you allocate time in your day to watch, listen and observe children in their environment? Are you missing spiritual moments ?*
- *How are you going to document these moments? What is your tool for documenting and observing children? Do you have a collective approach for this?*

- *How will you invite dialogue and discussion about your documentation to be discerned, reflected upon, acted upon?*
- *How can you use documentation and observation of children to bring about change in pedagogy and appearance in your early learning environments?*

Learning Story 6

Baby chickens: Narrative Observation 6

The class was involved in exploratory play during Exploration Time.

Baby chickens had hatched in the previous few days and many children were going over to the incubator to look at them.

Both Child 6 and Child 7 came up to me, laughing and smiling about their drawings, which were inspired by the chickens in their incubator in the foyer, just outside the classroom. The door was open, leading to an open space learning area where the incubator with the chickens was set up: children were able to come and go to observe the baby chickens.

I asked the girls where the chickens were and they guided me outside. We all sat down and watched the chickens. The girls had their clipboards with their drawings next to them and they started a conversation.

Child 6: "Baby chickens have to stay warm because they have just come out of the egg with wet wings."

Child 7: "They are fluffy."

Child 6: "They have claws."

Child 7: "They are all snuggling in. I wish I could hold them."

Child 6: "When they get bigger." Nodding her head.

Child 7 then decided to hold up her picture as if to show the chickens.

Child 6: "Look, they're looking at it—they think it's their mum and dad."

Child 7: "Sssshhhhh, they are cheeping."

Both girls stopped and bent towards the incubator to listen to the cheeping sound from the chickens: they were both smiling; and their heads were tilted towards the incubator.

They did not take their gaze off the chickens and were engaged with the cheeping noise, continuing to tilt their heads and listen, watching the movement of the chickens.

The girls showed me the diary they had been keeping of the stages of the chickens. The drawings were of the chicken's life stages and growth. This activity was not initiated by the teacher.

The interpretive summary of Learning Story 6

Indicators of spirituality	Interpretations from Narrative Observation 6
Connection to nature or a natural phenomenon	It appears that the two girls had a natural curiosity and connection to nature as they spent time looking and observing the baby chickens. The provocation began with eggs in the incubator. The girls had been engaged in observations, waiting for the chickens to hatch and then watching as the chickens grew and evolved: their connection to the chickens had begun at the earlier stage of the eggs, as this was their interpretation in the charts they had made.
Wonder and awe; joy	The girls' expressions appeared to be happy and interested. In the photographs for LS 6, both had smiles on their faces and also their gaze was down and they bent over towards the incubator. They smiled as they tilted their heads to listen to the sound of the chickens and noticed their feathers were fluffy. The smiles and the expressions on their faces as they were observing the chickens presented happy or joyful dispositions or expressions.
Pedagogical Condition: Reggio Emilia approach	**Interpretations from Narrative Observation 6**
The image of the child	The children in this story were able to use prior knowledge and relate this to their own theories about how chickens grow and hatch: the evidence is that they interpreted their theories in a chart with drawings. This Learning Story provided evidence of the children engaged in a multisensory environment where they gained an understanding of themselves in relation to aspects of the environment. There is evidence of the child in relationship with the other and with the environment. This Learning Story is evidence of children as co-constructors of learning, as together they produced their account of the chickens. This was not a required piece of work. It displayed resourceful, purposeful actions by the girls. This work had been initiated by the girls themselves during Exploration Time.
The environment as third teacher	There was a freedom in the learning environment to go and spend moments watching and observing the chickens: the children moved in and out of the classroom, observing, talking and staring at the chickens. The chickens were a provocation for the girls to further investigate and learn about the life cycle of this bird. The provocation of the chickens did not require an outcome for learning but was placed there for the children to observe and discover. They were in a relationship with the environment.
The hundred languages of children	The hundred languages of children depend on creating opportunities for children to express themselves through their different ways of thinking. The evidence in this Learning Story is the girls choosing to express themselves creatively through the medium of drawing.

Learning Story 7

Girls encounter with a spider in Year One: Narrative Observation 7

This observation took place during class Exploration Time, a time when play-based activities were encouraged. Quiet music played in the background. A child had brought in a spider, found in her parent's car, which she had transported inside a glass jar. The jar was placed in an area of the classroom where children could display interesting things.

Two girls became very interested in this spider and began to look at it closely. They did not take their gaze off the spider and began a conversation describing the spider. The girls moved around various parts of the classroom and they continued to investigate and have a conversation about the spider. They used a variety of equipment and materials as they moved around the classroom: they went from the curiosity table to the light table to an area which was set up with paper, pencils and another very strong light.

They carefully held and transported the jar with the spider even though the creature was dead. I decided to ask the girls some questions:

> HC: "I wonder does it look scary or interesting?"
>
> Child 8: "Interesting."
>
> HC: "Should we keep things like this alive?"
>
> Child 8: "Yes, because it's a creature."
>
> Child 8: "If it's poisonous, no, but if it's not then, yes, keep it alive."

Child 9 began to count out loud the number of legs that it had.

> Child 9: "1, 2, 3, 4, 5, 6, 7, 8. Three eyes! It's furry! Because brown is a colour you don't see very often."
>
> HC: "What about when you see it like this?"
>
> Child 8: "It looks beautiful."
>
> Child 8: "I feel like I'm on a trampoline with fluff."
>
> Child 9: "I feel like I'm touching cotton wool."

As she said this, her head was tilted to one side with a smile on her face.

> HC: "I wonder what you would do with this spider if it was alive?"

Child 9: "Leave it in its habitat."

Child 8: "I would set it free—because if it's free, it will be alive."

> HC: "I wonder what noise a spider makes and how would you find out?"

Child 9: "Listen to it."

Child 8: "If it has friends, it will talk to them."

The girls observed the spider with an accessible magnifying glass. They continued to observe the spider and took it over to a light area which was set up. There were magnifying glasses there for observation and other utensils. They smiled and touched the spider very gently; they felt the spider. The girls described the texture of the spider and touched it. They found this fascinating. They began to draw the spider and drew the parts of the spider which they talked about.

When they had finished their drawing, Child 8 wrote her name on the work and said:

Child 8: "Let's put our artwork here." (She said this to Child 9 and indicated next to the spider.)

Child 8: "Leave it here." (She left her 'artwork' next to the spider and so did Child 9.)

They decided to put their 'artwork' next to the spider. They called their work 'artwork'. Later, when the teacher called the children together in a group and asked all the children what they enjoyed or discovered during Exploration Time, Child 8 was the first to put up her hand wanting to share her spider experience with the group.

Child 8 "The best part was touching the spider. We thought it was alive. It was sticky."

They were then asked about what else they explored today.

Child 8 answered, "That spiders can speak."

When asked the question: "How do you think they speak?"

Child 8 replied, "They talk carefully, like a whisper, so, if we were spiders, we could hear them speak but, if we're not spiders, we can't hear them speak."

The interpretive summary of Learning Story 7

Indicators of spirituality	Interpretations from Narrative Observation 7
Imagination and creativity	The two girls used creative language in their description of how the spider felt when they touched it. They used their imagination as they drew the spider and they described their drawing as 'artwork'. which appeared to display an understanding that they had produced something creative.
Connection to nature or a natural phenomenon	It appears that the two girls had a natural curiosity and connection to nature as they were curious about the spider which had been brought in by another child. There is evidence here that the two girls had a natural desire to be connected to this natural creature: this provided an opportunity to see their own interconnectedness and relationship to the web of nature. The opportunity to be absorbed by the touch and the feel of the spider also maintained this relationship.
Wonder and awe	The animation of the girls in LS 7 could be interpreted as wonder and awe as they interacted with the spider.'They smiled and touched the spider very gently: they felt the spider. The girls described the texture of the spider and touched it.' Their sustained interest in the spider could also be evidence that they were in awe of this spider: they wondered about how spiders could speak and described the texture and feel of the spider.
Curiosity	The girls' natural curiosity and attraction to the spider led to further learning and discovery.
Pedagogical Condition: Reggio Emilia approach	**Interpretations from Narrative Observation 7**
The image of the child	The girls were asked a question and were able to draw on prior knowledge and formulate meaning about their understanding of sustainability and their awareness of being sensitive to another living thing. They verbally explained the best place for a spider: Child 9: 'Leave it in its habitat.' Child 8: 'I would set it free—because if it's free it will be alive.'
The environment as third teacher	There was a freedom in the learning environment to go and spend moments watching and observing the spider. The children moved around the classroom and used objects and areas which were set up for independent observation and discovery: the magnifying glasses, the light table, and the paper and pencils set alongside this light table. The environment offered the freedom for fluid, independent and multisensory discovery. The fact that the spider was put on a table for children to freely observe led to deeper discovery and learning for the two girls.

The hundred languages of children	The hundred languages of children depend on creating opportunities for children to express themselves through their different ways of thinking, and this is evident within LS 7. A connection with nature allowed the girls to have some real time to explore nature. They had time to see the spider, touch it and ask their own questions, and they formed their own language to reinforce their own experiences through their verbal descriptions of the spider. There is evidence in this Learning Story of the girls choosing to express themselves creatively through the medium of drawing.

Learning Story 8

Provocations and painting in Reception/One A: Narrative Observation 8

Child 10 was the last child to come over to the table. She was interested in what was occurring and was engaged with the materials. She did not ask what to do but just began creating with the materials which were available. (Before exploratory play had started in Exploration Time, all the children had had explained to them what activity and provocations were set up. This allowed them to choose freely what they wanted to do and to be independent and actively involved.)

Child 10 spent time alone creating her representation. Her attention was sustained as she added detail to her work with her eyes down and focused on what she was doing.

    HC: "Tell me about your painting."
Child 10: "Peace is my painting and it is a flower."
    HC: "Why is a flower peaceful?"

She spent some time before responding.

Child 10: "Because it's peaceful."

I noticed she started putting some other shapes and dots around her flower.

HC: "Would you like to tell me anything else about your painting?"

Child 10: "A little bit of rain" (as she painted the dots).

Child 10 was totally immersed in her painting; she did not acknowledge other children around her.

HC: "I wonder why rain is peaceful."

Child 10: "Because it helps make all the flowers grow." She nodded her head.

Child 10 continued with her painting and then placed it outside to dry. She then proceeded to another activity and another encounter within the environment.

The interpretive summary of Learning Story 8

Indicators of spirituality	Interpretations from Narrative Observation 8
Imagination and creativity	Evidence from LS 8 demonstrated that children were asked to represent an abstract phenomenon, such as peace, in a creative and imaginative way. Child 10 chose to paint a flower with raindrops to represent her understanding of peace. Being able to express herself creatively was an opportunity for a direct expression of her own emotion and understanding of the concept of peace. It offered an opportunity to express her connection to and to make meaning of the concept of peace. This mode of imagination and creativity demonstrated this child's natural spiritual disposition through which she is making connections and meaning in her life.
Connection to nature or a natural phenomenon	Through the opportunity to express peace in a creative way, Child 10 was also able to express her connection to nature through verbally expressing that the painting was peaceful because there was rain which the flower needed to grow.
Pedagogical Condition: Reggio Emilia approach	**Interpretations from Narrative Observation 8**
The image of the child	The evidence within LS 8 demonstrated the image of the child as a unique learner: in this narrative, Child 10 expressed her connection and understanding of her sense of oneness with the world. As she drew on prior knowledge about the need for nature to be cared for and the flower as a symbol of peace, she represented her thinking and construction of her own knowledge and relationship to the world. She was purposeful, and orchestrated her own interpretation of the concept of peace.

The environment as third teacher	There was a freedom in the learning environment to explore the concept of peace. The provocation was there as an invitation to engage. It was not there as an outcome for all children to achieve. The painting offered a mode with which children could engage and express their understanding and connection to a concept.
The hundred languages of children	The hundred languages of children depend on the creation of opportunities for children to express themselves in their different ways of thinking. There is evidence in this Learning Story that Child 10 was expressing herself creatively through the medium of painting.

Discovering spirituality

Figure 5.1

❧ *The very moment one gives close attention to anything, a rock, a leaf or anything that invites curiosity, it becomes a mysterious, awesome, indescribably magnificent world in itself: merely waiting to be explored.* ❧

Helena Card

5.1 Introduction

Throughout this chapter, evidence is presented in answer to the overall research question:

> *What indicators may be used to identify expressions of spirituality by four- to six-year-old children, and how the Reggio Emilia approach to education may offer a context for recognising and nurturing children's spiritual capacities?*

The data collected in response to this question are organised into the 15 Learning Stories, each of which captures an observation of the child in the educational setting. The 15 Learning Stories consider how the children's gestures, actions, vocalisations, creating, thinking out loud or imagining through play might be mediating expressions of spirituality. After each Learning Story, an interpretive summary is presented. As discussed in Chapter 4, a hermeneutic, multi-layered process is used for data analysis. Stage 1 consists of two layers (or parts) of deductive analysis. Stage 2 of the deductive analysis of the data is from the theoretical framework of the Reggio Emilia approach. Stage 1 of the multi-layered approach, with the two layers of deductive analysis, provides an entry point into the data.

Reflection and interpretation by the researcher on each Learning Story represent the initial part of the hermeneutic process (Gadamer 1976) as the researcher, through one horizon, which is the dialogue between the text (or children's observations and expressions), aims to challenge prior understanding and produce fresh insight and meaning from this dialogical encounter. Therefore, the fusion of horizons (Gadamer 1976) is the relationship, connections or what emerges from the data between the hermeneutics of the Reggio Emilia pedagogical environment and the affordances it allows for children's visible hermeneutic expressions of spirituality within this particular context and these conditions. A lens was used to distil and filter the subjectivity to allow for objectivity when interpreting the children's activity and interaction.

Stage 3 of the analysis includes data from Learning Stories, interviews with teachers, artefacts and digital photographs. In this stage, evidence is presented from the findings demonstrating how elements of the Reggio Emilia pedagogical approach offer conditions for the expression of spirituality to be exhibited. This presents new themes and constructs, thereby making the connection between the Reggio Emilia approach and the expressions of children's spirituality. The term 'the lens' was used to distil this next stage of data analysis and, as Merriam (2009) points out, classification schemes 'can be borrowed from sources outside the study … [whereby] the data base is scanned to determine the fit of prior categories and the data are sorted into the borrowed categories' (p. 137).

The findings address the four guiding questions of the research. The data provide evidence about the qualitative spiritual indicators demonstrated by young children within this case study and how the Reggio Emilia pedagogical approach provides conditions for the spiritual expression of children's spirituality. The findings present themes which emerge from the data addressing criteria that describe the manifestation of young children's spirituality bounded by this case study. The findings suggest that the Reggio Emilia approach is one which may nurture young children's spiritual expression.

5.2 More observations and interpretations

This chapter highlights many more Learning Stories with Narrative Observations and offers you interpretations and findings. I experienced so much joy as I observed children and their hundred languages evolved. I was able to sit alongside children as they took to the time to explore, ask questions and use their creative imagination. My aim as the researcher and observer was to open my senses and look deeply into the spiritual dimension of each child.

Learning Story 9

Creative materials in the Year One environment: Narrative Observation 9

Each child had to design an environment for sea creatures which they would then create in a jar. The class teacher invited the children to make something which was beautiful. She initiated the glitter and the bubbles in the final stage of the creation of the sea creatures' environments. The children were able to choose from a variety of materials, textures, shapes and sizes. Each jar was an individual creation.

The children had previously been involved in drawing their environment. From the drawing they had made, they were invited to reproduce this design in a jar with real objects. Various children gathered around the table.

I decided to interact with some of the focus children [children in the study] and asked for some responses on what they had created.

Three of the children were in the process of choosing objects and materials to put in their jars. I asked them about the environment for their sea creatures. All the children answered that the environments for their creatures were safe, happy and healthy. Child 11 expressed that if the sea creature did not have this kind of environment then it would die. Child 12 expressed that they had to keep oceans clean and not dirty otherwise the creatures would die.

The interpretive summary of Learning Story 9

Indicators of spirituality	Interpretations from Narrative Observation 9
Imagination and creativity	In LS 9, there is evidence that the children were interacting and learning through multisensory modes. They expanded their ideas and knowledge through drawing, the children drew and wrote about their theories and ideas. These ideas were then further expanded through the materials offered to create a sea creature environment. The jars in the demonstrate the creative ways in which the children represented their ideas. This led to further learning as the children experienced collaborative interactions with others and the environment as they used their imagination and creativity. The children worked alongside each other, not in isolation, and then verbalised their understandings.
Connection to nature or a natural phenomenon	The children in LS 9 were engaged in an inquiry about sea creatures. Through their engagement, they explored their understanding of sustainability: this was evident in the answer which they gave 'that the environments for their creatures were safe, happy and healthy.' This conveys their understanding of and sensitivity to the environment. Child 11 and Child 12 went on to further convey their understanding and sensitivity to the environment by their explanation that clean environments are necessary to keep sea creatures alive.
Pedagogical Condition: Reggio Emilia approach	**Interpretations from Narrative Observation 9**
The image of the child	LS 9 demonstrated that the children were relational in constructing their learning. They were working alongside each other, rather than in isolation. The children in this story were active agents in their learning as they discussed their ideas, hypotheses and points of view with others around them.
The environment as third teacher	The environment offered materials which were open-ended and multisensory, offering a relationship with the environment about which the children were able to communicate their understandings.

The hundred languages of children	The hundred languages of children were evident as the children were offered the mode of drawing to express their ideas, and then the opportunity to reproduce their ideas through materials and objects. This offered the children pathways towards different ways of knowing. The provocation and inquiry into sea creature environments did not require one answer but allowed the children to develop their own understandings.

Learning Story 10

An encounter with sand and sea materials: Narrative Observation 10

The Year One classroom environment provided many layers of interaction and provocation which stimulated and invited learning, interaction and curiosity. Children were involved in many areas of the room with a variety of activities.

I was observing the children and noticed that Child 13 was interacting with a sand tray and some natural objects from the sea. Child 13 and another child were around this sand tray, but Child 13 was the one who began to verbalise her thoughts, opinions and reactions to this experience. She explained that she was making a fish sea tank and that the fish was laying eggs. I was included in her interaction as I was sitting nearby and she looked at me when she spoke.

Child 13 moved and placed some objects together and then stated, "The babies and the nest."

She sat there, feeling the sand and arranging the objects in different ways. Child 13 had her eyes down and her hands were exploring through touching and investigating the natural materials. Her facial expression was a smile, and she was focused on her experience – feeling, manipulating and arranging the materials.

She changed a sponge arrangement and pronounced, "A tree." She then proceeded to change this around and, with a smile on her face, said, "It's like a bird's nest."

She turned towards me and showed me one of the pebbles and stated what it was: "It is like a real egg."

Child 13 remained with this experience for about 15 minutes, investigating the natural objects and exploring the sensory involvement with the different textures and surfaces of the materials.

The interpretive summary of Learning Story 10

Indicators of spirituality	Interpretations from Narrative Observation 10
Flow	In LS 10, there is evidence that Child 13 is engaged in an uninterrupted time. The Learning Story states that the children were involved in a variety of activities around the room. Others were around the child but she remained in an isolated activity, only interacting with the activity and, for a moment, with the researcher who was observing.
Connection to nature or a natural phenomenon	Child 13 was feeling and touching the sand with her eyes down and a smile on her face as she touched and moved the artefacts, feeling the textures.
Pedagogical Condition: Reggio Emilia approach	**Interpretations from Narrative Observation 10**
The image of the child	During this time of flow, Child 13 was allowed to interact in her own space. LS 10 demonstrates that the image of the child was valued by allowing the children time to explore, to discover and to investigate.
The environment as third teacher	The way the environment was set out facilitated this sensory experience. Child 13 was able to convey her feelings and her thinking through the hundred languages using gestures and sensation. Her eyes are directed down, as shown in the photograph, with a smile on her face. The photographs show her feeling the different textures of the materials.
The hundred languages of children	The hundred languages of children were evident as the child was offered a multisensory way through which to explore the materials, offering various media for new discoveries to make sense of the world. This is evident when Child 13 made the bird's nest with a pebble becoming an egg.

Learning Story 11

Exploring colours in the preschool environment: Narrative Observation 11

I entered the preschool outdoor area. Children were involved with materials in a variety of areas. One area was set up with open-ended materials on the wood-work table. There were various pieces of blocks, ranging from small to large, various hammers and nails, corks, paper and bits of leather for hammering, small, coloured blocks, masking tape and scissors.

I noticed Child 14 was making an object: he was in sustained concentration, not saying anything, just focused on his construction. He was constructing with coloured blocks of wood. I decided to ask him what he had made.

Child 14: "So when I am drawing and I don't know what colour to use. I look at this and it helps."

HC: "I wonder how it helps you."

Child 14: "It helps me with what colour to use."

HC: "What would you call this?"

Child 14: "A special colourful thing."

He covered the whole thing with masking tape to hold it together and he then looked at this. He was in sustained thinking for a period of time. He then placed coloured blocks on top of one another, and looked at this for a long time. He placed some of the coloured blocks over the colour arrangement.

With a pencil, he matched up the colours. He chose the colours and then realised that this area did not have all those that he needed. I suggested that he look over at another learning area which was set up, to see if he could find the colours. He nodded. He began matching his colours. I decided to ask him a question.

HC: "I wonder where colours come from."

Child 14: "From a rainbow."

HC: "Why do you think they come from rainbows?"

Child 14: "Because rainbows have got lots of colours."

Child 14 stopped and did not say anything, then he said:

"It comes from the rain and it comes from the clouds." (He was referring to where colours came from.)

I watched Child 14 find the colours he needed. He then proceeded inside to another learning area. The environment provided a variety of materials which were easily accessible to the children. He chose the colours which he needed and finished his creation. He put this in a safe place so he could use it later.

The interpretive summary of Learning Story 11

Indicators of spirituality	Interpretations from Narrative Observation 11
Flow	Child 14 was in sustained concentration: his head was down and he only interacted with the materials and, at times, with the researcher in response to questions. He remained in his own space of thinking and constructing with the elements in the environment, firstly outside, and then proceeded inside.
Creativity and imagination	Child 14 used his own creativity to design a colour block which would help him to locate colours. He utilised the open-ended materials in the environment to construct his artefact.
Pedagogical Condition: Reggio Emilia approach	**Interpretations from Narrative Observation 11**
The environment as third teacher	The materials in the environment provided the entry point for Child 14 to independently construct and design his artefact. It offered open-ended materials. He was able to move freely from outside to inside, independently selecting materials and elements from different spaces in the environment.
The hundred languages of children	Through designing this artefact and, when prompted, verbalising the intention of his creation, Child 14 was able to produce a concrete artefact which was meaningful and purposeful.
The image of the child	Child 14 was purposeful and resourceful as he independently constructed and represented his abstract thoughts into something which was concrete.

Learning Story 12

The creating table in the preschool environment: Narrative Observation 12

I noticed that Child 15 was using materials on the creating table. Child 15 was involved in her own interests and creating while turning around and looking at the surrounding elements within the environment. She moved towards the table, looking at the surroundings of the preschool space.

Child 15:   "I want to make a book."

Child 15 was staring for a sustained period of time at an umbrella which had glass beads hanging from it; her head and eyes were tilted towards this; she then looked around at what was occurring on the creating table.
She found a pipe cleaner and was holding this towards her face. When she felt this on her face, she smiled.

   Child 15 then watched and observed what was going on as she started to create what she had said was a 'book'. She stopped for a while, before turning and listening to the music which had been playing in the background. She then stopped and watched other things which were occurring around her and the other children.

   She turned her head to look at or to listen to various stimuli from the environment as she was involved in her own creative activity.

   Child 15 then chose some magazine pictures to put into her book.

Child 15:   "I'm sticking this on the next [page]."

She held up her picture to show to the co-educator, who was cutting out pictures nearby. As each child spoke around her, Child 15 would look at them and listen to their conversation and comments.

Child 15:   "Look."

She smiled at the picture of some cake which she had chosen, and then showed this to the co-educator.

Child 15:   "That page is done; I'm going to do the next page."

Child 15 worked through the pages in the book. The co-educator offered some guidance about how to stick the shapes in without making the pages stick together. Child 15 followed the ideas and worked through her book.

Child 15: "Look. I'm going to write about the sun."

She writes 'SUN' and says this out loud.
   The co-educator asked Child 15 what she was going to write about the sun.

Child 15: "Shining."

She then wrote some letters.
   As Child 15 was working on her own things, she was stopping to listen or to watch other children or things in the environment. She looked at the feature (an umbrella which had glass beads) which was hanging from the ceiling several times.
   The co-educator asked Child 15 what her book was about.

Child 15:   "Goldilocks and the Three Bears."
Co-educator: "Do you want me to help you write this?"
Child 15:   "Just talk about the letters" (which meant to tell her the letters).

The co-educator helped her to write 'Goldilocks'.

Child 15:   (looking at me) "What does this say?"
    HC: "It says Goldilocks."
Child 15:   "Goldilocks and the Three Bears."

She looked at the writing and then asked me to help her to write 'the Three Bears'. I wrote it on the back of the book and then we read this together.
   She continued making her book. As she was making and adding to her book, she leaned on the table and noticed that the table moved: she watched it go up and down, listening to the sound and moving the table: a smile crossed her face. Child 15 continued to add more elements to her book.

Discovering spirituality

> Child 15: (looking at her book and reading out loud) "Goldilocks and the Three Bears."

Child 15 then stood up, appearing to be finished: she moved to another area to put the book in a special place which had pockets for each child so that she could take the book home when the session finished.

On the way back, she passed the table and again looked up at the ceiling at the upturned umbrella frame, from which the glass beads were hanging. She stood there for a while, gazing upward at the different beads and the lights which reflected through them. Then she continued to move to the outside learning space.

The interpretive summary of Learning Story 12

Indicators of spirituality	Interpretations from Narrative Observation 12
Flow	Child 15 appeared to be in a state of flow, something that was demonstrated with the following evidence from the Learning Story:
	Child 15 is photographed with her eyes looking upward at the beads dangling from the umbrella. 'Child 15 was staring for a sustained period of time at an umbrella which had glass beads hanging from it: her head and eyes were tilted towards this …'
	There is further evidence which demonstrates periods of time when Child 15 was in this state of flow:
	'On the way back, she passed the table and again looked up at the ceiling at the upturned umbrella frame. There were glass beads hanging from the frame. She stood there for a while gazing upward at the different beads and the lights which reflected through them. Then she continued to move to the outside learning space.'
Curiosity and joy	Child 15 appeared happy and was curious as she turned around to watch or to listen to the sounds. She smiled when she felt the sensation of the pipe cleaner. There was a natural curiosity as she was attracted to various elements of the environment around her.

Pedagogical Condition: Reggio Emilia approach	Interpretations from Narrative Observation 12
The environment as third teacher	The aesthetics in the environment provided an avenue for natural curiosity and fascination, or for awe and wonder to occur. Child 15 had her eyes focused upwards and there were periods of time when she was looking at the umbrella and the beads. In addition, LS 12 provides evidence that Child 15 is interested and curious and connected to the multisensory elements of the environment. The photographs show her eyes down and focused on her creative activity and also the times when she is turning to look around at the environment or her head is tilted and her eyes are looking upwards. 'Child 15 then watched and observed what was going on as she started to create her what she had said was a "book". She stopped for a while and turned and listened to the music which had been playing in the background. She then stopped and watched other things which were occurring around her and the other children. She turned her head to look at or to listen to various stimuli from the environment as she was involved in her own creative activity.' The materials set out on the creating table offered an avenue to explore some meaning through writing and making a book. There was evidence of creative stimuli which led to making the book and also the opportunity for sensory exploration with the pipe cleaner: 'She then found a pipe cleaner and was holding this towards her face and felt this on her face, and her facial expression had a smile on it.'
The hundred languages of children	The creating table offered the avenue to explore the language of the book and the elements of the connection between print and meaning as Child 15 wrote the words, was supported by a co-educator and was able to demonstrate her understanding of a story through verbalising a familiar story, that of "Goldilocks and the Three Bears".

Learning Story 13

Designing the farm in Reception/One B: Narrative Observation 13

The classroom was involved in play-based activities during Exploration Time. A group of children were playing with some toy farm animals which were set up on tables in the room; various materials were also around the toy farm figures. I noticed the conversation which was occurring as the children played and interacted with the materials and with one another. A large drawing alongside the area was a design of a farm. It looked like they were all following this design.

Child 16 was playing in a group with some other children.

Child 16 announced, "We are designing a farm." Child 16 was interacting and participating in the design of the farm.

Child 16 said, "We need mud." He got a piece of material and took the time to fold it into an area and in such a way that it represented mud.

Child 16 said, "We need water." He placed some blue material out near the farm design area. Other children worked alongside him as he was designing and they were also designing parts of the farm.

Another child found what looked like a sun: he smiled and said, "Look at the sun."

Child 16 took the sun from the other child and then took some time to observe the sun carefully: looking down at it, his expression changed.

He said, "No, it's ugly and it's got a face; we can't have it. Suns don't have faces."

As he continued in his flow of learning, Child 16 was singing a tune to himself. He was singing out loud, and moving and changing the toy figures on the farm. Other children played and designed around him; all of the children had smiles on their faces as they were involved in the activity.

I had been observing from the side of the area and noticed the large drawing standing upright at the end of the farm area. I decided to ask Child 16 what it was.

Child 16 said, "It's a picture of the farm."

I asked whether he had drawn this and he nodded saying, "Yes."

Then I decided to ask a further question: "Did you try to make it on here?," pointing to the farm and the toy figures.

"Yes," said Child 16 and smiled, "tried to." Child 16 continued, with the other children around him, to construct ideas. He listened to each child's thoughts about the farm, and he and the others moved and changed the area. Child 16, along with a group of other children who were around him, stayed involved in this activity for about 20 minutes.

The interpretation of Learning Story 13

Indicators of spirituality	Interpretations from Narrative Observation 13
Flow, creativity and imagination	This Learning Story shows children involved in the flow of play as they used creativity and imagination to create a farm. They used materials to create their farm landscape, such as the toy figures, and used the materials to create features of the landscape. They were engaged with the activity for a period of uninterrupted time. 'Child 16 and a group of other children who were around him stayed involved in this activity for about 20 minutes.' Child 16 had drawn the farm first and he and a group of children worked together to construct this with concrete materials. This was clarified when, as the observer, I decided to ask a question. 'I had been observing from the side of the area and noticed a drawing which was standing upright at the end of the farm area. I decided to ask Child 16 what it was. Child 16 said, "It's a picture of the farm." I asked whether he had drawn this and he nodded saying, "Yes." Then I decided to ask a further question: "Did you try to make it on here?" pointing to the farm and the toy figures. "Yes," said Child 16 and smiled, "tried to."' Child 16 and the other children were involved in using their imagination to enter into the imaginative world of the farm: this offered them a way to think differently about their current understanding of everyday life experiences.
Pedagogical Condition: Reggio Emilia approach	**Interpretations of Narrative Observation 13**
The environment as third teacher	The environment provided conditions for imaginative play and provided conditions for co-constructing learning and meaning. The Learning Story states that Child 16 was involved with other children: Other children worked alongside him as he was designing and they were also designing parts of the farm. The environment provided multiple entry points for inquiry and meaning making through the aesthetic open-ended materials: this was evident as the children constructed their interpretation of the farm.

Learning Story 14

The human body and skeleton in Reception/One B: Narrative Observation 14

The children were involved in Exploration Time and a variety of provocations around the room were about the human body.

Child 18 had wandered around the room after she left an activity on the dough table and was looking at what the other children were doing. She wandered and looked around, perusing the area, watching what the other children were involved in. She noticed a table with some books and black paper around it, and with some wooden figurines with movable joints. The provocation on this table consisted of books about skeletons and the body, and paper was set out to invite children to draw their body with white chalk onto the black paper.

Child 18 looked at this and came over to the materials on the table: she decided to join in by first asking if she could.

Child 18: "Can I do a skeleton?"

She asked for a new piece of black paper. She was directing the question to the teacher. The teacher helped her to select the paper and also made a suggestion that she might like to use the pastels on the black.

I sat down at the table as Child 18 chose her seat to begin her drawing.

Child 18 began talking out loud, describing to no one in particular what she was about to do.

Child 18: "I am going to draw the outside first."

Child 18 began drawing the shape of a body.
She was looking at me and waited. I smiled at her and said,

HC: "Are you?"

Child 18: "Yes, the outside on this side [she showed me one side of the paper], then the bones on the back" (she showed me the other side of the paper).

She began drawing the outside of a body and features which seemed like body parts on the inside. Child 18 then stood up.

Child 18: "So imagine if you had one side, that you had this" (she pointed to herself). Then she turned around.

Child 18: "And you had bones on the back."

She then sat down, returning to her drawing. As she was drawing and representing, she continued to talk out loud.

Child 18: "Did you know the bone of the neck is longer than the skin part?"

She did not wait for an answer.

Child 17: "Yeah, it's weird."

Child 18 laughed to herself. As she was drawing, Child 18 was sharing some facts about the human body and still talking out loud, sharing facts and information.

Child 18: "The nose is just like a gigantic hole."

As Child 18 continued with her drawing, at the same time, some other children were around the table, looking at the pictures in the picture books on the human body.
    Child 19, one of the children who had joined the table was looking down at a picture of the epiglottis in the mouth. He stared at this picture for a long time. He then asked a question of another child, Child 20, who had joined the table.

Child 19: "What's that?"

He opened his mouth toward another child and Child 20 looked in.

Child 20: "I know."

He opened his mouth too and looked at Child 19's opened mouth.

Child 20: "That's it."

They took turns looking at the picture of the epiglottis, then looked into the inside of each other's mouths, then looked at each other's opened mouths and then at the picture.
    Child 18 was listening to the conversation and opened her mouth to show Child 19.

Child 20: "Wow, I can see it."

Child 19 kept looking down at the book and continued to look at other pictures. He moved to the floor alongside the table, and then to a chair on the other side of the table. He looked at the other pictures which were associated with the human body and spent some time looking at them closely with his head close to the pictures. Child 20 continued with his drawing; he was representing a skeleton.

Child 20:   "Me inside my body."

He was referring to his drawing and explaining what it was.

Child 20:   "Heart, and your leg bone and the brain, eyes, mouth."

I decided to ask a question.

    HC: "I wonder who made the body."

Both Child 18 and Child 20, without hesitation, shared their answer

Child 18 and Child 20: "God."

They both said this together and continued with their drawing. Child 18 then continued to speak.

Child 18:   "Because He made the world."
Child 20:   "Because He wanted to make the people."
    HC: "So what do you think you are made of?"
Child 18:   "I think wood."
Child 20:   "Maybe He [God] made the wood. Maybe he made the wood out of special wood."

Child 18 was labelling the body, competent with her literacy skills and knowledge of words and their purpose.

Child 18:   "Do we have 20 teeth?"

She did not wait for any answer.

Child 18:   "I think so, because I can count them: five on this side, five on that side."

She then counted her own teeth at the top and on the bottom and then said out loud:
"Yes, 20."

Child 18: "Do I have to label this side?" She looked at me.

She had already labelled one side of the body figure.

    HC: "It's up to you."
Child 18: "I don't want to."
Child 18: "Do you know my last name?"

Without waiting for an answer, she announced her name. Then both Child 18 and Child 20 played with the body figurines. They were each humming to themselves as they manipulated the body into different shapes and figures. They were smiling, making the shapes and designs and looking at how the joints moved.
  Child 20 then moved on to another activity, while Child 18 continued to draw another picture of the body with colours. Alongside, Child 19 came back up to the table from the floor with the book and was still looking at and exploring the books and the pictures.

The interpretive summary of Learning Story 14

Indicators of spirituality	Interpretations from Narrative Observation 14
Flow, creativity and imagination	This Learning Story shows children involved in the flow of play as they used creativity and imagination to draw and represent the human body and skeleton. They used materials to create their representations through this creative experience and, using their imagination, they entered into an understanding the body. As Child 18 was drawing, she discovered facts about her body: this offered her a way to think differently about her current understanding of everyday life experiences and knowledge. She verbally expressed her prior knowledge about teeth and the human body. As Child 20 drew her own body, she verbalised her theory about how she had interpreted the inside and outside of her body. Likewise, Child 20 had the experience of creating his skeleton and moving the figurine in different ways. The photographs show Child 19 in his own flow of thinking with his head down. He is shown moving away from the table and sitting on the floor in his own space in silence, with the other children interacting in the background.

Wonder and curiosity	Child 19 seemed curious and fascinated by his discovery of a particular part of the human body, the epiglottis. As he interacted with the others, his facial expression was directed towards this discovery. When he was looking at the book, his head was down, as he continued to explore the pictures and diagrams.
Asking bigger questions	Child 19 was stimulated by the provocation of the books through which he discovered the epiglottis and attempted to understand where this part of the body was. He directed a question to the other children about this part of the body. Child 18 and Child 20 both looked at, and into, each other's mouths and at the picture and connected that the epiglottis in their mouths was the same as the picture in the book.
Joy	Child 18 and Child 20 displayed joy or happiness as they hummed to themselves while playing with the movable wooden figurines. The smiles on their faces also indicated joy and happiness.
Talking about God or a supreme being	When asked the question about who made the human body, both Child 18 and Child 20 replied without hesitation that it was God, and presented the reasoning that He (God) made everything.
Attraction to a natural phenomenon	All the children were engaged with the phenomenon of the human body, either by discovering how to interpret this through drawing or by the pictures in the books which showed real parts of the body.
Pedagogical Condition: Reggio Emilia approach	**Interpretations from Narrative Observation 14**
The environment as third teacher	The environment provided conditions for imaginative play and for co-constructing learning and meaning. The Learning Story states that the children were alongside one another as they each interacted with the provocations on the table. The provocations were set out for the children to discover, inquire about and explore. There was no expectation of one answer. The environment allowed the children to co-construct knowledge through the provocations. For example, Child 19 became interested in the pictures of the body in the books on the table and this was his entry point for discovering new meanings. Multiple entry points for inquiry were offered through the aesthetic open-ended materials.

The hundred languages of children	Both Child 18 and Child 20 expressed themselves through the hundred languages as they were drawing and creating. They verbalised their theories and knowledge. Child 19 also expressed himself through non-verbalisation when he had his head down in the book, and then chose to verbalise his query as he was making meaning.

Learning Story 15

Investigating countries and identities in Year One: Narrative Observation 15

The class was involved in Exploration Time. Various provocations were set up around the room.

Child 21 had finished a painting of her family and said out loud that her grandparents came from England.

She went from her painting over to a table which had a globe set up on it.

She was looking at the globe with another child.

Child 21: "The United Kingdom is England. England is up."

HC: "Why do you think it's up?"

Child 21: "Because I've seen it before."

Another child was looking at all the countries on the globe and said out loud:
Child 22 "You know that Mexicans can speak 20 languages. Where's the United Kingdom? Do you know that 100 years ago in 1948, England was at war?" He was talking to Child 21.

Child 21: "That was years ago, with Italy?"

Child 22: "No. Against the Vikings."

They both looked at each other as they shared this information. Child 22 then looked at the globe.

Child 21: "We have to find the United Kingdom."
She went over to the table next to her. On it were little plastic tracing/drawing pads. It appeared that she was drawing a shape.

HC: "How is this going to help?"

Child 21: "I am going to draw England to help us find it."

Child 22 was looking at the shape of what Child 21 had drawn. He wanted to replicate this. He stared and observed the shape. He kept on going back to the map then the shape and back again.

Their fingers went over all the countries on the globe as they were looking. I decided to ask a question.

> HC: "What was the name you were looking for?"
>
> Child 21: "United Kingdom."

Once this was said, they found the word on the globe and were smiling.

Another child had been watching them both. He looked at the globe and the place on it which represented the United Kingdom.

Child 21 then copied it exactly onto one of the drawing pads which was set out near the globe.

Child 22 wanted to copy this too. He took one of the pads and drew the shape. He kept looking at the globe and at the drawing pad. He had a few attempts. The drawing pad allowed for new attempts because it had a plastic covering which could be lifted off to create a new image. The other child stood by him and helped by keeping his finger on the country.

The interpretive summary of Learning Story 15

Indicators of spirituality	Interpretations from Narrative Observation 15
Flow, creativity and imagination	Children were given the opportunity to freely explore equipment and materials.
Asking bigger questions	Bigger questions were asked about the children's identity with this prompted by the statement that Child 21's grandparents came from England.
Pedagogical Condition: Reggio Emilia approach	**Interpretations from Narrative Observation 15**
The image of the child	The children were active agents in their learning and co-construction of knowledge. Child 21 theorised and verbalised out loud, drawing on prior knowledge about where England was on the globe. Child 22 drew on prior knowledge about countries around the world. Through their conversation, Child 22 was helping Child 21 to discover where she was from. Child 21 seemed intent on the discovery and competently drew a map on a pad so that they could match the country's shape to the globe.

The environment as third teacher	No teacher was evident: the flow of conversation was between the children. They were active agents within their own environment. They utilised equipment, for example, the globe and the writing pads which were on the table, with this equipment set up around the room to assist them in their meaning-making and inquiry.

5.3 Qualitative indicators of spirituality observed in young children in everyday early childhood activities

5.3.1 Indicator of spirituality expressed as awe and wonder

As demonstrated in the Learning Stories with the Narrative Observations recorded, there were times when the children expressed moments of awe and wonder. In Learning Story (LS) 6, at the cheeping sound from the chickens, both girls stopped to listen and their facial expressions demonstrated a smile or amazement: they were intrigued and this was displayed in their facial expressions. They were totally immersed in the fascination of the chickens and their gaze was towards the incubator. 'Both girls stopped and bent towards the incubator to listen to the cheeping sound from the chickens; they were both smiling; and their heads were tilted towards the incubator.' They interacted with the chickens, holding up a picture to show the chickens: they were in awe that the chickens might have been looking at their drawing, as was described by Child 4.

In LS 6, the girls observing the chickens displayed a record of their observations through the drawings which they shared, which indicated further knowledge and theorising about the stages from egg to chicken and how chickens hatch. In the photographs, they presented a happy disposition and their gaze and facial gestures suggested they were intrigued by the chickens.

In LS 7, the two girls displayed awe and wonder as they touched, investigated and described the spider: they expressed that it was beautiful. The girls were smiling and in awe of the spider, with this displayed through their description of the spider. The photograph of the girls with the spider shows their interest as their eyes are fixed on the spider.

Child 8 and Child 9 in LS 7, while observing the spider, displayed times when they were immersed in discovering elements which they did not understand as they were searching for and wondering about answers to questions, such as whether spiders could talk. They discovered how to represent the spider, and theorised about the way spiders speak and how to care for living things. In the photograph, as they touch the spider with their fingers and describe what it feels like, they are both smiling.

This demonstrates that, within their play, children experience moments which can demonstrate wonder, engagement and curiosity.

Evidence in the data also demonstrates that, as the children express awe, wonder and curiosity, this can lead to pondering, questioning or discovering more about a phenomenon. For example, in LS 4, Child 4, through her gestures, smiles and gaze was in awe of the sound of thunder: she was also interested in discovering and touching the hail.

Further evidence is demonstrated in LS 14 with Child 19 immersed in the discovery of the epiglottis and his curious disposition as he looks with wonder at the pictures and inside the other child's mouth to discover new knowledge about his own body.

When children are immersed in awe and wonder, there is the tendency to ponder and question things that they do not understand. This state of meaningfulness (Ruddock & Cameron 2010) is linked to spirituality, whereby each human being seeks to find meaning for their existence, and meaning and connection to the world (Swinton & Pattison 2001; Zohar & Marshall 2000). This tendency to ponder and question may be occurring internally; however, as the children interacted with each other and the environment, the expression of awe and wonder was demonstrated and seen. Child 4 began to ponder and vocalise theories about the thunder, drawing on prior knowledge about God and how thunder is made. Her gaze demonstrated a disposition of wonder: as she touched the hail, her gaze was down, and could be interpreted as curious.

5.3.2 *Indicator of spirituality expressed as joy*

The indicator of the expression of joy occurred as children experienced and encountered their natural environment, as demonstrated by the data. The Learning Stories provide observations of the children's encounters with the environment or with one another, with joy expressed and demonstrated through their gestures, facial expressions, verbalisations and/or singing/humming as they experienced their environment.

In LS 4, Child 4 displayed her joy through clapping and dancing around as she heard the thunder. She had a smile on her face as she listened: she also had a smile on her face when discovering the hail on the ground. In the interpretive summary of this Learning Story, it states: 'Child 4 had an animated face with a smile on it as she gazes towards the sky which can represent an expression of joy. She claps her hands and is described as excited and she dances around with a smile on her face. Her gestures and movements suggest joy.'

The chickens in LS 6 provided moments of delight for the girls, Child 6 and Child 7, and they directed their gaze to the chickens with a smile on their faces. The interpretive summary of the Learning Story suggests that the girls presented a happy disposition. They smiled as they talked about their theories. They translated their theories into drawings which they were happy to go ahead and do; it was not a requirement to produce anything or to record anything on paper. In LS 12, as Child 15 put the pipe cleaner to her face and felt the sensation, she smiled and, in the interpretation, it is suggested that she was happy or joyful at the sensation. In LS 14, Child 18 and Child 20 also displayed a joyful disposition: their humming could suggest joy and happiness as they played with the wooden figurine.

According to researchers Hart (2003) and Kessler (2000), children's spirituality flows through their capacities for spontaneous joy and wonder. The data generated moments when the children expressed joy during their encounters in the learning spaces: it was expressed through their gestures and their happy disposition was displayed through smiling and other gestures. Nye (2009) supports the view that joy is a core strength through which children express their spirituality.

5.3.3 Indicator of spirituality expressed as flow of consciousness

The prevalence of the flow experience, as defined by Csikszentmihalyi (1997), was observed and recorded in the Learning Stories. Children were less concerned about the presence of others and were focused on their immediate experiences: this enabled 'flow' to be readily observed.

In each of the Learning Stories, the children were engaged in diverse ways: overall, the data were rich with examples where the children demonstrated flow and exhibited their tendency for the state of flow when unrestricted by time or any influences from or expectations of others.

The learning environments, with their aesthetic characteristics and the materials and provocations providing multiple possibilities of ideas and focus, fostered an orientation in the children in which they were engrossed in a state of flow or in sustained learning and discovery. It is often hard to describe this orientation and I have heard many educators including myself over time describe this orientation as children 'being in the zone'. The Learning Stories represented and described children in the flow of activities where there was little or no intervention either from the teacher or from myself as the participant observer. Child 1 was observed for a period of time in her own zone of discovery with the musical instruments with this interpreted as an expression of flow before a conversation was started by the researcher. Child 2 in LS 2, for the period of the observation, was involved and sustained in the imaginative role play and dialogue and was not distracted by others in the outdoor area, with this interpreted as an expression of flow. In LS 11, Child 14's behaviour was interpreted as evidence of the expression of flow with the photograph showing him with his head and eyes down. The interpretive summary of the Learning Story describes him as being in sustained concentration, only interacting with the materials until the researcher asks him a question and he engages in some dialogue. After the dialogue, he remains in his own sphere of concentration and space of thinking as he constructs and uses the elements in the environment: he moves from inside to outside while remaining in his own space of thinking. In LS 12, Child 15 gazes at a fixture hanging from the ceiling for a sustained period of time, with this act of gazing described in the interpretive analysis as an expression of flow. In LS 14, Child 19 demonstrates flow with his head down in his own space of thinking: he moves away from the table and sits on the floor in his own space and silence, with the other children interacting in the background.

As described through the work of Csikszentmihalyi (1997, 2002), this orientation, which children experience and educators observe, is a holistic sensation which occurs when a person experiences total involvement. Through the ordinary experiences of childhood, this sense of flow naturally and repeatedly occurs. Flow, according to Csikszentmihalyi (1997, 2002), is a time when there is an experience of concentrated attention and where one is free, allowing the feeling that the activity is managed by itself or by an outside influence, where pure attentiveness is apparent.

I offer my insights as a contribution to the notion of flow and allowing children to 'be' in the moment or allowing times of flow. Some thoughts on this after viewing my documentation and data is that all children need to be acknowledged for their strengths and intelligences. This helps children to feel valued and it lets them 'be' in the moment or flow. In the everyday children regularly relate to something greater than themselves if they are afforded the time to explore and discover. This relation and connection to something greater than themselves is their innate spirituality.

Researchers who have explored young children's spirituality have claimed that, when children are 'in flow', this state is a means through which to allow children's spirituality to be expressed (Csikszentmihalyi 1997, 2002). As the Learning Stories unfolded, there were also moments which occurred in the children's natural setting which displayed creativity and imagination, both of which are also expressions of children's spirituality (Hyde 2008a; de Souza 2009).

5.3.4 Indicator of spirituality expressed as curiosity and interest in mysterious things

In each of the Learning Stories, the children were engaged and expressed an interest in mysterious things, or demonstrated the curiosity to discover mystery as they interacted with their everyday environment. For Child 1, the notion of music showed how she exhibited her curiosity and interest in the sound of music. Child 3, with the guinea pig, was fascinated with the mystery of the living animal and expressed her interest, in particular, in the hair and legs of the animal as she drew them on her piece of paper. The spider too was mysterious and the girls, Child 8 and Child 9, were engaged and involved, expressing their curiosity through their discussions, interpretations and descriptions, and their gestures of joy and delight as they touched and looked carefully at the details of the spider.

The observation and questions about the chickens' growth and development presented a mystery and a fascination for the two girls, Child 6 and Child 7, who presented their ideas and theories about how they were formed. They openly discussed and analysed questions about which they were curious and which were mysterious to them. The environment allowed the girls to move to and from the chickens as their curiosity was sparked and they sought further questions.

The curiosity demonstrated by Child 21 and Child 22 in LS 15, as their curiosity led to discovery of a country and the origin of a particular child, was about discovering the mystery of knowing the unknown.

The concept of mystery is also connected to spirituality. Myers (1997) considered mystery to be something that can be explained as being beyond what we can name and understand, and that sometimes cannot be explained.

Hay and Nye (2006) claim that mystery jolts perception and meaning and suggest that, for young children, it is important to ponder and think about the meaning of a person's existence. This leads young children into questioning who they are, where they belong and how they are connected to their surrounding world.

5.3.5 Indicator of spirituality expressed as attraction to nature or a natural phenomenon

The children displayed periods of flow and engagement when they were immersed in creative activities. Flow and engagement were also clearly displayed when they were watching natural phenomena, and there were times when they were immersed in their own space. As a participant, I would merely observe these times as they appeared to be self-absorbed with their own curiosity, wonder and awe, and creativity. The environment provided opportunities to explore and discover natural phenomena. The following evidence from the data illustrates that the environment offered multisensory phenomena with which the children were engaged, and to which they were attracted and responsive in different ways: the spider; the opportunity for outside play; hearing the thunder and curiosity with the hail; the sand tray with sand, sea sponges and natural products from the sea; the classroom areas with animals and birds, such as the guinea pigs and the chickens. The data collected through actively engaging in observation support the evidence of these times, with the narratives presented in Learning Stories 3 to 7. The children were attracted to natural phenomena such as: the sound of musical instruments in LS 3; the natural materials in LS 4; the guinea pigs in LS 5; the baby chickens in LS 6; and the spider in LS 7. All of these phenomena were investigated with curiosity by the children, providing opportunities to observe them in their mystery-sensing discoveries.

Mystery sensing, according to Hay and Nye (2006), is a characteristic of children's spirituality and this sense of mystery can be awakened by 'down to earth and familiar phenomena' (p. 72). The children's mystery sensing, according to Hay and Nye (2006), is exhibited through their engagement and their imagination and creativity as they respond to the phenomena.

Discovering spirituality

In each of these Learning Story examples, it was recorded that the children were engaged, and that they responded in some way to the phenomena. This is supported by evidence, such as Child 1 in LS 1 tilting her head to listen to the sound of the instrument, and going on to represent the sounds of the music as 'waves and swirls' in her drawings.

In LS 2, this response to natural phenomena by Child 2 is described when he was observed to be curiously looking at the materials, showing his engagement in imaginary play with the dinosaurs and the materials.

Further evidence is demonstrated with the engagement with the guinea pig creatively represented as a drawing, in LS 5. In LS 7, the engagement with and attraction to the spider is evident: creative drawing was the medium used to represent each learning encounter and the 'artwork' produced by the two girls.

Child 4 was attracted to the sound of thunder: the photographs in LS 4 show her excitement and interest in the phenomenon as she verbalises her own theories about the thunder. Attraction to the natural phenomenon of weather was demonstrated as Child 4 became fascinated with the sound of thunder and the hail. She displayed a natural and excited curiosity as her head was tilted upward and she looked upward with her mouth open. Child 4 clapped and danced around, and was sufficiently curious to go over and pick up the hail. She was attracted to the hail and interested in feeling and touching it.

Creating an environment in a jar was an experience offered to the children in LS 9: they were clearly engaged as they created their own environment for a sea creature. They imagined and explored the phenomena of the environments they were creating which represented the sea for their sea creatures.

In all of these examples the data indicate that the children were attracted to natural elements of the physical environment and to nature more generally, such as the spider, the guinea pigs and chickens: the opportunity to be outside for play and inquiry led to the response or attraction to thunder and hail. In LS 10, Child 13 was attracted to and engaged with the natural phenomena of the sea artefacts:

> She sat there, feeling the sand and arranging the objects in different ways. Child 13 had her eyes down and her hands were exploring through touching and investigating the natural materials. Her facial expression was a smile, and she was focused on her experience—feeling, manipulating and arranging the materials.
> (LS 10)

The children's connectedness to the natural phenomena, across all four learning cohorts, demonstrated a connectedness to natural things and, according to the literature, this spontaneous attraction and connectedness to natural phenomena is an expression of spirituality (Vialle et al. 2008).

5.3.6 Indicator of spirituality expressed as care or empathy for another

Care and empathy can be demonstrated in various ways. For this case, the children in all cohorts were observed within their authentic learning environments. It appeared, from the evidence in the data, that the situations documented were times when the children worked collaboratively and respectfully with one another, allowing each other to experience flow and engagement. This respectful and collaborative attitude may be attuned to caring and empathy for one another. There were no recorded times when children were overcrowding each other's space or were not respectful of one another. Children either chose to interact on their own or in groups, for instance, in LS 14 where a group of children were amicably discussing the human body and co-constructing knowledge, each respectfully listening to one another and contributing to the conversation. In LS 15, Child 22 was intent on discovering the country from where Child 21's grandparents came and there was a collaborative effort to explore this and solve the problem together.

Through the everyday context of play, the example of Child 2 in LS 2 demonstrated a caring attitude towards another as he played with the toy dinosaurs and verbalised that he was putting the baby dinosaurs with the 'mother' dinosaurs, emphasising that the babies needed protection and to be looked after by their mothers. Child 2 emphasised the care and attention given to the baby dinosaurs through mentioning protection: this is an expression of the need for a sense of security and caring by another individual. He displayed careful attention to placing the babies close to the mothers for care and protection. Displaying care towards another for purpose, meaning and connection is an aspect which Myers (1997) advocates as an expression of the spiritual dimension.

Child 5, who was playing in the home corner area, demonstrated his care and attention to the other child in LS 5. His knowledge about routines to do with school and parents dropping off and picking up children was important: he looks directly at the other child when he states that he will pick her up. Child 5 also takes the other child's hand as they go to 'school'.

Care and empathy are important dimensions of the expression of spirituality. Adams et al. (2008) maintain that the spiritual intellect of children allows them to demonstrate a kindness and empathy towards others as they identify their belonging, meaning and purpose. Hart (2006) maintains that children have a spiritual capacity and, within this, is the deep compassion they demonstrate towards others. Furthermore, when children are involved in creating artwork or in other forms of creating, as seen in the Learning Stories, there is also the expression of empathy connected to art which McMurtary (2007) describes as 'the empathetic journeying with a created work in our imagination' (p. 95).

5.3.7 Indicator of spirituality expressed as creativity

The children's confidence and pleasure in creative pursuits were evident and their learning environments encouraged the expression of this indicator through the multisensory resources and materials that were available for them to pursue their creativity. There appeared to be no limits to the creative pursuits as the children's imagination guided their ideas and creative urges, with the teachers providing an unrestricted exploratory environment in which creativity was able to thrive. The children were able to theorise, to learn, discover, play and create.

Exploration Time, which is highly valued in the early years setting with its invitation for children to participate, is a time which is play-based, allowing the children to explore and discover their environment through creative and imaginative inquiry. Each teacher in the early years cohorts incorporated this time into their daily schedule. There were no particular outcomes expected during this time The teachers invite them [the children] in whatever way they want to take part in it. There were no particular outcomes expected during this time.

Creativity was evident and flourished through a variety of different modes. The data showed the many materials within the learning environments which children accessed to express their creativity, including: paints, wire, pencils, pens, sand, abstract materials, play equipment, toys, natural materials, loose parts and aesthetic materials.

Throughout the Learning Stories, patterns emerge which incorporate the children's flow, creativity and imagination. Each narrative presents a scenario where the children are oriented (Scheinfeld et al. 2008) in different ways during their encounters and learning experiences, and expressions appear in different forms.

In the preschool, Child 1 was uninterrupted in her flow and investigation of music, with the freedom to create, imagine and represent her meaning and discovery, making connections to her world. In their experiences with the guinea pigs and the chickens, all the children were attracted to, and mesmerised by, the creatures. Each child was able to be creative in representing their discoveries and observations: Child 3 with her drawing of the guinea pig, and Child 6 and Child 7 with their interpretations of the life cycle of chickens. There was also time for imagining further possibilities. The spider and the features of the environment cultivated a continuous flow or sustained attention by the two girls. In LS 8, Child 10 used the paints to creatively represent her understanding of peace. The representation of an environment for sea creatures was done firstly through drawing and, then, by using creative, aesthetic materials, an environment was created in a jar of blue water. The farm play in LS 13 was inspired by the creative drawings of Child 16 and then represented on the materials with the figurines and other artefacts. The opportunity to draw the human body and a skeleton in LS 14 was done with chalk on black paper by Child 18 and Child 20 who each designed their own representation of what their body and skeleton looked like.

In each of the experiences, the adult was an insignificant participant, only entering the experiences at certain times, and respecting the emergence of the experience, not knowing what to expect, but being open to boundless possibilities.

As children experience moments and activities in which they are oriented in creativity and imagination, they are also provided with opportunities to 'conceive what is beyond the known and what is obvious' (Hay & Nye 2006, p. 72). It is during these times, as creativity and imagination interface, described by Hyde (2008a) as being in the flow of consciousness, that children's spirituality is expressed.

5.3.8 Indicator of spirituality expressed as imagination

Time for creative experiences was provided and was uninterrupted as the children had the freedom to explore and discover concepts through creative modes. In LS 1, Child 1 was able to discover, imagine and represent music and sound through different media. In LS 7, Child 8 and Child 9 used imagination and were creative in describing and then in representing the spider. Facial gestures and curious, amazed faces were noted as the children interacted with elements in the environment. In my many discussions with teachers after they have some knowledge about children's spirituality, some common assertions can be compiled. All children need attention given to their hundred languages. It is a form of expression that includes spiritual expression and spiritual language which may occur through non-verbal interactions. We must be attuned to children in order to see the many ways in which children that they can express their spirituality.

I believe that we need to be attentive to the hundred languages, to learn to see things in the hundred languages, and a hundred more.

This particular indicator is evident throughout all the Learning Stories as the children were able to freely express themselves through creative experiences, with the environment offering a catalyst for these experiences through the hundred languages and the imagination to flourish. In each example, there is a connection with materials, areas or provocations which were accessible to the children for imaginative thinking.

In LS 13, the children were able to freely imagine and play with the artefacts and the materials to construct and design their farm. In their play, exploration and encounters, the children moved from real experiences to creative, imaginative experiences.

Berryman (1997) states that creativity is observed through the way that children show puzzled faces, frowns or looks of amazement when insight occurs. Montagu (1989) claims that childhood is a period in one's life when maximum creativity is present and defines creativity as a dialectic outcome that occurs between the child and the environment. There were times when children imagined and created and times when they were silent.

In allowing conditions that foster imagination and creativity, children's spirituality is nurtured and facilitated (Bode 1998; Watson 2007). Children's expression of spirituality may not be verbal; it could be through modes such as creativity and imagination (Hart 2003; Upton 2009). Uninterrupted time for play fosters imagination: in each Learning Story, imaginative activity occurred as playful conditions for children were provided.

5.3.9 Indicator of spirituality expressed as curiosity and engagement

The provocations in the environment which the teachers, encouraged were inspired by the Reggio Emilia approach. The environments provided opportunities for a sense of awe and wonder, which in turn, ignited curiosity. This curiosity led the children into a sense of discovery that linked to bigger questioning and theorising. For example, in LS 15, Child 21 began to question where her country of origin was located. Two other children became interested and intent on discovering the answer. The data and the evidence suggest that this sense of identity and connection to the world was important to Child 21. This evidence suggests that children strive and quest for their connection to the world around them and to foster a sense of identity.

Although an overall presence of flow was demonstrated by the data, this was when children were specifically engaged on their own: many examples were also generated through the data where groups of children were engaged. All the Learning Stories demonstrated a level of engagement with, or suggested curiosity aroused by, the various provocations and elements within the environment. The provocations around the classrooms both provided many entry points for engagement and prompted the children to be curious. The children in the Learning Stories were engaged through their senses or through different modes and multisensory pathways. The elements from the environment engaged and stimulated the children, inviting them into an encounter, to discover or to be curious, to theorise or to hypothesise. This was demonstrated through the questions they asked their peers and through self-discovery as they were given many opportunities to explore, inquire, construct, create, play and examine.

An example provided by one teacher demonstrates the children's curiosity to discover what makes a conscience. They were able to represent their theories through drawings and they constructed their own knowledge. Their wisdom stemmed from their own ability to theorise and hypothesise through their reasoning, verbal communication or through various other modes. The children's quest for answers to their curiosity and their analysis of their world offered them, in return, a foundation for building curiosity about their meaning and connection to the world.

5.3.10 Indicator of spirituality expressed as asking bigger questions

The Learning Stories provide examples of children in their everyday settings. Within this context, the religious tradition of the school is faith-based so God is a part of the tradition and the teaching. The examples in which the children referred to God or a supreme being were through prior knowledge. In LS 4, Child 4, who was interested in the thunder, claimed that she had been told about God by her mother. She drew on this knowledge to establish her own meaning and connection to explain where the storm clouds came from. In LS 14, Child 18 and Child 20, who were playing with the figurine, answered a question about who made the body by also claiming that this was God.

This indicator of an expression of spirituality poses questions concerning the connection of children's spirituality and religion. If one aspect of a definition of spirituality is, as Becker (1994, p. 257) describes, 'a code word for the depth dimension of human existence', then, as we work to understand young children, imagination through play moves children towards transcendence (Myers 1997). This transcendence may or may not be towards God; when it is towards God, as the examples have indicated, the question may be raised about the children's exposure to God within a particular tradition and context.

5.4 The Reggio Emilia pedagogical approach and conditions for the expressions of children's spirituality

From the observations in the Learning Stories, it appears that the environments were consistently inspired by the pedagogy of the Reggio Emilia approach. The headings of each section are related to key aspects of the Approach (Maynard & Chicken 2010). In the following sections, I have outlined each of the indicators of expressions of spirituality within the approach in relation to the information from the interpretation of the data.

5.4.1 A child-centred approach

Throughout all the Learning Stories, the children were involved in play-based discovery and learning: there was the freedom to express themselves in natural ways. The Reggio Emilia philosophy upholds a child-centred approach and views children as intrinsically curious and capable, valuing free play and discovery as a context for learning (Fraser 2006; Maynard & Chicken 2010; Rinaldi 2006). Within the approach, children are able to symbolically represent their ideas and theories and to make meaning through many media such as drawing, painting, dance and movement, singing, speaking, gesture and play, with the teacher having the role of observing and listening to the children (Edwards et al. 1998; Fraser 2006). The context of play as a setting is thus inspired by the Reggio Emilia philosophy. As was evident across the Learning Stories, the environment provided for the children was child-centred, offering many modes of meaning-making. Another characteristic within all the examples was the manner and attitude of the teacher or adult who was present: they were not directly teaching the children but were listening and observing the children and, at times, providing 'scaffolding' and support.

For example, in LS 3 the children had rich learning materials in the environment readily accessed by the children: pencils, pens and paper, as well as the guinea pigs, all set out and/or presented for the children to interact with easily in the flow of their activity. Finding the paper and equipment did not require an adult's assistance: the environment did this with no intervention required. As the child became curious about a certain provocation, in this case, Child 3's curiosity about the guinea pig, the invitation to observe and to draw was there, thus allowing the child to proceed. The result from this encounter was the representation of the guinea pig in Child 3's drawing, as shown in the photograph. The photographs in LS 3 show how the guinea pigs were positioned and where Child 3 was sitting as she observed and explored this natural phenomenon.

The evidence in the data, through the interpretation of each of the Learning Stories, was that the environment provided multiple ways for the children to interact, express themselves and communicate their thinking. There was no expectation for one common outcome from their thinking or expressions; instead, it was recognised that the children needed the opportunity to discover, explore and construct their own meaning-making. The environment was thus a key component, providing conditions in which the children's spirituality could be evident. This child-centred approach within this context was inspired by the Reggio Emilia pedagogical approach whereby materials, interactions and activities are designed to challenge and provoke children's thinking, communication and understanding.

The evidence suggests that as the child engages with others, whether they are adults or peers, and engages with the environment, this child-centred approach, where learning is activated by the child, provides conditions for the children's expressions of spirituality.

5.4.2 The image of the child

A recurring theme in the Learning Stories was the evidence presented of an image of the child which exemplified the description of the 'strong image of the child' which originated from the Reggio Emilia educational project (see the literature review in Chapter 3). This concept of the image of the child was respected by the educators of each of the four cohorts within the context of this setting.

The intent of the learning spaces was one that promoted this image of the child, allowing this image to belong and to be present. This image of the child, as Rinaldi (2006) describes, is the anchor of the Reggio Emilia philosophy and was developed as educators listened to and observed children. Each of the following Learning Stories presents a strong image of the child who is curious and who has a searching mind (Wexler 2004).

In the preschool, Child 1 presented a strong image of the child, a child who is a participator and a protagonist within her learning environment, where she displayed opportunities for both independence and interdependence (Kinney & Wharton 2008) as she discovered music and translated her theories into meaningful symbols. Throughout the other Learning Stories, the interpretation of the image of the child is one which describes the child as an activator of their own learning and theorising. Child 4 independently used prior knowledge to relate to her own theories about thunder and God. Child 5, through the dramatic role play, demonstrated an image of the child who could make connections to learning about the real world.

Within the other learning space in LS 6, we were presented with two children, Child 6 and Child 7, who presented an image of the child as 'active inquirer' (Scheinfeld et al. 2008, p. 3). The two girls were, as Kinney and Wharton (2008) describe, 'active social agents and participants' (p. 3) in their own learning. They were able to relate their understandings of the life cycle of chickens to symbolic representation. Both girls were eager to discover and participate in the environment, together exploring their learning and viewpoints (Kinney & Wharton 2008).

In LS 6, Child 6 and Child 7 also showed resourcefulness in using prior knowledge to construct a chart which represented their theories of how chickens hatch. The data demonstrated an image of the child as purposeful and independent in constructing meaning. It also demonstrated an image of the child as relational with peers and with elements in the environment.

The two girls in LS 7, Child 8 and Child 9, presented a strong image of the child displaying an identity with a sense of agency and one in which the discovery and construction of knowledge were self-steered and self-directed (Rogers 2011; Scheinfeld et al. 2008). The girls encountered their discovery within the environment, independently focused on the spider, and then co-constructed their knowledge through their dialogue and their other encounters in the environment.

Further evidence of the 'strong image of the child' is drawn from the data and the interpretation of LS 8. Here, Child 10 demonstrated an image of the child as a unique learner, drawing on prior knowledge about the need for nature to be cared for as she painted her interpretation of peace. Her construction of the symbol of peace demonstrated an image of the child in which the child was purposeful and orchestrated her own interpretations in her painting of the concept of peace through the flower and its need for rain.

In LS 9, the relational image of the child is demonstrated when the children constructed their learning about the sea creature environment together. The interpretive summary of the Learning Story constructed from the data drew on evidence that the children in LS 9 were active agents in their learning as they co-constructed their ideas, hypotheses and points of view.

An image of the child as purposeful and resourceful is demonstrated by the data in LS 11, as Child 14 independently constructed and represented his abstract thoughts into something which was concrete as he made his colour block. In LS 15, the image of the children is as active agents in learning as they discover the location of a country on the globe.

The teacher observed the children's activities from a distance: as the participant observer, I observed and listened to the children. As the adults alongside the children, we allowed their learning to emerge independently and, in accepting and valuing their motivation and thinking, we acknowledged their identity through the image of the child as an active agent in encountering and using the possibilities of emergent learning (Scheinfeld et al. 2008).

As the researcher, I reflected on these findings and related this image of the child to a postmodern perception of childhood (see the literature review in Chapter 3). This view of childhood, as supported by Rogers (2011), is one in which children are 'active subjects who can give voice, construct meanings and transcend normative barriers' (p. 124).

5.4.3 The hundred languages of children

In each of the four cohorts, the variety of ways in which children construct, and express meaning was demonstrated. The multiple ways in which children theorise and explore their theories through various modes were indicated by children in the four cohorts. There were indications and examples of the children seeking meaning to the varied experiences they encountered: they continually made connections, appearing to search for meaning in their lives. As I observed, listened and collected the data, I was conscious of a drive which the children displayed, one which was not activated by the teacher, but a drive which occurred naturally and revealed ways 'in which children think, question and interpret reality and their own relationships with reality' (Clark et al. 2005, p. 19). In order to do this, they required a vessel to convey their meaning(s) and I described this vessel, with reference to the Reggio Emilia approach, as the 'hundred languages' of children.

The children thus displayed tenacity and drive both in their search for meaning and to convey this meaning. According to Clark et al. (2005), the search for the meaning of life begins as children, and they maintain that the 'search for life and the meaning of life and of the self in life is born with the child and is desired by the child' (p. 19). According to Malaguzzi (1998), children convey this search for meaning through the 'hundred languages' (see the literature review in Chapter 3).

Each of the Learning Stories indicated that multisensory elements, such as textiles, paints, musical instruments, flexible, aesthetic materials, natural materials and artefacts were made accessible. These elements all supported the many languages which the children chose to express and connect their search for meaning. The languages that children use may be non-verbal or demonstrated through gestures or in their play (see the literature review in Chapters 2 and 3).

5.4.4 The environment as third teacher

In each of the Learning Stories, the environments were created and designed by the teachers who took their inspiration from the Reggio Emilia approach. In each Learning

Story, vibrant examples of environments were presented that engaged and amazed the children, environments which were responsive to all of the children and their need to construct, discover and encounter knowledge and possibilities. The message communicated through each environment was that it was owned by the inhabitants, not solely by the teacher, but by all who participated within the environment, through the features and the elements which were carefully and attentively designed within each classroom. The notion of the environment as third teacher is derived from the Reggio Emilia philosophy and, as Fillipini points out, educators in Reggio Emilia speak of 'space as a container that favours social interaction, exploration and learning, but also messages and being charged with stimuli toward interactive experience and constructive learning' (Fillipini 1990, cited in Gandini 1998, p. 164).

Within the Learning Stories, these learning environments indicated that investigation was encouraged and, in each example, the children were able to lead their own investigation, with the adult merely 'scaffolding' from time to time and listening attentively to the children. The photographs provide evidence that the children are the activators of learning with the teachers not appearing in the photographs. If, as the researcher, I was involved in the conversation or asked questions, this was then stated: otherwise, the child was at the centre of the observation and the experience. The environment fostered an understanding that all children were to be understood and respected. One can see from the examples that the children were given the right to express themselves in many ways, for example, the chart made by the girls with the chickens (LS 6), the interpretation of the guinea pigs (LS 3) and the spider (LS 7), and the evidence of meaning-making which Child 1 produced about her theory of music (LS 1). In each scenario, there was no expectation that there was only one answer or that only one way would represent the children's search for meaning. The environment thus acted as the 'third teacher' whereby it offered flexible, engaging and responsive conditions for the children to discover and construct their own learning (Gandini 1998).

As suggested by the review of the literature (Caldwell 2003; Fraser 2006; Malaguzzi 1998; Schroeder-Yu 2008), the organisation of the physical environment is crucial to the Reggio Emilia approach. The photographs of the environments in the Learning Stories suggest an attention to aesthetics and beauty that offered multisensory layers and media which provoked encounters and the involvement of the children.

Individual differences among the children were acknowledged, as the girls with the spider (LS 7) used the environment to guide the flow of their own wonderings and the girls with the chickens (LS 6) were attracted to the natural phenomena in the environment. In addition to the points mentioned above, this environment offered attention to aesthetic pathways and provocations for children to discover and explore (Feeney & Moravcik 1987). The ways of knowing and making sense of the world were supported through the many components and features of the environment, with this demonstrated by Child 1 in LS 1 as she was able to move from one area to the other in the environment, utilising the range of materials and equipment which were around and available to her. Throughout all the Learning Stories, the interpretive summaries emphasised the key role and the many ways in which the environment supported the children's interaction.

The 'natural' environment is an integral element of all environments inspired by the Reggio Emilia approach (Caldwell 2003). Through the photographs and the detailed descriptions of the context, the environments illustrated in the Learning Stories provided evidence and examples of the ways in which nature was included in each environment.

The children's attraction to nature and to natural phenomena was a provocation for further wonderings or for asking bigger questions which may be interpreted as different indicators of the expression of spirituality.

5.5 Pedagogical conditions which foster the visibility of the spiritual expression of children

5.5.1 Play and the spiritual dimension

As seen through the discussion and the literature review, the Reggio Emilia approach is associated with a child-centred pedagogy in which play is valued. This style of pedagogy suggests a context for listening to and observing children in their everyday encounters and experiences and in the way in which they perceive the world (Mountain 2011). The way in which Child 2 in LS 2 interacted with the dinosaurs through play and the conversation he initiated about care and routines was, as Mountain (2011) proposes, 'another way of experiencing life' (p. 266). In each of these learning spaces and examples, the child had the freedom to choose how they would play and interconnect within that space. The context and pedagogy of freedom and flexibility in learning spaces are claimed by researchers (Mountain 2011; Painton 2009; Winnicott 1971) to be a context in which expressions or aspects of children's spirituality are demonstrated. Each of the children discovered objects or materials in the environment with which they played and which they enjoyed. Upton (2009) describes this as a way in which the child's spirit is blended and expressed: she describes surroundings in the environment as 'an invitation to the spirit of the child' (p. 359).

Within early childhood learning environments, play is generally an integral part of the pedagogy. Play has also featured as a recurring theme in the literature discussing young children's spirituality (Adams et al. 2015) in which connections are made to creativity and imagination that are inherent within play. Dowling (2005, as cited in Adams et al. 2015) suggests that pedagogical approaches, such as Reggio Emilia, which endorse creativity and imagination in play 'are further examples of enhancing spirituality in early years settings' (p. 8).

5.5.1.1 Recognising and listening to the image of the child

Through this layer of analysis regarding the expression of children's spirituality, there is some suggestion that the 'image of the child' could extend to include and encompass the spiritual dimension. Each example has provided us with indicators related to the spiritual expression of children as they seek to find meaning in their world and how they are connected to their world. The views of Adams et al. (2008) support this idea: they advocate for the spiritual dimension of childhood, describing this dimension as the ways in which children 'experience the world' and make connections to their views and understandings (p. 117). As the present inquiry moved through the questions and more data were provided, a reconceptualisation began to evolve in the understanding of spirituality in young children. This might also suggest that a hypothesis regarding the image of the child might guide and suggest a reconceptualisation of the working definition of spirituality. This might influence the understanding of the image of the child to be extended to include the *spiritual* image of the child. My research and my work with children strongly suggests that with authentic and sincere listening by the adult, we can scaffold and nurture children's spiritual language and truly see the spiritual image of the child.

5.5.2 The hundred languages: a vessel to express spirituality

Similarly, through the examples in the Learning Stories, it could be verified that the spiritual expression of children was demonstrated through the hundred languages. When understanding spirituality in young children, it seems that one requires an openness and acceptance of the multiple modes of expression which young children use. Researchers, for example, Adams et al. (2008), with regard to young children's spiritual dimension, advocate that:

> Artistic media, such as paintings, drama, dance, mime and music may provide avenues for children through which the spiritual may be expressed. These media may involve language, but often they will not. They do, however, enable children to express their spirituality through the ordinary, everyday activities of childhood.
> (p. 130)

In the current study, different modes of expression were encouraged through the variety of materials which were offered to the children. In LS 9, for example, there were the different materials that the children each added to their own jar and the variety of materials, textures, shapes and sizes from which they could choose for their environments for the sea creatures.

In LS 9, curiosity and engagement were evident, as displayed through the children's use of materials. It was also noted that they were interested in the phenomenon of the sea creature. Their imagination was evident and seen through their individual creations within the jars, as depicted in the photographs and drawings.

The environment offered 'scaffolding' for the children's creations through the materials provided: each child was individually and independently able to choose and decide on materials. The materials were offered without restriction, allowing the final creations to be individual. The hundred languages were evident through different modes of meaning-making. For example, LS 9 demonstrated that the children were able to verbally express their theories about the sea creature: 'Child 11 expressed that if the sea creature did not have this kind of environment, then it would die.' Child 12 verbally expressed: 'That they had to keep oceans clean and not dirty otherwise the creatures would die.' The children were able to transfer knowledge from one process to another through expressing themselves with materials and objects, which extended the hundred languages. The children's comments provided evidence which showed that they were curious about natural phenomena, were able to form theories about bigger questions to do with sustainability, and were making meaning through the experience. Creativity and imagination were evident from the individual children's creations: the materials were provided as a provocation, but each child produced their own unique sea creature environment and theory. In LS 9, as the children participated, the hundred languages and the indicators of the expression of spirituality were entwined.

5.5.3 The environment and provocations: nurturing the spiritual child

In relation to the Reggio Emilia approach and its connection with spirituality, the environment is a key factor when affording young children's spirituality. In my many discussions with teachers involved in this study, the environment was the nucleus for cultivation and nurturing spiritual expression of children.

Through the guiding principle of the Reggio Emilia approach of the 'environment as the third teacher', it can be strongly suggested that this may be a way of nurturing the innate spirituality in that young children. have. The elements of the environment, inspired by the Reggio Emilia approach, encouraged times when children were in wonder and awe. Through her contemporary research on children's spirituality, Sagberg urges that, in order to 'nurture what it means to be human', we must provide an environment which cultivates children's spirituality (Sagberg 2008, p. 355). Sagberg suggests that we provide children with environments which have spaces provided for various experiences, wonderings and reflections.

In relation to indicators of spirituality, as children are provided with opportunities for awe and wonder, they are expressing their spirituality (Hart 2003). The elements of nature not only sparked and engaged the children's curiosity; in addition, moments of awe and wonder emerged as the children were experiencing and interacting with natural phenomena and with nature itself, for example, the guinea pigs, the chickens and the natural materials in the environment. A point to note is from the work of Hart and Ailoae (2006–07), who state that connection to the natural world is paramount in evoking moments of awe and wonder. These moments in children are when they are 'attuned to the existential' (Hart & Ailoae 2006–07, p. 351). In the opinion of Louv (2005, cited in Hart & Ailoae 2006–07), the loss of opportunity for awe in connection with nature may significantly impact on the spiritual development of young children. As the experiences and encounters of the children transpired, moments of awe and wonder emerged and these were noted in the data. It is evident that children really did want to ponder and wonder why things were happening.

Drawing on Nye's research reminds us that when we are empathetic to perceiving children's spirituality, research has provided us with clues through the indicators and expressions that children display. Not all of these expressions are verbal: through their wondering, as is evident in children's expressions, gestures and manner, they enter into the 'depth and breadth of the spiritual universe' (Nye 2009, p. 38). Each child within the Learning Stories displayed these moments: Child 3 with her encounter with the guinea pig (LS 3); the two girls (Child 6 and Child 7) with the chickens, their fascination with the life cycle and their attraction to a new life in the young chicken (LS 6); and the girls (Child 8 and Child 9) with the spider and the way they wanted to discover more about the creature (LS 7). This seemed an unlikely attraction for two young girls who were in awe of the features and qualities of the spider, perceiving it to be beautiful and enjoying their discovery of the creature.

5.5.3.1 Aesthetics

In the view of Crawford and Rossiter (2006), the aesthetic dimension and responses to aesthetics are linked to spirituality. In the Learning Stories, all the elements of these environments displayed aesthetic components. The description of the areas of the learning spaces showed spaces which were not like traditional classrooms. Attention was given to the way that materials were displayed, and an appreciation of beautiful objects in the learning spaces was evident.

As suggested by de Souza's (2009) research, environments which evoke responses to beauty nurture spirituality. The children were in various states—of flow or of curiosity or of awe and wonder—that seemed to be provoked by aspects of the aesthetics. They were in environments enriched with natural materials with which they could interact. Examples included: Child 2 with the dinosaurs in LS 2 with all the different materials, such as bark, acorns and pine cones; the children in LS 9 representing the sea creature environment in jars using interesting bits of paper, figurines, glitter and coloured water; the multisensory experience for Child 13 in LS 10 with the sand, sea sponges and sea artefacts; and, in LS 12, Child 15 experiencing the sensory experience of the pipe cleaner and also fascinated by the beads hanging from the umbrella frame suspended from the ceiling. Children who are able to enjoy beauty and aesthetics have time to wonder (Baumgartner & Buchanan 2010; Coles 1990), and this wonder is an expression of their spiritual dimension.

5.6 Emerging themes, categories and criteria

This next section outlines the emerging themes, categories and criteria that have been generated by the data and documentation. The Learning Stories were only one aspect of data collection from each cohort. At the end of each week, as the researcher, I would review field notes, observations and the interview transcripts and, in so doing, would reflect on the emergence of possible themes.

The interviews were also included in this process of analysis and, as the audio-recordings were transcribed, the codes and patterns were extracted and the same analytical process took place.

The previous stage of deductive analysis strongly suggested that indicators of spirituality in young children were evident. In addition, the second stage of the deductive analysis suggested that aspects of the pedagogical approach inspired by Reggio Emilia provided conditions in which these indicators of spirituality were able to manifest. The next layer of analysis was to trace certain criteria surrounding the emerging themes. As I went through the Learning Stories, and the field notes and the interview transcripts, codes, patterns and categories were extracted. Through connecting the codes and categories, certain criteria surrounding the themes were synthesised across the data. The documentation that was collected was like an engine room of children's thinking and inner capacity for spiritual expression. It provided insights into how the work of childhood is so deep to explore. It is only adults who look and appreciate children for who they are that this wonderful dimension is able to be seen and subsequently nurtured.

5.6.1 Deductive analysis

As the analysis process and distillation of the data deepened, a 'lens' was used in the analysis. The lens constitutes the deductive stage of the multi-layered analysis whereby the indicators of expressions of spirituality were viewed through the lens of the elements and guiding principles of the Reggio Emilia approach. At the end of the chapter, a matrix is provided to show the reader the themes that emerged and how the lens was used in the analysis process.

As the multi-layered analysis progressed, it is important to note that, in this case study, the notion of a lens helped with each stage and layer of the process. Nye (1998, p. 60) claims that adults often lack the means to interpret and understand children's spirituality and must 'look between the lines' when observing children's behaviour.

In order to truly understand children, the lived experience within and the 'texts of life' (Binder 2011) that occurred, my aim in this research was to explore and interpret some persuasive modes of looking at and seeing what really exists. These modes of looking at or 'seeing children' have been derived from the guiding principles of the Reggio Emilia educational project and experience (Ceppi & Zini 1998).

This case study was 'fit for purpose', as advocated by Mukherji and Albon (2010). At times, as Mukherji and Albon (2010) articulate, innovative approaches to research may fall into the category of a 'gimmick approach' (p. 170). I maintain that the lens assisted in creating and presenting a case which explicitly attempted to 'preserve the wholeness, unity and integrity of the case' (Punch 2005, p. 145).

It is crucial to unpack these elements of my researcher lens to provide the clear intention of the analytical approach. I note here that the language used in some of the terms describing the lens stem from and are respectful to the Reggio Emilia educational project: I have expanded their guiding principles with the work of Ceppi and Zini (1998) to form my lens and filter in the interpretive, analytical process of this research. The terms and notions stem from the Reggio Emilia educational project; however, the intention is not to replicate the approach (Robertson 2006), but to provide a filter which allows an interpretation within a contextual and cultural setting.

The lens I have used for this study came from ideas presented by a research project conducted by educators and researchers within Reggio Emilia. These possibilities of opening up the existing reality of particular learning environments, encounters within these environments, and how we perceive them. The lens is derived from key words stemming from Ceppi and Zini's (1998) 'critical analysis of the cumulative experience of the municipal early childhood system of Reggio Emilia' and identified 'desirable characteristics of a space for young children' (Ceppi & Zini 1998, cited in Caldwell 2003, p. 108).

Each of the following sections has, as its heading, one of the emerging themes and, at the end of the chapter, these are summarised into a matrix. In this matrix, I outline how the lens has guided the clusters of patterns, codes and themes into further emerging categories which are then explored in the discussion chapter.

5.7 Rich normality and ordinary moments: a context and criteria for spiritual indicators

Children come into this world with fresh eyes to see all that is beautiful, embrace all that is joyful. They do this with open hearts, true wonder, true awe and curious minds.

Helena Card

Each classroom was a vast tapestry of normality and ordinary moment-to-moment experiences: it was within this tapestry that the children, according to the data generated, constructed theories and expressed themselves in multiple ways.

A common thread connecting the data was the notion of rich normality (Ceppi & Zini 1998) and ordinary moments that existed across the learning spaces. The 'rich normality' (Ceppi & Zini 1998) of the social context within this case was what I, as the researcher, noticed by listening carefully and observing the children. As the researcher and participant observer, I used the pedagogy of listening. In a similar way to the teachers, I displayed the concept of listening with all the senses as I observed the children during my visits. My analytical process ensured that I clearly and succinctly viewed the information and the phenomena that contributed to the data that I was gathering. As I reviewed the data, my choice of the filtered lens and this view were supported by Altheide and Johnson (1994), who maintain that the social world is interpreted by the researcher and that data analysis is 'based on the value of trying to represent faithfully and accurately the social worlds or phenomena studied' (p. 292).

The lens of 'rich normality' (Ceppi & Zini 1998) requires viewing the harmony and existence of many elements of the didactic interchange between what we see as normal interactions of childhood and that which constitutes an 'exceptionality of experience' (Ceppi & Zini 1998). This enables a reconceptualisation of the childhood personality and experience to search for a new view and the positive position and value of normality.

This lens encompasses a whole harmony of viewing the environment as a place that speaks to us, allowing us to view the hermeneutical elements, the richness and the essence of what is occurring. This lens allowed the researcher to distil information as the data were analysed, and to illuminate the existing themes and patterns. I refer also to Giamminuti's (2009) study and research involving the Reggio Emilia philosophy and her lens in interpreting the findings within the research and the manner in which 'rich normality' (Ceppi & Zini 1998) was able to position the researcher. This offered a lens for viewing and allowing the 'surprise' of the possibilities which occurred. As stated by Giamminuti (2009): '[s]urprise is an element which is viewed as enriching daily experience and normality. The unexpected is valued in Reggio Emilia for the possibilities it offers' (p. 131). As I documented the children's experiences through the photographs and the Learning Stories, I was presented with data which offered many possibilities for my case and inquiry to unpack and interpret through this lens. As the process evolved, the natural setting and the social world positioned within this case were observed and documented. Knowing that the social world is an interpretive world (Altheide & Johnson 1994), and in order to distil, interpret and refine the data, I used the data analysis process which assisted in constructing a 'clearer reality and a more sophisticated reality' of the phenomenon of young children's spirituality (Stake 1995, p. 101). As the emerging patterns and codes were generated from the data, the analytical process was supported by the layering approach and, as Gillham (2000, p. 95) describes, different angles and 'kinds of evidence' emerged. The Learning Stories, the photographs, the observational field notes and the interviews were related to one another and the intent of the researcher was to 'weave this evidence into a coherent narrative' (Gillham 2000, p. 95). Yin (2003, p. 83) describes this as 'a chain of evidence': this is the researcher's interpretation and thick description of the human experience (Merriam 2009).

In the following paragraphs, extracts from my notes lead the reader into a narrative of the experiences which provided the data from the four cohorts to illuminate the theme of 'rich normality' (Ceppi & Zini 1998).

> A rainy afternoon on a visit to the preschool learning environment presented me with possibilities; the unexpected was about to occur, ordinary moments were everywhere, the possibilities were endless. I walked through to see whether any of my focus children were there; I was pleased to see that Child 8 was outside.
> (Field notes 14/3/2012)

As the researcher and participant observer, I was listening with all my senses to the children in the Learning Stories. As I was present in this moment, I referred to Forman, Hall and Berglund (2001), where they 'appeal to educators everywhere to find the marvel in the mundane, to find the power of the ordinary moment' (Forman et al. 2001, p. 53). Each Learning Story describes children in their ordinary settings. The ordinary moments in the following stories are used as an example of how 'rich normality' (Ceppi & Zini 1998) is connected to children's expression of spirituality.

In LS 4, the environment seemed to enhance the experience with the design of the preschool enabling children to flow between the inside and the outside: they had an instant connection to nature and the outside world. In this instance, the attention to the design of the environment illuminated this ordinary moment. As an adult participant who listened to Child 4 during that moment, I was able to capture the moment's memory and her actions and thoughts as she expressed herself through the language of gesture and animation using verbal reasoning to construct her theory about the natural phenomenon. What became evident as the data were analysed was that 'the most deliberate acts of children flow from a theory they have from the social or physical world' (Forman et al. 2001, p. 52). Child 4 related her experience to prior knowledge and made a connection to, and formed an understanding of, something greater than her, a transcendent being which she named and to which she referred as 'God'. This reference to God was pointed out, and noted, as prior knowledge which had been passed on to her because her mother had told her about God.

Each classroom presented a unique version of the children's ordinary moments and the 'rich normality' (Ceppi & Zini 1998), which were part of their identity as a collective group. It was during another visit that I became a participant in another ordinary moment in the 'rich normality' (Ceppi & Zini 1998) and was able to record moments within the stimulating early years' learning environment.

Within the ordinary moments in the 'rich normality' (Ceppi & Zini 1998) of the learning environments, various provocations were located around the room to engage the children. In LS 8, an account of 'rich normality' (Ceppi & Zini 1998) is provided. A group of children were actively involved on one particular table. The provocation was about creating a 'peaceful' drawing. The environment offered many stimulating and varied experiences. Paints and colours were arranged to be easily accessible to all the children. They were able to independently express themselves through the language of painting. A provocation was put out on the table, 'Peace, what are peaceful colours for you? Paint a peaceful picture using your peaceful colours.'

I quote what I wrote in my field notes after Child 10 finished her painting:

> Child 10's representation of peace became a theory which flowed from an abstract understanding of the concept of peace to a visual representation about Child 10's personal understanding of this notion.
>
> (Field notes 6/6/2012)

As the adult participant, I listened during my encounter with Child 10 as the dialogue evolved in the moment: the rich experience provided for the children and for Child 10 existed in the ordinary. The experience was possible because elements in the environment created the pathway for expression and there was the allowance for the child to have 'a moment to be fully in their experience' (Upton 2009, p. 354). Upton describes the world of the child as one where children continuously 'fly from moment to moment with joy and wonder' (p. 351). According to Upton (2009), it is within each moment that a child has the opportunity to express their spirituality. This example and how Child 10 expressed herself in recounting her moment showed that she was in a flow of consciousness, expressing joy and flowing through wonder and the beauty of her painting as she theorised and connected with wider knowledge and phenomena. These expressions demonstrated by Child 10 can be linked to the spiritual indicators identified within this inquiry. The analysis in the Learning Story highlighted the demonstrated indicators. As the adult who sat alongside this child, I opened myself to listening to her and was open to noticing how Child 10 expressed herself in multiple ways. The insights of Upton (2009) support this attitude and interpretation of the moment involving children:

> ... One must allow a child his/her moment of wonder. Children need to know that they are listened to. If we adults can allow a moment of space before answering their questions, we nurture this moment of spiritual curiosity .... When the children feel this empathy from us, they connect with our hearts. We must be teachers with 'listening hearts'.
>
> (p. 354)

As I participated alongside Child 10 with the intention of purposeful and open listening, the method of the pedagogy of listening became illuminated, supporting the understanding of the richness of listening whereby the listener is open to the other's thoughts, as supported by Rinaldi:

> If we believe that children possess their own theories, interpretations, and questions, and are protagonists in the knowledge-building processes, then the most important verbs in educational practice are no longer 'to talk', 'to explain' or 'to transmit' ..., but 'to listen'. Listening means being open to others and what they have to say, listening to the hundred (and more) languages, with all our senses.
>
> (Rinaldi 2006, pp. 125–126, cited in Clark et al. 2005)

At this point, the pedagogy of listening was part of the culture of the classroom and a way of understanding and listening to children, understanding their capacities and potential. For me allowing the pedagogy of listening with all my senses gave presence to the innate spirituality.

Within the 'rich normality' (Ceppi & Zini 1998) of these learning environments, the adult becomes a partner in the discoveries and the explorations of the children. The Reggio Emilia approach was the inspiration that led the teachers to provide learning activities that promoted a belief in the unexpected and a sense of open-ended, unlimited possibilities. The teachers created a context which offered a balancing of opportunities for multiple expressions, which included spiritual expression with the indicators for spiritual expression noted in the data. Spiritual indicators and expressions of spirituality were thus demonstrated, and the elements of the Reggio Emilia pedagogical approach were present within the context of the Learning Stories and among those who participated in the 'rich normality' (Ceppi & Zini 1998) of the everyday.

This example also presented evidence of expression through the hundred languages: painting was the vessel that transported Child 10's thoughts and connected her thought to meaning. The environment allowed her to find this mode of meaning: it offered multiple pathways for expression.

The experiences within each Learning Story occurred during children's normal encounters with their environments. The 'rich normality' (Ceppi & Zini 1998) provided conditions for the children to discover new ways of thinking and knowing during uninterrupted times of play. The conditions of 'rich normality' (Ceppi & Zini 1998) allowed indicators of the expressions of spirituality to be evident in the children.

However, when delving deeper and extracting further interpretation from the data, the findings also offer a redirection into the 'empirical world of the lived experience' (Denzin and Lincoln 2000, p. 179). The 'lived experience' is within the criteria of 'rich normality' (Ceppi & Zini 1998), a context in which the holistic environment naturally allows spirituality to be expressed and, as Sagberg (2008) suggests, allows for 'spirituality as a mark of being human' (p. 367) to be conveyed. When spirituality is expressed in the conventional, and in what I term the ordinariness of the normal, commonplace routines of childhood, that this leads to the heightened discovery of children's spirituality and to extraordinary moments.

5.7.1 Playful pedagogies: harvesting spiritual dispositions

Among the educators within this case study, a constant topic of conversation was the overcrowding of the curriculum. Their commitment to the Reggio Emilia approach allowed them to always seek a balance and create opportunities for playful pedagogies where children 'can construct their own worlds and develop a sense of themselves as creator' (Goouch 2008). In Goouch's examples of playful pedagogies, she draws on the Reggio Emilia approach where children are respected and allowed time for creating, being and interacting with others. In the case study site, a sense of timeless learning and importance was maintained regarding this time for children to play and to encounter possibilities.

Within the 'rich normality' (Ceppi & Zini 1998), and through providing time in their weekly programs which was centred on play, exploration, discovery and inquiry, the teachers provided the children with uninterrupted time, a time when play and open-ended possibilities were used as a guide for children to construct their learning.

It is during these times of playful pedagogy and timeless learning that children can be observed in the flow of consciousness: they can experience an awakening of the imagination. As I watched the children during these periods of uninterrupted time, I observed their engagement and involvement in exploring and playing where they were guided by the experience of the moment and followed their intuition into new spaces and new spheres of knowing. It was a time when flow was a means of opening up new ways of being and thinking, and of knowing and expressing the spiritual dimension and capacity of young children occurring in what Adams et al. (2008) describe as 'ethereal' moments (p. 55). It was a time when these indicators of the expression of spirituality appeared visible in the data and were able to flourish and exist as a natural part of the child's being.

It is through play that children independently relate to, and make meaning of, their world (Rogers 2011). They identify themselves in relation to their world and how they are connected to it, as they relate to others in the world.

Apart from co-creating and interweaving their meaning and relationship to the world and to one another, play, and a pedagogy that supports play, offers a pathway for spiritual expression. Each Learning Story, through the analysis process, noted the expressions of spirituality that occurred. The Learning Stories highlighted the context of and criteria for allowing a playful pedagogy to occur in the children's experiences and how focus was placed on 'enriching the children's expressive tools for self-steered meaning-seeking and construction, as well as time, space and materials for doing so' (Guss 2011, p. 124). The provision of a setting that invites playful pedagogy also supports a position on childhood, a postmodern perspective and view of children 'as active subjects who can give voice, construct meaning and transcend normative barriers' (Guss 2011, p. 124).

5.7.1.1 Uninterrupted time

Following is an example from my field notes from the Rec/One B of the classroom context, amidst a setting in which playful pedagogy was valued, where creativity was encouraged and where children were absorbed in the uninterrupted time to flourish in creative moments of flow.

> As I entered the classroom, groups of children were involved in play-based activities. As I entered the Rec/One B classroom, groups of children were involved in play-based activities. I observed that the children played alongside one another by allowing each other to be within their own flow of creativity and thinking. The environment was set up for the children to work independently and to be in control of their own learning, interaction and discovery. There was a sense of agency and independence among the children: as I observed, the teacher floated around engaging and participating at various points with different children, allowing them to direct the experience and the encounters.
>
> (Field notes 30/5/2012)

Uninterrupted time allowed the children to participate at their own pace: no deadline and no outcome were specified. Children were given this time to play and discover. It provided a time for the children in which spiritual indicators could be expressed.

5.7.1.2 Creativity, flow and imagination within uninterrupted time

Throughout the Learning Stories, patterns emerged which incorporated the children's creativity, flow and imagination. Each narrative presented a scenario where the children were oriented (Scheinfeld et al. 2008) in different ways during their encounters and learning experiences.

The learning environments, with their aesthetic characteristics, materials and provocations providing a variety of possibilities for ideas and focus, fostered an orientation in the children where they were engrossed in a 'flow' of sustained learning and discovery. This orientation is often hard to define and I have heard many educators, including myself over time, describe this orientation as children 'being in the zone'. However, through the work of Csikszentmihalyi (1997, 2002), this orientation which children experience and educators observe is considered to be a holistic sensation when a person experiences total involvement. Through the ordinary experiences of childhood, this sense of flow occurs naturally and repeatedly. Flow, according to Csikszentmihalyi (1997, 2002), is a time when there is an experience of concentrated attention and where one is free. This allows the feeling that the activity is being managed by itself or by an outside influence, giving rise to an attentiveness and what is described as a single flow, without outside interruptions or distractions.

In addition, flow is described as when the action of the activity in which one is involved and the awareness of this activity become merged (Csikszentmihalyi 1997, 2000). Each of the Learning Story examples demonstrates both the flow of consciousness and the awareness of the activity, with no attention given to the variety of activities going on around the child in the environment. Each of the children is photographed during Exploration Time when many activities are going on; yet each photograph demonstrates the flow of consciousness within each individual child's activity. Inspired by the Reggio Emilia approach, the environment is set out with attention to small details and with the intention that the environment act as the 'third teacher', providing opportunities for flow to occur naturally.

As the Learning Stories unfolded, moments occurred in the children's natural setting which displayed creativity and imagination, both of which are also expressions of children's spirituality (Hyde 2008a; de Souza 2009). As children experience moments and activities in which they are oriented in creativity and imagination, they are also provided with opportunities to go beyond the obvious and to conceive beyond the known (Champagne 2001; Hay & Nye 2006; Hyde 2008a). As suggested by Hyde (2008a), it is during these times, as creativity and imagination interface and children are in the flow of consciousness, that their spirituality is expressed. In each of the experiences, as subsequently outlined, the adult was an insignificant participant, only entering the experiences at certain times. There was no expectation for answers from the children but instead respect for the emergence of the experience. The adult did not know what to expect, but were open to various possibilities depending on where the child's direction of flow was going within the learning encounter.

5.7.1.3 Rhythm of flow: integrating the mind, body and spirit

Within this setting, the Reggio Emilia approach was embedded in everyday routines and interactions: the approach was connected to the students and the educators within the school. It unconsciously became a part of everyone's conversation and participation within the setting.

If someone was to spend time looking through the many memories recorded by the teachers in their special books on the welcoming tables, something would become very obvious: traces of the Reggio Emilia approach appear to be present and embedded in the way that things are done in the context of the day. It seems to be natural in this pedagogical approach to provide a criterion which allows children to think, to feel and to be in different ways, allowing their spiritual expression to be visible.

The pedagogy and the environment set up for children within this context. A 'rich normality' (Ceppi & Zini 1998) allows the teacher to understand how children express themselves with the hundred languages.

The Reggio Emilia approach nurtures spirituality because children's thinking is not stifled; they are allowed to explore many outcomes or expressions of learning. This is evident in the Learning Stories, where children were not expected to give direct answers: they were able to play, theorise and make meaning from their inquiries and encounters within the environment.

5.8 The system and scheme of the space

The term 'the system and scheme of the space' (Ceppi & Zini 1998), which describes the environment, the space, a system and a scheme, has been adapted from the research and suggestions made by Ceppi and Zini (1998). It presents a lens through which to view the environment as an evolving organism offering children multiple layers of experiences within their natural daily encounters and interactions. Within the case study, the environment was a living presence and integral to our understanding of how children express themselves through many modes and many experiences, and how their creativity is enhanced through the elements of the environment. The 'system of the space' is a system that endorses a welcome into the environment: it invites children and adults into a rich multisensory experience, a synthesis of cognition and creation (Caldwell 2003). It embraces aesthetics and beauty, and offers patterns within the scheme for exploring and creating: it provides a platform and an invitation through which to find oneself and to understand one's identity within life. All children, according to Ceppi and Zini (1998), are born with an innate capacity which allows them to explore, discriminate and interpret reality through their senses.

The multisensory environment, and the understanding of the space in which children interact and learn, are integral to the Reggio Emilia approach. Within this case study, it was fundamental to understand how and why the environment that we create for children and the modes in which children express themselves may help to redefine and reconceptualise childhood in relation to their spirituality.

The environment offered a multisensory, aesthetic, creative landscape within which the children could exist, belong and be. It provided opportunities for the children to have a variety of ways in which to express themselves. It also provided others, including myself as researcher and all those who interacted with the children, with the opportunity to see the many levels and dimensions where the children encountered and interacted. This is evident in the Learning Stories where the children freely accessed a variety of materials, had the opportunity for uninterrupted play, and could engage with materials or with other children.

> The search for life and for the self is born with the child, and this is why we talk of the child who is competent and strong, engaged in this search towards life, towards others and towards the relationships between the self and life.
> (Rinaldi 2006, pp. 111–112)

Viewing this inquiry and exploration through this lens strongly supported the researcher in the analysis as the layers became refined: the interpretive view of the natural environments revealed information about how the children existed within this setting.

5.8.1 Relational, interconnecting spaces

The environment inspired by the Reggio Emilia pedagogical approach creates a space for interconnecting and relational spaces, a space which cultivates relationships with the multisensory environment and with those who occupy the space. With regard to their spirituality, children require spaces which honour and respect their spiritual way of being and a space which allows their spiritual expression to be nurtured (Bellous & Csinos 2009). Balanced environments which allow for spiritual expression allow the spiritual style of expression to become visible and to exist, with this view supported through the work and research of Bellous and Csinos (2009). A holistic approach to the environment takes into account the relational and interconnecting pathways necessary for spiritual expression to exist, as children are connected to each other, to elements in the environment and to others.

Holistic learning can be described and interpreted by its honouring of the connections: between linear thinking and intuition; between subjects; between mind and body; with a sense of belonging in communities; and with the self and with others (Taggart 2001). As the research continued and I became immersed in the analysis of the data, each narrative provided a landscape where, as I looked at the Reggio Emilia approach, I saw these connections to holistic learning and how they had been woven into the fabric of the school. Examples portrayed children who were allowed to explore their world through the processes of thinking, using their intuition and perception to expand their connection to, and understanding of, their world. The connection between the body and mind was constantly being used as a vehicle for expressing the child's ideas and understanding. Furthermore, according to Swann (2008), it is through the hundred languages that the 'in-depth capacity and expressive vocabulary of each learning medium' (p. 36) reveals children's cognitive insights.

Many of the examples of children interacting in the environment portrayed an integration of thought, emotions and the senses. The pedagogy and practice provided the medium through which this occurred in the way that the learning spaces were designed and the multiple entry points offered to children to involve them and engage them. Miller (2006) describes such a setting, where there is an impact on the 'intellect, the body, emotions and spirit' (p. 6), as holistic. The educators in Reggio Emilia itself also describe the approach as holistic (refer to the literature review in Chapter 3).

Research conducted by Eaude (2005) generated findings which suggest that spirituality is seen to be embedded in the environments which teachers create, environments which emphasise the importance of multiple and varied experiences and relationships. Inspired by the Reggio Emilia approach, and as seen in the examples highlighted in the Learning Stories, spaces have been created where these experiences and relationships can occur. In the preschool, many of the children were intrigued by and engaged with their environment and the sensory experiences available. Moments of spiritual expression stimulated by the relationship and interactions with elements in the environment are highlighted in the extracts from the field notes and the photographs.

5.8.1.1 Beautiful spaces: where spirituality manifests

Provocations (see the literature review in Chapter 3) were used by the teachers to engage and invite the children's curiosity. Many of these provocations were related to nature; however, others were designed and placed with attention to beauty. These beautiful elements within the environment helped to shape the beliefs and practice of the learning spaces.

As the provocations served to offer possibilities for the children to transform experience and feelings into expressive modes, they were part of the style of pedagogy which was prevalent in this setting. The environment also presented some spaces with the intention of evoking a sense of inquisitiveness in the children. The educators who created these environments were inspired by the theory and knowledge from the Reggio Emilia approach:

> Educators in Reggio Emilia speak of space as a 'container' that favours social interaction, exploration and learning, but they also see space as having educational content, that is, as containing educational messages and being charged with stimuli towards interactive experience and constructive learning.
> (Edwards et al. 1998, p. 164)

The learning spaces within this case study hold two unique and connecting elements: they propose a sense of beauty through their aesthetic qualities and they contain materials which offer open-ended possibilities.

The materials and elements of the environment were presented with the intention of offering the children journeys of potential and opportunities to absorb and understand concepts in various ways. The children were also invited into an aesthetic experience which was provided by many of the natural materials, such as surfaces with different textures and colours. Lim (2005) implies that early childhood educators should reconsider beauty as a curriculum resource. The scholarly research which Lim (2005) conducted reveals 'the importance of cultivating a sense of beauty among young children' (p. 371).

As Curtis and Carter (2003) remind us, beauty and aesthetic elements serve to offer a pathway for the active imaginations that young children bring into their learning environments. Children use objects and materials to help them to represent the myriad of things that they are thinking about and discovering. These objects may offer creative experiences, they may engage the senses or they may provide the opportunity for intriguing discoveries as the child explores on their own or with peers or adults. All these flexible experiences which a beautiful environment offers lead to aesthetic experiences for young children which may ignite their imagination and thought to 'facilitate new perceptions' (Lim 2005, p. 370).

Aesthetic elements in their learning spaces may open new trajectories for children's perception and understanding. New perceptions foster a pathway to transcend from the 'known to the unknown' (Myers 1997, p. 86). When discussing the spiritual dimension of the child, the concept of transcendence is crucial, for it is through understanding what contributes to transcendence that an understanding of children's spirituality becomes clearer for educators. Champagne (2003) and Hyde (2004, 2008a) both maintain that a person embodies their spirituality and that spirituality is innately human. Other scholars (Hart 2003; Hay & Nye 2006; Ruddock & Cameron 2010) affirm that this innate spirituality manifests in the way each person seeks connection to, and to be relational with, their world, and that this means of finding and knowing leads to the process of transcendence. As Adams et al. (2008) explain, the transcendent process is 'a meta cognitive process which adds value to people's ordinary and everyday perspectives' (p. 15).

In relation to young children, this offers new ways of knowing and perceiving and, as Berryman (1985) suggests, young children 'live at the limit of their experiences most of the time' (p. 26). They seek clarity of vision, and to evoke their imagination, intelligence and curiosity through a learning environment which pays attention to beauty and aesthetics: as the scholarly research suggests, this leads to a journey of new perceptions. The data have generated moments in the Learning Stories where the environments have sparked children's curiosity and imagination, offering a realm of new possibilities and opportunities and discovering an outlook on the world and 'sensing how one fits in' (Adams et al. 2008, p. 49). Materials which provoke various responses also move children's thinking and expression to a richer, more meaningful response and, according to Werner and Kaplan (1963), can be viewed as having 'transcendence expressive qualities' (p. 37). As Myers (1997) suggests, transcendence describes the process of going over and beyond limitations and obstacles, and this transcendence, according to Adams et al. (2008), is the essence of spirituality. In each of the Learning Stories, the possibilities were not predicted by the teachers as the children encountered the elements in the environments. The children perceived and interpreted the environment through being active agents, forming their own perceptions and responses.

5.8.1.2 Aesthetics and beauty as an activator for learning

A distinctive characteristic of this setting was the appearance of the learning spaces, which did not look like the traditional institutions and classroom settings that are more familiar to all of us. The traditional early learning classroom, with its rows of desks and bright colours, abounds with pinboards of colourful posters, signs and visuals that create a 'noise', a collage of information which is overwhelming and, at times, becomes just a blur of colour and words. However, in the study's setting, there seemed to be no evidence of visual noise: there was a blending of the aesthetics using natural materials, plants and multisensory materials.

The preschool learning space, being separate from the early learning classrooms, had a different layout and a larger outside space, with greater opportunity to invent and create spaces in distinctive ways. The garden areas, small tables, hidden spaces, access to multiple materials and a variety of equipment suited the layout and the connection between the design of the indoor and outdoor areas. The many elements imposed and offered a sense of intrigue: the way in which they were placed appeared to send an invitation and ask anyone who entered to examine, touch and discuss. Thus, provocations were evoked and inspired. The identity of the elements in the environment, ranging from the tables and chairs to the natural objects and multisensory materials, would go through a process of metamorphosis, as the children and adults worked and interacted within this environment. Nothing remained the same as these elements were interconnected, utilised, changed, theorised and expressed.

The attention given to these classrooms and learning areas has been inspired by the Reggio Emilia approach in which: colours are softer; there is attention to light and colour; aesthetics and beauty are valued; and materials, lights and natural elements are all present to create a harmonious learning space. Desks were arranged to invite collaboration and dialogue and for setting up provocations which engaged curiosity and wonder. There was no hint of rows of tables and shares with no room to move and interact, converse and co-construct knowledge.

In what appeared to be part of the natural practice of this setting, a thread of attention to aesthetics was woven through the areas of the early learning classrooms. Provocations were set out waiting for someone to explore the possibilities, for the construction of theories or for the pure wonder that they inspired. The aesthetics were prominent, the fundamental characteristic which contributed to the uniqueness of this setting.

The aesthetic aspect of the setting was clearly an element used in encouraging the expression of spirituality. As the children flowed through these spaces, it seemed there was a connection to the multisensory environment and a rhythm in which the children naturally engaged. The connection to aesthetics within a space invites the child into a journey of contemplation and provides times where spirituality becomes apparent.

I recall some extracts from my field notes:

> I walked into the Reception/One A classroom during Exploration Time which is a play-based discovery time in the classroom, a very relaxed environment. Various provocations were around the room to engage children. I looked at how the aesthetics directed the flow of imagination and creativity, how these indicators of spirituality were present and alive in the classroom. The simple, yet provocative way in which the teacher had designed the spaces aesthetically allowed for the expression of spirituality – from the guinea pigs which sat in the middle of a set of tables which provoked bigger questions and thoughts, wonder and awe as each child watched with intent the way the animals moved, and how they paid attention to their detail. In the foyer, caterpillars were eating leaves on a plate which had been set up: different groups of children go out and stare at this natural phenomenon, trying to form theories about the life cycle, trying to connect to the wonder of nature. They hold up the magnifying glasses, look at the caterpillars from different directions.
>
> The children are fascinated: some laugh out loud excitedly, some just stare, others describe to each other with great detail what this looks like. A simple provocation creates many levels of engagement. The life cycle of the butterfly started with this provocation of the caterpillars: it will be a learning journey to explore and emerge. A table was set with real-life caterpillar pictures: the striking colours and beautiful patterns were explored by the children. Beautiful photos capturing various caterpillars were arranged; a mirror was placed underneath the plant with the caterpillars; magnifying glasses were placed around for the children to view and discover the caterpillars.
>
> The Year One class is offered the opportunity to represent their image of the caterpillars through observational drawings. The colourful photos are scattered on a table; the paint pots have the matching colours which are corresponding to the colourful pictures, creating a visual balance. An opportunity to be creative and to use their imagination in their representations, at the same time, marvelling at the beauty of the provocations, the natural experience of viewing the live creatures and having the time to be absorbed and have moments of flow. I note how I felt intrigued myself, how I became immersed in the flow, watching the children create.
>
> (Field notes 22/4/2012)

A table was set up in the foyer area between the learning spaces: the provocations on the table were set out by the educators in this area with the intention that the children's interest and curiosity would be engaged.

> In the foyer area, I too joined the children in fascination. I was attracted by the beautiful assembly and layout which was set up: the colours, the arrangement, the attention to materials like the magnifying glass which offered another dimension for seeing and perceiving. At one time, I found myself just looking close up at a section of the caterpillar, noticing the way its body was so beautifully patterned.
>
> (Field notes 22/4/2012)

As children have the freedom to interact with the aesthetics and elements of beauty in the environment, they are also able to enjoy 'life's mysteries' (Baumgartner & Buchanan 2010, p. 92). As they reflect and wonder, they are also asking and inquiring: according to Coles (1990), that inquiring and questioning are at the heart of spirituality.

Likewise, in the current study, the opportunities through the aesthetic provocations in the environment offered the children time and space to appreciate beauty, to marvel at the mystery and splendour of nature. The caterpillar and the magnifying glasses, the stimulus pictures all created a myriad of items about which to marvel. This engaged the children and they were offered the time to encounter and marvel leading to awareness and an appreciation of the unknown. Scholarly research (Baumgartner & Buchanan 2010; Coles 1990; Myers 1997) suggests that these opportunities may be seen as ways in which children express their spirituality and as ways that facilitate spiritual development.

5.9 Osmosis

The lens in the current study is derived from the Reggio Emilia educational project and extends the concept of spaces and relationships. This lens supports the understanding that unstimulating environments will dull our perceptions (Ceppi & Zini 1998). This lens, according to the Reggio Emilia educators, describes the interface of materials and objects in the environment as operating through a process of osmosis whereby children absorb the environment through their senses. The exchange of information between the materials and the senses ignites curiosity, serving to invite new knowledge and perceptions. The multisensory aspects spiral the imagination and creativity into a different mode of awareness and children 'flow' through the rhythm and connection of the materials and the creative opportunities.

Caldwell (2003) reveals, in her interpretation of the Reggio Emilia approach, that osmosis is in the characteristics of the space. The multisensory aspects of a space allow children to discover using their body and all of their senses. Caldwell (2003) describes the richness of the sensory experience as: '[s]ensory navigation that exalts the role of synaesthesia in cognition and creation, fundamental to the knowledge building process and the formation of the personality' (p. 108).

5.9.1 Creativity and expression

The value of creativity as an element woven through aspects of the curriculum was highlighted through the ways in which the teachers allowed the children to discover and explore phenomena.

The Year One class was involved in an ongoing theme of 'creation', a theme that integrated many subject areas. The class teacher provided a context and the criteria for the children to express their learning as they explored the cycle of the changing seasons through creativity and expression, and an artist was invited to work alongside the children and the teacher to harvest the creativity. As the children expressed their creative ideas, there was a sense of a deep and collective understanding of the changing world through the seasons.

The children were invited by the artist to represent their understanding of the cycle of the seasons through patterns. These patterns were then used to create a collective representation of the cycle of the seasons. The portrait of the seasons sits in the garden area of the school as a memory of the children's interpretations. Throughout the school, there was an emphasis on creativity and art. Children were offered many media though which they could express themselves. Visiting artists were readily welcomed into the school to work alongside the children on various projects.

From the very early years in the preschool, art and creativity had a special emphasis and place in the school. Each year, the preschool would hold an art exhibition and, throughout the time of my data collection and observations, the preschool children were preparing for their art exhibition. The theme for that year was 'Splitting Image' and the children were invited to create a portrait of themselves from the back and the front. It was a beautiful provocation for creativity and open-ended questions and discovery.

Throughout the time of my visits, many children were seen looking at and observing themselves in mirrors placed around the preschool learning space.

The children were theorising through this creative venture. The art exhibition posed the question to children about a 'splitting image' and they were asked to draw their interpretation. Materials were freely accessible to the children; small tables were set with paints and brushes; various mirrors were placed around the painting area. All the photographs demonstrate that the children were able to express themselves through creativity and imagination. As the children painted, their vocalisations were recorded.

5.10 Narration

Through the use of this lens in the current study, examples of the emerging themes were presented. The field notes I collected, and the photographs I took of the children interacting within their environments, were collated into Learning Stories providing narratives of the experience. These provided a visible and transparent view of the children and their expressions and provided data for interpretation within the case study. It also provided credibility and reliability for the research. Documentation used by the educators of Reggio Emilia offers a narrative of the possible, a way of seeing, of positioning oneself in the rich possibilities of interpretation. Rinaldi (2006) posits the following view of documentation:

> Documentation not only lends itself to interpretation but is itself interpretation. It is a narrative form, both intrapersonal and interpersonal communication, because it offers those who document and those who read the documentation an opportunity for reflection and learning.
>
> (pp. 70–71)

The lens of documentation is also embellished by Rinaldi who offers the further view that: '[d]ocumentation is thus a narrative form. Its force of attraction lies in the wealth of questions, doubts and reflections that underlie the collection of data …' (Rinaldi 2006, p. 71).

In relation to the design of the case and its limitations and boundaries, documentation opened up the finding of the concentrated narrative lens on the school setting and environment. The lens of narration (Ceppi & Zini 1998), affiliated within Reggio Emilia-inspired thinking, suggests that the school provided:

> [v]isibility and transparency of the children's processes of research and cognition … [s]elf representation, the capacity of each space to narrate all the choices and references that generate the school environment, like a hologram.
>
> (Ceppi & Zini 1998, p. 25)

Thus, I have captured the visibility of children interacting in natural environments and used the field notes, observations and photographs in the form of Learning Stories. These were designed so that, as the researcher, I would provide integrity both in terms of the nature of this research, confined within the boundaries of the case study by the individual school setting and environment, and in terms of the findings within the 'hologram' of the setting of the research.

5.10.1 Respecting the voice and agency of the child

A common element which emerged from the data was the child as an active agent in the learning process as they encountered and were absorbed and engrossed as a participant in the learning space. As the interviews were analysed and the layering process applied, the teachers offered multiple aspects which supported this emerging theme of children as active agents in learning. To respect the child in such terms demonstrates the role of the educator and adult, as being one which respects the strong image of the child. The teacher and children become co-constructors of knowledge and theories.

The lens of 'narration' (Ceppi & Zini 1998) is one which values documentation opening up a landscape of understanding:

> An environment that documents not only results but also the processes of learning and knowledge building, that narrates the didactic paths and states the values of reference. The environment generates a sort of psychic skin, an energy-giving second skin made of writings, images, material, objects and colours, which reveals the presence of the children even in their absence.
> (Ceppi & Zini 1998, p. 25)

Viewing the child through this lens provides a context in which to revisit the child and the learning which they encounter. Allowing children to draw their theories and to record the children's drawings and the documented conversation which sits alongside the drawings presents a way of seeing the agency with which a child approached theories and makes meaning of abstract and complex concepts.

Strong parallels exist between documentation and Max van Manen's description of human science research (Felstiner, Kocher & Pelo 2006). I transcribed this parallel with a view that the lens of 'narration' (Ceppi & Zini 1998) allowed the documentation to reflect the phenomenon of daily life within the 'hologram' or environment of the research setting where a particular pedagogy and practice inspired by the Reggio Emilia approach were taking place.

> Pedagogy requires a phenomenological sensitivity to lived experience [children's realities and life-worlds]. Pedagogy requires a hermeneutic ability to make interpretive sense of the phenomena of the life-world in order to see the pedagogic significance of situations and relations of living with children.
> (van Manen 1990, p. 2, cited in Felstiner et al. 2006)

As I presented the Learning Stories within the case and viewed them through the lens of 'narration' (Ceppi & Zini 1998), and certainly through the power of this understanding of narration, this suggested that the principles of Reggio Emilia, in relation to documentation, offer a pedagogical lens for understanding children. As I worked through interpreting and connecting themes within the Learning Stories, the lens of 'narration' (Ceppi & Zini 1998) refined, distilled, extracted and concentrated my observations into ideas, concepts, themes and my findings. In relation to thinking about this research and the integrity of this case study research, 'narration' (Ceppi & Zini 1998) provided me with an authentic and reliable tool for interpreting data but also provided a broader lens for affiliating and connecting the inquiry itself with the Reggio Emilia approach.

If children are considered meaning-makers and are respected for their theories and participation in their own learning, we are illuminating their agency and their active roles in their learning (Kim & Darling 2009). Through respecting the strong image of the child where the child is seen as powerful and competent, inquisitive and a natural researcher who is searching for ways of being and understanding their world (Malaguzzi 1998), we are recognising the child as a capable agent in their everyday discoveries and encounters. When adults respect children in this way, they are able to open themselves to treating children as active subjects and are open to recognising that young children have a distinct perspective of the world (Kim & Darling 2009).

The lens of 'narration' (Ceppi & Zini 1998) assists in affiliating the real-life situations of children and in understanding how their sense of agency and active roles in learning also relate to their expressions of spirituality, thus leading to more understanding about this phenomenon in relation to young children.

Children's ways of being are illuminated through the Learning Stories. They are seen as children with rights rather than needs (Malaguzzi 1993; Rinaldi 1998a). This understanding of children is integral to the Reggio Emilia approach (Hewett 2001) and opens up the expanse of children's capacities and ways of being in, and perceiving, their learning environments. Included in children's ways of being is their innate spirituality and this can only be illuminated through a pedagogy which respects the holistic nature of the child.

Not only is the child an active agent but, according to Hewett (2001) who expands on the image of the child, the child is an active constructor of knowledge, an active researcher and an active social being. The umbrella of the child as an active agent encompasses a broad image of the child: one could suggest that this image is of the child who strives to be noticed and has the right to be noticed for their immense capacity as a human being. As a human being they are also a spiritual being.

In this study, the lens of 'narration' (Ceppi & Zini 1998) captured moments of the children's learning and provided avenues for further thought and perception about children and learning. The children were shown to be social agents in constructing their learning and knowledge. They were observed as expressing their meaning through multiple ways. All teachers were asked to comment on the data and the emerging themes and categories.

Allowing time for children to play and to inquire is a fundamental principle of the Reggio Emilia approach. The data provided evidence that this attention and the time given to children to immerse themselves in the environment were considered to be special, suggesting that this principle of Reggio Emilia formed an integral part of all the teacher's pedagogy and approach to teaching and working with children within this context and the field of my research.

5.10.2 *Constructiveness*

For the case study to hold its credibility and its strength, the case needed to connect to wider theoretical perspectives. The theoretical orientation of constructivism provides a concept of how knowledge is constructed. Thus, through the lens of 'constructiveness' (Ceppi & Zini 1998), this study was taken deeper into this orientation with this lens providing a connection between the school and the setting of the inquiry and between the concept of research and a place for research. When we view research as an 'openness' to an individual's learning and experimentation, we are respectfully allowing the lens of 'constructiveness' (Ceppi & Zini 1998) to increase the depth of the inquiry. We then allow knowledge to be constructed through experimentation: one can also term this a form of 'alchemy' that informs learning. In this way, we can relate to Ceppi and Zini's (1998) reference to 'constructiveness' and the lens which I imposed on this case study to enrich its authenticity. When defining constructiveness, Ceppi and Zini offer:

> … school as a workshop for research and experimentation, a laboratory for individual and group learning, a place for constructivism. A place for the alchemic composition of knowledge and desires, for perceiving and constructing reality, for the development of its own 'ecology of the artificial'.
>
> (1998, p. 23)

The lens of 'constructiveness' (Ceppi & Zini 1998), in this case, assisted with investigating the phenomenon of spirituality in young children and watching the phenomenon occur in the natural setting; in watching it construct itself through the lived experience, it may be considered as a 'developing network' (Caldwell 2003, p. 109). Within the laboratory of research which, in this scenario, was the setting of the case study, we assumed the lens of 'constructiveness'(Ceppi & Zini 1998) where 'the composition of knowledge does not take place in a linear way but as a developing network, based on dynamic interweaving of interconnected elements' (Caldwell 2003, p. 109).

As part of their construction of knowledge, there are many moments when each child searches for their own identity. The manner by which they discover this identity is understood by the way that they perceive themselves (Moriarty 2011). They require time to discover and to construct this identity and, as the Learning Stories indicated, during time within the learning environments, there were moments which could signify times when children pursued their identity and sense of belonging.

The evidence from the Learning Stories indicates that children construct meaning and knowledge as they interact with each other during the rhythm and flow of a learning environment which allows children to activate learning, and in an environment which supports relational spaces where children can be in conversation and learning opportunities together (Curtis & Carter 2003). Elements which invited children to collaborate and connect with each other as they discovered new knowledge about themselves and their world were encompassed in the space in which these children were together and in the Reggio Emilia pedagogy. Materials on the tables and the environments were provocations and provided open-ended and flexible entry points for children's meaning-making and encounters. Each contributed in a different way, bringing self-discoveries or some joint construction of new learning. There was a sense of flow and uninterrupted time for these children to encounter these realisations, to inquire through play and exploration. My place as participant observer was to 'scaffold' questions at times, but mostly just to observe and to listen to these children. Research by Sewell (2009) indicates that, as children learn together in a communal environment, there is a strong sense of identity which develops, extending towards a strong sense of who they are as humans. These reciprocal connections and a constructivist attitude (Ceppi & Zini 1998) towards a community of learners can also contribute to a spiritual essence (Sewell 2009).

The children were provided with unlimited pathways, requiring no set answer, along which to explore and answer the questions they pondered. In LS 15, two children (Child 21 and Child 22), through conversation and inquiry evoked by the environment, were able to trace one child's identity and nationality, co-constructing knowledge and information, leading to an awareness of where Child 21 came from, familiarising themselves with a globe and gaining information by locating different countries. This relational encounter may offer a deeper interpretation about children constructing knowledge together and gaining a sense of their own identity. Through offering a way to be connected to others in the transmission of knowledge and learning, children are able to delight in a mutual exchange of ideas and interpretations. The environment was characteristic of a constructivist approach which, apart from allowing the children to acquaint themselves with and experience new knowledge, also enlightens us to the fact that 'the different expressions of spirituality served to strengthen their intellectual, social and emotional connections, as well as to deepen their capacity for connection' (Sewell 2009, p. 14). The constructivist lens on this data stemming from the Reggio Emilia philosophy enlightened the interpretation, with the lens distilling the everyday experience of these children for further interpretation and a deeper layer of analysis. According to Malaguzzi (1998), we can deduce that children are attuned to being communicative from the very first moment of their life. Young children are not passive in receiving information (Kim & Darling 2009; Malaguzzi 1998): they are active participants when they encounter learning. It is through communicating with peers, as shown by the children detailed in the Learning Stories, that 'children construct a productive way of being in the world with others and learning alongside them' (Kim & Darling 2009, p. 144).

Another point generated by the data is that in everyday activities, as children engage with each other, they express their spirituality: this may suggest that 'everyday spirituality is always pedagogical possibility' (Bone 2007, p. 247, cited in Sewell 2009).

Table 5.1 in the next sub-section represents a summary and overview of the multi-layered data analysis which indicates the process and the stages of analysis, and the interpretations and findings emerging from the data.

5.10.3 *Overview of the multi-layered data analysis*

Table 5.1 Overview of data analysis

Stage 1: Deductive Analysis	
Qualitative indicators of expressions of children's spirituality demonstrated in the Learning Stories	*Reggio Emilia approach*
Flow Creativity Imagination Caring for another Attraction to a natural phenomenon Attraction and connection to nature Wonder and awe Engagement and curiosity Talking about God or a supreme being	The environment The image of the child The hundred languages of children

Emerging themes Reggio Emilia-inspired pedagogical elements in which expressions of spirituality are visible	Stage 2: Lens to distil and illuminate data and evidence (deductive analysis)	Pedagogical conditions and emerging categories
The environment Play, inquiry, discovery, exploring Curiosity Co-construction of theories and knowledge Reciprocal communication with: - the environment - one another - materials	Rich normality	Playful pedagogies: - uninterrupted time - authentic openness of experience - authentic environment
	Spaces as relationships	Relational spaces Multisensory opportunities for children Children work alongside each other or in relationship with the environment Aesthetics in the environment as an activator for learning
The hundred languages of children Engagement/flow-engaging experiences Opportunities given in valuing the child's right to: - inquire - explore - discover	Narration	Multidimensional: pedagogical conditions which allow for: - Multiple entry points to learn and make meaning
	Osmosis	Child-directed rhythm and flow of experiences and engagement: - Provocations to inspire learning with no expectation of one outcome, new ways of knowing Multiple modes of expressing meaning
The image of the child and evidence of the characteristics of broadening this image of the child: - social being - constructor of knowledge and identity - agent in own learning - orchestrating - purposeful - independent - resourceful	Constructiveness	Recognising through pedagogy the child's right to: - participate - be curious - be questioning No expectation of one answer or outcome

Discovering spirituality

Provocations for educators:

How can you use different lenses to view children, taking inspiration from the Reggio Emilia approach?

Are your observations and documentation of children shared with the community, with parents?

Is your dialogue inhibiting the strong image of the child, or can it be used as a tool to honour authentic and sincere listening to children?

Have you considered that there is a spiritual image of the child?

Do your environments reflect a less 'institutional' setting for children to grow and flourish?

Taking the notion of 'flow', how can you afford children the time and the space for this to occur in the everyday of their learning environment?

The next chapter discusses the final stage of analysis and the categories which emerged from the findings. The findings are discussed in relation to the guiding questions of the research. and open up some essential understanding about the spiritual dimension of young children.

Spirituality
A natural phenomenon in children's lives

Figure 6.1

❧ The concept of spirituality must find its way back to educational philosophy, it is an important ingredient for raising the whole child in order to make the future a better world and to add joy to learning ❧

Helena Card

6.1 Introduction

This chapter discusses the findings of the research in relation to the overall research questions and the guiding research questions.

The phenomenon of young children's spirituality is a debate fraught with many scholarly views and research; although many definitions of spirituality have been offered by academics, a single definition is not agreed upon (Adams 2013; Watson 2003). Best (2000) suggests that spirituality is, 'particularly resistant to operational definition' (p. 10) and argues that spirituality is better described rather than defined. Given that spirituality is present and exists in young children as highlighted in the literature review it cannot be ignored as part of a child's development. Through exploring the overall research question and the guiding research questions, this research suggests how the Reggio Emilia context offers a context for how spiritual capacities in young children may be visible, recognised and described.

The overall research question is:

> What indicators may be used to identify expressions of spirituality by four- to six-year-old children, and can the Reggio Emilia approach to education offer a context for recognising and nurturing children's spiritual capacities?

The four guiding research questions are:

Question 1: What are the qualitative indicators of expressions of spirituality that may be demonstrated by young children in their everyday early childhood activities?

Question 2: In what ways can the Reggio Emilia pedagogical approach provide conditions for the expression of children's spirituality?

Question 3: How can young children's expression of spirituality be described?

Question 4: What are the specific elements of the Reggio Emilia pedagogical environment that nurture children's spiritual dimension?

6.2 Identifying children's spirituality as expressions of spirituality

This section addresses the first guiding research question:

> What are the qualitative indicators of expressions of spirituality that may be demonstrated by young children in their everyday early childhood activities?

This research found that there were indicators and expressions of spirituality. These are collated in Table 6.1. The indicators were developed initially from the research literature and were further refined from the analysis of the Learning Stories. Each Learning Story provided an account of the observation of experiences in children's interactions which occurred during moments of their daily routines. The Learning Stories were analysed for qualitative indicators of expressions of spirituality which were developed from the reviewed literature. Table 6.1 provides a summary of the data analysis which revealed the following main indicators of spiritual expression: flow; creativity; imagination; caring or empathy for another; attraction and connection to nature and natural phenomena; joy; wonder and awe; curiosity and engagement; and talking about God or a supreme being.

Table 6.1 Indicators and expressions of spirituality

Indicators of spirituality	Expressions of spirituality
Flow	- Demonstrating flow of consciousness (sustained engagement, not noticing or aware of others in the environment, total immersion in activity)
Creativity	- Participating in creative activities and demonstrating creative abilities through painting, making, constructing, drawing - Aesthetic awareness/noticing beauty
Imagination	- Expressing imagination through various 'languages' and modes
Caring or empathy for another	- Expressing empathy - Demonstrating relationships with others
Attraction and connection to nature and natural phenomena	- Demonstrating intrigue and sustained interest in a natural phenomenon - Demonstrating an interest in mysterious things: asking bigger questions - Displaying an interest and interaction with nature
Joy	- Expressing joy through verbal means or through gesture, smiling
Wonder and awe	- Communicating and expressing moments of awe and wonder through verbal and/or other modes - Demonstrating moments of awe and wonder, questions out loud (may be to another child or participant observer) - Demonstrating moments of awe and wonder (silence, no questions)
Curiosity andengagement	- Sustaining involvement in a particular encounter - Encountering the environment (materials, natural phenomena and other children or adults in the environment) - Demonstrating a curiosity to theorise and hypothesise (through actions of reasoning, verbal communication, or various other modes)
Talking about God or a supreme being	- Using prior knowledge about a supreme being - Stating a connection to something bigger than themselves

The data suggested that expressions of spirituality were evident as the children interacted in their natural everyday environments and that these expressions could be seen and observed. Evidence was also provided that expressions of spirituality could be witnessed and were present as young children played and naturally interacted in their learning environment. The evidence from the data suggests a deeper understanding of expressions of spirituality and that spirituality is a natural capacity in young children. The findings suggested evidence in relation to how the Reggio Emilia approach provided conditions for young children's spirituality to be visible and to be recognised as dimensions. Three categories of dimensions of spirituality emerged from the findings. These categories describe spiritual dimensions and were facilitated by the conditions of the Reggio Emilia approach as: interconnectedness, meaning making, and being relational and multidimensional. Further discussion of the emerging dimensions is presented later in this chapter. Pedagogical conditions for spirituality

This section addresses the second guiding research question:

In what ways can the Reggio Emilia pedagogical approach provide conditions for the expression of children's spirituality?

Within this study, spirituality, as viewed through the lens of the Reggio Emilia approach, is by three main areas of the pedagogical approach: the image of the child; the environment as the third teacher; and the hundred languages of children. Within these three main areas, other pedagogical conditions stemmed from the guiding principles of the Reggio Emilia approach which created conditions, allowances and opportunities for children to express their spirituality. This extension of the principles of the Reggio Emilia approach was informed by the work of Ceppi and Zini (1998) and these conditions are discussed in this section.

This study contributes to knowing and understanding what children's spirituality may look like and the pedagogical conditions that nourish it. The data from this study suggest that children themselves must be afforded the opportunities for spiritual capacities to exist and flourish and that this cannot be ignored as a natural part of childhood. The data analysis of this study demonstrated that certain aspects of the Reggio Emilia pedagogical approach provided conditions for the expressions of children's spirituality.

The Reggio Emilia approach suggests an awareness of the 'hundred languages' with which children are born (Rinaldi 2013, p. 20): it also correlates with the possibility proposed by Champagne (2001) that children's spirituality can be communicated without words. Viewing through the lens of the Reggio Emilia approach, and listening to the strong and powerful image of the child, empower recognition of the expression of spiritual indicators which young children naturally display through their hundred languages.

Silent episodes of imaginative play were demonstrated in the data. In LS 10, Child 13 was engaged in an isolated activity in the learning space, only interacting with her activity comprising artefacts from the sea on a sand tray; feeling the textures and moving the sea artefacts, she was interacting within her own space and made a tree and a bird's nest from the artefacts. In LS 11, Child 14 was immersed in his activity, his head down, and only interacting with the materials at hand and with the researcher when he was questioned. The environment allowed him to interact freely and to move from inside to outside, allowing for sustained, silent and uninterrupted interaction with multiple materials. He was in control of his own thinking, moving from abstract to concrete, expressing himself creatively and discovering new knowledge and meaning.

It can be suggested that these examples from the data demonstrate the expressions of spirituality, as children's everyday encounters and experiences become 'imbued with the spiritual' (Bone 2007, p. 348). These examples from the data demonstrate that allowances and spaces were made for the children to have opportunities for new experiences and new interpretations of the materials which they encountered. This is supported by Miller and Athan (2007), who state that making allowance for such experiences is linked to an understanding of spiritual reality whereby pedagogy and the recognition of spiritual experience are linked: 'classroom pedagogy is part of spiritual reality; and every moment in a classroom, a spiritual opportunity' (Miller & Athan 2007, p. 17).

According to Trotman (2006), the solitary imaginative space displayed by the children as they were immersed in their own creations and thoughts can also be viewed as sacred, a private space 'in which fantasy, daydreams, reflections, thoughts, meditations, anxieties find form in our consciousness' (Trotman 2006, p. 5).

Rinaldi (2013) and the Reggio Emilia philosophy maintain that the rich child has rights and potential, with a hundred languages with which to communicate and express, thus supporting the argument of my research and this book, whereby spirituality can be meaningfully exhibited in multiple ways by young children in various modes of expression or 'languages'.

Underpinning the Reggio Emilia approach is the notion that spaces are made for children to make visible the Reggio Emilia interpretation of the strong image of the child (Malaguzzi 1994; Rinaldi 2006) and to allow visibility and the recognition of the hundred languages through which children can express themselves in their everyday encounters. In LS 1, Child 1 was able to represent music and a bird through creative expression. She independently investigated and discovered the materials: she was in control and demonstrated agency as an active constructor of knowledge.

The evidence in this study suggests that spirituality could be considered a mode of expression within the hundred languages of children within a learning environment inspired by the Reggio Emilia approach. Therefore, this research suggests that the conditions and pedagogical environment which transpires from the Reggio Emilia approach allows spirituality to be expressed and present. Once this is understood and observed, it can then be nurtured through such an approach.

Spirituality

In response to the second guiding research question, it was found that spirituality in connection to the Reggio Emilia philosophy is expressed in what the children do in their play, their interactions in the environment and how they connect to, and identify themselves with, elements in their world in a daily early childhood context. Table 6.2 summarises the findings.

This study suggests the viewpoint that spirituality may be viewed as a natural human disposition and that, in young children, it may be expressed in what they do in play and in actions, gestures and artwork, through the modes of many 'languages' or of expression. Chapter 5 presented the Learning Stories which provided many examples of children displaying expressions of spirituality as they played, created, imagined and encountered their environment.

Table 6.2 Conditions for expressions of children's spirituality

Reggio Emilia pedagogical approach	*Evidence from data*
Hundred languages of children	As children interact with specific elements in a learning environment inspired by the Reggio Emilia approach, spirituality, as an intrinsic aspect of the child, is expressed through the hundred languages
Image of the child	Spirituality integrates all aspects of the human person and, in children, this is apparent through the lens of the strong image of the child. The Reggio Emilia approach recognises the advocacy and agency of young children and describes this as the image of the child and how the child exists as a young person. The Reggio Emilia approach involves a respect for the child as capable of making decisions and engaging with life on their own terms.
Environment as the third teacher	An environment inspired by the Reggio Emilia approach allows children to explore and discover in a variety of different modes and provides conditions for children's spirituality to have the freedom to flourish as they search and perceive the meaning and purpose of their world, wonder and make new discoveries.
Pedagogy of listening	The Reggio Emilia approach provides pedagogical conditions in which listening to the strong image of the child supports the recognition and understanding of the spiritual expressions which young children naturally display through their hundred languages as they respond to the environment in different ways.

Alongside the indicators of expressions of spirituality that emerged from the data, various themes were developed from the triangulated data analysis. Several conditions became apparent, the presence of which seemed to be required for spiritual indicators to be expressed and manifested in this early childhood setting. The image of the child influences the view of children. The data from the interviews revealed that the educators proposed a strong image of the child which was indicative of their approach to designing their pedagogy and practice for young children.

Evidence revealed that, through allowing the child to interact with the environment, the child's agency was respected and flow was able to occur as the children moved from one activity or interaction to another without restrictions of time or directed approaches and expectations. Overall, the data suggested that the context of the environment across the cohorts was one of child-centred learning, with the teacher in the background.

The findings from this research showed that, within the conditions of this early childhood setting, spiritual expression manifested and was present and visible through indicators. This study has proposed that the conditions in which spiritual expression was present were in criteria linked to the pedagogical position and practice which existed in each of the learning cohorts at the setting. Furthermore, the data provided evidence of the qualitative expressions of spirituality as each of the children in the study naturally proceeded with their daily activities within the learning cohorts.

The second guiding research question explored the way that the Reggio Emilia approach provided conditions for expressions of spirituality, with this able to occur through the pedagogy of listening, the way that the environment was designed, a particular view of the image of the child and the view that children express themselves and make meaning through the hundred languages. This was inspired by the Reggio Emilia approach and allowed the observer to listen to the children. The notion of listening through this pedagogy was not restricted to the verbal but included all aspects of children's modes of expression and communication. This was evident in the Learning Stories where not only verbal modes of expression were recorded but gesture, silence, flow, engagement, involvement, drawings and artefacts were observed, listened to and recorded. The environment allowed for multiple entry points and multiple modes of expression and for the child to be an active protagonist able to explore and discover in a meaningful context.

6.3 Descriptions of children's expressions of spirituality

This section discusses the aim of the final stage and layer of data analysis. It addresses the third guiding research question:

How can young children's expression of spirituality be described?

Spirituality

This research has highlighted that spirituality may be intrinsically present and expressed by young children in these learning environments. To fully understand the intrinsic nature of young children, it is important to describe this nature within a pedagogical environment and how spirituality is intrinsic to all aspects of learning (Nye & Hay 1996). This research suggests that understanding children's expression of spirituality and recognising it will contribute to nurturing and supporting spiritual development in the early years. Thus, this research builds on Dowling's (2010) scholarly input, whereby it is suggested that no guidance is available to early childhood practitioners on how to describe spirituality in order to incorporate the support or nurturing of spiritual development in the early years.

As the expressions of spirituality were interpreted in this study, the final layer of analysis explored the broader criteria and categories in which spiritual expression were visible. These were informed by Stage 2 of the deductive analysis of the data under 'Pedagogical conditions and emerging categories'.

The data demonstrated that the Reggio Emilia pedagogical elements and conditions that were present allowed spiritual expressions to be observed and noticeable. Further synthesis and the last stage of the data analysis in this research suggest that, with the Reggio Emilia approach present, children's spiritual expressions of spirituality could be characterised and described as dimensions as the children were observed interacting in various ways in the context of this context and environment, on their own with materials and phenomena or with others.

This forms a further stage in the hermeneutic conversation (Gadamer 1976) in which, in a middle space, the researcher extends the dialogical engagement (Hyde & Australian Catholic University 2005) with the text, representing the sociocultural context within which the child and the researcher speak and act. The final layer and stage of analysis proposes descriptions of children's expression of spirituality as the following suggested dimensions: interconnectedness, making meaning, and being relational and multidimensional. A summary of the final stage and layer of data analysis is outlined in Figure 6.2.

As shown in Figure 6.2, the dimensions that emerged from the data analysis are in relation to the unique pedagogical approach inspired by Reggio Emilia which was present during the observation times and when expressions of spirituality were evident. The following sections are the descriptions of the expressions of children's spirituality as suggested dimensions in relation to the pedagogical context of this study.

6.3.1 Interconnectedness

This research suggests that, in the context of a Reggio Emilia-inspired early learning environment, interconnectedness is a dimension of spirituality. The observations provided data in the form of field notes or Learning Stories as children took part in a variety of experiences, with each child having the opportunity to engage in various encounters

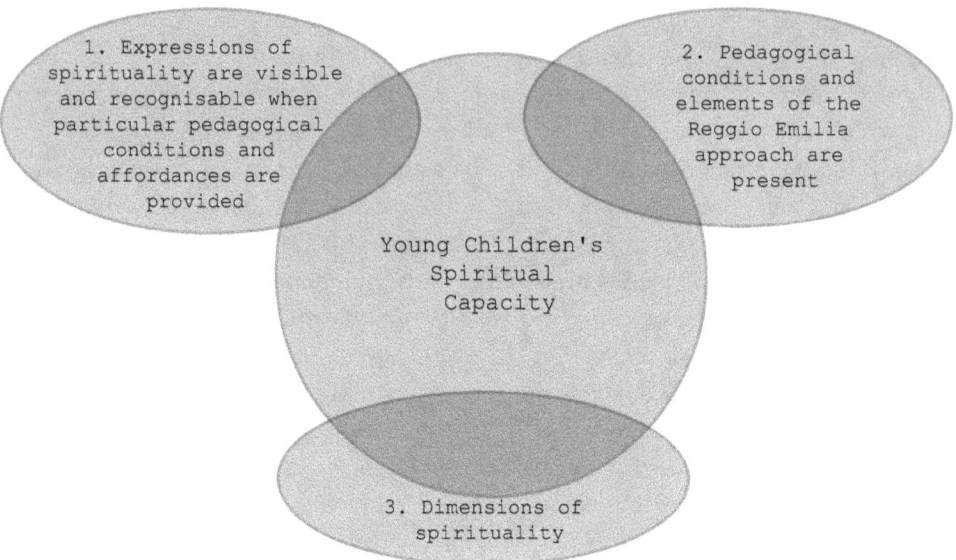

Figure 6.2 Summary of final stage of data analysis

and with specific elements and conditions in the environment. The conditions of playful pedagogies: uninterrupted time, authentic open experiences and authentic environment were evident and suggested in the data. To support this statement, data were generated from observing the many experiences of the children in which they were connected with emotions of joy and wonder and in which they were engaged in learning, discovering and expressing themselves through various modes. Their minds were engaged with the child-centred activities and environments where they could wonder, notice, hypothesise and discover themselves and their connections to the world, drawing on prior knowledge or discovering new knowledge.

For example, in LS 2, Child 2 was able to draw on prior knowledge of family and, in connection with the materials in play, also formed a connection to the notion of family and mother–baby relationships. The children in LS 14 and LS 15 were observed as they interacted with the materials, allowing them to use prior knowledge to connect to new knowledge. The children in LS 14 used their knowledge of the body and their interaction with the materials provided to develop new knowledge: as Child 18 was drawing her body, she also verbally expressed her own knowledge of facts about the body. The two children then explored the bigger questions of bones and where they came from and, when asked by the researcher, claimed to know who made the bones. Child 19 was looking at his throat, then looking at the diagram of the epiglottis and making new discoveries about his body. The flow of learning was evident, as was the time for self-expression during unhurried, uninterrupted, enabled immersion in a task or encounter. Further evidence of interconnectedness is drawn from observations from the Learning Stories, such as LS 1 where connection with materials initiated creative expression through the hundred languages, and Child 1 was observed in a state of flow. This evidence can be considered as an integration of mind, body and soul whereby spirituality emphasises the connectedness of all things: ideas, people, forms, nature and community. Based on research on children's spirituality, I argue that the connectedness within the individual integrates mind, heart and soul, and that the child is immersed in the full functioning of mind and body when they are fully engaged in tasks. This aligns with Csikszentmihalyi's (2000) statement: '[f]or the soul works in unison with the entire self. It is not separated but part of an interconnectedness with a larger system' (p. 145).

The study's findings suggest that the Reggio Emilia approach provided a time for children to make visible their advocacy and agency. For example, in LS 15, the children were active agents in their learning and co-construction of knowledge. Child 21 theorised and verbalised out loud, drawing on prior knowledge about where England was on the globe. Child 22 drew on prior knowledge about countries around the world. Through their conversation, Child 22 was helping Child 21 to discover where she was from, with Child 21 seeming intent on the discovery and competently drawing a map on a pad so they could match the country. The children in this Learning Story were discovering themselves in the broader context of the world and they were abstracting themselves into the concrete by connecting to a thought about the map. They were able to see themselves as part of a planet, that is, as part of a bigger picture, and visualise themselves in relation to a wider world.

Each observation was noted during a time when children were provided with an environment of multisensory experiences. This study suggests that the Reggio Emilia philosophy and pedagogy provided a theoretical framework for recognising expressions of spirituality as children connected to the environment and theorised or verbalised, spent moments in silence as they connected with materials in the environment, and connected through gestures. The many possibilities within spaces (Moss & Petrie 2002) are where children actively create and inhabit, and where they reveal their thoughts and interpretations about life. The children in this research were shown through the data to be active agents within their inquiry and discovery: they connected with the multisensory layers of the environment whether through the materials, nature or their own imaginative play.

The examples were found through observation at times when the children were involved in their own learning and there were times of not knowing, of discovery or of discovering the unknown. In LS 7, Child 8 and Child 9 were observed with the spider and showed their curiosity and connection to nature, leading to further knowledge and construction of what was unknown. Bone (2014) refers to this as being 'spiritually in-between' (p. 409) and supports the spiritual sense of uncertainty in the actual moment of, or in the moment just before, knowing what happens. It is through this unknown and the discovery of the unknown possibilities that they are interconnected. Space was created in the timetable and allocated to uninterrupted time which fostered play and discovery. This allowed for spiritual expression to be noticed as a consciousness of being interconnected between the self and the elements in the learning environment which then provided a link to further understanding and interconnectedness to the wider world.

6.3.2 Making meaning

Making meaning, in the context of this study where learning spaces were inspired by the Reggio Emilia approach, can be viewed as a description of a dimension of children's spirituality. Children are curious and I recognised, as the data were analysed, that their drive to express spirituality comes from a sense of curiosity and fascination with the world, evident from an early age, and, as in this study, from age four, each child sought engagement and involvement within their learning environment to make meaning. Within each of the Learning Stories presented, the focus was on the children: the role of the teacher and/or researcher was as a facilitator of the co-construction of knowledge, neither a dictator of knowledge nor a provider of questions which demanded one right and correct answer. All the children were curious and inquisitive by nature and were allowed to explore their curiosity. They formulated an understanding of the meaning of life through their discoveries and their encounters. Each child, as demonstrated by the data, was capable, resourceful and intelligent, and expressed themselves in 'one hundred ways' (Edwards et al. 1998) in a variety of symbolic and graphic ways. In LS 1, Child 1 was observed graphically expressing her theories of music and the sound she was hearing. In LS 4, Child 4 verbally announced her ideas about where thunder came from as she heard the sound of thunder. The observations of the children showed times when they graphically expressed their concepts of ideas: in LS 6, Child 6 and Child 7 chose to show their understanding of the chicken's life stages and growth on the chart that they both drew.

The Reggio Emilia approach, incorporating the hundred languages (Malaguzzi 1998; Rinaldi 2006) that provide children with the means for expression, can be refined into categories: symbolic and poetic understandings (Swann 2008) or representations of their understanding of the world. In LS 9, the hundred languages of children were evident as the children were offered multiple ways to express their meaning-making and understandings which did not require a direct, single answer. They were able to express their knowledge about a sea environment and sustainability through the mode of writing and then used materials to create and simulate this environment. Through not requiring one single answer, the provocation and inquiry into the sea environment allowed the children to develop their own understandings and to construct meaning. This construction of meaning and understanding provided the means by which they also expressed their spiritual nature and their noetic understanding (Nye 2009) of their surroundings, with this observed through their questioning and curiosity about elements in their daily environment. Plunkett (1990, cited in Meehan 2002a) points out that the spiritual is 'the source of ultimate meaning' (p. 16).

Spirituality and expressing spirituality in young children involves searching and perceiving the meaning and purpose of their world. The Reggio Emilia philosophy suggests a framework in which the construction of meaning or co-construction of meaning underpins the pedagogical approach. The data in this study were from observing the children in a play-based environment during Exploration Time which is scheduled in the daily timetables of the learning cohorts, providing times of deep play and unhurried or uninterrupted time. Hyde (2014) states that during these times of 'deep play, children are able to use both verbal and nonverbal communication as a means to discover and unpack the meaning of an event or story in their lives' (pp. 134–135). The non-verbal responses may be intuitive, involving no words: children then use other means to express and make visible their meaning-making. The multidimensional conditions in the environment provided the multiple entry points for children to make meaning: the environment provided conditions for authentic, relational experiences through which the children could interact with each other and with the elements in the environment to make meaning. According to Hyde (2014), when children construct their meaning in this way, they are expressing their spirituality. The collation of Table 5.1 from observations in the Learning Stories showed examples where children were constructing meaning in multiple ways through their hundred languages and through the indicators of spiritual expressions which were evident during these times and within these conditions.

In concluding, I suggest that this dimension of spirituality is reflected in the reciprocal experiences of the children's pedagogical context. It was represented in their everyday expressions of making meaning and discovering new knowledge through imaginative and creative play and interaction which allowed for new moments of reflection and thinking from within and for the children to make meaning and sense of the world around them.

6.3.3 *Being relational and multidimensional*

This research suggests that being relational and multidimensional can also be considered as a dimension of spirituality in young children within the context of a Reggio Emilia-inspired environment. It can be interpreted from the evidence in the data from this study that young children are on a quest to make meaning of and to perceive their world as they connect and relate to each other or with the elements of their environment. The pedagogical environment across all the cohorts within this study was inspired by the Reggio Emilia approach. The educators in Reggio Emilia offer us the view that 'children construct their knowledge of the world by acting on the environment' (Swann 2008, p. 36).

The environment is important to the Reggio Emilia approach. This approach pays particular attention to factors such as light, colour, nature, aesthetics and multisensory materials. The environment illustrated through the data provided evidence that the educators in the early learning cohorts made an overall attempt to provide an environment which was not a traditional environment where the child is 'filled' with knowledge, but instead one in which the child interacts with a stimulating environment. The environment had activities and encounters for the children which were multisensory and multidimensional (providing multiple entry points). These kinds of conditions in the environment were a critical element in this study providing for each child the pathway, fluidity and creative thinking which could take them beyond their capabilities. No end point or right answer stopped or halted learning: each child was facilitated and had conditions that provided unknown possibilities. From this evidence, it can be suggested that this style of environment is one which engages the spiritual and the whole dimension of children, as Meehan points out:

> A curriculum that aims to promote spiritual development must be holistic and integrative. A curriculum is holistic where feelings, emotions, values, beliefs, behaviour, aspirations, and the intellect are catered for ... An integrative curriculum engages the mind, body and spirit ...
>
> (Meehan 2002a, p. 22)

For spirituality to be developed and to manifest (Coburn 1968; Priestley 1985), it is pivotal that the environment must be holistic.

Another point to discuss in light of considering this research is that evidence was found that the young children were searching for meaning and definition in their world through their interactions. For example, in LS 11, Child 14 was exploring colours: he was engaged and relating to the environment and the multi-layered aspects it offered to design his artefact about colours. He was relational with the researcher when she asked a wondering question which he then related to his artefact and the elements, such as a rainbow, in the natural environment. Even though he was observed in a state of flow, he was relational with the environment both outdoors and indoors and when the researcher interacted with him.

In a further aspect of their curiosity, the children were observed to problem solve as they encountered materials or each other. For instance, in LS 13, the children worked together and with the materials to design and problem solve as they engaged with the materials. They worked to design a farm, using materials to represent aspects of the farm, such as mud and water. They also tried to recreate and design the farm from the graphic images which were drawn. The children were involved together in their construction, with the environment and the materials providing multiple entry points for problem solving as they took turns to represent their drawing and construct their interpretation of the farm. This evidence closely aligns with what the literature defines as spiritual intelligence. When we consider the notion of 'holistic', we must include the mind and its intelligence (Adams et al. 2008; Emmons 1999; Gardner 1999; Hyde 2004; Painton 2009; Zohar and Marshall, 2000).

Spiritual intelligence naturally exists in young children, as Painton (2009) points out from her scholarly input and work with children:

> Spiritual intelligence is boys' and girls' capacity to be awake and aware of a deeper dimension of themselves that leads to wisdom and intuition, compassion and other-worldly experiences. It refers to the inner world of the child.
> (p. 368)

The current study revealed the conditions which allowed the children to be active agents in expressions and meaning-making through relational and multidimensional aspects of the environment.

6.4 Implications of a Reggio Emilia-inspired environment in relation to children's expression of spirituality

This study suggests that the Reggio Emilia approach has specific elements in the environment that it inspires which may allow the expressions of spirituality in young children to be recognisable. This section refers to the fourth guiding research question:

What are the specific elements of the Reggio Emilia pedagogical environment that nurture children's spiritual dimension?

Reggio Emilia philosophers support the idea of children's deep need for beautiful aesthetic environments in which natural materials are prominent. The photographs and the Learning Stories all demonstrated and provided evidence to support this idea. The classrooms were constructed differently to other classrooms: the attention to detail and aesthetics within each learning environment were inspired by the Reggio Emilia approach.

The data indicated that the children were engaged in multiple ways that incorporated multisensory involvement as they encountered their daily environments and experiences. This multisensory involvement and engagement can be correlated with the description of holistic education which Miller, 2007, cited in Binder 2011) defines as:

> the relationship between linear thinking and intuition, the relationship between mind and body, the relationships among the various domains of knowledge, the relationship between the individual and community, the relationship to the earth, and our relationship to our souls.
> (p. 13)

As the children's experiences were collated and documented in the Learning Stories, the manifestation of spiritual indicators and the children's spiritual dimension became evident. The Reggio Emilia philosophy and its approach to documentation and observation of children allowed these indicators to be evident, as presented by the Learning Stories. The indicators of spirituality expressed by the children became noticeable as the observations and field notes were collated, interpreted and analysed. Brussat and Brussat (1996) note that, as we read the texts of children's experiences and fully listen to children through the pedagogy of listening, we then allow ourselves to be exposed to the spirituality of young children and are able and open to reading the signs of spirituality which appear in the texts of children's lives

This study explored the connection of children's spiritual expression to the core philosophy of the educators of Reggio Emilia, whereby children are invited to explore the world using their hundred languages for expressing and making visible their understandings of themselves and of the world (Gandini et al. 2005). As indicated by the study and supported by researchers and scholars in the literature review (Goodliff 2013; King 2013; Meehan 2002a), contemporary understandings of spirituality are associated and linked to all human experiences. Certain spiritual expressions and indicators become prevalent when we carefully allow the time to observe children in their everyday encounters. These expressions and indicators were made evident in the data and summarised in Table 6.1. A shift in thinking towards a pedagogy, which not only recognises spiritual qualities in children but also supports these qualities, is timely and must be integrative to fully understand young children's spiritual capacity (Meehan 2002a).

6.5 Reggio Emilia approach to nurturing children's spiritual expressions

This section continues the discussion on the fourth guiding research question:

What are the specific elements of the Reggio Emilia pedagogical environment that nurture children's spiritual dimension?

A discussion is necessary at this point to identify whether a pedagogy, where the aim is to promote and nurture young children's spirituality, must be holistic, integrative and one which engages mind, body and spirit. The findings generated from the data in this study indicated certain pedagogical attitudes and conditions offered by the Reggio Emilia approach that are required to foster spirituality. Meehan (2002a) supports this statement by adding:

> Stimulating a sense of the spiritual requires students to have opportunities for using their imaginations, for creativity, exploration, wonder, awe, a sense of

mystery and an environment where students are at ease asking questions, but questioning received views.

(p. 22)

As revealed by the literature review, imagination, creativity, wonder and awe are all characteristics associated with spirituality. The findings from the Learning Stories, as summarised in Table 6.1, represent the dispositions demonstrated by the children in this study and are indicators of expressions of spirituality.

Reviewing the evidence which emerged from the data, it can be confidently suggested that Reggio Emilia offers a pedagogical approach where the learning process is fostered by research with children as they play and interact, and their spiritual dimension is nurtured.

This study presented evidence of qualitative indicators of expressions of spirituaity which were present as the children interacted in their everyday environment, one inspired by the Reggio Emilia pedagogy. Scholarly contributions have advocated that knowledge about children's spirituality is essential if it is to be nurtured and not lost or misunderstood (Crompton 1998). Many advocate that nurturing children's spiritual development enables and leads them to a deeper understanding and appreciation of themselves as whole persons (Hay & Nye 2006; Liddy 2002; Myers 1997; Nye & Hay 1996). When spirituality is intentionally nurtured in young children, as Grajczonek (2012) claims, then this intentional attention to the spiritual dimension of children's lives would afford a holistic approach to learning. As Stage 2 of the deductive analysis suggests, certain pedagogical conditions unique to the Reggio Emilia approach were evident and presented in Table 5.1. The evidence from this research suggests that young children's spiritual dimension is nurtured by the Reggio Emilia approach and the highlighted elements that are unique to this pedagogical approach.

The work provides evidence that the provocations (inspired by the Reggio Emilia approach) offered possibilities for explorations, with the children displaying an urge to discover more about their world by inquiring and interacting with their environment through imagination, creativity, curiosity and through asking bigger questions. For example, the provocation with the jar and blue water in LS 9 was linked to a bigger question about the environment and sustainability: the children were able to make the artefacts and express their thoughts through creative imaginative experiences demonstrating the use of one hundred languages or multiple ways of representing their meaning and understanding.

In LS 9, when three of the children were in the process of choosing objects and materials to put in their jars for their sea creatures, I asked them about the environments they were creating. All three children expressed concern about the environment for their creatures that they wanted to be safe, happy and healthy. Their understanding of, and sensitivity to, the environment were evident and they all answered with conviction.

Child 11 stated that if the sea creature did not have this kind of environment, then it would die. Child 12 expressed the view that they had to keep oceans clean and not dirty, otherwise the creatures would die. The children were able to use prior knowledge and apply this to analysing natural environments which preserved the life of natural creatures. They were able to transfer knowledge from one process to another through expressing themselves with materials and objects which extended the hundred languages. Their wonder and experience with the sea environment emphasised the empathy they had for ecological sustainability and natural phenomena.

6.5.1 Signs and expressions of children's spirituality

Hay and Nye (2006) describe children's natural and varied interactions as the texts of children's lives and suggest that we can potentially read these texts through the signs which children present. Further scholarly input (Binder 2011) suggests that the texts, including signs and expressions of meaning within children's lives, are an essential core for defining and exploring young children's spirituality. Each child offers educators, and those who are involved in researching young children, their unique 'signature', providing an opportunity for interpretation and understanding of childhood. This is supported through the hermeneutic approach and analysis of this study and, as Sargeant and Harcourt (2012) state, 'much of the research of young children requires careful engagement with a range of childhood languages including, oral, text, artefacts and behaviour' (p. 8). Binder (2011) advocates that reading these signs 'is the act of understanding the inner life which we all possess' (p. 22). As stated by Binder (2011) and Hay and Nye (2006), the reading of these signs also enables the potential for transforming educational practices.

My study's data led to a final discussion and summary of the study where the spiritual cosmologies (Binder 2011), or the curious nature of children to study and answer questions which exist in our universe, offer that notion of interrelationship and connection to self and others (Buchanan 2009). Throughout the Learning Stories, the children became immersed in constant curiosity with a sustained flow of engagement. For example, in LS 14, Child 19, who was discovering his epiglottis, was first engaged with others then became totally immersed in his own discovery and inquiry as he stared at the pictures while working out his body parts. Child 8 and Child 9 with the spider in LS 7 were involved in an encounter with each other as they co-constructed their ideas, concepts and understandings, as well as being involved in an encounter and engagement with the environment, which supported their inquiry and investigation. The researcher and a teacher were present, observing and listening as the two girls were immersed in their attraction to a natural phenomenon and their related inquiry.

The opportunity to stand back, observe and listen was an example of the way listening could value and support the strong and powerful image of the child and understand their relationship with life. As Davies (2011) states, this notion of listening means 'opening up the ongoing possibility of coming to see life, and one's relation to it, in new and surprising ways' (p. 120). This captured moment of encounter opened up an opportunity for me as researcher to be:

> Open to the understandings one has of self and the other, and the relations between them, creatively evolving into something new. Open listening opens up the possibility of new ways of knowing and new ways of being, both for those who listen and for those who are listened to.
>
> (Davies 2011, p. 120)

Adams (2009) refers to children's spiritual expressions as 'voices' and she states that, for children's spiritual voices to be heard in learning situations, this element of education cannot be ignored. All the Learning Stories, which were collated and then documented, were developed by the researcher taking an approach which involved listening deeply to the children in order to recognise their spiritual 'voices'.

In concluding, I argue that, to recognise and understand the spiritual dimension of young children and to nurture their spiritual expression, early childhood practitioners need to be challenged to create learning spaces where there is a willingness to listen to and to hear the many languages of young children.

6.6 Limitations

This study is bounded by a particular context with the findings interpreted to answer the overall research question. The understanding of children's innate spirituality is still recognised as a broad topic, with many scholarly disparities regarding the meanings of what spirituality may look like. This is acknowledged in the current study by stating that the research presents this particular context by viewing spirituality through a particular lens and child-centred pedagogical approach. This unique aspect of the case identifies a gap in the scholarly work about pedagogical approaches which are conducive to spiritual nurture and that provide allowances for the expressions of spirituality in young children.

This study acknowledges that the global debate on spirituality is a contentious one. The review of the literature supports the fact that spirituality is an ontological feature of the human person which can exist within religion or outside any religious tradition. This research presents a case bounded by context and conditions which suggests that, for young children, spirituality is visible through expression and is present when certain pedagogical conditions are constructed within a learning environment.

Future research could be undertaken by broadening the sample size to additional cultural, religious and demographic educational sites which are influenced by the Reggio Emilia approach with this age group of children.

The following section discusses spirituality and religion in relation to the limitations and boundaries of the case.

6.7 Spirituality and religion

One element that became apparent within this study and the early childhood setting was that there was little evidence of instances when children talked about a 'supreme being'. Perhaps this is an essential consideration when reconceptualising spirituality and childhood. While the children in this study were within a Catholic context which is linked to a supreme being named 'God' with a specific tradition and doctrine, some evidence from the data suggested that the religious aspect appeared to have little significance in the spirituality of young children. Here, I refer to the two Learning Stories (LS 4 and LS 14) where there was a mention of God. The reference to God, in this context, originated from what the children had been taught or had had explained to them. Child 18 and Child 20 in LS 14 were discussing an authentic situation in relation to what they knew and understood about God. In LS 4, links to a supreme being were part of the culture of the family, with the reference to God by Child 4 originating from information provided by her mother.

Although within this research spirituality for young children appeared to be areligious, further thought may consider it to be part of a spiritual nature. This is explored through the data which demonstrated that expressions of spirituality can be considered as being innate in the child or noetenous (Nye 2009). A distinction thus evolved in the data in relation to spirituality and religion in which spirituality in young children is a capacity that displays certain indicators which they demonstrate, and which this study suggests may or may not be associated with a specific religion. This may require further research and inquiry; nevertheless, this discussion warrants mentioning in relation to this overall study. In addition, this leads to an indication that children's spirituality is present and will be displayed by the child when certain conditions are present. Furthermore, these expressions of spirituality may constitute the spiritual dimension of children.

Through the evidence collated within this study and this setting, the dimension of children's spirituality has been made accessible. Reggio Emilia has been the pedagogical approach which has made visible this ontological dimension of children and how it can be described. The expressions are a result of the context in which this study is situated: this study suggests opening the door to recognising young children's expressions of spirituality within a particular context and pedagogical approach.

6.8 Encouraging spirituality: rethinking the soulfulness of the everyday

While my conclusions in this study have been based on the evidence that I collected. There is an element that must be considered when we delve into the wonderful accounts of children's everyday lives. Play encompasses moments for rejoicing the expressions of spirituality in young children. It provides the soul which cultivates and affords children's innate spiritual lives. It offers us the provocation to rethink childhood to include the spiritual dimension and question ourselves how we offer environments to children where the fabric of their being can be nurtured. It offers us the provocation to rethink childhood and reconceptualise children to include and honour their spiritual dimension. Children and childhood can best be treasured as respected beings in our communities whose voice is sought and whose spiritual agency is honoured. I believe that all children deserve a sanctuary in which there is a time and a space where children can be in closer contact with the biological, psychological and spiritual rhythms of their lives. Children cannot be neatly defined and used as means for measuring success through standardised means. They cannot be categorised; they need to be understood holistically.

6.8.1 Children's encounters in their natural environment: the extraordinary in the ordinary

My own intention with this research was to capture children in their everyday encounters. These encounters were filled with spiritual moments. It tests us to think about the fact that ordinary moments can be in themselves extraordinary. Especially when we adopt the lens of rethinking the potential of every child and their spiritual dimension. It is essential that we offer environments which stimulate and invite all the senses to be active. Through encounters with a wide variety of aesthetic materials and with nature, children can explore the sensuousness and beauty of colour, texture, movement, lines and space. As children immerse themselves and become comfortable with the composition and materials of their environment, they are able to communicate their understandings, emotions and big questions. Their fluency with the aspects of their learning environment, opens up new opportunities for collaboration and encounter, deepening their relationship with the world and themselves.

As the adults that work alongside children, I invite you to think about the narration of everyday moments that children have. One of the delights of my research was the documentation of children: the pedagogical narration. This is recognised as a hallmark of the Reggio Emilia educational project. My learning stories presented ordinary moments. As educators and carers of children, this is core if we want to truly understand

and rethink childhood. When we strive to pay attention to everyday, ordinary moments, these ordinary moments are indeed the fabric of children's lives. They offer us the extraordinary in the ordinary and tender glimpse into children's hearts and minds and their true human capacity.

6.9 The soulfulness of play

Young children express spirituality in their everyday lives. My Master's Thesis provided me with theoretical evidence that young children express spirituality when a pedagogy and practice which nurtures spirituality is put into place. My research highlighted a connection between a pedagogy inspired by the work of the educational project of Reggio Emilia. In essence, a rich pedagogical framework which valued the image of the child as capable and full of potential supports the spiritual dimension of the child. In this current day and age, we are constricted by so many uncertainties, that it may be that we have forgotten to take the time to understand our soul and our spirit. Early childhood education offers an opportunity and platform to nourish the soul and to deeply understand young children and their innate spiritual capacity. If we allow this window of opportunity to be opened, then we can also reflect on ourselves as the adults who accompany children in their natural learning environments. The pedagogy and practice that we create for young children has a direct effect on their holistic and spiritual development.

The basic elements of play provide a window into the soul of children, developing and nurturing their expression of spirituality and developing the whole child. Returning to the foundations of our natural curiosity and questioning can support not only children to reach their full spiritual potential but also help us as adults and early childhood educators to fully understand the world of the child and their spiritual dimension.

6.9.1 Wisdom and wonder in play

One of my favourite phrases is "I wonder". It opens a delightful mode of inquiry. As adults, we can limit ourselves from this inquiry through our own hesitation with wondering; we forget to let our thoughts go. Sometimes we get stuck gazing through a fixed lens, trapped in a prejudice of thinking we know what is right, and when it is OK to know and to wonder and question. The incredible gift of wonder is that it invites us to soften our tired and focused eyes for a moment, to exhale, pause and be open to unknown possibilities. Wonder provides a resting space between our litany of beliefs and opinions where we can explore like a young child with uncharted possibilities and trajectories. Wonder provides a medium for the unravelling of the clenched working mind, a threshold into the mysterious that no thought can lead us to. It unleashes the freedom to travel with our mind to new and incredible theories and ponderings.

These reasons suggest that wonder is not easy. The conditional logical mind that rules over our lives loves to hold on. Its identity is formed from walls of knowledge gathered for decades, and fed through educational institutions which have a factory mentality of filling humans with knowledge and expecting this knowledge to be stored and tested and stacked neatly into data, diagrams, and performance of an individual's capability. This kind of identity limits possibilities and detracts from the natural and innate wonder that exists in all of us. The innate wonder that builds our intelligence and our wisdom of the world around us. This needs to be unleashed in our children every day, not governed by data and politics.

At times, wonder may not be comfortable, but it is a necessity if we are to truly grow beyond the confines of the consensual or the acceptable. Wonder may, at times, be unsettling to our psyche and way of preferred thinking as we lose the control of what we know. Wonder will enlighten and educate your heart and your mind and those of the children in your life. This is integral in their growth and development. Wonder ignites and nurtures the spiritual dimension.

6.9.2 Play and wonder raises the child

As educators, if we want to navigate the spiritual dimension, we need to accept it and to think and dig deeply into the child's world. We need to be open to asking ourselves questions and reflect on what are observing. When children are playing, do we specifically ask ourselves, "I wonder what they are learning?", "I wonder how they are developing?" and "I wonder what they know that I do not know?" If we allow ourselves to really deepen this thought and soften our eyes, quiet our mind, and open our listening heart, what else could there be? This kind of wondering and allowance that we are granting ourselves can open us to the nuance of the intelligence of play. It is when we are truly listening to and engaging with their innate spirituality.

Have we perhaps lost the innocence of play, to have a relationship with parts of life that only the heart and soft eyes can see? We may remember being in close conversation with a butterfly and begin in awe of its ability to fly. We may remember having hands and feet lost and embraced in the moist texture of the earth, covering ourselves in mud and feeling this through our senses, discovering how we can express our feelings. Or finding the joy of touching a wriggly worm, being enchanted by the moon, stars and the vastness of space. Looking at the ordinary as extraordinary. Do we remember the feeling of inhabiting our twisting body with abandon, sipping tea with an imaginary friend or dancing and twirling with fairies? Do we remember staring up at the clouds, being in wonder of our expansive earth. What was it like to jumble into the middle of a puddle and tumble through fallen leaves as they crunch, and swirl and let out a laugh of delight? We may remember the circumstance, but can we truly remember the feel and essence of the feeling? For most of us, this is an unreachable state. Somehow, the soulfulness of play has been lost and the unique portal which play provides for us, the portal into the reproductive spaces between our busy thoughts, plans and the necessity of what we think matters, the heavy load of a crowded curriculum and what we think our children should learn rather than what they can experience in the ordinary. Over the last few years, we may have lost touch with the deeper rhythms of life, mystery, wonder and possibilities, the invisible or uncertainty that children continually point us back to in a hundred ways each and every day in their natural settings.

Today, more than ever, we need to return to this simplistic notion of wonder and possibilities and unleash the capable in our children, this is essential for holistic education and necessary to nurture spirituality. Unfortunately, the essential is being paved over with the concrete, literal, measurable, fast-paced and unmindful world that we think life is, the one that we are now preparing children for more than ever before. We can take that first step to pause, rethink and reconceptualise children and childhood if we are truly committed to understanding and nurturing the whole child and their innate spirituality.

6.9.3 Play is the conception period for ideas, innovation and gifts the world needs

If we want to raise mature, openhearted youth and adults, then for educators and the adults that walk beside children this begins by simply letting children play. By respecting the soulfulness of play, we then allow it to do its job of nurturing children in ways that we cannot. Play, especially unstructured play, is essential. It is the perfect field for children's innate spirituality to manifest and be made visible. Slowly and mysteriously, it provides a period of initiation as it nourishes and cultivates their mysteries, wonder and questions tending to the subtle nudges and whispers of the soul and mind, their curiosities. The instinctive qualities of curiosity, wonder, openness, exploration, awe and imagination stoke the fire of creativity and support children to keep dreaming their dreams alive, recognise the children incredible potential so that they can then leap into the world and share these gifts within their communities and their lives. They are the essence of what is to become our future. We need to recognise the intrinsic nature of young children and how they can offer their pondering and points of view to the world. We need to honour the agency of each child, allow them the time for their spiritual capabilities and expressions to manifest. What better way to allow this to happen than within their natural ability to play.

In this present time, there is a great urgency for children to move and think in unstructured and divergent ways and to freely explore and embody their learning environment. Children's formative years are similar to the experience of a butterfly submerged in metamorphosis. It is like a metaphor; the butterfly pumps blood into its strengthening wing by pushing the boundaries of its chrysalis; in a similar fashion, children pump blood into their own wings by submerging and giving themselves fully to their play, and their theories about their connectedness to the world. The improvisation, non-attachment to linear movement, direction and outcomes become inherent and visible when we let a child immerse in unstructured play. It keeps the child open and responsive to the heartbeat of the inner soul. Children have the flexibility to adapt, change and explore phenomena as the rhythm of play changes and they go about in their divergent manners.

6.9.4 Play is training for the unexpected, the unknown

The unpredictability, the openness to possibilities and the opportunities that play affords rather than the predictabilities of linear thought, unleash the child's soul, the true expressions of spirituality, deep learning, and intelligence. It's no wonder that we are more frequently seeing a generation of children who would rather succeed at fitting in rather than fail at standing out and being unpredictable and open to possibilities. These old mindsets about children and learning harbour systems that fit children with cookie-cutter, outdated systems and ideas that no longer work or serve the new emerging world. As educators, we need to unleash our own freedom and expect the unexpected and the unknown to occur. With this insight, we are letting ourselves be free to truly and authentically 'see' and 'listen' to children, valuing their individual theories and thoughts about the world.

6.9.5 Space and flow: the rightful place in child development

Our current world is driven more by rationality and power than by intuition and space and flow are now losing their rightful place in child development. Classroom environments are cluttered with curriculum and a surplus of students, children are tired as they are scheduled and schooled both at school and outside school. How often do we stop in the business of a child's education to allow them to become open, present and fully engaged? How much is the connection of children with their natural, spontaneous curiosity when they are regularly spoken down to, whisked off to a piano or music lesson, expected to line up, be still, not talk or trudged off to football, soccer or netball practice and, to top it all off, find time for homework? This hustle and bustle, the pressure of a crowded curriculum, and an overzealous approach to extra-curricular activities does not connect with play. Rather, it disconnects the child from their natural, curious spontaneity. How much time do we allow for the nurturing of the soft stirring of a child's soul, when more information is piled into them rather than pulled out? Children need the room within our cluttered existence to think for themselves, traverse the richness of their imaginations, contemplate and question ideas about the world, and wonder about theories which are yet to be born into the world. They can offer us a new wisdom about our world.

Being immersed in this style of over-cluttering is unavoidable today, but what is not is the ability to not forget to allow play and recognise children's spiritual expression. We become consumed by the symptoms of a society that has completely forgotten to slow down, to be in the flow of play or total immersion, to be quiet, to belong in nature, in awe and in wonder and to allow children to touch that which lies between the clutter of daily existence, where the voice of the heart, other worlds and the hundred languages are all seen and heard. The Reggio Emilia approach and philosophy encompasses the metaphor that children have a hundred languages to explore and experience. Within these hundred languages is the language of spirituality, which can be unleashed by simply letting children play. It is a much harder effort to engage and educate the heart and nurture a child's innate spirituality in a cluttered classroom and life. It is an essential must to allow a space between the educator's words, learning outcomes and in the minds of children if the heart and spirit are to be heard and acted upon: for the language of spirituality to be present. Space must be made for the flow of imagination, exploration and intuition. Otherwise, children will eventually disassociate from their wonderings and imagination will concretise and the ability to be inspired by awe and wonder will eventually calcify and disappear entirely. We cannot let this happen; we need to preserve the sacredness of childhood as we navigate the spiritual dimension.

6.9.6 *Let play be the teacher, guide, and nurturer*

Letting children play is a crucial and essential step towards creating a better future. In the Reggio Emilia approach to education, the classroom, or environment, is considered the 'third teacher'. Open, uncluttered space filled with beauty, natural materials, intelligent materials to engage children, natural light inspires and offers a beautiful container and chrysalis for change, evolving, learning and development.

6.9.6.1 What if we saw play as being a teacher as well and an essential part of everyday practice?

What if the essence and soulfulness of play is the soil which supports and cultivates the child? Can we let him/her flourish naturally, organically and at his/her own pace? Can we trust the immense, innate and immeasurable wisdom of play to let a child flourish and be raised in ways we can never imagine?

If we allow ourselves to see play as a powerful and wise teacher that believes that we have no way of knowing everything, then we can release our control of knowledge and make room for nuanced knowledge and guidance. If we can learn to trust play and have the courage to rethink the forgotten child that resides within each individual, we can allow ourselves the courage to wonder beyond the literal and concrete of our tired and conditioned eyes and return to soft eyes that see all. If we are able to let go a little of the obsession with assessing, testing, reporting and structure as a whole, we can allow uncertainty to be fluid, open and grounded in the essential and let ourselves dance with children in their awe- and wonder-filled spaces. We can allow their full expression to flourish and nurture their creative and innate spirits.

Play becomes an obsession when we fully understand its capacity for the holistic development of children. Let play become your obsession.

6.10 Summary

This chapter has discussed the findings in relation to the four guiding research questions that relate to the overall research question. It considered the examples of children's qualitative expressions of spirituality, collated in Table 6.1. These indicators were expressions of spirituality by children between the ages of four and six years. The data provided evidence of what these qualitative indicators of the expressions of spirituality looked like and how they were observed in the children's everyday activities. The findings highlighted conditions in which the indicators of spirituality manifested and the categories which described the expressions of spirituality. The literature review in Chapter 2 guided the development of the spiritual indicators and expressions demonstrated by the children. From the discussion, it emerges that spirituality is a vital element to consider and to be recognised in early childhood education. Young children experience involvement and connection through wonder and awe, which evoke a curiosity to discover bigger questions and theories about their place and meaning in the world.

This chapter has also outlined the pedagogical conditions in relation to the second guiding research question. In summary, the conditions and the pedagogy which existed and were described and displayed in the Learning Stories were inspired by the Reggio Emilia approach, as outlined in Chapter 3. The data provided evidence that the indicators of expressions of spirituality were present when viewed through the Reggio Emilia approach and, in pedagogical practice, when this approach was implemented. This approach provided conditions in which children could explore, find their place in the world, engage and create. Links to the environment, the conditions and how we document and observe children's daily activities and carefully listen to children's verbal and non-verbal interactions emerged as being integral for understanding and observing children's expressions of spirituality.

This chapter proceeded to answer the third guiding research question and how the data suggested that expressions of spirituality could be described as spiritual dimensions which emerged as the data was further analysed, namely: interconnectedness, making meaning, and being relational and multidimensional. With the Reggio Emilia philosophy connected under the umbrella of holistic education, we allow children to contextualise intent and meaning (Bone, 2005). The chapter discussed the fourth research question and how specific elements of the pedagogical environment nurture the spiritual dimension of young children. While scholarly input suggests that spirituality is evident within a holistic pedagogical environment which recognises the strong image of the child (Edwards et al. 1998) and where the child is an active agent in their own learning and experiences. Children within such an approach are provided with conditions in which they interconnect, belong and discover a way of living (Benson & Roehlkepartain 2008; Binder 2011). While the Reggio Emilia approach can be linked to the umbrella of holistic education, this study is different from other studies which have focused on holistic education in that it provides evidence on the unique aspects and elements of the Reggio Emilia approach which engage and nurture children's spirituality.

This chapter offers the readers an invitation to use play and encounters in the everyday to guide their own understanding of the spiritual dimension. It invites educators to become obsessed with play.

Provocations for educators:

- *Can your context use the guiding questions of the case study to explore the Reggio Emilia approach and children's expression of spirituality?*
- *How do you consider play in your setting? Is this time considered sacred and essential?*
- *Do you agree with the powerful, soulful nature of play?*
- *How can you advocate for children's right to play?*

Revelations
What research is telling us about young children and spirituality

Figure 7.1

❧ *The child's mind is an open book to their innate spiritual capacity, it is our role as adults to clearly see, connect, understand and nurture this capacity* ☙

Helena Card

7.1 Introduction

The study, as presented in this book, opens new ground in research, rethinking spirituality in young children and exploring spirituality in connection to the unique pedagogical approach of Reggio Emilia.

The main aim of this work was to identify:

> What indicators may be used to identify expressions of spirituality by four- to six-year-old children, and how can the Reggio Emilia approach to education offer a context for recognising and nurturing children's spiritual capacities?

This research explored the idea, within the particular context of a Reggio Emilia-inspired pedagogical approach, that children's expressions of spirituality were observed and present. The research highlighted evidence that children's spirituality is an everyday phenomenon which naturally exists. Throughout this chapter, I will discuss the importance of linking pedagogy to practice in relation to young children's spirituality. The chapter will then discuss the implications for educators in early childhood to recognise and understand that spirituality is intrinsic in young children and to carefully consider the pedagogical approach they design for young children. I will address the implications for considering spirituality in a secular society and present some concluding remarks and suggestions for further research. This chapter will highlight the unique contribution of this study in understanding and recognising the particular dimension of childhood, spirituality, which has been overlooked in early years education.

7.1.1 Theoretical framework

The sociocultural theoretical framing of this research, which also aligns with the Reggio Emilia approach, recognised the agency of young children as active meaning-makers, and creators and co-constructors of knowledge. Adopting a sociocultural approach acknowledges one of the main guiding principles of the Reggio Emilia approach with the strong image of the child (Malaguzzi 1994; Rinaldi 2006) as the constructor of knowledge. In addition, this sociocultural theoretical framework supported the concept that children create and construct how they express their spirituality. The study presented an analysis of data demonstrating children's everyday actions and experiences in this particular child centred learning context.

The wider theoretical foundation of the research highlights the principles of the Reggio Emilia philosophy in which spiritual expression can be recognised and nurtured. It suggests that a space needs to be made in the everyday learning of young children which allows expressions of spirituality to be present. The findings in this research highlights that a sociocultural approach such as Reggio Emilia in an early years setting allowed, and provided for, space and time in the daily program for expressions of spirituality to flourish and to be noticeable.

7.2 Pedagogy and spirituality

This study explored the idea that, when the Reggio Emilia approach was implemented, indicators of expressions of spirituality were observed to be present. Material objects or natural phenomena provided a multidimensional or multisensory exploration or relational connection for the child to communicate their expressions of spirituality as summarised in the previous chapter. While it is recognised, of course, that there are other pedagogical approaches which are child-centred and play-based which can also provide stimulating environments and be conducive to young children's creativity, imagination and flow, this study explores children's expression of spirituality and connection to the Reggio Emilia approach, and suggests a juxtaposition or viewpoint about young children's spiritual capacity.

This study also acknowledged the contested spiritual debate, and has not confined spirituality to one sole definition. In the opening chapter I proposed a position regarding children's spirituality in this research and I continue to acknowledge this, rather than one sole definition. As the researcher and for the purposes of this study I continue to advocate this original position. This stance recognises that spirituality is intrinsic to young children and that it is an integral part of their being. This research also adopts the position that spirituality in young children takes the form of inbuilt curiosity, questioning, wonder and awe about where they came from or how they exist in relation their everyday world. Additionally, my research and work proposes that spiritual expression and spiritual capacity is an aspect of young children's natural identity.

The evidence presented through the Learning Stories comprised indicators of the expression of spirituality: flow, creativity, imagination, caring for another, attraction to a natural phenomenon, attraction to nature, joy, wonder and awe, engagement, wisdom and curiosity. These indicators, as discussed in the literature reviewed in this study, are associated with children's spirituality. In addition, as the data were analysed, other themes emerged in relation to the pedagogical conditions inspired by the Reggio Emilia approach. The findings highlighted the elements and conditions within the pedagogical environment, with these summarised and categorised in Table 6.2. The research demonstrated that a multisensory, multidimensional environment, such as that which has been offered and inspired by the Reggio Emilia approach, is essential, first, to invite and to recognise spirituality and then, in turn, to nurture the spiritual expression of young children. Through further analysis of the data, evidence which emerged from the study suggested that spirituality within this context could be considered in terms of the following dimensions: interconnectedness, making meaning, and being relational and multidimensional.

The findings presented evidence of instances when the children were offered opportunities to be creative within an environment which provided the materials and multiple ways which engaged the children through activities and encounters. The teacher and the researcher were present, not to instruct, but principally to watch, listen and observe while the environment engaged the child. The emphasis on creativity through multiple modes, as supported by Dowling (2005), is a key principle in the Reggio Emilia approach. My research argues that, on the basis of the evidence, the Reggio Emilia approach, with this emphasis on creativity, engages children and they demonstrate spiritual indicators of the expression of spirituality. This is also supported by Dowling (2005), who suggests 'that the Reggio Emilia approaches to nurturing creativity are further examples of enhancing spirituality in early years settings' (cited in Adams et al. 2015, p. 8).

Analysis of the data revealed that the indicators of expressions of spirituality could be considered as part of young children's hundred languages (Malaguzzi 1998; Rinaldi 2006) and the way in which they make meaning and construct theories and perceptions about their lives. Thus, offering multiple 'opportunities for a freedom to envision more life-giving and life-enhancing ways of being' (Hyde 2008b, p. 36).

This research suggests that, to fully understand children's spirituality, the pedagogical approach which allows spirituality to evolve within young children has a valid place in the discussion of reconceptualising a pedagogy which values and recognises the image of the child (Malaguzzi 1994; Rinaldi 2006) to also include their spirituality. The data within this study revealed that, through interconnectedness and relational experiences with the environment and with others, and through authentic encounters and wholeness, children can interpret what is meaningful to them and to discover their world. As Meehan (2002a) suggests, for spirituality in young children to evolve they need to have opportunities 'for using their imaginations; for creativity, exploration, wonder, awe' and situations in which children are able to ask many questions (p. 22). Meehan (2002a) further asserts that these are essential components of a learning environment or curriculum designed to promote spiritual development. A pedagogy that includes certain conditions to allow such learning to manifest is paramount for spiritual expressions to be seen; this study has explored the possibility that the Reggio Emilia approach offers a pedagogy whereby spiritual expression can be seen. An attitude such as the Reggio Emilia philosophy and approach, which is open and accepting towards children, is essential and, as Watson (2013) clearly points out, educators, 'can make no assumptions about the spiritual identity each child brings to the classroom and must make space for an individualised encounter with each child' (p. 127).

This research, based on the synthesis of the findings, suggests that spirituality is a natural part of young children's lives: an ontological capacity which can be expressed in multiple ways and through multiple modes. Gang, Lynn and Maver (1992) support this view, stating that '[s]pirituality does not become a subject matter, but rather the thread that runs through and permeates all activity' (p. 57), that spirituality is about participation in life and is the core of what it means to be human. Meehan (2002a) asserts that 'the spiritual is rooted in the essence of being human' (p. 22); Rinaldi (2004) advocates that children are the 'best expressions of our being human' (p. 2).

The study revealed that spirituality is a reality and exists, which raises implications for educators in terms of reacting to and nurturing this intrinsic aspect of young children. The observable expressions of spirituality capture the environmental qualities of the Reggio Emilia approach, which are necessary for this visibility of children's spirituality to occur, to be recognised and to be nurtured.

7.3 Considering spirituality in a secular world

One consideration which my work poses is as follows: if the spiritual capacity of young children is not developed or nurtured it can be impeded, thwarted, stopped from developing and it can go underground and become invisible. This study has explored the spiritual debate and the contested interpretations of spirituality; it has adopted the argument that children are spiritual beings and that spirituality and spiritual expression are part of their natural identity. My work also premises that young children have a natural capacity for spirituality, and that this is not always related to religion.

Taking the above points into consideration imposes a responsibility for those adults working with children in education to nurture this natural capacity be open to considering new understandings of spirituality within our secular world. Policy makers who have used the term spirituality in relation to young children will need to think about supporting educators in recognising what expressions of spirituality look like and how pedagogy can nurture this. Natsis (2016) states that Australia is facing a new frontier in the educational discourse of spirituality. The study asserts that we are transitioning into a globalised and secular society where educators are faced with the question of how to respond to the intrinsic nature of spirituality in young children. Therefore, it could be considered that this recognition of spirituality and nurturing must be linked to learning and has a significant place in the design of pedagogy and learning for young children in today's society.

7.4 Listening to the expressions of spirituality

My involvement in this study as the researcher and participant observer, collecting the data and observing the children, involved a deep listening, a listening which goes beyond the normal understanding of listening. It is one which I have fashioned and modelled from the Reggio Emilia philosophy and their principle of the pedagogy of listening. For me to fully understand this dimension in children, I needed to go beyond listening and to 'listen' with all my senses, not just hearing the children's verbal expressions but listening and seeing their expressions of spirituality through different modes of expression.

This study revealed that the reality of young children's expressions of spirituality existed in their natural everyday encounters. As adults and educators, this requires an attentiveness to children to listen to and acknowledge these expressions and perhaps for educators to change their views about how to listen to children in order to notice expressions of spirituality. Therefore, there is a suggestion that the adults who work alongside young children should be open to listening differently to children, with an awareness of their gestures and non-verbal communication and also through their creativity and imagination. Champagne (2001) identifies listening to young children as 'active and responsive' in order to understand and recognise spirituality (p. 289). Champagne (2001) advocates that attentive listening to children is crucial if we are to fully understand and recognise young children's expressions of spirituality.

7.5 The Reggio Emilia approach and expressions of spirituality: a spectrum to consider for learning

In light of the evidence presented, a challenge has emerged for early childhood educators about how pedagogy at this stage should be inclusive of the understanding of the whole child and of the necessity to recognise and nurture the spiritual dimension as an integral part of each child's development. It is necessary to point out that the focus of this study, although it was conducted in a Catholic setting, was centred on the Reggio Emilia approach and the evidence which was analysed and presented. It is important to acknowledge that there may have been influences from the Christian, Catholic ethos of the school and this can be acknowledged as a limitation within the study. However, the case and the boundaries of the study were clearly stated in relation to the specific pedagogical approach within this context. It must also be noted that the researcher's focus was to examine and explore spirituality separately from religion through the lens of the Reggio Emilia approach, thereby allowing the study to be unique and different from other studies by providing an exploration of young children's spirituality as it occurs in a natural everyday setting. This study may recommend and warrant an importance for understanding young children's spirituality within a broader conversation. Furthermore, because of its importance, many actions must be taken and further study conducted to provide researchers, parents, and educators more information on the spiritual development of young children.

Working within this wider view of spirituality would permit the broader understanding of children's spirituality, which is outside religious tradition and orientation. This does not, of course, dismiss any religious framework or directives from religious organisations that oversee early childhood sites. Within a Catholic context or a faith-based early years setting, the challenge is to develop wider recognition and understanding of spirituality as an integral part of early childhood development. This suggests that changes in attitude toward children are essential. The suggestion is a provocation for further investigation to look at religious education programs to ensure that, within the early years, indicators of spiritual expression are acknowledged. If this acknowledgement occurs alongside the development of the understanding of God in the Catholic tradition, the Reggio Emilia approach could then be considered as a pedagogical approach in which these expressions and indicators are present and which is then further developed in relation to Catholic identity. Consequently, this is an area of research which may require further investigation and research.

Furthermore, the scholarly input, and the wider understanding of spirituality which suggest that spirituality is an inherent quality of the human being, including adults and children, have offered more scope to fully understand spirituality. In Chapter 1, i provided a variety of definitions of children's spirituality and highlighted the contentious debate about a single definition. However, in Chapter 1, I :argued the position of my study regarding children's spirituality; that it was intrinsic, they are spiritual beings and that spiritual expression is part of their natural identity. This is where this study has a particular contribution. This study contributes to, and builds on, the understanding of young children's spirituality and, as recommended by Mata (2014) and Schein (2013), to deepen the knowledge about how this concept and phenomenon is present in young children. The study recommends a necessary understanding of young children's spirituality so that it may no longer go unnoticed or misunderstood, but instead be included as an essential element of thinking and learning in new times and when designing programs for early years education.

7.6 Image of the child: the Reggio Emilia view of the child

My work and research indicated that children's spirituality requires a catalyst in which certain conditions and allowances are essential for children's spirituality to flourish and be evident. The Reggio Emilia philosophy and approach to childhood offer one style or catalyst for these conditions and the support of children's spiritual development. In developing and acknowledging a framework, such as the Reggio Emilia approach, that recognises and encourages spirituality within the various contexts of children's early childhood activities, it is anticipated that more children will be able to fully experience their spiritual capacities and lives. The study highlighted that one of the guiding principles of the Reggio Emilia approach was the understanding of the image of the child (Malaguzzi 1994; Rinaldi 2006), as acknowledged and described by the educators of

Reggio Emilia, with this image affecting the style of practice which is offered to children. The study proposes that if we understand this image of the child, then a child's spirituality can be identified through an approach such as that of Reggio Emilia.

7.7 Language of spirituality

Language is a system of symbols and signs. Within the Reggio Emilia philosophy, this system of symbols and signs is present in young children in many ways; it is not restricted but covers an array of ways and means by which children express themselves. The hundred languages (Malaguzzi 1998; Rinaldi 2006) become a way, a means and a vessel for young children to express themselves through multiple ways. As the data have revealed, the expressions, gestures, silence and flow in the relationships which children have within the early years setting exhibited their spiritual expressions. Through the children's imagination, conditions in the environment and their creativity, the language of spirituality became visible, and was heard and seen within a pedagogy which listened to children in multiple ways. The Learning Stories provided many examples of children expressing themselves through their hundred languages (Malaguzzi 1998; Rinaldi 2006). Hall (2012) supports this claim and adds:

> a child's spirituality can be recognised and expressed through the Hundred Languages of Children as we ask the child to make a 'hundred ways of listening … marvelling … to discover … to invent … and to dream …'
>
> (Hall 2012, p. 36)

Once the data were synthesised and presented in Chapter 6, the evidence suggested that conditions were pertinent for spirituality, first, to be expressed and then to be understood so educators could nurture this dimension. Furthermore, Chapter 6 suggested further identification and ways to describe children's expressions of spirituality within the Reggio Emilia context in terms of the following dimensions: interconnectedness, making meaning, and being relational and multidimensional. This identification requires a pedagogical attitude, such as the Reggio Emilia approach, which does not consider children to be empty vessels in need of filling up, but rather recognises how young children express themselves and what they already know. Both the naturalistic, multidimensional learning environments observed and also the evidence of expressions of spirituality which was revealed through the findings of this research accounted for this situation, in which children were not expected to produce single-outcome learning tasks. Instead, time was allocated in the learning program for children to be able to explore and express themselves in an environment which validated self-discovery and during which they were free to imagine, create and experiment. The child's right to play was afforded and prioritised.

This study proposes that the language of spirituality was used in children's conscious and unconscious reactions and expressions and was embedded in the everyday, in the ordinary moments of children's encounters. My work suggests that spirituality is naturally present, but that it is necessary for it to be seen and recognised. The challenge is to listen and hear this phenomenon of spirituality, to carefully understand how this relates to the whole dimension of the child, and to provide a pedagogy which will nurture spirituality.

7.7.1 Welcoming spirituality

In early childhood settings, it is essential to provide a community which welcomes every aspect of the child. This community needs to be aware that their child is an integral and nucleic part of the community. We have to learn to welcome the child as a human child, to acknowledge that they are a competent protagonist in learning, and finally to acknowledge their spirituality. In so doing, we are setting the stage for holistic learning and an appreciation of the spiritual dimension.

> children are the best expression of the potentiality of human beings
> Carla Rinaldi (2013, Thinker in Residence speaker)

We need to welcome an archaeology of childhood which includes the spiritual dimension. To do this we need to rethink the intrinsic dignity of each child's capacity to go beyond the known into the unknown, in order to understand fully how they express themselves as humans.

This understanding of the archaeology of childhood also needs to be afforded and time given to treasure play as sacred, This is a thought that I ask you to carry with you as we welcome the spiritual dimension to be nurtured as part of the human being. Play is spiritual expression in a pure, honest and undisturbed flow of ideas, natural curiosity and inner knowing. It is the most honourable opportunity we can offer young children. It is a sanctuary for joy, freedom, curiosity, beauty and peace.

Surely this is what every educator in early childhood would want for each human child that is welcomed into the learning environment. With this thinking, we can only contribute generously and positively to the next generation in our world.

7.8 Some further considerations

This inquiry, and its findings, have emerged in a specific context. It is a response to the complexity of understanding spirituality in young children. I have captured and presented moments from the children's rich naturalistic environments. The Adelaide Thinkers in Residence program (2012–2013), with the involvement of Carla Rinaldi, offered a challenge to re-imagine childhood, and she continues to advocate this through the lens of the Reggio Emilia philosophy. When considering re-imagining childhood, my research suggests that this may also involve a reconceptualisation of the early childhood pedagogy towards understanding the full capacity of childhood in our society in which the inclusion of the spirituality of children is recognised. This reconceptualisation is about choosing to implement a pedagogical approach, such as the Reggio Emilia approach, which allows indicators of the expression of spirituality to be present and, thus, a pedagogical approach which provides the space and the time for expressions of spirituality to be noticed.

This book, and my work, provokes thinking about how we can access or witness young children's interior life, which includes the spiritual, and why this is an important factor to consider in present-day early years education. The study has provided evidence that the spiritual capacity can be noticed in young children and, therefore, compels a pedagogical approach in which spirituality can be facilitated and be nurtured. It raises the question: does early years education today recognise and accept that the basic expression of spirituality can be recognised through children's creativity, imagination, ability to ask bigger questions, attraction to natural phenomena, connection to nature, caring for another, wonder and awe, curiosity and engagement or during times of flow? This recognition and consideration require a shift in thinking about education and pedagogical approaches, and acceptance that the spiritual dimension does exist and is present in children's development and must not be ignored.

This book, and my research, highlights that educators need to examine how the process of human development involves the whole child. To fully recognise spirituality in early years education requires going beyond knowledge acquisition and entering the domains of meaning and purpose. Furthermore, this study suggests that early childhood educators require an understanding about the various modes through which children can express themselves. If the hundred languages (Malaguzzi 1998; Rinaldi 2006) of children are ignored, then spirituality may not be seen or allowed to be present. It is proposed that this study will advance dialogue about early childhood spiritual development among researchers, parents, early childhood educators and other stakeholders dedicated to the growth and development of young children living in the 21st century.

The review of the literature highlighted the developing interest and scholarly work surrounding spirituality and supported the view that it is part of the natural human condition and that it can be seen and witnessed in young children. The literature review revealed an accumulation of knowledge involving young children and spirituality which presents a valid argument for providing a space in early years teaching practice for spirituality to be expressed, to be noticed and to flourish. This presents an ethical argument for spirituality to be recognised as an integral part of educating the young child.

My research with children argues that young children's spirituality is core to their whole development and, as revealed in the literature review, is connected to what it is to be human. Children are vulnerable within current education systems and are victims of the political decisions which drive educational programs. In addition, our modern society's demands, the drive to become perfect or to achieve academically are at the forefront of the approach to education. This contributes to a fragmentation within our educational approach, one which is driven by outcomes and academic achievement. Educational approaches have become distracted by the factory approach of filling children's heads with information and controlled knowledge. Recognising spirituality as a dimension and a natural part of children's being will prevent the industrialisation of, or factory-belt approach to, education and provide children with the right to exercise their existing means and ways of acquiring knowledge and to express their meaning making. If we choose to ignore the existence of the spiritual dimension, it will then become invisible with children's abilities and expressions never made visible within an education system that only values knowledge that can be tested. The difficult task of nurturing the whole person will be likely to disappear from the list of educational priorities as it is considered so elusive to measure. A truly ethical approach to education is to acknowledge the whole human identity: this cannot be done through ignoring the spiritual aspect of being human.

My work, and my research, contributes to determining what kind of pedagogical framework is conducive for nurturing spiritual development in young children. Glazer (1999) suggests that 'education is about transformation' (p. 238). Goodliff (2013) suggests that including the spiritual dimension in a pedagogical approach is 'nurturing the full humanity of young children'. She proceeds to advocate that allowances should be provided for children to participate in spaces where the 'language is recognised' (Goodliff 2013, p. 1068). Rinaldi (2006) offers the image and construct of the 'rich child, an active subject with rights and extraordinary potential and born with a hundred languages' (p. 17), which underpins the Reggio Emilia approach and philosophy. This resonates with a holistic understanding of children's spirituality. Another connection and comparison of the Reggio Emilia approach is the pedagogy of listening (Rinaldi 2006). This is based on the opinion and belief that the child is a social being and requires encounters and interaction with their world to make meaning: as the educators alongside children, we can be ardent listeners. This pedagogy is similar to Bronfenbrenner's (1979) explanation of the two-way nature of children's impact on their environment and the multiple possibilities of the spaces created in their learning environments (Moss & Petrie 2002). This study suggests that the Reggio Emilia approach and the way in which the environment is considered as the third teacher allow for this multisensory entry for children and, in turn, provide conditions for indicators of expressions of spirituality to be present, to be described as dimensions and to exist.

The Reggio Emilia philosophy, as supported by Moss and Petrie (2002), is a pedagogy where children actively create, inhabit and encounter spaces to reveal their thoughts, curiosity and questions, meanings and interpretations of life. As educators and researchers, we can be the ardent listeners where the notion of listening to the meaning-making of children and their quest to be, do and know involves an openness to listen, interpret and understand: it is not 'just with our ears, but with all our senses ...' (Rinaldi 2006, p. 20).

By observing spirituality through the lens of the Reggio Emilia approach, this study suggests that it offers an entry point, viewpoint and juxtaposition into understanding the inner lives of children and respecting and honouring the whole human being, including spiritual capacity. The study has provided evidence that expressions of spirituality in young children can be seen. The pedagogy and practice offer the conditions and the allowance for expressions of spirituality to be naturally present. Rinaldi (2004) states that: '[b]ecause we believe in the pedagogy of listening, the experience in Reggio tries to honour the children by listening to that expression of the human being' (p. 4).

7.8.1 A contribution to different thinking in early childhood education

This study offers a contribution to early childhood education and practice by putting forward a viewpoint which has not been widely considered and honoured. This study has provided an original perspective and contribution by offering a unique viewpoint, which suggests that the Reggio Emilia pedagogical approach offers a multisensory, multidimensional environment and makes visible the indicators of expressions of spirituality in young children. The approach also offers a pedagogical approach which can nurture this human dimension of young children. This research highlights that it is essential to use a style of pedagogy where knowledge and encounters with a learning space are not driven by predetermined outcomes, suggesting instead a pedagogical approach which allows the whole child to develop and to be seen. When the explorations and experiences of children also influence the spiritual side of human development, then a high-quality early childhood education, incorporating natural materials and beautiful, aesthetic spaces (Bailie 2012; Harris 2007; Kirmani & Kirmani 2009; Schein 2013; Surr 2012; Wilson 2008) is an essential pedagogical consideration. This study goes further to suggest that once spirituality is recognised, a pedagogical approach, such as that of Reggio Emilia, with the elements described above, is necessary and will influence the human side of development. The study suggests that this style of pedagogical approach has the potential to also nurture young children's spiritual development and must be considered as part of a high-quality early childhood program.

Further empirical research is necessary to build on this viewpoint to instil a global understanding and commitment to nurturing this intrinsic capacity in young children.

Investigation of children's spirituality and the part schooling should play in its development would need to include how the educator can articulate spirituality as one of their aims in teaching young children and all children.

7.8.2 A new description for spirituality: educating the head, hearts and souls of children

I have been very fortunate to dedicate so much time and effort into understanding young children's spirituality. I hereby offer a new description with my own vindications and beliefs about spirituality in children. Spirituality in children is:

> An innate capacity and desire to know and to experience life through creativity, imagination, wonder and awe. Spirituality exists and is intrinsic. Children are spiritual embryos who yearn to be connected to their world through discovery, respect and the right to be inquisitive and curious. Spirituality in young children is expressed through their everyday extraordinary moments and deserves the right to flourish in beautiful, aesthetic learning environments.

7.8.3 Possibilities for early childhood: towards a new tomorrow

In summary, my research suggests that when early childhood educators select pedagogies, it is important to include strategies which recognise and accommodate children's expressions of spirituality. This requires an understanding that spirituality can be nurtured through an environment and approach where interconnectedness, meaning-making, and being relational and multidimensional are integral. A holistic, multidimensional, multisensory approach, such as that of Reggio Emilia, is one that would consider the spiritual aspects of children's lives (Adams 2009; Adams et al. 2008; Baumgartner & Buchanan 2010; Hyde 2008a; Yust 2007) and their learning and would create an environment where these aspects are present. The curriculum continues to be stretched as more and more content is demanded by society and early childhood educators seem to be expected to prepare children for every eventuality. Educators have an important role to play in developing these future citizens and one way to do this is to acknowledge and nurture children's spirituality. I adopt Motha's (2011) argument that spirituality exists in the core of each human, regardless of race, gender, culture or religion. Educating our young children to be cognitively intelligent is not enough, and driven by stringent academic outcomes is not enough; we must extend the discourse of spirituality into a broader educational context and nourish children's spirituality.

Based on this knowledge, this book contributes to the process of further developments in understanding and educating the future generation involved in education in the early years of childhood in relation to comprehending and recognising the spiritual indicators of young children's expressions of spirituality. This book and research suggests that once the spiritual capacity of young children is fully understood, seen and expressed in the way that young children express it, then the challenge is to apply a pedagogical approach inspired by the Reggio Emilia approach which will nurture spirituality and allow it to flourish within early childhood settings.

I would argue, then, that the inclusion of further ongoing explorations and discussions around children's spirituality is not a sidebar to the main business of education, but rather an essential component that underpins the work of early learning centres, primary schools and secondary schools. Early learning centres and schools seem to be expected to prepare children for every eventuality. These educational institutions have an important role to play in developing these future citizens; one way to do this is to acknowledge and nurture children's spirituality and no longer allow it to be silenced.

Continuing the discourse of spirituality and expanding studies into primary and secondary schools with cross-sections of cultures, genders and religions is crucial to consider. I am hopeful that the development of a wider discourse about young children's spirituality will be present not only in early childhood education settings but also in other educational institutions.

What can we do?

Nurturing spirituality in young children while understanding our own

Figure 8.1

> ❦ We can be open to understanding our own spirituality and use this to guide us as we navigate young children's spiritual dimension. ❧
>
> *Helena Card*

My research has been my life-long passion, ambition and contribution to preserving the wonderful and exuberant time of childhood. To do this, we, as educators, can take some time to reflect on our practice and how we might construct and reconceptualise our view of children to provide settings which are conducive to nurturing them holistically, in mind, body and spirit. I am offering educators the following resources to try to understand their own spirituality as they provide and afford learning environments for children.

8.1 Spiritual moments

8.1.1 Spiritual moments in everyday life

Everyone experiences spiritual moments in time during their everyday life. It is how we respond to these moments in time that impact our own spiritual awareness. Children have spiritual moments in time when they have generous amounts of time to play, explore, discover and participate.

Becoming aware of spiritual moments as educators is very important if we truly desire to understand spirituality in young children. As educators, some of these reflective activities can support your own understanding of spirituality in order to better understand and nurture young children's innate spirituality.

- *As educators, how do you as adults allow spiritual moments for yourself?*
- *Think about moments that have given you feelings of peace and joy, moments when you have the time to let your mind flow without being hurried or pressured.*
- *Are you still curious, do you allow yourself to be vulnerable and ask questions?*
- *Do you spend time being creative?*
- *Think about reflective moments.*
- *Think about times of wonder and awe, do you give yourself time to experience this*
- *What ties these reflective moments and moments of awe and wonder together?*

8.1.2 Spaces to ignite spiritual moments

What I know about spirituality through my research and the accounts within this book is that young children must have a right to beautiful learning spaces if we are going to afford and nurture their innate spirituality and expressions. If are creating spaces, they need to be aesthetically beautiful, filled with real and authentic materials and objects to ignite real experiences and rich language. These kinds of environments are likely to be filled with moments of wonder, awe, creativity and inner peace and flow.

- *What qualities and characteristics would this space need?*

8.1.3 Spiritual moments with nature

As the research detailed, nature is a poignant aspect which ignites spiritual expressions in young children. They can explore the outdoors with nature, but it is so important and essential that nature is also brought indoors into the learning environment for close exploration and discovery. It is a poignant source for wonder and awe, and provides a provocation for the emergence of bigger questions to ask. Educators take some time to experience nature.

- *Go for a walk outdoors, try to look for moments that touch you and ignite inner feelings.*
- *Immerse yourself in how nature is present, and what is it showing or telling you.*
- *Notice the beauty of nature and natural objects.*
- *Can you put your feelings into words? What big questions are arising from these moments?*

8.1.4 Children and big questions

As children explore and interact with nature and natural objects, they may be unable to completely articulate their big questions, but they are exploring curiosities and questions about how life works. Listening to children ponder and ask questions is a way that we, as educators, can be the attentive and respecting adults who can nurture these spiritual moments for children.

8.1.4.1 Provocations for educators

- *Has your understanding of spirituality changed as you have read through this book? If so, in what ways?*
- *How can you make spirituality visible in your setting?*
- *What bigger questions does spirituality pose for you as an adult?*

8.1.4.2 Spiritual moments: ideas and activities to share with children

Spaces and relationships are conducive to nurturing expressions of spirituality and spiritual moments. Here are some suggestions for educators working with children.

- *Be attentive, be present with children.*
- *Make time in your daily routines to sit, wonder and observe children.*
- *Encourage quiet time.*

- *Include Exploration Time in your daily programming. Allow the time for this to happen. Value this time and make evident to your community why this time is so important.*
- *Try not to be too hurried in the overcrowded expectations of assessment and progress.*
- *Treat each moment as a moment to truly see spirituality.*
- *Find objects and wonder about them with the children.*
- *Keep play spaces decluttered and organised, but expect them to become disarrayed after, so that children have explored them and this can filter through the environment in multiple ways.*
- *Offer children time to play alone or with other children without any interruptions from you as the adult. Watch, observe, document, listen.*
- *Step back, enjoy.*
- *Do not interfere.*
- *Allow agency.*
- *Try not to suggest to the child to do something different than what they have chosen to do.*
- *Pay specific attention to the learning environment; make it beautiful and inviting. There is so much to benefit from learning and discovering in a beautiful, less institutional environment.*
- *Notice little things, like the shape of leaves, and the way the wind blows objects. Help children to notice, experiment and be curious in their environments.*
- *Explore methods of supporting a sense of interconnectedness with the natural world to encourage an appreciation of its beauty and value on our planet.*

Weaving the tapestry of Spirituality

Figure 9.1

❧ *Everyone's most useful assets is not the head full of knowledge, but a heart full of love an ear ready to listen, and a hand willing to help, a soul willing to guide and nurture* ❧

Helena Card

Throughout this book, I have provided you with a framework of theory, practice and provocations for discussion. In doing so, I have emphasised that a common language of agreed values about children is necessary in every early childhood setting, if we are to entwine ourselves into understanding them and reconceptualising our idea and belief in childhood which includes the spiritual dimension.

This chapter is a practical way in which you can begin to weave the tapestry of spirituality into your planning and work within early childhood. The following table can be modified as a vision statement of core beliefs in early childhood. It can be a stepping stone for actioning learning environments which value childhood and support their innate spirituality to grow and flourish (Table 9.1).

I have designed that table as a provocation for thoughts about children in early childhood settings. I believe that if the core beliefs of your educational space considers these points as a crucial part of practice and beliefs. Then together with a rich pedagogical approach such as Reggio Emilia, this is conducive to providing a setting and a tapestry for nurturing the spiritual dimension of each child.

Table 9.1 The child and practical implications in the early childhood setting

The child...	Practical Implication in the early childhood setting
is a spiritual child	• Learning through open-ended inquiry and natural curiosity • Engagement of imagination and discovery • Time for pondering and wondering
has life experiences	• Connections between home and learning encouraged • Positive experiences shared • Inclusion of family, community, culture and or faith/Church • Meaningful connections to life experiences and prior learnings • Valuing of diversity and respect for difference
has innate capacities and spiritual expression	• Sustained engagement in authentic learning tasks • Comprehensive teacher knowledge of the student • Diverse opportunities to encourage and demonstrate capabilities and spiritual expression • Cognitively challenging learning experiences through exploration, investigation and problem solving • the right to beauty in the learning environment

The child…	Practical Implication in the early childhood setting
is holistic and sensory	- Learning through collaborative interactions with others and the environment
- Self-directed tasks to support independent learning
- Attentive listening to the early learner's ideas, hypotheses, questions and points of view
- Multisensory spaces for inquiry-based learning
- Spaces where the hundred languages can come to life
- Opportunities to learn through head, heart and hands
seeks meaning and connections	- Time and space to imagine, innovate and create
- Time for flow
- Enjoyment of learning
- Authentic learning opportunities connected to real-world opportunities
- Connection to nature and natural materials
- Use of technologies as a tool for accessing and creating information
- Timely teacher feedback to support and guide learning
thrives and flourishes in relationships	- A sense of belonging, where all learners feel safe and valued
- Teacher respects learning opportunities to be open-ended
- Learning experiences based on reciprocal relationships
- Creation of flexible spaces for engagement of small groups or pairs
- The active involvement of parents, caregivers and significant others in the learning process
- Children's work and learning documented and celebrated within the community
- Creating a sense of 'holding and nurturing' the child

Source: Helena Card 2024

Provocations for educators
How can you change the tapestry or intention of your learning environment?
Do the points in the table above resonate with your beliefs and practice?
Do you consider the child to be the active protagonist who will urge you to discover more about the spiritual dimension?

Creating the spiritual tapestry

Figure 10.1

❧ Creating a spiritual tapestry in early childhood is about weaving together experiences, values, relationships, and rituals that nurture a child's inner life, sense of wonder, and connection to something greater than themselves ❧

Helena Card

Think about the practicalities in your early learning environment. Do you spend time with the children in contemplation? For faith-based settings, this could be in prayer. For other settings, it could be in the form of ritual. I have offered you a pedagogical approach to consider, the Reggio Emilia approach. However, there are additional practices that you can introduce into your learning settings. Those who are faith-based can weave wonderful moments into the teaching day which align with your particular doctrine or beliefs. First and foremost, I hope this book has inspired you, and has encouraged d you to become advocates in nurturing the spiritual dimension of young children.

Some practicalities to consider:

- *Set up a ritual to contemplate or share positive things that have happened in the day.*
- *Inform children of gratitude and how this is a state of being where 'the other' is recognised and valued.*
- *Write or draw in gratitude journals.*
- *Listen to the child with interest, be in the moment with children, listen with your whole self.*
- *Incorporate a time for mindfulness. Allow children to have this time. So often we are rushed to meet outcomes and expectations. Children need quiet times to reflect, contemplate and to be still.*
- *Introduce time for breath and presence. Establish your own breath and presence practices and model these for children.*
- *Notice how the very simple act of taking a deep breath can change how you feel. Try it yourself and encourage children to try it with you.*
- *Create a beautiful space where you can gather to be present, to give thanks, to pray (if this is relevant in your context), to reflect, to centre or to just be.*
- *Always have opportunities to be present in nature, invite children to be connected with nature.*
- *Create a feeling of belonging for all children; be relational with children.*

Potential benefits of spiritual nurturing to children

My research, and this book, has enlivened the awareness of spirituality in young children and the benefits of a pedagogy which connects the head, heart and hands of children. It provides all educators with some tools and insights to navigate the spiritual dimension in childhood. It suggests implementing and believing in a pedagogy that helps to safeguard children from commercialism and materialism, and provides a passage for spirituality to gain its rightful place in young children's development and growth.

Among the various understandings of young children's spirituality, I have provided you with some core traits, characteristics and expressions of spirituality which are forever present in the everyday lives of children. It provides you with a table of indicators of expressions of spirituality. This book offers you the opportunity and entry points to see, hear and experience young children's spirituality. It offers you, as educators, time to reflect on holistic development of young children.

In our world, the time is running out for the adoption of a common reverence towards global warming and ecological appreciation. Connection to nature has had a common thread in all the learning environments I have talked about in this book. Realising that we are all part of the same universe carries the potential of embedding a profound realisation, appreciation and respect for life and to respect our coexistence with nature and our world. In order to grow and sustain in today's environment, we need to evoke growth and improvements in the world. We need to recognise that each person and each child is in relationship with their mind, body and spirit and eagerly desires to connect to the world. Life and learning needs to be viewed through a spiritual lens that scopes the whole person as being of potential and possibility. We can learn; we can grow; we can keep spirit at the core of education

It is time for educators to rethink their practice, reconceptualise childhood and care about the innate spiritual capacity contained within each child. I hope that this book can impart a renewed vigour and meaning into educators' practice by enriching children's lives. Above all, think about the child as a spiritual being, one who is relying on us to deeply nurture and care for this quality and dimension of their being. We can be the protagonists and advocates in reviving this mostly unnoticed and unarticulated dimension of young children.

> *Follow your hearts, teach with your hearts, listen with your hearts, learn with your hearts and senses. I invite you to dance with the spirit as you work and learn with children.*
>
> Helena Card

Figure 10.2

References

Adams, K 2009, 'The rise of the child's voice; the silencing of the spiritual voice', *Journal of Beliefs & Values*, vol. 30, no. 2, pp. 113–122.

Adams, K 2013, 'Spiritual development in schools with no faith affiliation: The cultural ambivalence towards children's spirituality in England', in J Watson, M de Souza & A Trousdale (eds.), *Global Perspectives on Spirituality and Education*, Routledge, London, pp. 21–32.

Adams, K, Hyde, B & Woolley, R 2008, *The Spiritual Dimension of Childhood*, Jessica Kingsley Publications, London.

Adams, K, Bull, R & Maynes, M 2015, 'Early childhood spirituality in education: Towards an understanding of the distinctive features of young children's spirituality', *European Early Childhood Education Research Journal*, vol. 24, no. 5, pp. 760–777.

Adler, P & Adler, P 1987, *Membership Roles in Field Research*, SAGE Publications Inc., Thousand Oaks, CA.

Aird, E 2004, 'Advertising and marketing to children in the United States', in P Pufall & R Unsworth (eds.), *Rethinking Childhood*, Rutgers University Press, New Brunswick, NJ, pp. 141–153.

Altheide, DL & Johnson, JM 1994, 'Criteria for assessing interpretive validity in qualitative research', in NK Denzin & YS Lincoln (eds.), *Handbook of Qualitative Research*, SAGE, London.

Anning, A 2009, 'Chapters 1 and 3', in A Anning, J Cullen & M Fleer (eds.) 2009, *Early Childhood Education: Society and Culture*, SAGE Publications Ltd, London.

Anning, A, Cullen, J & Fleer, M (eds.) 2009, *Early Childhood Education: Society and Culture*, SAGE Publications, London.

Apps, L & Macdonald, M 2012, 'Classroom aesthetics in early childhood education: 1', *Journal of Education and Learning*, vol. 1, no. 1, pp. 49–59.

Arendt, H 1998, *The Human Condition*, University of Chicago Press, Chicago, IL.

Atkinson, P & Hammersley, M 1998, 'Ethnography and participant observation', in N Denzin & Y Lincoln (eds.), *Strategies of Qualitative Inquiry*, SAGE, Thousand Oaks, CA, pp. 1–34.

Atkinson, R 1995, *The Gift of Stories: Practical and Spiritual Applications of Autobiography, Life Stories and Personal Myth Making*, Bergin & Garvey, Westport, CT.

Australian Government Department of Education [AGDE] 2022, Belonging, Being and Becoming: The Early Years Learning Framework for Australia (V2.0), Australian Government Department of Education for the Ministerial Council, viewed 1 July 2024, EYLF-2022-V2.0.pdf (acecqa.gov.au) https://www.acecqa.gov.au/sites/default/files/2023-01/EYLF-2022-V2.0.pdf

References

Australian Government Department of Education, Employment and Workplace Relations (DEEWR) 2009, Belonging, Being & Becoming, The Early Years Framework for Australia 2009, produced by the Australian Government Department of Education, Employment and Workplace Relations for the Council of Australian Governments, viewed 13 February 2011, www.earlyyears.sa.edu.au/files/…/Student_Engagement_and_Qua.pdf

Bailie, PE 2012, Connecting children to nature: A multiple case study of nature centre Preschools, Doctoral dissertation, University of Nebraska-Lincoln, viewed 13 November 2016, http://digitalcommons.unl.edu/teachlearnstudent/24

Barbarin, O & Wasik, B 2011, *Handbook of Child Development and Early Education: Research to Practice*, Guilford Press, viewed 21 March 2013, https://unisa.edu.au/patron/FullRecord.aspx?p=454787

Barr, A, Gillard, J, Firth, V, Scrymgour, M, Welford, R, Lomax-Smith, J, Bartlett, D, Pike, B & Constable, E 2008, *Melbourne Declaration on Educational Goals for Young Australians*, Ministerial Council on Education, Employment, Training and Youth Affairs, Melbourne, viewed 18 January 2016, http://apo.org.au/node/29859

Baumgartner, JJ & Buchanan, T 2010, 'Supporting each child's spirit', *Young Children*, vol. 65, no. 2, pp. 90–95.

Beck, C 1986, 'Education for spirituality', *Interchange*, vol. 2, no. 17, pp. 148–158.

Beck, C 1990, *Better Schools: A Values Perspective*, Falmer Press, New York.

Becker, W 1994, 'Spiritual struggle in contemporary America', *Theology Today*, vol. 51, no. 2, pp. 256–277.

Beckwith, I 2004, *Postmodern Children's Ministry: Ministry to Children in the 21st Century*, Zondervan, Grand Rapids, MI.

Bell, J 1987, *Doing Your Research Project: A Guideline for First-Time Researchers in Education and Social Science*, Open University Press, Milton Keynes.

Bell, J 2010, *Doing Your Own Research Project*, 5th ed., Open University Press, McGraw-Hill Education, Maidenhead.

Bellous, JE & Csinos, DM 2009, 'Spiritual styles: Creating an environment to nurture spiritual wholeness', *International Journal of Children's Spirituality*, vol. 14, no. 3, pp. 213–224.

Bennett, JB 2003, *Academic Life: Hospitality, Ethics, and Spirituality*, Anker Publishing Company, Bolton, MA.

Benson, PL & Roehlkepartain, EC 2008, 'Spiritual development: A missing priority in youth development', in PL Benson, EC Roehlkepartain & KL Hong (eds.), *New Directions for Youth Development, Spiritual Development*, Jossey-Bass, San Francisco, CA, pp. 13–28.

Benson, PL, Roehlkepartain, EC & Rude, SP 2003, 'Spiritual development in childhood and adolescence: Toward a field of inquiry', *Applied Developmental Science*, vol. 7, no. 3, pp. 204–212.

Bentz, V & Shapiro, J 1998, *Mindful Enquiry in Social Research*, SAGE, Thousand Oaks, CA.

Berger, I 2010, 'Extending the notion of pedagogical narration through Hannah Arendt's political thought', in V Pacini-Ketchabaw (ed.), *Flows, Rhythms, and Intensities of Early Childhood Curriculum*, Peter Lang Publishing, New York.

Berryman, JW 1985, 'Children's spirituality and religious language', *British Journal of Religious Education*, vol. 7, no. 3, pp. 120–127.

Berryman, JW 1997, 'Spirituality, religious education, and the dormouse', *The International Journal of Children's Spirituality*, vol. 30, no. 1, pp. 9–22.

Best, R (ed.) 1996, *Education, Spirituality and the Whole Child*, Continuum International Publishing Group Ltd, London.

References

Best, R (ed.) 2000, *Education for Spiritual, Moral, Social and Cultural Development*, Continuum, London.

Binder, MJ 2011, '"I saw the universe and I saw the world": Exploring spiritual literacy with young children in a primary classroom', *International Journal of Children's Spirituality*, vol. 16, no. 1, pp. 19–35.

Bode, B 1998, 'Evaluation: A personal knowledge of the nature of learning', in PA Kienel, OE Gibbs & SR Berry (eds.), *Philosophy of Christian School Education*, Association of Christian Schools, Colorado Springs, CO.

Bone, J 2005, 'Breaking bread: Spirituality, food and early childhood education', *International Journal of Children's Spirituality*, vol. 10, no. 3, pp. 307–317.

Bone, J 2007, 'Everyday spirituality: Supporting the spiritual experience of young children in three early childhood education settings', PhD thesis, Massey University, Palmerston North, New Zealand, viewed 15 May 2011, https://mro.massey.ac.nz/bitstream/10179/623/1/02whole.pdf

Bone, J 2010, 'Metamorphosis: Play, spirituality and the animal', *Contemporary Issues in Early Childhood*, vol. 11, no. 4, pp. 402–414, viewed 4 November 2010

Bone, J 2014, 'Spirituality and early childhood education in New Zealand and Australia', in J Watson, M de Souza & A Trousdale (eds.), *Global Perspectives on Spirituality and Education*, Routledge, New York.

Bone, J, Cullen, J & Loveridge, J 2007, 'Everyday spirituality: An aspect of the holistic curriculum in action', *Contemporary Issues in Early Childhood*, vol. 8, no. 4, pp. 344–354.

Bonner, A & Tolhurst, G 2002, 'Insider–outsider perspectives of participant observation', *Nurse Researcher*, vol. 9, no. 4, pp. 7–19.

Bosacki, SL 1999, 'Spiritual literacy: Can schools provide nourishment for children's brains and souls?' *International Journal of Children's Spirituality*, vol. 4, no. 1, pp. 91–95.

Boyatzis, C 2005, 'Children's religious and spiritual development', in R Paloutzian & D Ratcliff (eds.), *Children's Spirituality: Christian Perspectives, Research and Applications*, Cascade Books, London, pp. 166–181.

Boyatzis, C & Newman, B 2004, 'How shall we study children's spirituality?', in D Ratcliffe et al. (senior eds.), *Children's Spirituality: Christian Perspectives, Research and Applications*, Wipf & Stock Publishers, Eugene, OR, pp. 166–181.

Boynton, HM 2011, 'Children's spirituality: Epistemology and theory from various helping professions', *International Journal of Children's Spirituality*, vol. 16, no. 2, pp. 109–127.

Brearley, L 2001, 'Exploring creative forms within phenomenological research', in R Barnacle (ed.), *Phenomenology*, RMIT Press, Melbourne, pp. 74–84, viewed 25 November 2012, https://search.informit.com.au/documentSummary:dn=740311673997182:res=IELHSS

Bredekamp, S 1993, 'Reflections on Reggio Emilia', *Young Children*, vol. 49, no. 1, pp. 13–21.

Broadhead, P 2010, '"Insiders" and "outsiders" researching together to create new understandings to shape policy and practice. Is it possible?', in A Campbell & S Groundwater-Smith (eds.), *Connecting Inquiry and Professional Learning in Education: International Perspectives and Practical Solutions*, Routledge, London.

Bronfenbrenner, U 1979, *The Ecology of Human Development: Experiments by Nature and Design*, Harvard University Press, Cambridge, MA.

Bruner, JS 1977, *The Process of Education*, Harvard University Press, London.

Bruner, JS 1996, *The Culture of Education*, Harvard University Press, London.

Brussat, F & Brussat, MA 1996, *Spiritual Literacy: Reading the Sacred in Everyday Life*, Scribner, New York.

References

Buchanan, MT 2009, 'The spiritual dimension and curriculum change', *International Journal of Children's Spirituality*, vol. 14, no. 4, pp. 385–394.

Buchanan, MT & Hyde, B 2008, 'Learning beyond the surface: Engaging the cognitive, affective and spiritual dimensions within the curriculum', *International Journal of Children's Spirituality*, vol. 13, no. 4, pp. 309–320.

Bunge, M 2006, 'The child, religion, and the academy: Developing robust theological and religious understandings of children and childhood', *The Journal of Religion*, vol. 86, no. 4, pp. 549–579.

Burkhardt, MA 1989, 'Spirituality: An analysis of the concept', *Holistic Nursing Practice*, vol. 3, no. 3, pp. 69–77.

Burman, L 2009, *Are You Listening? Fostering Conversations That Help Young Children Learn*, Redleaf Press, Saint Paul, MN.

Caldwell, L 2003, *The Reggio Approach to Early Childhood Education: Bringing Learning to Life*, foreword by C Rinaldi, Teachers College Press, New York.

Carey, S 2003, *The Whole Child: Restoring Wonder to the Art of Parenting*, Rowman & Littlefield Publishers Inc., New York.

Carr, D 1995, 'Towards a distinctive conception of spiritual education', *Oxford Review of Education*, vol. 21, no. 1, pp. 83–98.

Carr, M 2001, *Assessment in Early Childhood Settings: Learning Stories*, SAGE, London.

Carroll, N 1999, *Philosophy of Art: A Contemporary Introduction*, 1st ed., Routledge, Abingdon.

Carson, R 1956, *The Sense of Wonder*, Harper & Row, New York.

Ceppi, GE & Zini, ME 1998, *Children, Spaces, Relations: Metaproject for an Environment for Young Children*, Reggio Children, Piazza della Vittoria, Reggio Children & Domus Academy Research Centre, Milan.

Champagne, E 2001, 'Listening to … listening for …: A theological reflection on spirituality in early childhood', in J Erricker, C Ota & C Erricker (eds.), *Spiritual Education. Cultural Religious and Social Differences: New Perspectives for the 21st Century*, Sussex Academic, Brighton.

Champagne, E 2003, 'Being a child, a spiritual child', *International Journal of Children's Spirituality*, vol. 8, no. 1, pp. 43–53.

Chan, KH 2010, 'Rethinking children's participation in curriculum making: A rhizomatic movement', in V Pacini-Ketchabaw (ed.), *Flows, Rhythms & Intensities of Early Childhood Education Curriculum*, Peter Lang Publishing Company, New York, pp. 113–131.

Chandler, CK 1992, 'Counselling for spiritual wellness: Theory and practice', *Journal of Counselling and Development*, vol. 71, no. 2, pp. 168–175.

Chawla, L 1990, 'Ecstatic places', *Children's Environments Quarterly*, vol. 7, no. 4, pp. 18–23.

Clark, A 2005, 'Listening to and involving young children: A review of research and practice', *Early Child Development and Care*, vol. 175, no. 6, pp. 489–505.

Clark, A, Kjorholt, A & Moss, P (eds.) 2005, *Beyond Listening: Children's Perspectives on Early Childhood Services*, The Policy Press, Bristol.

Claxton, G 2002, *Building Learning Power*, TLO Limited, Bristol.

Coburn, JB 1968, 'The new mood in spirituality', in E James (ed.), *Spirituality for Today*, SCM Press Ltd., London, pp. 15–85.

Cole, S 2011, 'Situating children in the discourse of spirituality', in NN Wane, EL Manyimo & EJ Ritskes (eds.), *Spirituality, Education & Society*, Sense Publishers, Rotterdam, pp. 1–14.

Coles, R 1990, *The Spiritual Life of Children*, Houghton Mifflin, Boston, MA.

Coles, R 1997, *The Moral Intelligence of Children*, Bloomsbury, London.

Cooke, B 1994, *Sacraments and Sacramentality*, Twenty-Third Publications, Mystic, CT.

Coolican, H 2004, *Research Methods and Statistics in Psychology*, 4th ed., Hodder Arnold, London.

Copple, C 2003, 'Fostering young children's representation, planning, and reflection: A focus in three current early childhood models', *Journal of Applied Developmental Psychology*, vol. 24, no. 6, pp. 763–771.

Crawford, M & Rossiter, G 2006, *Reasons for Living: Education and Young People's Search for Meaning, Identity and Spirituality: A Handbook*, ACER Press, eBook Collection (EBSCO*host*), Camberwell, VIC, viewed 12 June 2013.

Creswell, J 2009, *Research Design: Qualitative, Quantitative, and Mixed Methods Approaches*, 3rd ed., SAGE Publications Inc., Thousand Oaks, CA.

Creswell, J 2012, *Research Design: Qualitative, Quantitative and Mixed Methods Approaches*, 4th ed., SAGE Publications Inc., Thousand Oaks, CA.

Creswell, JW 1998, *Qualitative Inquiry and Research Design: Choosing Among Five Traditions*, SAGE Publications, Inc., Thousand Oaks, CA.

Creswell, JW 2003, *Research Design, Qualitative and Mixed Methods Approaches*, SAGE Publications, Inc., Thousand Oaks, CA.

Crompton, M 1998, *Children, Spirituality, Religion and Social Work*, Ashgate Publishing Ltd., Burlington, VT.

Crotty, M 1998, *The Foundations of Social Research: Meaning and Perspective in the Research Process*, Allen & Unwin, Sydney.

Csikszentmihalyi, M 1997, *Creativity: Flow and the Psychology of Discovery and Invention*, Harper Collins, New York.

Csikszentmihalyi, M 2000, *Flow Theory*, Oxford University Press, Oxford.

Csikszentmihalyi, M 2002, *Flow: The Classic Work on How to Achieve Happiness*, Rider & Co, London.

Cullen, J 2009, 'Adults co-construction of an early childhood curriculum', Chapter 6 in A Anning, J Cullen & M Fleer (eds.) 2009, *Early Childhood Education: Society and Culture*, SAGE Publications, London, pp. 80–90.

Cullen, J, Hedges, H & Bone, J 2009, 'Planning, undertaking and disseminating research in early childhood settings: An ethical framework' [online], *New Zealand Research in Early Childhood Education*, vol. 12, pp. 109–118. Available at ISSN: 1174–6122, viewed 8 January 2015, http://search.informit.com.au.ezlibproxy.unisa.edu.au/documentSummary;dn=055340906250874;res=IELHSS

Cupit, G 2002, 'Spirituality in early childhood educative care', *Every Child*, vol. 8, no. 4, pp. 4–5.

Curtis, D & Carter, M 2003, *Designs for Living and Learning: Transforming Early Childhood Environments*, Redleaf Press, Saint Paul, MN.

Dahlberg, G, Moss, P & Pence, A 1999, *Beyond Quality in Early Childhood Education and Care: Postmodern Perspectives*, Falmer Press, Oxon.

Dahlin, B 2009, 'On the path towards thinking: Learning from Martin Heidegger and Rudolf Steiner', *Studies in Philosophy and Education*, vol. 28, no. 6, pp. 534–537.

Davies, B 2011, 'Open listening: Creative education in early childhood settings, OMEP XXVI world conference, 11–13 August 2010, Gothenburg, Sweden', *International Journal of Early Childhood*, vol. 43, no. 2, pp. 119–132.

References

de Souza, M 2009, 'Promoting wholeness and wellbeing in education: Exploring aspects of the spiritual dimension', in M de Souza, LJ Francis, J O'Higgins-Norman & D Scott (eds.), *International Handbook for Spirituality, Care and Wellbeing*, Volume 3 of the series *International Handbooks of Religion and Education*, New York, pp. 677–692.

Dei, GJS 2005, 'The challenge of inclusive schooling in Africa: A Ghanaian case study', *Comparative Education*, vol. 41, no. 3, pp. 267–289.

DeLyser, D 2001, '"Do you really live here?" Thoughts on insider research', *The Geographical Review*, vol. 91, no. 1, pp. 441–453.

Denzin, NK & Lincoln, YS 2000, 'The discipline and practice of qualitative research', in NK Denzin & YS Lincoln, (eds.), *Handbook of Qualitative Research*, 2nd ed., SAGE Publications, Inc., Thousand Oaks, CA, pp. 1–28.

Norman K Denzin, Yvonna S Lincoln, 1995, 'Transforming Qualitative Research Methods: Is it a Revolution', *Journal of Contemporary Ethnography*, pp., 349–358, Vol. 24, no. 3.

Department for Education and Child Development (DECD) 2013, *Universal Access to Preschool Education*, Government of South Australia, viewed 17 March 2013, http://www.decd.sa.gov.au/childrensservices/default.asp?navgrp=earlychildhoodreform&id=universalaccess

Department for Education and Children's Services (DECS) 2007, *Learner Wellbeing Framework for Birth to Year 12*, Department of Education and Children's Services, Government of South Australia.

Derrida, J 1976, *Of Grammatology*, Johns Hopkins University Press, Baltimore, MD.

Dewey, J 1897, 'My pedagogic creed', *School Journal*, vol. 54, no. 1, pp. 77–80.

Dewey, J 1910, *How We Think*, DC Heath & Co, New York.

Dewey, J 1980, *Art as Experience*, Penguin Group Inc., New York.

Dillon, JJ 2000, 'The spiritual child: Appreciating children's transformative effects on adults', *Encounter: Education for Meaning and Social Justice*, vol. 13, no. 4, pp. 4–18.

Dowling, M 2004, 'Hermeneutics: An exploration', *Nurse Researcher*, vol. 11, no. 4, pp. 30–39.

Dowling, M 2005, *Young Children's Personal, Social and Emotional Development*, Paul Chapman, London.

Dowling, M 2010, 'Spiritual growth', *Nursery World*, pp. 18–20, 13 May.

Duncan, S 2011, 'Breaking the code', *Exchange*, vol. 33, no. 4, pp. 13–17.

Eaude, T 2003, 'Shining lights in unexpected corners: New angles on young children's spiritual development', *International Journal of Children's Spirituality*, vol. 8, no. 2, pp. 151–162.

Eaude, T 2005, 'Strangely familiar? Teachers making sense of young children's spiritual development', *Early Years: An International Journal of Research and Development*, vol. 25, no. 3, pp. 237–248.

Eaude, T 2009, 'Happiness, emotional well-being and mental health: What has children's spirituality to offer?' *International Journal of Children's Spirituality*, vol. 14, no. 3, pp. 185–196.

Edwards, A 2001, 'Qualitative designs and analysis', in G MacNaughton, SA Rolfe & I Siraj-Blatchford (eds.), *Doing Early Childhood Research: International Perspective on Theory and Research*, McGraw-Hill/Open University Press, Maidenhead, pp. 155–175.

Edwards, A 2002a, 'Responsible research: Ways of being a researcher', *British Educational Research Journal*, vol. 28, no. 2, pp. 157–168.

Edwards, C, Gandini, L & Forman, G (eds.) 1998, *The Hundred Languages of Children: The Reggio Emilia Approach – Advanced Reflections*, 2nd ed., Ablex Publishing Company, Westport, CT.

Edwards, CP 2002b, 'Three approaches from Europe: Waldorf, Montessori and Reggio Emilia', *Early Childhood Research and Practice*, vol. 4, no. 1, pp. 2–14.

References

Edwards, S & Hammer, M 2006, 'The foundations of early childhood education: Historically situated practice', in S Edwards, M Fleer, M Hammer, A Kennedy, A Ridgeway, J Robbins & L Surman (eds.), *Early Childhood Communities: Sociocultural Research in Practice*, Pearson Education, Melbourne, pp. 193–208.

Elkind, D 1988, *The Hurried Child: Growing Up Too Fast Too Soon*, revised ed., Addison-Wesley Publishing Company, Reading, MA.

Elkins, D, Hedstrom, L, Hughes, L, Leaf, J & Saunders, C 1998, 'Towards a humanistic phenomenological spirituality', *Journal of Humanistic Psychology*, vol. 28, no. 4, pp. 5–18.

Elliot, E 2010, 'Thinking beyond a framework: Entering into dialogues', in V Pacini-Ketchabaw (ed.), *Flows, Rhythms, & Intensities of Early Childhood Education Curriculum*, Peter Lang Publishing Inc., New York, pp. 3–20.

Emmons, RA 1999, *The Psychology of Ultimate Concerns: Motivation and Spirituality in Personality*, Guilford Press, New York.

Emmons, RA 2000, 'Is spirituality an intelligence? Motivation, cognition, and the psychology of ultimate concern', *International Journal for the Psychology of Religion*, vol. 10, no. 1, pp. 3–26, Psychology and Behavioral Sciences Collection, EBSCO*host*, viewed 22 May 2013.

Etheridge, S 2004, '"Do you know you have worms on your pearls?" Listening to children's voices in the classroom', in P Pufall & R Unsworth (eds.), *Rethinking Childhood*, Rutgers University Press, New Brunswick, NJ, pp. 87–103.

Ezzy, D 2002, *Qualitative Analysis: Practice and Innovation*, Allen & Unwin, Crow's Nest, NSW.

Farnsworth, EB 1996, 'Reflexivity and qualitative family research: Insider's perspectives on bereaving the loss of a child', in MB Sussman & JF Gilgin (eds.), *The Methods and Methodologies Of Qualitative Family Researchs*, Haworth Press, New York, pp. 399–415.

Feeney, S & Moravcik, E 1987, 'A thing of beauty: Aesthetic development in young children', *Young Children*, vol. 42, no. 6, pp. 7–15.

Felstiner, S, Kocher, L & Pelo, A 2006, 'The disposition to document', in A Fleet, C Patterson & J Robertson (eds.), *Insights: Behind Early Childhood Pedagogical Documentation*, Pademelon Press, Jamberoo, New South Wales, pp. 55–76.

Ferrer, JN 2002, *Revisioning Transpersonal Theory: A Participatory Vision of Human Spirituality*, SUNY Press, Albany, NY.

File, N 1995, 'Applications of Vygotskian theory to early childhood education: Moving toward a new teaching–learning paradigm', *Advances in Early Childhood Education and Day Care*, vol. 7, pp. 295–317.

Fillipini, T (1990), Introduction to the Reggio approach. Paper presented at the annual conference of the National Association for the Education of Young Children, Washington, DC.

Fischer, KW & Bidell, TR 2006, 'Dynamic development of action, thought, and emotion', in W Damon & RM Lerner (eds.), *Theoretical Models of Human Development: Handbook of Child Psychology*, Wiley, New York, pp. 313–399.

Fleer, M 2006, 'A sociocultural perspective on early childhood education: Rethinking, reconceptualising and reinventing', in S Edwards, M Fleer, M Hammer, A Kennedy, A Ridgeway, J Robbins & L Surman (eds.), *Early Childhood Communities: Sociocultural Research in Practice*, Pearson Education, Melbourne, pp. 3–14.

Fleer, M & Richardson, C 2009, Cultural–historical assessment: Mapping the transformation of understanding, in A Anning, J Cullen & M Fleer (eds.), *Early Childhood Education: Society and Culture*, 2nd ed., SAGE Publications Ltd, London, pp. 130–144.

References

Forman, G 1994, 'Different media, different languages', paper presented at the Study Seminar on the Experience of the Municipal Infant–Toddler Centres and Preprimary Schools of Reggio Emilia, Reggio Emilia, Italy, 30 May–10 June.

Forman, G, Hall, E & Berglund, K 2001, 'The power of ordinary moments', *Childcare Information Exchange*, pp. 52–55, September 2001.

Forster, D, McColl, M & Fardella, J 2007, 'Spiritual transformation in clinical relationships between social workers and individuals living with disabilities', *Journal of Religion and Spirituality in Social Work: Social Thought*, vol. 26, no. 1, pp. 35–51.

Foucault, M 1989, *The Order of Things: An Archaeology of the Human Sciences*, Routledge, London.

Foucault, M 1991, *The Archaeology of Knowledge*, Routledge, London.

Fowler, J 1981, *Stages of Faith: The Psychology of Human Development and the Quest for Meaning*, Harper Collins Publishers Inc., New York.

Fowler, JW & Dell, ML 2006, 'Stages of faith from infancy through adolescence: Reflections on three decades of faith development theory', in EC Roehlkepartain, PE King, L Wagener & PL Benson (eds.), *The Handbook of Spiritual Development in Childhood and Adolescence*, SAGE, Thousand Oaks, CA.

Fraser, S 2006, *Authentic Childhood: Experiencing Reggio Emilia in the Classroom*, 2nd ed., Thompson Nelson, Scarborough, Ontario.

Freebody, PR 2003, *Qualitative Research in Education: Interaction and Practice*, SAGE, London.

Fried, J 2001, 'Civility and spirituality', in VM Miller & MM Ryan (eds.), *Transforming Campus Life: Reflections on Spirituality and Religious Pluralism*, Peter Lang, New York, pp. 261–280.

Froebel, F 1887, *The Education of Man*, D Appleton and Company, New York.

Gadamer, HG 1975, *Truth and Method*, Sheed and Ward, London.

Gadamer, HG 1976, *Philosophical Hermeneutics*, University of California Press, London.

Gandini, L 1998, 'Educational and caring spaces', in C Edwards, L Edwards, L Gandini & G Forman (eds.), *The Hundred Languages of Children: Advanced Reflection*, Ablex Publishing Corporation, New York.

Gandini, L 2005, 'The evolution of the atelier: Conversations from Reggio Emilia', in L Gandini, L Hill, L Caldwell & C Schwall (eds.), *In the Spirit of the Studio: Learning from the Atelier of Reggio Emilia*, Teachers College Press, New York.

Gandini, L, Hill, L, Caldwell, L & Schwall, C (eds.) 2005, *In the Spirit of the Studio: Learning from the Atelier of Reggio Emilia*, Teachers College Press, New York.

Gang, PS, Lynn, NM & Maver, DJ 1992, *Conscious Education: The Bridge to Freedom*, Dagaz Press, Montpelier, VT.

Gardner, H 1983, *Frames of Mind: The Theory of Multiple Intelligences*, Basic Books, New York.

Gardner, H 1994, *The Arts and Human Development*, Basic Books, New York.

Gardner, H 1999, *Intelligence Reframed, Multiple Intelligences for the 21st Century*, Basic Books, New York.

Gardner, H 2001, 'Introductions', in Project Zero & Reggio Children (eds.), *Making Learning Visible: Children as Individual and Group Learners*, Reggio Children, Reggio Emilia, Italy.

Gardner, H 2011a, *Frames of mind: The theory of multiple intelligences*, Basic Books, New Youk, USA, e-book, accessed 21 May 2013, https://unisa.eblib.com.au.ezlibproxy1.unisa.edu.au/patron/FullRecord.aspx?p=665795

Gardner, H 2011b, *Truth, Beauty and Goodness Reframed: Educating for the Virtues of the Twenty-First Century*, 1st ed., Basic Books, New York.

Gendler, JR 2007, *Notes on the Need for Beauty*, Da Capo Press, Cambridge, MA.

References

Giacopini, E 2010, The Other Way to Listen Conference, Bold Park Community School, Perth, WA, 11–14 August.

Giamminuti, S 2009, 'Pedagogical documentation in the Reggio Emilia Educational Project: Values, quality and community in early childhood settings', PhD thesis, University of Western Australia, School of Education, viewed 20 January 2013, www.uwa.edu.au/__data/assets/pdf.../Giamminuti-Stefania-PhD.pdf

Giamminuti, S 2012, 'The semiotics of entering: beauty, empathy and belonging in Reggio Emilia', in A Fleet, C Patterson & J Robertson (eds.), *Insights: Behind Early Childhood Pedagogical Documentation*, Pademelon Press, Jamberoo, New South Wales, pp. 189–216.

Giesenberg, A 2007, 'The phenomenon of preschool children's spirituality', PhD thesis, Faculty of Education, Queensland University of Technology, viewed 28 September 2010, QUT Digital Repository, https://eprints.qut.edu.au/view/year/2007.html

Gillham, B 2000, *Case Study Research Methods*, Cassell, New York.

Glassman, M 2001, 'Dewey and Vygotsky: Society, experience, and inquiry in educational practice', *Educational Researcher*, vol. 30, no. 4, pp. 3–14.

Glazer, S (ed.) 1999, *The Heart of Learning: Spirituality in Education*, Penguin Group Inc., New York.

Goodliff, G 2013, 'Spirituality expressed in creative learning: Young children's imagining play as a space for mediating their spirituality', *Early Childhood Development and Care*, vol. 183, no. 8, pp. 1054–1071.

Goodsir, K & Rowell, P 2010, 'Learning stories – narratives of the complex ways that children learn', extract from *Putting Children First, the Magazine of the National Childcare Accreditation Council (NCACA)*, vol. 35, pp. 12–13.

Goodwin, WL & Goodwin, LD 1996, *Understanding Qualitative and Quantitative Research in Early Childhood Education*, Teachers College Press, New York.

Goouch, K 2008, 'Understanding playful pedagogies, play narratives and play spaces', *Early Years: An International Journal of Research and Development*, vol. 28, no. 1, pp. 93–102.

Grajczonek, J 2011, 'Belonging, being, becoming: The early years learning framework for Australia: Opportunities and challenges for early years religious education', *Journal of Religious Education*, vol. 59, no. 3, pp. 23–35.

Grajczonek, J 2012, 'Interrogating the spiritual as constructed in belonging, being and becoming: The early years learning framework for Australia', *Australasian Journal of Early Childhood*, vol. 37, no. 1, pp. 152–160.

Greenstreet, WM 1999, 'Teaching spirituality in nursing: A literature review', *Nurse Education Today*, vol. 19, pp. 649–658.

Groome, T 1996, 'What makes a school catholic? Abridged version', in K Treston (ed.), *The Contemporary Catholic School: Context, Identity, and Diversity*, Falmer Press, London, pp. 107–125.

Groome, T 1998, *Educating for Life: A Spiritual Vision for Every Teacher and Parent*, Crossroad Publishing Company, New York.

Guss, FG 2011, 'Meeting at the crossroads: Postmodern pedagogy greets children's aesthetic play-culture', in S Rogers (ed.) *Rethinking Play and Pedagogy in Early Childhood Education: Concepts, Contexts and Cultures, Routledge*, Abingdon, Oxon.

Haiman, PE 1991, 'Developing a sense of wonder in young children: There is more to education than cognitive development', *Young Children*, vol. 46, no. 6, pp. 52–53.

Haldane, J 1992, 'Aquinas and the active intellect', *Philosophy*, vol. 67, no. 260, pp. 199–210.

Hall, C 2012, 'Recognising spirituality', *The Challenge*, vol. 16, no. 1, pp. 34–37.

References

Hardt, J, Schultz, S, Xander, C, Becker, G & Dragan, M 2012, 'The spirituality questionnaire: Core dimensions of spirituality', *Psychology (Irvine)*, vol. 3, no. 1, pp. 116–122.

Harklau, L & Norwood, R 2005, 'Negotiating researcher roles in ethnographic program evaluation: A postmodern lens', *Anthropology and Education Quarterly*, vol. 36, no. 3, pp. 278–288.

Harris, K 2007, 'Re-conceptualizing spirituality in the light of educating young children', *International Journal of Children's Spirituality*, vol. 12, no. 3, pp. 263–275.

Hart, T 2003, *The Secret Spiritual World of Children*, Inner Ocean Publishing Inc., Berkeley, CA.

Hart, T 2004, 'The mystical child: Glimpsing the spiritual world of children', *Encounter: Education for Meaning and Social Justice*, vol. 17, no. 2, pp. 38–49.

Hart, T 2005, 'Spiritual experiences and capacities of children and youth', in EC Roehlkepartain, PE King, L Wagener & PL Benson (eds.), *The Handbook of Spiritual Development in Childhood and Adolescence*, SAGE Publications, London, pp. 163–177.

Hart, T 2006. "Spiritual Experiences and Capacities for Children and Youth."in EC Roehlkepartain, PE King, L Wagner, and PL Benson (eds.), *The Handbook of Spiritual Development in Childhood and Adolescence*, SAGE, Thousand Oaks, CA, pp. 163–178.

Hart, T 2009, 'Transforming self and subject: Toward an integrative spiritual pedagogy', in M de Souza et al. (eds.), *International Handbook of the Religious, Moral and Spiritual Dimensions in Education*, Springer, New York, pp. 1149–1163.

Hart, T & Ailoae, C 2006–07, 'Spiritual touchstones: Childhood spiritual experience in the development of influential historic and contemporary figures', *Imagination, Cognition and Personality*, vol. 26, no. 4, p. 345.

Hatherly, A & Sands, L 2002, 'So what is different about learning stories?', *The First Years: Nga Tau Tuatahi New Zealand Journal of Infant and Toddler Education*, vol. 4, no. 1, pp. 8–12.

Hay, D & Nye, R 1996, 'Investigating children's spirituality: The need for a fruitful hypothesis', *International Journal of Children's Spirituality*, vol. 1, no. 1, pp. 6–16.

Hay, D & Nye, R 2006, *The Spirit of the Child*, revised ed., Jessica Kingsley Publications, London.

Hay, D, Reich, KH & Utsch, M 2006, 'Spiritual development; Intersections and divergence with religious development', in EC Roehlkepartain, PE King, L Wagener & PL Benson (eds.), *The Handbook of Spiritual Development in Childhood and Adolescence*, SAGE Publications, London, pp. 46–59.

Heidegger, M 1978, *Basic Writings*, Routledge, London.

Helminiak, DA 1996, 'A scientific spirituality: The interface of psychology and theology', *International Journal for the Psychology of Religion*, vol. 6, no. 1, pp. 1–19.

Hemming, PJ 2013, 'Spaces of spiritual citizenship: children's relational and emotional encounters with the everyday school environment', *International Journal of Children's Spirituality*, vol. 18, no. 1, pp. 74–91.

Herr, K & Anderson, GL 2005, *The Action Research Dissertation: A Guide for Students and Faculty*, SAGE Publications Inc., Thousand Oaks, CA.

Hewett, V 2001, 'Examining the Reggio approach to early childhood education', *Early Childhood Education Journal*, vol. 29, no. 2, pp. 95–100.

Hill, S & Millar, N (2015), 'Case study research: Creating the case', in O Saracho & B Spodek (eds.), *Handbook of Research Methods in Early Childhood Education*, Information Age Publishing Inc., Charlotte, NC.

Hogan, MJ 2009, 'On spirituality and education', *Thinking Skills and Creativity*, vol. 4, no. 2, pp. 138–143.

References

Hughes, E 2007, 'Linking past to present to create an image of the child', *Theory into Practice*, vol. 46, no. 1, pp. 48–56.

Hyde, B 2004, 'The plausibility of spiritual intelligence: Spiritual experience, problem solving and neural sites', *International Journal of Children's Spirituality*, vol. 9, no. 1, pp. 39–52.

Hyde, B 2008a, *Children and Spirituality: Searching for Meaning and Connectedness*, Jessica Kingsley Publications, London.

Hyde, B 2008b, 'I wonder what you think really, really matters? Spiritual questing and religious education', *Religious Education: The Official Journal of the Religious Education Association*, vol. 103, no. 1, pp. 32–77.

Hyde, B 2014, 'Nurturing spirituality through a dispositional framework in early years contexts', in J Watson, M de Souza & A Trousdale (eds.), *Global Perspectives on Spirituality and Education*, Routledge, New York.

Hyde, B & Australian Catholic University 2005, *Identifying some characteristics of children's spirituality in Australian Catholic primary schools: A study within hermeneutic phenomenology*, [electronic resource], viewed 12 January 2012, https://dlibrary.acu.edu.au/digitaltheses/public/adt-acuvp82.04092006/index.html

Hyde, B & Rymarz, R 2009, *Religious Education in Catholic Primary Schools: Contemporary Issues and Perspectives for RE Teachers*, David Barlow Publishing, Macksville, New South Wales.

Hyde, B, Yust, K & Ota, C 2010, 'Silence, agency and spiritual development', *International Journal of Children's Spirituality*, vol. 15, no. 2, pp. 97–99.

Iannone, RV & Obenauf, PA 1999, 'Toward spirituality in curriculum and teaching', *Education*, vol. 119, no. 4, pp. 737–743.

Jacobs, J 2003, 'Spirituality and virtue', in D Carr & J Haldane (eds.), *Spirituality, Philosophy and Education*, Routledge, London, pp. 41–55.

James, A 2004, 'Understanding childhood from an interdisciplinary perspective: Problems and potentials', in P Pufall & R Unsworth (eds.), *Rethinking Childhood*, Rutgers University Press, New Brunswick, NJ, pp. 25–37.

Janzen, MD 2008, 'Where is the (postmodern) child in early childhood education research?' *Early Years: An International Journal of Research and Development*, vol. 28, no. 3, pp. 287–298.

Johnson, CN & Boyatzis, CJ 2006, 'Cognitive-cultural foundations of spiritual development', in EC Roehlkepartain, PE King, L Wagener & PL Benson (eds.), *The Handbook of Spiritual Development in Childhood and Adolescence*, SAGE Publications, London, pp. 211–223.

Johnson, JE, Christie, JF & Yawkey, TD 1999, *Play and Early Childhood Development*, 2nd ed., Addison Wesley Longman, New York.

Jordan, B 2009, 'Scaffolding learning and co-constructing understandings', in A Anning, J Cullen & M Fleer (eds.), *Early Childhood Education: Society and Culture*, 2nd ed., SAGE Publishing Company, London, pp. 39–52.

Katz, L 1998, 'What we can learn from Reggio Emilia', in A Edwards, L Gandini & G Forman (eds.), *The Hundred Languages of Children: The Reggio Approach – Advanced Reflections*, 2nd ed., Ablex Publishing Company, Westport, CT.

Kemp, E 2001, 'Observing practice as participant observation – linking theory to practice', *Social Work Education: The International Journal*, vol. 20, no. 5, pp. 527–538.

Kemple, KM & Johnson, CA 2002, 'From the inside out nurturing aesthetic response to nature in the primary grades', *Childhood Education*, vol. 78, no. 4, pp. 210–218.

References

Kendall, S 1999, 'The role of picture books in children's spiritual development and meaning making', *International Journal of Children's Spirituality*, vol. 4, no. 1, pp. 61–76.

Kennedy, A 2006, 'Images of children: A picture tells a thousand words' in M Fleer et al. (eds.), *Early Childhood Learning Communities: Sociocultural Research in Practice*, Pearson Education Australia, NSW, pp. 15–26.

Kennedy, A & Duncan, B 2006, 'New Zealand children's spirituality in Catholic schools: Teachers' perspectives', *International Journal of Children's Spirituality*, vol. 11, no. 2, pp. 281–292.

Kessler, R 2000, *The Soul of Education: Helping Students Find Connection, Compassion, and Character at School*, Association for Supervision and Curriculum Development, Alexandria, VA.

Kim, BS & Darling, LF 2009, 'Monet, Malaguzzi, and the constructive conversations of preschoolers in a Reggio-inspired classroom', *Early Childhood Education Journal*, vol. 37, no. 2, pp. 137–145.

Kind, S 2010, 'Art encounters: Movement in the visual arts and early childhood education', in V Pacini-Ketchabaw (ed.), *Flows, Rhythms & Intensities of Early Childhood Education Curriculum*, Peter Lang Publishing Company, New York, pp. 113–131.

King, U 2009, *The Search for Spirituality: Our Global Quest for Meaning and Fulfilment*, Canterbury Press, London; Norwich.

King, U 2013, 'The spiritual potential of childhood: Awakening to the fullness of life', *International Journal of Children's Spirituality*, vol. 18, no. 1, pp. 4–17.

Kinney, L & Wharton, P 2008, *An Encounter with Reggio Emilia Children's Learning Made Visible*, Routledge, London.

Kirmani, M & Kirmani, S 2009, 'Recognition of seven spiritual identities and its implications on children', *International Journal of Children's Spirituality*, vol. 14, no. 4, pp. 369–383.

Knill, P 2004, *Minstrels of Soul*, EGS Press, Toronto, ON.

Krauss, SE 2005, 'Research paradigms and meaning making: A primer', *The Qualitative Report*, vol. 10, no. 4, pp. 758–770.

Kroeger, J & Cardy, T 2006, 'Documentation: A hard to reach place', *Early Childhood Education Journal*, vol. 33, no. 6, pp. 389–398.

Labouvie-Vief, G 1994, *Psyche and Eros: Mind and Gender in the Life Course*, Cambridge University Press, New York.

Lawrence-Lightfoot, S & Davis, JH 1997, *The Art and Science of Portraiture*, Jossey-Bass, San Francisco, CA.

Lee, W 2006, 'Documentation of learning stories: A powerful assessment tool for early childhood: part 1', *Reflections*, vol. 23, pp. 4–9.

Lichtman, M 2006, *Qualitative Research in Education; A User's Guide*, SAGE Publications Inc., Thousand Oaks, CA.

Liddy, S 2002, 'Children's spirituality', *Journal of Religious Education*, vol. 50, no. 1, pp. 13–19.

Lillard, AS 1998, 'Playing with a theory of mind', in ON Saracho & B Spodek (eds.), *Multiple Perspectives on Play in Early Childhood*, State University of New York Press, Albany, NY.

Lim, B 2005, 'Aesthetic experience in a dynamic cycle: Implications for early childhood teachers and teacher educators', *Journal of Early Childhood Teacher Education*, vol. 25, no. 4, pp. 367–373.

Lindner, E 2004, 'Children as theologians' in P Pufall & R Unsworth (eds.), *Rethinking Childhood*, Rutgers University Press, New Brunswick, NJ, pp. 54–68.

Lodico, MG, Spaulding, DT & Voegtle, KH 2010, *Methods in Educational Research: From Theory to Practice*, Jossey-Bass, San Francisco, CA.

Louv, R (2005) *Last child in the woods: saving our children from nature-deficit disorder*. Algonquin Books of Chapel Hill, Chapel Hill, NC.

Love, PG 2001, 'Spirituality and student development: Theoretical connections', *New Directions for Student Services*, vol. 95, pp. 7–16.

Ludlow, S 2014, 'Applying contemporary early childhood theory & pedagogies to the process of intentionally scaffolding children's emergent spiritual awareness', in L Tolbert (ed.), *Exploring and Engaging Spirituality for Today's Children: A Holistic Approach*, Wipf and Stock, Eugene, OR, pp. 243–256.

Lyotard, JF 1984, *The Postmodern Condition: A Report on Knowledge*, Manchester University Press, Manchester.

MacNaughton, G 2009, 'Exploring critical constructivist perspectives on children's learning', in A Anning, J Cullen & M Fleer (eds.), *Early Childhood Education: Society and Culture*, 2nd ed., SAGE Publishing Company, London, pp. 53–64.

Major, CH & Savin-Baden, M 2010, *An Introduction to Qualitative Research Synthesis: Managing the Information Explosion in Social Science Research*, Routledge, New York.

Malaguzzi, L 1993, 'For an education based on relationships', *Young Children*, vol. 11, no. 93, p. 10.

Malaguzzi, L 1994, 'Your image of the child: where teaching begins', *Child Care Information Exchange*, vol. 96, no. 3, pp. 52–56.

Malaguzzi, L 1998, 'History, ideas and basic philosophy: An interview with Lella Gandini by Loris Malaguzzi' in C Edwards, L Edwards, L Gandini & G Forman (eds.), *The Hundred Languages of Children: Advanced Reflection*, Ablex Publishing Corporation, New York.

Marrero, E 2000, 'The competent reflector: A Reggio Emilia inspired religious education model', unpublished doctoral project, Claremont School of Theology, Claremont, CA.

Marshall, G & Rossman, B 2011, *Designing Qualitative Research*, 5th ed., SAGE Publications Inc, Thousand Oaks, CA.

Martalock, PL 2012, 'What is a wheel? The image of the child: Traditional, project approach and Reggio Emilia perspectives', *Dimensions of Early Childhood*, vol. 40, no. 1, pp. 3–11.

Maslow, AH 1954, *Motivation and Personality*, Harper, New York.

Maslow, AH 1968, *Toward a Psychology of Being*, D. Van Nostrand Company, New York.

Maslow, AH 1971, *The Farther Reaches of Human Nature*, Viking Press, New York.

Mata, J 2014, 'Sharing my journey and opening spaces: Spirituality in the classroom', *International Journal of Children's Spirituality*, vol. 19, no. 2, pp. 112–122.

Matthews, G 2004, 'Children as philosophers', in P Pufall & R Unsworth (eds.), *Rethinking Childhood*, Rutgers University Press, New Brunswick, NJ, pp. 38–53.

Matthews, GB 1980, *Philosophy and the Young Child*, Harvard University Press, Cambridge, MA.

Mayer, J 2000, 'Spiritual intelligence or spiritual consciousness?', *The International Journal for the Psychology of Religion*, vol. 10, no. 1, pp. 47–56.

Maynard, T & Chicken, S 2010, 'Through a different lens: Exploring Reggio Emilia in a Welsh context', *Early Years: An International Journal of Research and Development*, vol. 30, no. 1, pp. 29–39.

McCreery, E 1996, 'Talking to young children about things spiritual', in R Best (ed.), *Education, Spirituality and the Whole Child*, Cassell, London, pp. 196–206.

McGhee, M 1992, *Philosophy, Religion and the Spiritual Life*, Cambridge University Press, Cambridge.

References

McGhee, M 2000, *Transformation of Mind: Philosophy as Spiritual Practice*, Cambridge University Press, Cambridge.

McKechnie, L 2000, 'Ethnographic observation of preschool children', *Library and Information Science Research*, vol. 22, no. 1, pp. 61–76.

McMurtary, MJ 2007, 'Realms of engagement – toward an understanding of the contribution of the arts to children's spiritual development', *International Journal of Children's Spirituality*, vol. 12, no. 1, pp. 83–96.

Meehan, C 2002a, 'Promoting spiritual development in the curriculum', *Pastoral Care in Education*, vol. 20, no. 1, pp. 16–24.

Meehan, C 2002b, 'Resolving the confusion in the spiritual development debate', *International Journal of Children's Spirituality*, vol. 7, no. 3, pp. 291–308.

Mercer, J 2005, *Welcoming Children: A Practical Theology of Childhood*, Chalice Press, Saint Louis, MO.

Merriam, SB 2009, *Qualitative Research: A Guide to Design and Implementation*, Jossey-Bass, San Francisco, CA.

Miller, JP 2000, *Education and the Soul: Toward a Spiritual Curriculum*, SUNY Press, Albany, NY.

Miller, JP 2006, *Educating for Wisdom and Compassion: Creating Conditions for Timeless Learning*, Corwin Press, SAGE Publications Company, Thousand Oaks, CA.

Miller, JP 2007, *The Holistic Curriculum*, 2nd ed., University of Toronto Press, Toronto, ON.

Miller, L & Athan, A 2007, 'Spiritual awareness pedagogy: The classroom as spiritual reality', *International Journal of Children's Spirituality*, vol. 12, no. 1, pp. 17–35.

Millikan, J 2003, *Reflections: Reggio Emilia Principles Within Australian Contexts*, Pademelon Press, NSW.

Millikan, J 2010, 'The hundred languages of children and a hundred hundred more: A symbiotic relationship between the visual arts and learning in Reggio Emilia', *Australian Art Education*, vol. 33, no. 2, pp. 12–25.

Millikan, J & Giamminuti, S 2014, *Documentation and the Early Years Learning Framework: researching in Reggio Emilia and Australia*, Pademelon Press, Jamberoo, NSW.

Ministerial Council for Education, Early Childhood Development and Youth Affairs (MCEECDYA) 2008, *Melbourne Declaration on Educational Goals for Young Australians*, MCEECDYA, Canberra, ACT.

Ministry of Education 1996, *Te Whāriki: he whāriki mātauranga mo ngā mokopuna o Aotearoa, Early Childhood Curriculum*, Learning Media, Wellington.

Moffett, J 1994, *The Universal Schoolhouse: Spiritual Awakening through Education*, Jossey-Bass, San Francisco, CA.

Montagu, A 1989, *Growing Young*, 2nd ed., Bergin & Garvey, New York.

Montessori, M 1964, *The Montessori Method*, Schocken Books, New York.

Mooney, C 2000, *Theories of Childhood, An Introduction to Dewey, Montessori, Erickson, Piaget & Vygotsky*, Redleaf Press, USA.

Moore, T 1996, *The Education of the Heart*, Harper Collins, New York.

Moran, M, Desrochers, L & Cavicchi, N 2007, 'Progettazione and documentation as sociocultural activities: Changing communities', *Theory into Practice*, vol. 46, no. 1, pp. 81–90.

Moriarty, MW 2011, 'A conceptualization of children's spirituality arising out of recent research', *International Journal of Children's Spirituality*, vol. 16, no. 3, pp. 271–285, edu.au/digitalthesis/public/adt-acuvp291.16032011/index.html

Moss, P & Petrie, P 2002, *From Children's Services to Children's Spaces: Public Policy, Children and Childhood*, Routledge Falmer, London.

Motha, J 2011, 'The contemplative educator', in NN Wane, EL Manyimo & EJ Ritskes (eds.), *Spirituality, Education and Society: An Integrated Approach*, Sense Publishers, Rotterdam.

Mountain, V 2007, 'Educational contexts for the development of children's spirituality: Exploring the use of imagination', *International Journal of Children's Spirituality*, vol. 12, no. 2, pp. 191–205.

Mountain, V 2011, 'Four links between child theology and children's spirituality', *International Journal of Children's Spirituality*, vol. 16, no. 3, pp. 261–269.

Mukherji, P & Albon, D 2010, *Research Methods in Early Childhood: An Introductory Guide*, SAGE Publications Ltd, London.

Myers, BK 1997, *Young Children and Spirituality*, Routledge, London.

Myers, D 2002, *Intuition: Its Powers and Perils*, Yale University Press, New Haven, CT and London.

Natsis, E 2016, 'A new discourse on spirituality in public education: Confronting the challenges in a post-secular society', *International Journal of Children's Spirituality*, vol. 1, no. 1, pp. 1–12.

Nemme, K 2008, 'Nurturing the inner lives of children: an exploration of children's spirituality in three educational settings', PhD thesis, Faculty of Education, University of Wollongong, http://ro.uow.edu.au/theses/651

New, R 1998, 'Theory and praxis in Reggio Emilia: They know what they are doing and why', in C Edwards, L Edwards, L Gandini & G Forman (eds.), *The Hundred Languages of Children: Advanced Reflection*, Ablex Publishing Corporation, New York.

New, R 2007, 'Reggio Emilia as a cultural activity theory in practice', *Theory into Practice*, vol. 46, no. 1, pp. 5–13.

Norris, C 1987, *Derrida*, Collins, London.

Nye, R 1998, 'Psychological perspectives on children's spirituality', PhD thesis, University of Nottingham, viewed 23 May 2013, http://eprints.nottingham.ac.uk/11177/1/243253.pdf

Nye, R 2004, 'Christian perspectives on children's spirituality', in D Ratcliff, A Catterton, C Boyatzis, K Lawson, M McQuitty, S May, S Morgenthaler, B Posterski & C Stonehouse (eds.) *Children's Spirituality: Christian Research, and Applications*, Wipf & Stock Publishers, Oregon, pp. 90–107.

Nye, R 2009, *Children's Spirituality: What It Is and Why It Matters*, Church House Publishing, London.

Nye, R & Hay, D 1996, 'Identifying children's spirituality: How do you start without a starting point?' *British Journal of Religious Education*, vol. 18, no. 3, pp. 144–154.

O'Leary, Z 2004, *The Essential Guide to Doing Research*, SAGE, London.

O'Murchu, D 1998, *Reclaiming Spirituality: A New Spiritual Framework for Today's World*, Crossroad Pub. Co., New York.

Olmsted, S 2012, *Imagine Childhood; Exploring the World through Nature, Imagination and Play*, Shambhala Publications Inc., Boston, MA.

Painton, M 2009, 'Children's spiritual intelligence', in M de Souza, LJ Francis, J O'Higgins-Norman & D Scott (eds.), *International Handbook of Education for Spirituality, Care and Wellbeing*, Springer, Netherlands, viewed 10 October 2013, http://ezlibproxy.unisa.edu.au/login?url https://doi.org/10.1007/978-1-4020-9018-9

Palmer, PJ 1998, *The Courage to Teach: Exploring the Inner Landscape of a Teacher's Life*, Jossey-Bass, San Francisco, CA.

Palmer, PJ 1999a, 'Evoking the spirit in public education', *Educational Leadership*, vol. 56, no. 4, pp. 6–11.

References

Palmer, PJ 1999b, 'The grace of great things; reclaiming the sacred in knowing teaching and learning', in S Glazer (ed.), *The Heart of Learning: Spirituality in Education*, Penguin/Putnam, New York, pp. 15–32.

Palmer, PJ 2003, 'The heart of a teacher: Identity and integrity', in A Lieberman (ed.), *The Jossey-Bass Reader on Teaching*, Jossey-Bass, San Francisco, CA, pp. 3–25.

Pascual-Leone, J 2000, 'Mental attention, consciousness, and the progressive emergence of wisdom', *Journal of Adult Development*, vol. 7, no. 4, pp. 241–254.

Peters, M & Burbules, N 2004, *Post-structuralism and Educational Research*, Rowman and Littlefield Publishers Inc., Blue Ridge Summit, PA.

Piaget, J 1929, *The Child's Perception of the World*, Routledge & Kegan Paul, London.

Piaget, J 1968, *Six Psychological Studies*, Random House, New York.

Piaget, J 1976, *The Child's Perception of the World, Littlefield*, Adams & Co., North Brunswick, NJ.

Piaget, J 2002, *Language and Thought of the Child*, 3rd ed., Routledge, Abington, Oxon.

Plunkett, D 1990, *Secular and Spiritual Values*, Routledge, London.

Podmore, V 2009, 'Questioning evaluation quality in early childhood', in A Anning, J Cullen & M Fleer (eds.), *Early Childhood Education: Society and Culture*, 2nd ed., SAGE Publications Ltd, London, pp. 158–168.

Priestley, JG 1985, 'The spiritual in the curriculum', in PC Souper (ed.), *The Spiritual Dimension of Education*, Department of Education, University of Southampton, Southampton.

Puhakka, K, Hart, T & Nelson, PL 2000, *Transpersonal Knowing: Exploring the Horizon of Consciousness*, State University of New York Press, Albany, NY.

Punch, KF 1998, *Introduction to Social Research: Quantitative & Qualitative Approaches*, SAGE Publications Ltd., London.

Punch, KF 2003, *Developing Effective Research Proposals*, SAGE Publications Ltd., London.

Punch, KF 2005, *Introduction to Social Research: Quantitative & Qualitative Approaches*, 2nd ed., SAGE Publications Ltd., London.

Rahner, K 1966, 'Gedanken zu einer Theologie der Kindheit', trans. D Bourke as 'Ideas for a theology of childhood', *Schriften zur Theologie* vol. 8, pp. 313–329.

Ratcliff, D 2001, 'Rituals in school hallway: Evidence of a latent spirituality of children', *Christian Education Journal*, vol. 5, no. 2, pp. 9–26.

Ratcliff, D 2004, *Children's Spirituality: Christian Perspectives, Research and Applications*, Cascade Books, Wipf & Stock Pub, Eugene, OR.

Ratcliff, D 2010, 'Children's spirituality: Past and future', *Journal of Spiritual Formation and Soul Care*, vol. 3, no. 1, pp. 6–20.

Ratcliff, D, Catterton, A, Boyatzis, C, Lawson, K, McQuitty M, May, S, Morgenthaler, S, Posterski, B & Stonehouse, C (eds.) 2004, *Children's Spirituality: Christian Research, and Applications*, Wipf & Stock Publishers, Eugene, OR.

Ratcliff, D & May, S (eds.) 2004, 'Identifying children's spirituality, Walter Wangerin's perspectives and an overview of this book', in D Ratcliff et al. (eds.) 2004, *Children's Spirituality: Christian Research, and Applications*, Wipf & Stock Publishers, Eugene, OR.

Ratcliff, D & Nye, R 2006, 'Childhood spirituality: Strengthening the research foundation', in E Roehlkepartain, P King, L Wagner & P Benson (eds.), *The Handbook of Spiritual Development in Childhood and Adolescence*, SAGE Publications Inc, London, pp. 473–483.

Reggio Emilia Australia information exchange website, viewed November 2010, www.reaie.org.au/

References

Ridgeway, A & Hammer, M 2006, 'Spaces that educate', in S Edwards, M Fleer, M Hammer, A Kennedy, A Ridgeway, J Robbins & L Surman (eds.), *Early Childhood Communities: Sociocultural Research in Practice*, Pearson Education, Melbourne, Victoria, pp. 95–117.

Riemer, F, Quartaroli, M & Lapan, S 2012, *Qualitative Research: An Introduction to Methods and Designs*, eBook Collection (EBSCO*host*), San Francisco, CA, Jossey-Bass, viewed 29 May 2013.

Rinaldi, C 1998a, 'Projected curriculum constructed through documentation – progettazione: An interview with Lella Gandini', in C Edwards, L Gandini & G Forman (eds.), *The Hundred Languages of Children: The Reggio Emilia Approach – Advanced Reflections*, 2nd ed., Ablex Publishing Company, Westport, CT.

Rinaldi, C 1998b, 'The space of childhood', in G Ceppi & M Zini (eds.), *Children, Spaces and Relations: Metaproject for an Environment for Young Children*, Reggio Children & Domus Academy Research Centre, Milan.

Rinaldi, C 2001, 'Documentation, dissensus and debate: Some possibilities of learning from Reggio', in C Guidici, R Rinaldi & M Krechevsky (eds.), *Making Learning Visible: Children as Individual and Group Learners*, Reggio Children, Reggio Emilia.

Rinaldi, C 2004, 'The relationship between documentation and assessment', *The Quarterly Periodical of the North American Reggio Emilia Alliance*, vol. 11, no. 1, pp. 1–5.

Rinaldi, C 2006, *In Dialogue with Reggio Emilia: Listening, Researching and Learning*, Routledge, Oxon.

Rinaldi, C 2013, *Re-imagining Childhood: The Inspiration of Reggio Emilia Education Principles in South Australia*, Adelaide Thinkers in Residence, Government of South Australia, Adelaide, SA.

Ritskes, E 2011, 'Indigenous spirituality as resistance', in NN Wane, EL Manyimo & EJ Ritkes (eds.), *Spirituality, Education & Society*, Sense Publishers, Rotterdam, pp. 15–36.

Robertson, J 2006, 'Focusing the lens: Gazing at "gaze"', in A Fleet, C Patterson & J Robertson (eds.), *Insights: Behind Early Childhood Pedagogical Documentation*, Pademelon Press, Jamberoo, NSW, pp. 147–162.

Robertson, M & Gerber, R 2001, *Children's Ways of Knowing: Learning Through Experience*, Australian Council for Educational Research (ACER) Press, Camberwell, VIC.

Robinson, E 1977, *The Original Vision: A Study of the Religious Experiences of Childhood*, Religious Experience Research Unit, Manchester College, Oxford.

Rodari, G 1996, *The Grammar of Fantasy: An Introduction to the Art of Inventing Stories*, Teacher and Writers Collaborative, New York.

Rodger, A 1996, 'Human spirituality: Towards an educational rationale', Ch. 4, in R Best (ed.), *Education, Spirituality and the Whole Child*, Cassell, London, p. 19.

Roehlkepartain, E, King, PE, Wagener, L & Benson, P (eds.) 2006, *The Handbook of Spiritual Development in Childhood and Adolescence*, SAGE Publications Inc., London.

Rogers, S (ed.) 2011, *Rethinking Play and Pedagogy in Early Childhood Education: Concepts, Contexts and Cultures*, Routledge, Abingdon, Oxon.

Rogoff, B 2003, *The Cultural Nature of Human Development*, Oxford University Press, Oxford.

Rose, S 2001, 'Is the term "spirituality" a word that everyone uses, but nobody knows what anyone means by it?' *Journal of Contemporary Religion*, vol. 16, no. 2, pp. 193–207.

Rossiter, G 2010a, 'A case for a "big picture" re-orientation of K-12 Australian Catholic school religious education in the light of contemporary spirituality', *Journal of Religious Education*, vol. 58, no. 3, pp. 5–18.

Rossiter, G 2010b, 'Religious education and the changing landscape of spirituality: Through the lens of change in cultural meanings', *Journal of Religious Education*, vol. 58, no. 2, pp. 25–36.

References

Ruddock, B & Cameron, RJ 2010, 'Spirituality in children and young people: A suitable topic for educational and child psychologists?' *Educational Psychology in Practice*, vol. 26, no. 1, pp. 25–33.

Rudge, L 2010, *Holistic Education: An Analysis of Its Pedagogical Application*, Lambert Academic Publishing, Saarbrücken.

Sagberg, S 2008, 'Children's spirituality with particular reference to a Norwegian context: Some hermeneutical reflections', *International Journal of Children's Spirituality*, vol. 13, no. 4, pp. 355–370.

Saracho, ON & Spodek, B 1998, *Multiple Perspectives on Play in Early Childhood Education*, State University of New York Press, Albany, NY.

Sargeant, J & Harcourt, D 2012, *Doing Ethical Research With Children*, McGraw-Hill/Open University Press, Maidenhead, Berkshire.

Scheibel, H 1995, 'Filosoti er for Born [Philosophy for children]', Kroniken I Politiken. *Politiken*, 28 April (newspaper article).

Schein, D 2018, *Inspiring Wonder, Awe, and Empathy*, Redleaf Press, Saint Paul, MA.

Schein, DL 2013, 'Research and reflections on the spiritual development of young Jewish children', *Journal of Jewish Education*, vol. 79, no. 3, pp. 360–385.

Scheinfeld, DR, Haigh, KM & Scheinfeld, JP 2008, *We are all Explorers: Learning and Teaching with Reggio Principles in Urban Settings*, Teachers College Press, New York.

Schroeder-Yu, G 2008, 'Documentation: Ideas and applications from the Reggio Emilia approach', *Teaching Artist Journal*, vol. 6, no. 2, pp. 126–134.

Sedan, J 2005, *Child Spirituality*, The Open University, Milton Keynes. Retrieved 22 August 2023, https://www.open.edu/openlearn/body-mind/childhood-youth/childhood-and-youth-studies/childhood/child-spirituality.

Sewell, A 2009, 'Evoking children's spirituality in the reciprocal relationships of a learning community', *International Journal of Children's Spirituality*, vol. 14, no. 1, pp. 5–16.

Silverman, D 2000, *Doing Qualitative Research: A Practical Handbook*, SAGE, Thousand Oaks, CA.

Singer, W & Gray, C 1995, 'Visual feature integration and the temporal correlation hypothesis', *Annual Reviews of Neuroscience*, vol. 18, pp. 555–586.

Smart, N 1996, *The Religious Experience*, 5th ed., Prentice-Hall, Upper Saddle River, NJ.

Soler, J & Miller, L 2003, 'The struggle for early childhood curricula: A comparison of the English foundation stage curriculum, "Te Whariki" and Reggio Emilia', *International Journal of Early Years Education*, vol. 11, no. 1, pp. 57–67.

Spilka, B & McIntosh, D 1997, *The Psychology of Religion: Theoretical Approaches*, Westview/Harper, Boulder, CO.

Spodek, B & Saracho, O 2003, 'On the shoulders of giants: Exploring the traditions of early childhood education', *Early Childhood Education Journal*, vol. 31, pp. 3–10.

Stack, GJ 1998, 'Materialism', in E Craig (ed.), *Routledge Encyclopaedia of Philosophy*, Routledge, New York, pp. 170–171.

Stake, R 1995, *The Art of Case Study Research*, SAGE Publications Ltd, Thousand Oaks, CA.

Stake, R 2006, *Multiple Case Studies Analysis*, Guilford Press, New York.

Steiner, R 1995, *The Kingdom of Childhood: Introductory Talks on Waldorf Education*, Association of Waldorf Schools of North America Publications, Anthroposophic Press, Fair Oaks, CA.

Stewart, D & Mickanus, A 1990, *Exploring Phenomenology: A Guide to the Field and Its Literature*, Ohio University Press, Athens, OH.

Strong-Wilson, T & Ellis, J 2007, 'Children and place: Reggio Emilia's environment as third teacher', *Theory into Practice*, vol. 46, no. 1, pp. 40–47.

Surman, L, Ridgeway, A & Edwards, S 2006, 'Program planning: Negotiating the curriculum', in S Edwards, M Fleer, M Hammer, A Kennedy, A Ridgeway, J Robbins & L Surman (eds.), *Early Childhood Communities: Sociocultural Research in Practice*, Pearson Education, Melbourne, pp. 174–190.

Surr, J 2012, 'Peering into the clouds of glory: Explorations of a newborn child's spirituality', *International Journal of Children's Spirituality*, vol. 17, no. 1, pp. 77–87.

Swanborn, P 2010, *Case Study Research: What, Why and How?* SAGE Publications, London.

Swann, AC 2008, 'Children, objects, and relations: Constructivist foundations in the Reggio Emilia Approach', *Studies in Art Education: A Journal of Issues and Research in Art Education*, vol. 50, no. 1, pp. 36–50.

Swinton, J & Pattison, S 2001, 'Spirituality: Come all ye faithful', *Health Service Journal*, vol. 111, no. 5786, pp. 24–25.

Tacey, C 2005, 'Why do boys like to build and girls like to draw? Gender issues in a small British military community', Ch. 7 in D Hirst & K Nutbrown (eds.), *Perspectives on Early Childhood Education: Contemporary Research*, Trentham Books Limited, UK, pp. 63–67.

Tacey, D 2000, *Re-enchantment: The New Australian Spirituality*, Ashgate Publishing Limited, Aldershot.

Tacey, D 2004, *The Spirituality Revolution: The Emergence of Contemporary Spirituality*, Bruner-Routledge, Hove.

Tacey, D 2006, 'Spirituality as a bridge to religion and faith', in K Engebretson, M de Souza, G Durka & A McGrady (eds.) 2006, *International Handbook of the Religious, Moral and Spiritual Dimensions in Education*, Springer, New York, pp. 201–213, viewed 29 March 2013, http://link.springer.com.ezlibproxy.unisa.edu.au/content/pdf/10.1007%2F1-4020-5246-4_15

Taggart, G 2001, 'Nurturing spirituality: A rationale for holistic education', *International Journal of Children's Spirituality*, vol. 6, no. 3, pp. 325–329.

Tarr, P 2003, 'Reflections on the image of the child: Reproducer or creator of culture', *Art Education*, vol. 56, no. 4, pp. 6–11.

Thomas, G 2013, *How to do Your Research Project: A Guide for Students in Social Sciences and Education*, SAGE Publications Ltd., London.

Thomas, P & Lockwood, V 2009, 'Nurturing the spiritual child: Compassion, connection and a sense of self', *Research in Practice Series*, vol. 16, no. 2, pp. 26–27.

Trotman, D 2006, 'Evaluating the imaginative: Situated practice and the conditions for professional judgement in imaginative education', *International Journal of Education & the Arts*, vol. 7, no. 3, pp. 1–19.

Turner, T & Krechevsky, M 2003, 'Who are the teachers? Who are the learners?', *Educational Leadership*, vol. 60, no. 7, pp. 40–43.

Unluer, S 2012, 'Being an insider researcher while conducting case study research', *The Qualitative Report*, vol. 17, no. 29, pp. 1–14. Retrieved from http://nsuworks.nova.edu/tqr/vol17/iss29/2

Upton, M 2009, 'Moment to moment spirituality in early childhood education', in M de Souza, LJ Francis, J O'Higgins-Norman & D Scott (eds.), *International Handbook of Education for Spirituality, Care and Wellbeing*, Springer, Springer, New York, viewed 10 October 2013, http://ezlibproxy.unisa.edu.au/login?url https://doi.org/10.1007/978-1-4020-9018-9

van Manen, M 1984, *Doing Phenomenological Research and Writing: An Introduction*, Monograph No. 7, University of Alberta, Edmonton, AB.

References

van Manen, M 1990, *Researching Lived Experience: Human Science for an Action Sensitive Pedagogy*, State University of New York, New York.

van Manen, M 1997, 'From meaning to method', *Qualitative Health Research*, vol. 7, no. 3, pp. 345–370.

Vaughan, F 2002, 'What is spiritual intelligence?', *Journal of Humanistic Psychology*, vol. 42, no. 2, pp. 16–33.

Vecchi, V 2010, *Art and Creativity in Reggio Emilia: Exploring the Role and Potential of Ateliers in Early Childhood Education*, Routledge, London.

Vialle, W, Walton, R & Woodcock, S 2008, 'Children's spirituality: Grappling with student ethics in postgraduate work-based degrees', in P Kell, W Vialle, D Konza & G Vogl (eds.), *Learning and the Learner: Exploring Learning for New Times*, University of Wollongong, pp. 143–160, viewed 10 June 2013, http://ro.uow.edu.au/cgi/viewcontent.cgi?article=1042&context=edupapers

von Eckartsberg, R 1998, 'Introducing existential-phenomenological psychology', in R Valle (ed.), *Phenomenological Inquiry in Psychology: Existential and Transpersonal Dimensions*, Plenum Press, New York, pp. 3–20.

Vygotsky, LS 1962, *Thought and Language*, MIT Press, Cambridge, MA.

Vygotsky, LS 1978, 'The role of play in development', in M Cole, V John-Steiner, S Scriber, E Souberman (eds.) *Mind in Society: The Development of Higher Psychological Processes*, Harvard University Press, Cambridge.

Walters, K 2006, *Capture the Moment: Using Digital Photography in Early Childhood Settings*, Early Childhood Australia, Canberra, ACT.

Wane, NN, Manyimo, EL & Ritskes, EJ (eds.) 2011, *Spirituality, Education & Society: An Integrated Approach*, Sense Publications, Rotterdam.

Warming, H 2005, 'Participant observation: A way to learn about children's perspectives', in A Clark, A Kjorholt & P Moss (eds.), *Beyond Listening: Children's Perspectives on Early Childhood Services*, The Policy Press, Bristol, pp. 51–70.

Watson, J 2000, 'Whose model of spirituality should be used in the spiritual development of school children?', *International Journal of Children's Spirituality*, vol. 5, no. 1, pp. 91–101.

Watson, J 2003, 'Preparing spirituality for citizenship', *International Journal of Children's Spirituality*, vol. 8, no. 1, pp. 9–24.

Watson, J 2007, 'Spiritual development: Constructing an inclusive and progressive approach', *Journal of Beliefs and Values*, vol. 28, no. 2, pp. 125–136.

Watson, J 2013, 'Knowing through the felt-sense: A gesture of openness to the other', *International Journal of Children's Spirituality*, vol. 18, no. 1, pp. 118–130.

Watson, J, de Souza, M & Trousdale, A (eds.) 2014, *Global Perspective on Spirituality and Education*, Routledge, New York.

Webster, S 2004, 'An existential framework of spirituality', *International Journal of Children's Spirituality*, vol. 9, no. 1, pp. 7–19.

Werner, H & Kaplan, B 1963, *Symbol Formation*, Wiley, New York.

Wexler, A 2004, 'A theory for living: Walking with Reggio Emilia', *Art Education*, vol. 57, no. 6, pp. 13–19.

White, J 1996, 'Education, spirituality and the whole child: A humanist perspective', in R. Best (ed.), *Education, Spirituality and the Whole Child*, Cassell, London, pp. 30–42.

Whitfield, PT 2009, *The Heart of the Arts: Fostering Young Children's Ways of Knowing*, Springer US, Boston, MA.

References

Wills, R 2012, 'Beyond relation: A critical exploration of 'relational consciousness' for spiritual education', *International Journal of Children's Spirituality*, vol. 17, no. 1, pp. 51–60, Academic Search Premier, EBSCO*host*, viewed 25 October 2013.

Wilson, R 2008, 'Developing the whole child: Celebrating the spirit of each child', *Early Childhood News, The Professional Resource for Teachers and Parents*, viewed 23 May 2013, http://www.earlychildhoodnews.com/earlychildhood/article_view.aspx?ArticleID=545

Winnicott, DW 1971, *Playing and Reality*, Tavistock, London.

Wood, E 2009, 'Developing a pedagogy play', in A Anning, J Cullen & M Fleer (eds.), *Early Childhood Education: Society and Culture*, 2nd ed., SAGE Publications Ltd, London, pp. 27–38.

Wright, A 2000, *Spirituality and Education*, Routledge Farmer, London.

Wright, S 2010, *Understanding Creativity in Early Childhood*, SAGE Publishing Ltd, London.

Wright, S 2012, *Children Meaning-Making and the Arts*, Pearson, Melbourne.

Wurm, JP 2005, *Working the Reggio Way: A Beginner's Guide for American Teachers*, Redleaf Press, USA.

Yeu, H 2011, 'Deconstructing the metaphysics of play theories: Towards a pedagogy of play aesthetics', in S Rogers (ed.), *Rethinking Play and Pedagogy in Early Childhood Education: Concepts, Contexts and Cultures*, Routledge, Abingdon, Oxon, pp. 126–138.

Yin, RK 1994, *Case Study Research: Design and Methods*, 2nd ed., SAGE, London.

Yin, RK 2003, *Case Study Research: Design and Methods*, 3rd ed., SAGE, Thousand Oaks, CA.

Yin, RK 2009, *Case Study Research: Design and Methods*, 4th ed., SAGE, Thousand Oaks, CA.

Yin, RK 2012, *Applications of Case Study Research*, 5th ed., SAGE, Thousand Oaks, CA.

Youngquist, J & Pataray-Ching, J 2004, 'Revisiting "play": Analyzing and articulating acts of inquiry', *Early Childhood Education Journal*, vol. 31, no. 3, pp. 171–178, March.

Yust, KM 2007, 'Childhood and spiritual wisdom: Constructing a critical conversation for the 21st century', *International Journal of Children's Spirituality*, vol. 12, no. 1, pp. 5–8.

Zohar, D & Marshall, I 2000, *SQ Spiritual Intelligence: The Ultimate Intelligence*, Bloomsbury, London.

Index

Pages in **bold** refer to tables.

Adams, K. 10, 13, 37, 41, 56, 92, 168, 177–178, 187, 193–194, 223
Adelaide Thinkers in Residence program 7, 241–242
aesthetics 83, 97–100, 180–181, 194–196; *see also* beauty
aesthetic sensitivity 103–106; *see also* beauty
Ailoae, C. 180
Albon, D. 182
Altheide, D. L. 183
Anderson, G. L. 18
Anning, A. 74, 100
Arendt, H. 82
Athan, A. 210
Atkinson, P. 85
attraction to nature 166–167
awareness sensing 42
awe *see* wonder

beauty 97–100, 102–109, 194–196; aesthetic sensitivity 103–106; as an activator for learning 194–196; as a basic need and desire 104; as a bridgebuilder 104; defining 103–104; learning environments 104–105; nature and 106–107; *see also* aesthetics
Beckwith, I. 62
Bellous, J. E. 191
Belonging, Being and Becoming: The Early Years Learning Framework for Australia 12, 37
Benson, P. L. 37, 40

Berger, I. 82
Berglund, K. 184
Best, R. 206
Binder, M. J. 11–12, 59, 79, 222
Bone, J. 8, 10, 14, 39, 58, 215
Bonner, A. 17
Boyatzis, C. 5, 30, 57
Boynton, H. M. 29–31, 37
Brearley, L. 88
Bruner, J. 72–73
Burman, L. 81

Caldwell, L. 84, 196–197
Cardy, T. 68–70
care and empathy 168
Carr, D. 39
Carr, M. 81, 128
Carroll, N. 104
Carter, M. 98, 193
case study 5, 13–15; aims/purpose 6, 16, 119–120; boundaries 20; contribution 15; data collection 126–129; ethnographic approach 20; exploration of a particular phenomenon 120–121; listening and valuing young children 125–126; lived experience 120; naturalistic settings 19–20, 121–125; participants 21, 129–132; phases 125; questions 119–121; teacher as researcher and participant observer 126
Catholic perspective 60–63
Ceppi, G. E. 14, 74, 182, 190, 201, 209

Champagne, E. 8–11, 42–43, 127, 193, 209, 238
child-centred approach 172–173
children 2–4; as active agents 100–102, 199–201; daily encounters 50–51; image 7–9, 71, 73–78, 173–175, 239–240; lived experience 120; Reggio Emilia pedagogical approach *see* Reggio Emilia approach; spiritual dimension *see* spirituality; ways of being 51; ways of knowing 50
Clark, A. 76–77, 123, 175
cognitive development theory 70–71
Cole, S. 11, 14
Coles, R. 8, 10, 39, 56, 121, 196
connectedness 47–49; *see also* relationships
consciousness 52, 54, 57, 164–165
constructiveness 201–203
constructivism 37, 68–70; social 18, 101; theoretical orientation 201
Cooke, B. 50
Coolican, H. 123
Crawford, M. 5, 98, 180
creativity 169–170; expression and 197; Gardner on 92; imagination and 91–96; as a personal trait 92; uninterrupted time 188–189
Creswell, J. 20, 126
critical spiritual education 31
Crompton, M. 63
Csikszentmihalyi, M. 90, 92, 164–165, 189, 215
Csinos, D. M. 191
Cullen, J. 17, 100
Cupit, G. 77
curiosity: engagement and 171; mysterious things 165–166
Curtis, D. 98, 193

Dahlberg, G. 73, 79
data collection: field notes 127; interviews 128–129; Learning Stories (LS) *see* Learning Stories (LS); observations 127; tools and methods 127–130
Davies, B. 77, 223
deductive analysis 181–182
Dell, M. L. 38, 61
DeLyser, D. 17

Derrida, J. 33
Descartes, R. 32
de Souza, M. 34, 38, 52, 57, 97, 180
Dewey, J. 18–19, 68–70, 95; image of the child 71
documentation 69–70, 79–82; interpretation 80–82; narration *see* narration; spiritual indicators 82; as a tool 80–81
Dowling, M. 177, 213, 236
Duncan, S. 106

early childhood education 58–63; Catholic perspective 60–63; connecting people and communities 63; considerations 241–246; diversity and 59; learning framework 60; practical implications **252–253**; well-known approaches 58
Eaude, T. 39, 46–48, 63, 192
Edwards, A. 17, 123
Elliot, E. 95–96
Ellis, J. 99
Emmons, R. A. 56
empathy 168
empirical studies 5
environment 82–85; aesthetics and beauty 83, 97–100; creativity and imagination 91–96; multisensory 83; as third teacher 83, 99, 109, 175–177, 179, 189, 209, 230, 243; wonder and awe 96–97
existential intelligence 53, 55
Exploration Time 131–132
expressions of spirituality *see* indicators and expressions

faith 30
Farnsworth, E. B. 17
Ferrer, J. N. 87
field notes 120, 127
field visits 125, 130–131
flow 92, 164–165; rhythm 189–190; uninterrupted time 188–189
Forman, G. 184
Foucault, M. 33
Fowler, J. 38, 61
Fraser, S. 68–69, 71, 89, 96
Froebel, F. 69, 90

279

Gandini, L. 94
Gang, P. S. 236–237
Gardner, H. 76; beauty 104; creativity 92; existential intelligence 53, 55; *Intelligence Reframed* 54–55; meaning-making through manipulating symbols 79; multiple intelligences theory 19, 53–55, 68, 71–72, 78–79
Gendler, J. R. 104
Gerber, R. 19
Giacopini, E. 77
Giamminuti, S 84–85, 183
Giesenberg, A. 8, 31–32, 125
Gillham, B. 124, 184
Glazer, S. 243
Goodliff, G. 8–9, 11, 13, 243
Grajczonek, J. 14, 37, 60, 62, 221
Gray, C. 55
Greenstreet, W. M. 38
Groome, T. 49, 62

Haiman, P. E. 127
Haldane, J. 32
Hall, E. 184
Hammersley, M. 85
Harcourt, D. 17, 19, 222
Hardt, J. 51
Harklau, L. 17
Harris, K. 82, 86, 97, 99
Hart, T. 9–11, 29, 38, 41, 43–46, 76, 87, 97, 164, 168, 180
Hatherly, A. 82
Hay, D. 9–11, 29–31, 34–35, 41–42, 46–47, 53, 77–78, 93, 125, 166, 222
Helminiak, D. A. 51
Herr, K. 18
Hewett, V. 101, 200
historical phases of research 29–31
Hogan, M. J. 54
human development 54
hundred languages 7, 14, 19, 52, 67, 71–72, 75–76, 78–79, 105, 125, 132, 170, 175, 178–179, 186, 209–210, 212, 215–217, 221–222, 230, 236, 240, 242–243
Hyde, B. 9, 29–30, 41, 46, 61, 102, 125, 170, 189, 193, 217

Iannone, R. V. 57
identity 49, 202; indigenous spirituality and 63; multiple 63
image of the child 7–9, 71, 73–78, 173–175, 239–240; recognising and listening to 178
imagination 49, 170–171; creativity and 91–96; uninterrupted time 188–189
indicators and expressions 15–16, 43–50, 162–172, 207–212; asking bigger questions 171–172; attraction to nature 166–167; awe and wonder 9, 43–44, 49, 96–97, 162–163, 226–228; care and empathy 168; conditions 210–213, **211**; creativity 169–170; curiosity in mysterious things 165–166; descriptions 212–219; flow 164–165; imagination 49, 170–171; joy 163–164; nurturing 219–222; signs 222–223
indigenous spirituality and identity 63
intelligence 54–56; existential 53, 55; multiple 19, 53–55, 68, 71–72, 78–79; spiritual 54–56, 218–219
Intelligence Reframed (Gardner) 54–55
interconnectedness 213–216
interpretive summary: baby chickens (LS6) 134; colours (LS11) 148; creating table (LS12) **151–152**; creative materials (LS9) 143–145; designing farm (LS13) **154**; girls encounter with a spider (LS7) **137–138**; human body and skeleton (LS14) 158–160; investigating countries and identities (LS15) 161–162; music (LS1) **23**; nature (LS3) **113**; outdoor play materials (LS2) 25–**26**; playful moments (LS5) **117**; provocations and painting (LS8) **139–140**; rainy, stormy day (LS4) 115; sand and sea materials (LS10) 146; *see also* Learning Stories (LS); narrative observation
interviews 125, 128–129
intuition 36

Jacobs, J. 32–33
Johnson, C. 30, 57
Johnson, C. N. 30, 57
Johnson, J. M. 183
joy 163–164

Kaplan, B. 193–194
Kemp, E. 126
Kessler, R. 92–93, 164
Krauss, S. E. 37
Krechevsky, M. 80–81
Kroeger, J. 68–70

language 240–241; *see also* hundred languages
Learner Wellbeing Framework (DECS) 12
learning framework for early years 60
Learning Stories (LS) 3–4, 19, 21, 81–82, 131; baby chickens (LS6) 133–134; colours (LS11) 147–148; construction of 125, 128; constructiveness 201–203; creating table (LS12) 149–151, **152**; creative materials (LS9) 144–145; data collection 125–129; designing farm (LS13) 153, **154**; field notes 120, 125, 127; girls encounter with a spider (LS7) 135–138; human body and skeleton (LS14) 155–160; indicators of spirituality 162–172; intent 81, 124, 128; investigating countries and identities (LS15) 160–162; music (LS1) 22, **23**; narration 198–203; narrative approach to 128; nature (LS3) 112, **113**; outdoor play materials (LS2) 24–26; playful moments (LS5) 116–117; provocations and painting (LS8) 138–140; rainy, stormy day (LS4) 114; Reggio Emilia approach 172–177; sand and sea materials (LS10) 145–146
Lee, W. 128
Lichtman, M. 20, 124
Liddy, S. 34, 48
Lillard, A. S. 91
Lim, B. 98, 193
listening 132, 237–238; as an approach to life 76; case study research 125–126; open 77; pedagogy 76–78, 127; responsive 81
lived experience 120
Love, P. G. 10
Lynn, N. M. 236–237
Lyotard, J. F. 33

Malaguzzi: image of the child 7; Reggio Emilia educational project 66–67, 69

Marrero, E. 83
Marshall, I. 55, 59
Mata, J. 13, 239
Matthews, G. 32
Maver, D. J. 236–237
McCreery, E. 8, 42
McGhee, M. 32
meaning-making 78–79, 216–217
Meehan, C. 218, 220–221, 236–237
Melbourne Declaration of Educational Goals for Young Australians 12–13
Merriam, S. B. 142
Mickanus, A. 32
Miller, J. P. 52, 90, 192, 219
Miller, L. 210
Millikan, J. 68, 80, 83–85
modes of spirituality 42–43
Montessori, M. 52, 58
Moran, M. 68, 70
Moss, P. 82, 243
Motha, J. 10–11, 245
Mountain, V. 92, 177
Mukherji, P. 182
multi-layered data analysis **203–204**
multiple intelligences 19, 53–55, 68, 71–72, 78–79
multisensory aspects of space 196–197
Myers, B. K. 37, 55, 166, 168, 194
Myers, D. 36
mystery 165–166; sensing 42

narration 198–203
narrative observation: baby chickens (LS6) 133–134; colours (LS11) 147–148; creating table (LS12) 149–151; creative materials (LS9) 143; designing farm (LS13) 153; girls encounter with a spider (LS7) 135–138; human body and skeleton (LS14) 155–158; investigating countries and identities (LS15) 160–161; music (LS1) 22; nature (LS3) 112; outdoor play materials (LS2) 24–25; playful moments (LS5) 116; provocations and painting (LS8) 138–139; rainy, stormy day (LS4) 114; sand and sea materials (LS10) 145–146; *see also* interpretive summary; Learning Stories (LS)
Natsis, E. 237

Index

naturalistic settings 19–20, 121–125
nature: attraction to 166–167
Nemme, K. 53
New, R. 79, 101
Norris, C. 33
Norwood, R. 17
Nye, R. 9–11, 34–35, 40–42, 46–47, 50, 53, 76–78, 93, 120, 125, 164, 166, 180–181, 222

Obenauf, P. A. 57
observations 120, 127; field notes 127; naturalistic 126
Olmsted, S. 90
O'Murchu, D. 10
ontological concept 28–29
open-ended interview questions 128
open listening 77
ordinary moments 182–187; see also rich normality
osmosis 196–197
Ota, C. 102
the other 87

Painton, M. 56, 219
Palmer, P. J. 38
Pascual-Leone, J. 54
Pataray-Ching, J. 91
pedagogy 235–237; listening 76–78, 127; relationships 85–87
Pence, A. 82
Petrie, P. 243
phenomenology 87–88, 120–121; aspects 88; hermeneutic 88
philosophy 31–32
Piaget, J. 37, 70–72
Plato 32
play 88–91, 127, 177–178; as being a teacher 230–231; Fraser on 89; as a recreational activity 90; Rogers on 89; soulfulness 226–231; spirituality and 90–91; theorists 90; unpredictability 229; unstructured 228–229; Vygotsky on 89; wisdom and 226–227; wonder and 226–228
Plunkett, D. 217
postmodernism 33, 73

provocation 83–85
psychology 54–57

qualitative research 121–122

Ratcliff, D. 29–31, 39–40, 120
Reggio Emilia approach 2, 4, 6–8, 51–53, 238–239; documentation 69–70, 79–82; environment 82–85; history and context 67–68; as a holistic pedagogy 6–7, 14; image of the child 7–9, 71, 73–78, 239–240; origins 66–70; philosophy 68–70; teachers as researchers 85–87; theoretical perspectives 70–73
Reich, K. H. 10
relational consciousness 42
relational spirituality 9, 43–44
relationships 47–49; pedagogy 85–87; reciprocal 87; as relational practice 86
religion 28–30, 34–37, 63, 224
research 5–6; contemporary 40–41; gap 13–15; phases 29–31; questions 6, 119–121
rich normality 182–187; see also ordinary moments
right to spirituality 107
Rinaldi, C. 7, 52, 68–69, 76, 80, 82, 86, 93–94, 97, 99, 173, 186, 198, 210, 237, 241–244; experience and philosophy of Reggio Emilia 16; teacher researcher for 126
Ritskes, E. 63
Robertson, M. 19
Rodari, G. 84
Rogoff, B. 42
Rossiter, G. 5, 98, 180

Sagberg, S. 120, 179, 187
Sands, L. 82
Saracho, O. N. 75, 90–91
Sargeant, J. 17, 19, 222
Scheibel, H. 32
Schein, D. 13, 239
search for meaning 47
secular world 237
sense of belonging 49, 202
sense of search 47

Sewell, A. 202
signs 222–223
Singer, W. 55
social constructivism 101
sociocultural approach/theory 18–19, 100–102, 234
soul 52
space: aesthetics and beauty 194–196; beautiful elements 192–194; multisensory aspects 196–197; relational and interconnecting 191–192; system and scheme 190–191
spiritual intelligence 54–56, 218–219
spirituality 2–3, 27–28; as an innate quality 10; as an ontological concept 28–29; benefits 255–256; categorising 41–42; characteristics 46; concept 9, 11–12; contemporary research 40–41; debate 10–11; fundamental beliefs 2; humanist perspective 35; modes 42–43; philosophy 31–32; postmodernism 33, 73; Reggio Emilia pedagogical approach *see* Reggio Emilia approach; religion and *see* religion; right to 107; secular world 237; studies and research 8–9; understanding 29–34; virtue 33; western secular society 63; working definition 39–40
spiritual moments 132–133, 248–250; ideas and activities 249–250; with nature 249; spaces 248
spiritual sensitivity 42
Spodek, B. 75, 90–91
Steiner, R. 52, 58
Stewart, D. 32
Strong-Wilson, T. 99
Swanborn, P. 129
Swann, A. C. 191–192

Tacey, D. 34, 36
teacher: play as being a 230–231; as researcher and participant observer 126; as researchers in Reggio Emilia approach 85–87

theology 29
thinking 54
Tolhurst, G. 17
transcendence 55
Trotman, D. 210
Trousdale, A. 34
Turner, T. 80–81

understanding 87
uninterrupted time 131, 171, 187–189, 216–217
Unluer, S. 17
unstructured play 228
Upton, M. 177, 185
Utsch, M. 10

value sensing 42
van Manen, M. 199
Vialle, W. 60
virtue 33
Vygotsky, L. S. 18–19, 68, 70, 89, 127

Warming, H. 85–86, 123
Watson, J. 34, 46, 58–59, 78, 236
ways of being 51
ways of knowing 50
Werner, H. 193–194
Whitfield, P. T. 75
wisdom 9, 43–45, 226–227
wonder 9, 43–44, 49, 96–97, 162–163, 226–228
Wright, A. 31, 33, 97
Wright, S. 92, 95

Youngquist, J. 91
Yust, K. 102

Zini, M. E. 14, 74, 182, 190, 201, 209
Zohar, D. 55, 59

For Product Safety Concerns and Information please contact our EU
representative GPSR@taylorandfrancis.com
Taylor & Francis Verlag GmbH, Kaufingerstraße 24, 80331 München, Germany

www.ingramcontent.com/pod-product-compliance
Lightning Source LLC
Chambersburg PA
CBHW051147290426
44108CB00019B/2639